Theatre: A Way of Seeing

Theatre
A Way of Seeing
Third Edition

Milly S. Barranger
The University of North Carolina,
Chapel Hill

Wadsworth Publishing Company
Belmont, California
A Division of Wadsworth, Inc.

Theatre Editor: Peggy Randall
Editorial Assistant: Nancy Spellman
Production Editor: Angela Mann
Interior and Cover Designer: Andrew H. Ogus
Design Assistant: Anne Kellejian
Print Buyer: Barbara Britton
Permissions Editor: Robert M. Kauser
Copy Editor: Jennifer Gordon
Page Dummier: Barry Age/Beach City Graphics
Photo Researcher: Stephen Forsling
Technical Illustrator: Carole Lawson
Compositor: Thompson Type
Cover Photographer: Gerhard Kassner
Cover Photograph: *The Forest*, a production by
Robert Wilson

Printed in the United States of America 19

1 2 3 4 5 6 7 8 9 10 — 95 94 93 92 91

Library of Congress Cataloging-in-Publication Data

Barranger, Milly S.
 Theatre, a way of seeing / Milly S. Barranger. — 3rd ed.
  p.   cm.
 Filmography: p.
 Includes bibliographical references and index.
 ISBN 0-534-14418-7
 1. Theater.   I. Title.
PN2037.B32   1991   90-12779
792 — dc20

To Heather

Features

Theatre *as a way of seeing* is the subject of this book. We will talk about the experience of *theatre* — who sees, what is seen, where, and how it is seen — largely from our own viewpoint as audiences engaged in the direct experience of a complex, living art. We will also try to place ourselves in the creative process of those artists engaged in creating the theatre event. Many persons — writers, directors, actors, designers, technicians, managers, producers — contribute to what is truly a collective, all-encompassing art.

Theatre is where people make art out of themselves for others to watch, experience, think, and feel. Chiefly through the actor, theatre is humanness, aliveness, and presence. Nor does theatre exist in any book. A book, like this one, can only *describe* the passion, wisdom, and excitement that comes with experiencing theatre — in its motion, color, and sound.

This edition has been revised and updated to discuss theatre as an experience of art, life, and human imagination: spaces, people, plays, language, artists, designs, staging, forms, and productions. For this purpose, the book is divided into thirteen chapters. Ten of the thirteen deal with the complex answer to the question: What is theatre? There are discussions of theatre aesthetics, theatrical spaces, theatre artists, artistic process, dramatic forms, elements, and conventions. Two chapters discuss playreading and theatre language, and the last examines theatre criticism — its form and influence on our theatregoing. In addition, there are diagrams, definitions, quotations, sections from texts of plays, and photo essays illustrating theatre's variety, color, tools, and styles. If instructors want to change the order of the chapters, they will find that they can readily do so. None of these discussions, of course, takes the place of sitting with others in a darkened theatre and experiencing the actors, text, scenery, costumes, changing lights, music, and sound effects in a carefully crafted event demonstrating the wonders of the human imagination.

Written for the basic course, this book *introduces* students to theatre as a way of seeing men and women in action: what they do and why they do it. After all, Shakespeare said that "All the world's a stage,/And all the men and women merely players . . ." (*As You Like It*). Because many students are probably discovering theatre for the first time and perhaps even attending their first performances, I have limited to eleven the "model" plays, ranging from the Greeks to the moderns, used as examples of trends, styles, and forms in theatrical production: *Oedipus the King*, *The Trojan Women*, *Hamlet*, *Tartuffe*, *Ghosts*, *The Cherry Orchard*, *The Caucasian Chalk Circle*, *Waiting for Godot*, *A Streetcar Named Desire*, *Buried Child*, and *Fences*. Each of these plays has a special place in the history of theatrical writing and performance from the past to the present. They also represent, in combination, the extraordinary range and magnitude of human expression and theatrical achievement.

In addition, the complete text of Samuel Beckett's *Rockaby*, along with extensive excerpts from *The Three Sisters*, *The Bald Soprano*, *Marat/Sade*, and *Buried Child* are included in an effort to keep the book (and its material) self-contained, at least for use in the classroom.

In this revised edition of *Theatre: A Way of Seeing*, the reader will also find sections discussing the "new" director-collaborators (for example, Peter Brook, Robert Wilson, and Martha Clarke); current stage technology, especially sound and computers; and photo essays on contemporary stages, environmental performance, women playwrights, new stage design, and great actors.

I have also provided tools to help students with questions of history, biography, definition, and example. A list of these tools appears on pages xiv–xv. Included are synopses of the model plays and short biographies of playwrights, actors, directors, designers, and critics. Other elements that should be useful for teachers and students include study questions; suggested plays and books to read; lists of films and videotapes providing "recorded" performances of some of the model plays and featuring such distinguished actors as Laurence Olivier, Jessica Tandy, James Earl Jones, Derek Jacobi, Irene Worth, Marlon Brando, Vivien Leigh, John Malkovich, and many others. These recommended films represent work by such directors as Peter Brook, Elia Kazan, Alan Schneider, and Ariane Mnouchkine. An expanded glossary of theatre terms, as well as projects that require special work outside the classroom and attendance at performances, are included in the appendixes. All terms that appear in boldface in the text are defined in an expanded glossary. Wherever possible, terms are briefly defined within the text itself, but the glossary provides more extensive explanations.

Finally, this book is in no way a definitive treatment of theatre practice, history, or literature but an attempt to put students in touch with theatre as a performing art and humanistic event. Most important, it introduces students to theatre as an *immediate* experience, engaging actors and audiences for a brief time in a special place. The Greeks called that special place where audiences sat to watch performances a *theatron*, or "seeing place." Let us make theatre as a way of seeing our guide to understanding and enjoying the theatre.

My thanks are due to colleagues and students for their encouragement and assistance in the preparation of the several revisions of this book. Those who advised on this manuscript at various stages are Georgia A. Bomar, East Texas State University; Robert H. Bradley, Southwest Missouri State University; Sharon Broom, PlayMakers Repertory Company, Chapel Hill; Bill G. Cook, Baylor University; Marilyn J. Hoffs, Glendale College; Edward T. Jones, York College of Pennsylvania; William Leonard, Western Kentucky University; Craig Turner, The University of North Carolina at Chapel Hill; Douglas R. Vander Yacht, Western Washington University; and Berenice Weiler, Weiler/Miller Associates.

Milly S. Barranger
The University of North Carolina,
Chapel Hill

While we are watching, men and women make theatre happen before us. In the theatre we see human beings in action — what they do and why they do it — and we discover our world's special qualities by seeing them through others' eyes.

Discovering Theatre

Theatre—like dance, music, opera, film, and video—places human experience before a group of people—an audience. In this first chapter, we want to ask: What is theatre? What makes theatre different from other arts? How is theatre *a way of seeing*? Let us concern ourselves with those crucial elements of theatre's uniqueness: its immediacy, doubleness, aliveness, and entertainment.

The Immediate Art

Theatre is an art that takes place in the present moment, as we watch. For theatre to happen, two groups of people, actors and audience, must come together at a certain time and in a certain place. There, the actors present themselves to the audience in a story usually involving some aspect of being human. The audience shares in the story and the occasion.

Theatre possesses a living quality because it involves two groups of people: actors and audiences. Although dance, music, opera, film, and video share with theatre the human being as performer, they do not imitate human reality in theatre's special way. As director Peter Brook writes, "A man walks across this empty space whilst someone else is watching him, and this is all that is needed for an act of theatre to be engaged." Unlike other arts, theatre presents human beings playing fictional characters who move, speak, and "live" *before* us, creating recognizable events and places. For a short time we share an experience with them that is entertaining, provocative, imitative, and magical.

Theatre, then, is a *living* art form, continually before us in present time until that final moment when William Shakespeare's Hamlet is lifted from the stage to Fortinbras' command: "Take up the bodies," or when Samuel Beckett's tramps do not move from the appointed place for their meeting with "Godot" who never comes. In its immediacy, theatre bears a unique relationship to the aliveness (and humanity) it mirrors. What are these parallels between theatre and life? There are four essential ones:

actors	humanity
simulation	reality
rehearsal	spontaneity
audiences	society

It is far easier to sit in the theatre and discover the similarities (and differences) between theatrical performances and life than it is to sort out the many elements that contribute to the theatre event. Let us consider the special place where it happens, or what Peter Brook calls "the empty space."

The Special Place

At the heart of the theatre experience, as Peter Brook suggests, is the act of seeing and being seen. That requires a special place. We are told that the word *theatre* comes from the Greek word *theatron*, meaning "seeing place." At one time or another during the history of Western culture, this place for seeing has been a primitive dancing circle, a Greek **amphitheatre**, a church, an Elizabethan platform stage, a marketplace, a garage, a street, or a **proscenium** theatre (see glossary). Today, it may be a Broadway theatre, a university playhouse, or a renovated warehouse. But neither the stage's shape nor the building's architecture makes a theatre. Rather, the use of space to imitate human experience for an audience to see makes that space special—a seeing place. And this seeing place, *theatron*, or theatre is where we learn about ourselves and others. It is the place where we perceive the how, the what, and the why of our humanness.

Types of Contemporary Theatres

Today's theatres are found in large cities as well as in small towns. Just as their locations are diverse, so theatre buildings and stages differ in size and shape.

London's National Theatre, located on the south bank of the Thames River, was completed in 1976. This huge complex contains three theatres (the Lyttelton, the Olivier, and the Cottesloe), rehearsal rooms, workshops, offices, restaurants, and foyers. The Lyttelton Theatre, seating 890, has a conventional proscenium stage; the proscenium opening can be altered by changing its width and height.

The Olivier (named for the English actor Laurence Olivier) has an open stage and 1,150 seats. The audience encircles the stage.

Interior of the 400-seat Cottesloe black box theatre. Modeled on an Elizabethan courtyard with balcony above and flexible seating below, it has been used largely for experimental work, staged readings, and seminars.

The Guthrie Theater, Minneapolis, built in 1963, houses a large auditorium (1,441 seats) encircling the unique seven-sided **thrust stage**. No seat is more than fifty-two feet from the center of the stage. The photo shows the audience's relationship to the actors and stage.

The Oregon Shakespearean Festival Theatre in Ashland (founded in 1935) is an open-air theatre. The audience sits in front of a platform stage. A multilevel building serves as a permanent background for plays by Shakespeare and other playwrights. Compare this photo with the picture of Shakespeare's Globe on page 41.

In the Arena Stage, built in 1960 in Washington, D.C., the audience completely surrounds the stage action. Lighting instruments are visible above the stage, and scenery and furniture are minimal. Actors enter and exit through the alleyways, called voms, for the Roman *vomitorium* or entranceways into the seats in the early amphitheatres.

The Grand Illusion

Theatre creates the *illusion*, as we watch, that we are sharing an experience with others for the first time. As members of the audience we tacitly agree with the actors that, for the time of the performance, the play is a living reality. We know that theatre is not life, but we suspend this knowledge for the few hours we watch the play. We share with the actors the illusion that life is being lived on stage as we observe their actions, which can be repeated night after night. As we watch and listen, we share their experiences — both spontaneous and rehearsed. Moreover, actors contribute further to the illusion, for they are both actors and characters. We are simultaneously aware that Oedipus, the central figure in *Oedipus the King*, is Sophocles' central character and that he is being played by an actor named John Gielgud. Theatre's grand illusion is twofold: that the actors are other than who they are in the present moment, and that life is taking shape before us *for the first time*.

In the theatre we both believe in what is happening before us ("suspend our disbelief," as the poet Coleridge said) and disbelieve in the pretense. We give way to theatre's magic and illusion as our minds and emotions are involved, yet we exist apart.

Audience, Space, and Actor

The three basic components of theatre are the actor, the space, and the audience; the history of theatre has been, in one sense, the record of the changing physical relationships of actor and audience. The audience has moved from the hillside of the Greek amphitheatre to a place before the Christian altar, to standing room around the Elizabethan theatre's platform stage, to seats in a darkened hall before a curtained proscenium stage, to the floor of a modern environmental production.

In the same historical sequence, the actor has moved from the dancing circle of the Greek theatre to the church, to the open stage of the Elizabethan theatre, to the recessed stage of the proscenium theatre, to the environmental space of some contemporary productions. The effect of historical trends and social institutions on theatre are important but not crucial to this discussion of theatre as a way of seeing. What is crucial is an understanding of the common denominators, unchanged since the legendary Thespis, credited with being the first actor, stepped apart from the Greek chorus and created dialogue for the listener. It is no accident that the Greek word for actor is *hypokrites*, meaning "answerer." That first actor literally answered the chorus' questions. At its most basic, theatre's common factors are *actor, space, text,* and *audience.*

Whether the physical space becomes more elaborate or less so, whether the performance occurs indoors or out, the actor–audience relationship is theatre's vital ingredient. In one sense, the formula for theatre is simple: *A man or woman stands in front of an audience in a special (or prepared) place and performs an action, usually interacting with another performer.*

The Living Experience

The actor–audience relationship distinguishes theatre from that extraordinarily popular medium of our culture, *film.* When we go to a movie, we sit in a darkened room looking at a screen filled with light images. We respond to the large image of the actor as though Marlon Brando, John Malkovich, or Mel Gibson were a living physical presence. But, in film, the story, the actors, and the locations are recorded on tape months before we see the movie. In contrast, the actor in the theatre exists before us in the moment.

Although films and videotapes are often made from plays, and many stage plays—from *Hamlet* to *A Streetcar Named Desire* to *Driving Miss Daisy*—have been made into highly popular films, theatre and film are different. Films and videos use actors as characters-in-action who express themselves in dialogue, but they are subordinate to the photographic images that the director and film editor have arranged. Unlike theatregoers, film audiences are in the presence of *images* from the past whose speech is reproduced through recorders and electronic sound systems, not human beings speaking and moving in the present. And just as the film or televi-

FIGURE 1.1

This still from the 1951 movie version of Tennessee Williams' play A Streetcar Named Desire *captures for all time a moment between Vivien Leigh (as Blanche DuBois) and Marlon Brando (as Stanley Kowalski). Each time we see the movie (and it may be ten times), we can experience again this interaction between these two particular actors. A similar moment in the theatre is lost to us even as it takes place before us on the stage.*

sion audience does not experience the actors' flesh-and-blood presence, the film actor does not experience the audience's instant response.

Theatre is "alive"—in immediate communion with its audience—and has been for 2,500 years. Film is a twentieth-century technological invention, a means of recording and preserving that "aliveness" for all time. The television program "Live from Lincoln Center" is one highly successful effort to record on videotape a stage performance with its audience. From our homes we can watch opera stars Luciano Pavarotti and Joan Sutherland and hear the audience's enthusiastic response, but we are twice removed from the original event. We know that both theatre and film/video are equally convincing in their story-telling powers, but their modes of presentation are vastly different.

For example, the great performances of Marlon Brando and Vivien Leigh as Stanley Kowalski and Blanche DuBois in *A Streetcar Named Desire* are captured in the 1951 film (see Figure 1.1). But the wonderful theatrical performances of Laurette Taylor, Jessica Tandy, Vanessa Redgrave, Kathleen Turner, and others in plays by Tennessee Williams are lost to us as the performance ends (see Figure 1.2). Theatre is an evanescent art, lasting only those two or three hours it takes to see the play. The experience

FIGURE 1.2

A tender moment between actors Jessica Tandy as Blanche DuBois and Karl Malden as Mitch in the original New York production of A Streetcar Named Desire *(1947), directed by Elia Kazan.*

can be repeated night after night as long as the show is running, but once the play is closed and the cast is dispersed, that performance is lost.

Although admittedly frustrating, this intriguing quality of theatre, which critic Brooks Atkinson calls the "bright enigma," is the source of its vitality and our pleasure.

Entertainment

Entertainment takes many forms: rock concerts and videos, movies and dances, games and sports events. Watching a basketball game, for example, is entertaining. What is it about the theatre that makes its entertainment value different, say, from an athletic event? What do games and theatre have in common? What are their differences?

There are historical precedents for relating theatre to athletic events. The Greeks celebrated their civic achievements with both theatre festivals and Olympian games. The Romans programmed athletic contests and theatrical events in their *ludi* — festivals with races, games, and entertainments. The Elizabethans accommodated bear-baiting spectacles, like modern bullfighting, in some of their playhouses. Today, such sports as baseball, basketball, football, and tennis compete for television time with news and dramatic programming.

FIGURE 1.3

Star player (Michael Jordan of the Tarheels, the University of North Carolina, Chapel Hill, and now an NBA player for the Chicago Bulls) contributes to the entertainment value of this athletic event through his consummate skills, honed in practice with his teammates. Note the spectators' riveted attention in the background. Sports and theatre have much in common — not the least of which are the performers and audience.

In both theatre and basketball, for example, we, as amateurs, take pleasure in observing the skill of the performers and especially "the stars" (see Figure 1.3). But part of the pleasure in watching a basketball game is finding out who's going to win, and it is this unpredictable or random quality of the sporting event that distinguishes it from the theatre's ritual quality. Both sets of performers must be capable of physical effort, self-expression, technique, comprehension, and emotional involvement — all within limits set by the rules. Although both actors and athletes hone their skills before performance — calling it "rehearsal" or "practice" — only the actors know how the show will end before they begin because the theatre event is meaningfully organized and crafted from beginning to end: Oedipus will always blind himself; Hamlet will always die in the duel with Laertes; Blanche DuBois will always be taken to an asylum; and Godot will never arrive. In contrast, the Chicago Bulls, an NBA team, will either win or lose, depending upon their efforts and those of the competing team.

The theatre's actors, directors, and designers plan their event with great care from beginning to end. The players in a basketball game, on the other hand, never know how things will turn out until the very last second before the buzzer sounds.

Each night, actors re-create the same characters and re-enact the same story; at predetermined times, actors move, speak dialogue, handle properties, make gestures; the stage lights change and the scenery shifts on *cue*. And although we take pleasure in observing the skill, talent, and intelligence of the performers in both basketball and theatre, there is a special pleasure that results from our participation with actors in an activity that for them is a ritualized performance.

If any random quality exists in theatrical performance, it comes from the particular *feedback* the performers get from each separate audience, which may vary from attentive rapport to an impatient shifting about in seats. Certain kinds of feedback, like laughter and applause, are almost second nature to us. But there is another, less tangible kind of communication between actor and audience. Like the Zen archer who becomes one with the arrow in flight, a great actor can establish an emotional kinship with the audience. The audience's attention, breathing, energy, and tensions send out signals to the actor and vice versa. For a brief interval, an emotional oneness is achieved between them. At the end of such a performance, the audience's applause is like the breaking of a spell, releasing energy and tension. These are those very special moments we remember in the theatre, *when the actor's emotional life melds with the audience's humanity.*

The Collaborative Art

In much the same way as most sports events, theatre is a team effort — a collaboration among artists, not athletes. Directors, designers, and actors combine their talents, ideas, and imaginations to create a special world. Working together, they transform an empty space into an environment where actors live out the characters' make-believe lives within fictional worlds. And the audience, as we have seen, becomes part of this collaboration, responding from night to night to the success or limitations of the team's collective effort.

"Magic Time" — The Taming of the Shrew, *1990*

Getting to the audience's "magic time" requires months of preparation. When asked to restage *The Taming of the Shrew* for the New York Shakespeare Festival's open-air theatre in Central Park, director A. J. Antoon set Shakespeare's battle of the sexes between Petruchio (Morgan Freeman) and Katherina (Tracey Ullman) in America's Old West of the 1880s.

Updating Shakespeare is no longer an oddity nor is the nontraditional casting of Morgan Freeman as Shakespeare's "unwanted husband." This time-warped production of the Bard's comedy is also familiar to us as *Kiss Me Kate,* a musical version of Shakespeare's story about a most unlikely couple—the strong-willed bridegroom and the bad-tempered bride.

This photo essay follows the hard work and many talents that go into the making of a production. Designers, craftspeople, technicians, director, and actors follow a process from early production conferences through technical and dress rehearsals to the magic of opening night.

For the Old West concept, scenic designer John Lee Beatty created a Main Street setting of a Western town that reminds us of a Hollywood backlot facade decorated with murals of stampeding horses. Here, Beatty paints finishing touches on the rustic scene.

Top, the Old West costumes are created in the costume shop by craftspeople — cutters and drapers, seamstresses, milliners, etc. The cutter/drapers work on the heroine's plain gingham dress, designed by Lindsay Davis (far left) for Kate to wear in Act I. The basic garments are completed with chaps, guns, holsters, buckskins, hats, and bonnets.

Center, in the audio booth, composer Claude White and technician Ted Lehrman prepare the "show tape" for audio sound track and cues. In this production, tumbleweeds even dance about on stage to White's musical score.

Bottom, lighting designer Peter Kaczorowski and his assistant (Jeanne Koenig) work at a temporary lighting desk set up with monitors and headsets in the theatre's auditorium. Kaczorowski talks by headset to technicians in the lighting booth as he sets light levels and cues for the show during technical rehearsals.

For the actor's process, director A. J. Antoon (left) has a "line rehearsal" with the play's hero and heroine. He listens as Morgan Freeman and Tracey Ullman quietly rehearse only their lines without concern for "acting" their roles.

Kate uses her more marriageable younger sister Bianca (Helen Hunt) for target practice. Each time Kate fires her gun, one of the six balloons around Bianca pops. These balloons are the responsibility of the properties department and crew.

Morgan Freeman and Tracey Ullman rehearse a scene in which Petruchio lassos and captures his unruly wife in a play whose sexual politics modern audiences often regard as offensive—as an endorsement of male supremacy and female submissiveness.

Left, for the dress rehearsal actor William Duff-Griffen applies makeup and moustache before his makeup mirror in the theatre's dressing rooms. Playing a traveling ham-actor, he makes up to resemble a pink-cheeked W. C. Fields.

Right, following dress rehearsal, the cast has a "photo call" arranged by the theatre's press representative (Richard Kornberg, left). Tracey Ullman and Morgan Freeman stand in costume as the photographer arranges the pose.

On opening night (July 12, 1990) at the Delacorte Theatre in Central Park, the audience watches an early scene. The city's lights brighten the skyline behind the outdoor stage.

Over months and weeks, many talents have been coordinated in the creation of this "Wild West" staging of Shakespeare's *Taming of the Shrew,* which one critic called an old-fashioned Western that leaves the audience feeling that the good folks (man and woman alike) have won in this classic "shootout between the sexes."

Life's Double

Theatre is a way of seeing men and women in action, of observing what they do and why they do it. Because human beings are both theatre's subject and its means of expression, theatre is one of the most immediate ways of experiencing another's concept of life — of what it means to be human.

It has been said by Shakespeare and others that there is a doubleness about the theatrical experience that provides a sense of life reflected before us in a special mirror — the stage. For instance, the audience experiences the actor both as actor — the living presence of another human being — and as fictional character. We experience Laurence Olivier as Hamlet, Marlon Brando as Stanley Kowalski, and Jessica Tandy as Blanche DuBois. Likewise, the performing space is a stage and at the same time an imaginary world created by the playwright, designer, director, and actor. Sometimes this world is as familiar to us as a New Orleans tenement or a Midwestern farmhouse. The stage might resemble a modern living room or a hotel room or a front yard. Sometimes it is unfamiliar, like Hamlet's blighted castle at Elsinore, Oedipus' plague-ridden city of Thebes, or Othello's storm-tossed island of Cyprus.

The Elizabethans thought the theatre mirrored life. Shakespeare had Hamlet describe the purpose of acting, or "playing," in this way:

> . . . the purpose of playing, whose end, both at the first and now, was and is to hold as 'twere the mirror up to Nature, to show Virtue her own feature, scorn her own image, and the very age and body of the time his form and pressure. (3, ii)

Hamlet speaks here of the Elizabethan idea that the stage, like a mirror, shows audiences both their good and bad qualities along with an accurate reflection of the times.

The Elizabethan idea of the stage as a mirror, related as it is to the act of seeing, can help us understand the dynamics of theatre. Looking into a mirror is, in a sense, like going to the theatre. When we look into a mirror we see our double — an image of ourselves — and possibly a background

▼▼▼

Shakespeare's greatest tragedy, *Hamlet* (c. 1601) tells the story of a man who confronts a task that seems beyond his powers.

Although the Danish court is celebrating King Claudius' wedding to Queen Gertrude, her son Prince Hamlet still mourns the death of his father. The ghost of his father appears and tells Hamlet that he was murdered by Claudius. Hamlet swears to take vengeance, but he must first prove to himself that Claudius is guilty. He has a group of strolling players put on a play in which a similar murder is depicted. Claudius' reaction to the play betrays him and Hamlet plots revenge (see Figure 1.4).

By accident he kills Polonius, the Lord Chamberlain and father to Ophelia, a young woman who loves Hamlet. Hamlet is exiled for killing Polonius, and Ophelia is driven mad.

Laertes, Polonius' son, vows revenge and challenges Hamlet to a duel. To ensure that Hamlet is killed, Claudius poisons Laertes' sword and prepares a cup of poison for Hamlet to drink during the duel. In the closing scene, Gertrude accidentally drinks from the poisoned cup and dies, Hamlet kills Claudius, and Laertes — after mortally wounding Hamlet — is killed in turn by Hamlet with the poisoned sword. Hamlet's cousin Fortinbras is made king of Denmark.

Hamlet is a tragedy about the power of evil to corrupt the innocent, bring chaos to a kingdom, and paralyze the human will. It contains some of the greatest poetry written by Shakespeare.

and anyone standing around the reflection. The image can be made to move; we make certain judgments about it; it communicates to us certain attitudes and concerns about our humanness. Our humanity as reflected in the mirror has shape, color, texture, form, attitude, and emotion; it is even capable of limited movement within the mirror's frame. Onstage the actor's living presence as a fictional character — as Oedipus, Othello, Hamlet, or Blanche DuBois — creates the doubleness that is theatre's special quality. It is both a stage world and an illusion of a real world.

Theatre is life's double, but it is also something more than a reflection of life. It is a form of art — *a selected reflection*. It is life's reflection *organized meaningfully*.

Discovery

Theatre people often call the beginning of a performance "magic time" because performances usually start with a certain magical effect. The house lights dim, the front curtain goes up (if there is one), and the audience *discovers* a hidden world.

In one sense, then, theatre is *discovery*. Let us briefly examine two plays to see how this discovery process works. Starting with two actors on a bare platform, the complex world of *Hamlet* gradually reveals itself. As the

FIGURE 1.4
Roger Rees as Hamlet in the 1984 Royal Shakespeare Company production, Stratford-on-Avon, directed by Ron Daniels. In this famous scene, Hamlet decides not to murder Claudius (Brian Blessed) while he is praying, because his enemy's soul would go to heaven.

ghost appears to Hamlet demanding that he avenge his father's murder by his uncle Claudius, Shakespeare shows us a fallen and disordered world. Appearances are deceptive. The innocent appear to be guilty, and the devious seem honest. We find out about Claudius' villainy, Hamlet's "madness," Ophelia's suicide, and the murderous plots that end in the fatal duel. Hamlet's delayed revenge results in the destruction of two families and a kingdom. Witnessing that destruction, we discover that Shakespeare's revenge play is, in truth, a complex tragedy about the power of evil and political disorder to paralyze the human will and corrupt the imagination.

In Samuel Beckett's *Waiting for Godot* (1953), a curtain rises to reveal two tramps, Vladimir and Estragon, waiting under a wasted tree for someone named Godot. During the next two hours Beckett's tramps eat, sleep, joke, suffer, quarrel, despair, and hope while waiting out their lives. As we watch the play we discover that, like Vladimir and Estragon, we are also waiting for things to happen and time to pass.

The playwright, too, is engaged in a process of discovery. It is not unreasonable, then, that many plays begin and end with questions. When theatre emerged from the Dark Ages after the decline of the Greek and Roman cultures, one of the earliest recorded pieces was the *Quem Quaeritis*

▼▼▼

Jaques' speech from Shakespeare's *As You Like It* provides us with one of the
most famous discussions on the similarities between theatre and life:

All the world's a stage,
And all the men and women merely players.
They have their exits and their entrances,
And one man in his time plays many parts,
His acts being seven ages. At first the infant,
Mewling and puking in the nurse's arms.
And then the whining school-boy, with his
  satchel
And shining morning face, creeping like snail
Unwillingly to school. And then the lover,
Sighing like furnace, with a woeful ballad
Made to his mistress' eyebrow. Then a soldier,
Full of strange oaths, and bearded like the pard,
Jealous in honor, sudden and quick in quarrel,
Seeking the bubble reputation
Even in the cannon's mouth. And then the
  justice,

In fair round belly with good capon lined,
With eyes severe and beard of formal cut,
Full of wise saws and modern instances,
And so he plays his part. The sixth age shifts
Into the lean and slippered Pantaloon,
With spectacles on nose and pouch on side,
His youthful hose, well saved, a world too wide
For his shrunk shank, and his big manly voice,
Turning again toward childish treble, pipes
And whistles in his sound. Last scene of all,
That ends this strange eventful history,
Is second childishness and mere oblivion,
Sans teeth, sans eyes, sans taste, sans
  everything.
(2, vii)

trope, lines of chanted dialogue, which begins with the question: Whom seek ye? The first words of *Hamlet*, spoken by the guard on the fog-shrouded battlements, are "Who's there?" The next-to-last lines of the two acts of *Waiting for Godot* are also questions — the same questions, in fact:

ESTRAGON: Well, shall we go?
VLADIMIR: Yes, let's go.

[*They do not move.*] *Curtain* (Act I)

VLADIMIR: Well, shall we go?
ESTRAGON: Yes, let's go.

[*They do not move.*] *Curtain* (Act II)[2]

Theatre searches for answers about human nature and society: Who are we? Where have we been? Where are we going in this life? It discloses what it means to be a human being in certain situations and under certain conditions. In Sophocles' *Oedipus the King*, Oedipus searches for the cause of the plague and discovers his own identity. Shakespeare's Othello seeks revenge and finds out, too late, that he has killed an innocent wife and has been destroyed himself by Iago's malevolence. In Beckett's *Waiting for Godot* (Figure 1.5), Vladimir and Estragon keep their appointment with the ab-

Waiting for Godot, by the Irish playwright Samuel Beckett, was first produced at the Théâtre de Babylone, Paris, in 1953. On a country road in a deserted landscape marked by a single leafless tree, Estragon and Vladimir are waiting for someone named Godot. To pass the time, they play games, quarrel, make up, fall asleep. In comes Pozzo, leading Lucky by a rope tied around his neck. Pozzo demonstrates that Lucky is his obedient servant, and Lucky entertains them with a monologue that is a jumble of politics and theology. They disappear into the darkness, and Godot's messenger (a boy) announces that Mr. Godot will not come today.

In Act II, a leaf has sprouted on the tree, suggesting that time has passed, but the two tramps are occupied in the same way. They play master-and-slave games, trade hats, argue about everything. Pozzo and Lucky return, but they are not the same: The master is blind and the slave is mute. Godot again sends word that he will not come today, but perhaps tomorrow. As the play ends, Vladimir and Estragon continue waiting, alone but together. In this play Beckett demonstrates how each of us waits for a Godot — for whatever it is that we hope for — and how, so occupied, we wait out a lifetime.

FIGURE 1.5

The first American production of Beckett's Waiting for Godot *was directed by Alan Schneider in 1956 at the Cocoanut Grove Playhouse in Miami. Tom Ewell played Vladimir (center) and Bert Lahr was Estragon.*

sent Godot and perhaps discover in their waiting something essential about themselves and others. "We have kept our appointment and that's an end to that. We are not saints, but we have kept our appointment," says Vladimir. "How many people can boast as much?" Estragon answers: "Billions."

Audience Expectations

A modern audience enters a theatre lobby with an air of excitement and a sense of anticipation. There is usually a last-minute crush at the box office to pick up tickets, then to get programs and find seats. An audience is not an unruly crowd but a very special group assembling for a special occasion; it is the final, essential participant in the theatre event. The audience is the assembled group for which all has been written, designed, rehearsed, and produced.

What, then, are our expectations as we wait for the house lights to dim and the curtain to rise? Our expectations are essentially the same whether we are in the Shubert Theatre on Broadway or the Guthrie Theater in Minneapolis.

1. *As audiences, we expect plays to be related to life experiences.* (It goes without saying that audiences expect plays and performances to hold their attention and to be entertaining.) This does not mean that audiences actually expect to have experienced the events taking place on stage. None of us would willingly exchange places with Oedipus or Blanche DuBois. Instead, we expect the play's events (and also the actor's performances) to

Tennessee Williams' *A Streetcar Named Desire* was first produced at the Barrymore Theatre, New York, in 1947. Her family's Mississippi estate sold, Blanche DuBois arrives at the New Orleans tenement home of Stella and Stanley Kowalski, her pregnant sister and brother-in-law. Blanche's faded gentility clashes with Stanley's brutish masculinity. As she seeks protection from the world, she competes with Stanley for Stella's affections but finds herself no match for his sexual hold over her sister. She tries to charm Mitch, Stanley's poker-playing friend, into marrying her. However, Stanley destroys Blanche's hopes for marriage by telling Mitch about her past drunkenness and promiscuity. As Stella reproaches Stanley for his cruelty, her labor pains begin and Stanley rushes her to the hospital.

Blanche is visited by a drunken Mitch, who accuses her of lying to him and makes an effort to seduce her. Stanley returns to find Blanche dressed for a party, fantasizing about an invitation to go on a cruise with a wealthy friend. Angered by her pretensions, Stanley starts a fight with her that ends in rape. In a final scene some weeks later, Blanche, her tenuous hold on reality shattered, is taken to a mental hospital.

The tragedy of *Streetcar* reveals human duplicity and desperation in Williams' modern South, where fragile people are overcome by violence and vulgarity.

be *authentic* in feelings and experiences. We are moved by *A Streetcar Named Desire* because it rings true in terms of what we know about ourselves and others. It confirms what we have studied, read, and heard about human behavior. Williams' characters and situation may not be literally a part of our lives; yet we all recognize the need for fantasies, self-delusion, and refuge from life's harsh realities. In short, we go to the theatre expecting the performance to be an authentic representation of some aspect of life as we know it or can imagine it.

2. *Most of us go to the theatre expecting the familiar.* These expectations are based largely on plays we have already seen or on our experiences with movies and television. Audiences enjoy the familiar in plots, characters, and situations. For this reason, daily television soap operas, like "The Young and the Restless" and "As the World Turns," are popular with all ages. Also, audiences frequently have difficulty understanding and enjoying plays from the older classical repertory or from the contemporary avant-garde. We are not as comfortable with the concerns of Oedipus or Estragon as we are with the domestic affairs of Roseanne Barr or Bill Cosby.

All audiences come to the theatre with certain expectations that have been shaped by their previous theatregoing experiences. If those experiences have been limited to musicals, summer stock, or local community theatre, then they may find the first experience of a play by Anton Chekhov or Samuel Beckett a jarring, puzzling, or even boring experience. But masterpieces somehow ring true! In them we find authentic life experiences, even if the language is difficult, the situations strange, or the production techniques unfamiliar.

The response to the first American production of *Waiting for Godot* is a good example of audiences confronted with the unfamiliar and having their expectations disappointed on their first experience with the play. Audiences in Miami and New York were baffled by it. But in 1957, Jules Irving and Herbert Blau's San Francisco Actor's Workshop presented *Waiting for Godot* to the inmates of San Quentin Prison. Because no live play had been performed at San Quentin since Sarah Bernhardt appeared there in 1913, the director and actors were apprehensive.

Of the 1,400 convicts assembled to see the play, possibly not one had ever been to the theatre. Moreover, they were gathered in the prison dining room to see a highly experimental play that had bewildered sophisticated audiences in Paris, Miami, and New York. What would be the response? It was simply overwhelming. The prisoners understood the hopelessness and frustration of waiting for something or for someone that never arrives. They recognized the meaninglessness of waiting and were aware that if Godot finally came, he would probably be a disappointment.[3]

By now, *Waiting for Godot* is no longer considered experimental, and most audiences are no longer baffled by it. It has become a classic of the modern theatre, exemplifying how initial audience expectations can change over a period of years in response to an unusual, profound play.

Even though audiences desire to see the familiar—this is probably the reason there are so many revivals of *Arsenic and Old Lace* and *Charley's Aunt*—they also appreciate and look forward to novel experiences in the theatre. Imagine the surprise of audiences in 1970 when director Peter Brook reinterpreted Shakespeare's *A Midsummer Night's Dream*, exploring the complications of young love in a white boxlike setting with actors in mod clothing on trapezes (Figure 1.6). Most audiences around the world were delighted with the new concept for staging a very old play, although a few were dissatisfied by not having their expectations fulfilled.

Like all great art forms, the theatre gives us a heightened sense of life and self-awareness. Great theatre also provides a sense of *new* possibilities. We go to plays (whether consciously aware of our reasons) to realize a fuller, deeper understanding of our lives, our society, and our universe. When we are satisfied, we no longer cling to our need for the familiar.

3. *Another facet of audience expectations is more difficult to pin down—the collective response.* We experience a performance as a group—as a collective

FIGURE 1.6

A radical adaptation of Shakespeare's A Midsummer Night's Dream *directed by Peter Brook in 1970 for Britain's Royal Shakespeare Company. Oberon (Alan Howard) and Puck (John Kane) speak Shakespeare's lines while seated on trapezes like acrobats.*

thinking and feeling presence. We have already remarked how theatre is a collective art. Psychologists tell us that being in an audience satisfies a deeply felt human need: the need to participate in a collective response, whether with laughter, tears, appreciative silence, or thundering applause. As part of an audience, we become very much aware of group dynamics at the conclusion of a powerful and moving play. Sometimes when audiences are deeply moved, there are moments of silence before the beginning of applause. At other times applause is instantaneous, with audiences leaping to their feet clapping and shouting "bravo." The response to a great performance, as it was to Laurence Olivier's Othello, is immediate and unrestrained.

Even though applause is a theatregoing convention, it is also a genuine expression of our appreciation and approval of a performance. One major element of our experience of live theatre is this sharing of feelings with others around us. Sometimes this even happens in movie houses, especially in horror films, but rarely does it happen when we sit before the television set at home—because we are usually watching alone, or else we are distracted by movements around us. An audience by definition is a sharing with others—of laughter and tears, expectations and delight.

Summary

Theatre takes place as we watch actors present themselves to us in stories usually about human beings. The heart of the theatrical experience is the act of seeing and being seen; hence, we have subtitled this book "A Way of Seeing."

Theatre, like life, happens within the present moment. Theatre has an immediacy that most other art forms do not have or require. For theatre to happen, two groups of people — actors and audience — must come together in a certain space. There the actors present themselves to the audience. The space, the actor, and the audience are the three essential ingredients of the theatre event. Most effectively of all the arts, theatre captures the experience of what it means to be human because human beings are both its medium and its subject: The actor (the medium) on the stage is also Hamlet (the subject) at Elsinore castle.

Comparing theatre with film and other forms of entertainment helps clarify the special qualities of the theatre. Theatre's *immediacy* — living actors presenting themselves before a live audience — is one of the most notable differences between theatre and film. Although both the theatre and sporting events entertain us, there is a random and unpredictable quality in sports that is not found in the carefully crafted, rehearsed, and performed play.

Theatre requires the participation of people with varied skills: playwrights, directors, actors, designers, and producers. They work together to bring a story to life before an audience. Theatre, unlike painting and sculpture, is a collaborative art, but the collaboration is not complete until the audience is also engaged.

Theatre is an act of discovery. When the curtain goes up, we discover a world that is both familiar and unfamiliar to us. We discover new ways of learning about ourselves, our society, and our world. Great plays always raise questions about what it means to be a human being. Great performances communicate this knowledge to us in fresh, entertaining, and challenging ways.

Questions for Study

1. How does theatre differ from other art forms, such as film, television, music, dance, and painting?

2. What did the ancient Greeks mean when they called their theatre a "seeing place" or *theatron*?

3. What types of theatres are we likely to find today on our campuses and in our cities?

4. What is special about theatrical space?

5. Why are the actor, the space, and the audience the theatre's three unchanging components?

6. What do we mean when we say that each night in the theatre there is an "illusion of the first time"?

7. How does Shakespeare define the "purpose of playing"?

8. What do we mean when we say that theatre is an *immediate* art?

9. How does the theatre's quality of entertainment differ from the entertainment of a sports event like basketball or football?

10. What do we mean when we say that theatre is a *collaborative* art, a team effort?

11. What kinds of *audience feedback* are we likely to experience in the theatre?

12. How are human beings both theatre's subject and its means of expression?

13. What did Shakespeare mean by writing in *Hamlet* that a performance is like a mirror held up to nature?

14. Why does Brooks Atkinson call theatre a "bright enigma"? What does it mean?

15. *Plays to Read*: Sophocles' *Oedipus the King*, Shakespeare's *Hamlet*, Williams' *A Streetcar Named Desire*, Beckett's *Waiting for Godot*.

16. *Suggested Reading*: *The Empty Space* by Peter Brook (New York: Atheneum, 1968).

There are, for example, privileged places, qualitatively different from all others — a man's birthplace, or the scenes of his first love . . . as if it were in such spots that he had received the revelation of a reality other than that in which he participates through his ordinary daily life.
MIRCEA ELIADE, *THE SACRED AND THE PROFANE: THE NATURE OF RELIGION*[1]

Since its beginnings, theatre has been a place for seeing — for viewing, presenting, perceiving, understanding. Places for theatre to happen are found in all societies, ancient and modern. Throughout history the theatre space has been arranged so that audiences can see and performers can be seen.

Chapter 2

The Seeing Place: Traditional Spaces

L et us begin the discovery of theatre with the places, stages, and auditoriums where it all happens. All cultures, no matter how primitive or sophisticated, have theatrical performances and places for *seeing* these events. The earliest theatrical spaces were areas for performance of rituals dealing with life and death.

Ritual and Theatre

The Special Place

When we examine the origins of ritual and theatre, we discover that the earliest actor always performs in a special or privileged place. The priest, the guru, the dancer, or the actor performs in a threshing circle, or in a hut, a building, or an enclosure that is shared with the onlooker or audience. In some ritual spaces, a circular area is surrounded by spectators in much the same way that the semicircular Greek amphitheatre is configured. In others, special buildings are constructed for the occasion and often destroyed at the end of the rite in the same sense that a modern production is "struck," or removed at the end of the play's run. Some groups moved from place to place in early societies, like today's touring companies.

Since the publication of Sir James Frazer's *The Golden Bough* in 1890, theatre historians have connected the origins of theatre with agrarian and fertility rites and with *special places* for enactment of these rites. Primitive people staged mock battles between death and life in which the king of the old year, representing death, perished

FIGURE 2.1

The shaman of early hunting cultures was both a healer and an artist. As well as healing the sick, the shaman brings psychic calm and confidence to the tribe by revitalizing and intensifying its notions of the world. The annual hunting rites carried out by the shaman are a good example. The photo shows a Siberian shaman's coat and mask. (From Shamanism: The Beginnings of Art.*)*

in a duel with the champion of the new year. In these rituals we can see the beginnings of theatrical modes of today: *enactment, imitation,* and *seasonal performances*—all held in special or privileged spaces so designated by the community.

Dramatic overtones were added to ceremonies designed to win favor from supernatural powers. The rain dance ceremonies of the Indian Americans of the Southwest were meant to ensure that the tribal gods would send rain to make crops grow. Early societies acted out seasonal changes—patterns of life, death, and rebirth—until their ceremonies became formalized dramatic rituals. Harvest rituals, for example, celebrated abundant food supplies. Imitation, costume, makeup, masks, gesture, and pantomime were theatrical elements in these early rituals. (See Figure 2.1.)

Whereas primitive ritual was concerned with the protection of the tribe, theatre's most common objective is to please and entertain rather than to pacify, protect, or heal. And its audiences are not secondary to what's going on onstage, as they may very well be in the practice of ritual magic. Theatre's audiences, as we have seen, are central and indispensable to the theatrical experience.

FIGURE 2.2

The shaman's role in energizing the successful hunting life of the tribe is shown in rock paintings. This cave painting shows reindeer and a shaman in a bison mask. Artistic ability represents an important part of the shaman's effectiveness: Dramatic gifts and theatrical effects (mime, masks, costume, dance, drum-beating) give the tribe superior power over animals and success in the hunt.

Theatre, on the other hand, deals with the mystery, history, and ambiguity of human events. Plays speak to us of individuals, as well as of groups. They hold the mirror up to our joys and our sorrows, to our questions and tentative answers about life. Theatre aims to provoke thought while entertaining us, rather than to provide concrete answers. We spoke in the previous chapter about the playwright's concern for the human condition. Shakespeare demonstrates the sensitivity of a supreme dramatic artist in this speech by Hamlet:

> What a piece of work is a man, how noble in reason, how infinite in faculties; in form and moving how express and admirable, in action how like an angel, in apprehension how like a god: the beauty of the world, the paragon of animals! And yet to me what is this quintessence of dust? (2, ii)

Hamlet speaks about himself, but he also speaks in universal terms about all of us. He raises questions about human nature; insights are there for those who want them. But even so, the play's essential function is to entertain. For without diversion, all else in the theatre must inevitably fail and audiences become bored, restless, "turned off." Although ritual performances are often entertaining, their objective is largely practical: Crops will grow, the hunt will succeed, warring tribes will be placated or defeated. (See Figure 2.2.) In ritual, entertainment is a bonus for the onlooker; in theatre we share in a complex experience that is simultaneously entertaining, imitative, provocative, subversive, and even magical.

Although theatre evolved from early ritual and those special places reserved for enactment of communal rites, theatre differs from ritual in several essential ways. Unlike participants in a ritual, actors create fictional characters. Actors also present themselves on a stage, or in a special place, using the playwright's words to create a sense of place and life. That the actor appears *on a stage* is important not only for an actor, and for the other artists and technicians involved, but also for the audience.

What is certain in these early beginnings is that theatre, as we know it now, is a kind of ritual act performed not in a hut or other temporary structure that will be dismantled after the ceremony, but in a permanent building that will be used again and again. Theatrical space as we know it in modern terms has two components: the *stage* and the *auditorium*. And the first such permanent theatre building we know of in our culture stands in the curve of a hillside in Greece.

The Greek Theatre

The most celebrated theatre of fifth-century Athens, called the Theatre of Dionysus in honor of the fertility god, was an open-air structure located on the slope of the hill below the Acropolis.

In time, there were two performance areas cradled within the curve of the hillside: the dancing circle (or *orchestra*), and the area backed by the scene building (or *skene*). The chorus, usually portraying ordinary human society, performed in the dancing area. One actor (later three) portrayed mythical and historical characters, first in an "empty space" and later in front of the rectangular scene building, which formed a neutral background easily representing many places — a palace, temple, house, cave, or whatever was needed. A late addition to the theatre was the wooden scene building erected on a stone foundation. The actors may also have performed in the *orchestra*, although no one knows for sure. The chorus, actors, and audience all entered the theatre through passageways called *parodoi*, and the audience stood, or were seated on the ground and later on wooden or stone benches, on the hillside "auditorium."

In the ancient Greek theatre there were no barriers between the performing area and the auditorium. The audience on the hillside had an unbroken view of actor and chorus as they do in the photo of the Theatre

FIGURE 2.3

The Theatre at Delphi is typical of ancient Greek theatres. It is built on a hillside with seats on three sides surrounding the stage. The temple of Apollo is in the background. Eventually, scene buildings were built behind the playing area. Audiences could look past the stage to the mountains and the sea in the distance. The photo shows the stone benches placed on the hillside for the audience, the flat dancing circle or stage at the foot of the hill, and the remains of the stone foundation of the scene building.

at Delphi (see Figure 2.3). The spectators in the lower tiers near the orchestra, in fact, were so near the chorus that they were practically an extension of it.

The Chorus as Spectator and Commentator

The Greek chorus, which was eventually reduced from fifty people to fifteen or twelve by the time Aeschylus, Sophocles, and Euripides were writing for the festivals, shared the audience's reactions to events and characters, and sometimes interacted with the actors. Functioning as the play's community or society, the chorus gave advice, expressed opinions, asked questions, and generally set the ethical framework by which events were judged. They frequently served as the "ideal spectator," reacting to characters and events as the playwrights hoped audiences would. Their costumes and masks added spectacle — movement, song, and dance — to the occasion, and their moods heightened the story's dramatic effectiveness.

Aeschylus and the Athenian Festivals

Aeschylus (525/4–456 B.C.), Sophocles, Euripides, and Aristophanes are four Greek playwrights whose work has survived. Aeschylus began at an early age to write tragedies for the annual festivals in the Theatre of Dionysus, Athens, winning thirteen first prizes during his lifetime.

Sometime before or during Aeschylus' career, the features of Greek tragedy became fixed: At an Athenian festival, three groups of players, each consisting of a chorus and two (later three) actors, competed in acting four sets of plays. Each set contained three tragedies and a **satyr play**, a burlesque of Greek myth, for **comic relief**. The plays were based on Greek legend, epic poems, or history. Costumes were formal, masks elaborate, physical action restrained; violent scenes occurred offstage. The playwright expanded and interpreted the characters and stories of legend or history.

Although Aeschylus wrote over seventy plays, we have inherited scripts for only seven: *The Suppliants, The Persians, The Seven Against Thebes, Prometheus Bound, Agamemnon, The Libation Bearers,* and *The Eumenides.* These last three comprise the *Oresteia* (458 B.C.), the only surviving Greek trilogy, or sequence of three tragedies. Its satyr play is missing.

We know little about Aeschylus as a person except that he fought at Marathon (490 B.C.) and probably at Salamis (480 B.C.) during the Persian Wars. His epitaph, which he wrote himself, shows that he was most proud of his military record:

Under this monument lies Aeschylus the Athenian, Euphorion's son, who died in the wheatlands of Gela. The grove of Marathon with its glories can speak of his valor in battle. The long-haired Persian remembers and can speak of it too.

Unlike the chorus, the actor, representing a heroic figure like Oedipus or Orestes, stood apart in the performance space, just as he stood apart from ordinary mortals in life. Thus, the dancing circle and the chorus formed a kind of bridge between actor and audience, serving as both commentator and spectator for the deeds it witnessed (see Figure 2.4).

Theatre Space as Social Commentary

The arrangement of spaces in the Greek theatre indicates how the Greeks saw their world: Classes separated physically by space and social status found themselves on common ground when faced with spectacles of terror and misfortune. They found mutual comfort in being part of a cosmos dominated by gods and heroes. Sophocles' *Oedipus the King* speaks to

One of several Greek playwrights whose work survives today, Sophocles wrote three plays about Oedipus. *Oedipus the King* (427 B.C.) is generally considered the greatest of Greek tragedies. (*Antigone*, 441 B.C., and *Oedipus at Colonus*, 406 B.C., are the other two.)

Oedipus the King tells the story of a man who flees from Corinth to avoid fulfilling a prophecy that he will kill his father and marry his mother. On his journey he kills an old man (an apparent stranger but actually his real father, the king of Thebes) at a place where three roads meet. He then proceeds to Thebes and solves the riddle of the Sphinx. As a reward, he is made king and married to the widowed queen, who is actually his mother, Jocasta. He rules well and has four children.

The play opens with Thebes stricken by a plague. Declaring that he will rid the city of the infection, Oedipus has sent his brother-in-law Creon to consult the Delphic oracle about the cause of the plague. As he pursues the plague's source, Oedipus comes face to face with himself as his father's killer, as his mother's son and husband, and as his children's father and brother. When the truth is learned, Jocasta kills herself and he puts out his eyes. By his own decree, Oedipus is exiled from Thebes and wanders blind into the countryside.

Oedipus the King explores human guilt and innocence, knowledge and ignorance, power and helplessness. Its fundamental idea is that wisdom comes to us only through suffering.

FIGURE 2.4

The National Theatre Company of Greece performs today in the Epidaurus Festival Theatre. The photo shows the chorus in the orchestra *and two actors, with one standing above them on the stone steps leading into the modern scene building or* skene *and the other kneeling (center).*

master and slave when the chorus concludes: "Count no man happy until he has passed the final limit of his life secure from pain."

From the classical to the Hellenistic period (c. 990–30 B.C.), the Greek theatre underwent changes: Wooden seats were replaced by stone; the addition of the scene building made the actors' area more complex, providing a scenic background and dressing area; a raised stage was probably added sometime after the fifth century for the actors to perform on. (See Figure 2.5.) But the theatres remained in the open air, with well-defined places for the audience to sit and for the actors and chorus to perform. As we shall discover in a later chapter, the division of space and other conventions such as the formal entrances, choral odes, and two to three actors dictated the structure of the plays performed there. The plays of Aeschylus, Sophocles, Euripides, and Aristophanes were shaped by the theatre's conventions.

Medieval Theatre

The medieval theatre (c. 950–1500) began in churches with Latin playlets performed by priests. (An early example is the *Quem Quaeritis* trope mentioned in Chapter 1.) Gradually, performances moved out of the churches into the marketplaces. Lay performers replaced priests; scripts grew longer and more complex, mixing the serious with the boisterous and farcical.

Like the Greek and Roman amphitheatres, the medieval European theatre was an open-air festival theatre. There were few permanent structures. The plays, grouped in *cycles*, dealt with Biblical events and ranged from the creation to the destruction of the world. One cycle contained as many as forty-two plays. They were performed in spring and summer months on religious holidays such as Corpus Christi, Easter, and Whitsuntide.

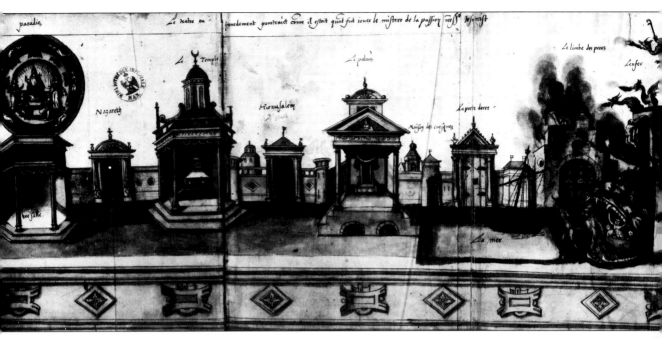

FIGURE 2.6

The fixed stage used for the Valenciennes Passion Play in 1547. The mansions or huts represent (from left to right) specific locations: Paradise, Nazareth, the temple, Jerusalem, the palace, the golden door, the sea, and Hell's Mouth.

Productions were sponsored by town councils, often with the help of local priests. Religious confraternities or secular trade guilds usually produced them; they hired a director or stage manager and recruited actors from the local population, who turned out en masse to be part of the event.

Types of Medieval Staging

Precursors of the medieval *fixed stage* are to be found in the permanent Greek and Roman theatres and in the Christian churches with their aisles, naves, and raised altars. The *movable stage* had its beginnings in the medieval processions that celebrated religious and state occasions. We can see the influence of the medieval theatre on our own fixed and movable stages, open-air theatre buildings, amphitheatres, street theatre, festival theatres, and holiday parades.

The Fixed Stage   One of the best-known fixed stages was constructed in 1547 for the Valenciennes Passion Play, in northern France (see Figure 2.6). Other important medieval fixed stages include the Roman amphitheatres, the "rounds" in Cornwall, England (see Figure 2.7), and the stages, like the Valenciennes stage, set up in public squares in France.

The fixed stage at Valenciennes was a rectangular platform with two chief areas. One contained the "mansions," or huts, which depicted specific locales; the other was the *platea*, an extended playing space. There

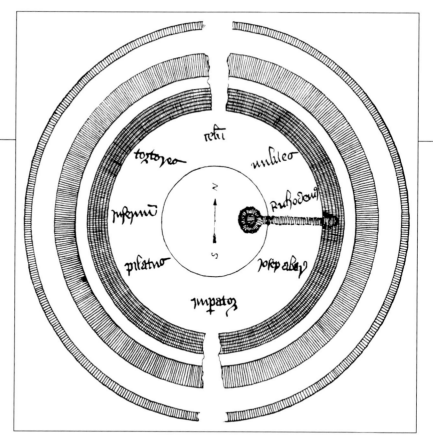

FIGURE 2.7

A Cornish circular amphitheatre (fixed stage). A typical permanent open-air theatre in Cornwall (also called a round) was made out of earth with circular turf benches surrounding a level area 130 feet in diameter. Openings on two sides of the earthen mound provided entrances and exits. This diagram (of the fourteenth-century theatre at Perranzabulo) shows the staging for a Biblical cycle called The Resurrection of Our Lord Jesus Christ. *There are eight scaffolds located in the round's center. Action requiring a specific locale took place on the scaffolds, progressing from one scaffold to another around the circle. The audience, seated on the earthen tiers of seats, could follow the scenes with ease.*

were no scene changes as we know them in our theatre. The actor merely went from hut to hut to indicate change in locale. Heaven and hell were usually represented on each end of the stage, with earthly scenes of humor, travail, and so on occurring between them. The fixed stage made it possible to present numerous scenes and actors, along with the necessary costumes, **properties**, and special effects.

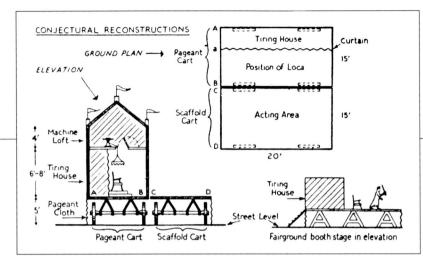

FIGURE 2.8

Glynne Wickham's drawing is a conjectural reconstruction of an English pageant wagon and ground plan of the overall playing arrangement. The drawing shows the essential features of what was to be the Elizabethan playhouse: a platform acting area, a tiring-house with a recessed area (the loca) for interior scenes and costume changes, and an area above the cart for machinery.

In the Roman and Cornish amphitheatres, the audience probably viewed the action from two or three sides. When the stage was the platform type, viewers might be grouped around three sides of the playing areas. Or they might gather at the front only. Whichever way, the stage was always in the open air; there was a definite performing space for the actors and a definite audience area. The actor was close to the audience, and performances sometimes continued from dawn to dusk.

The Pageant Wagon Although fixed stages were common in many parts of Europe, theatrical space sometimes took on entirely different forms. In Spain and England, for example, the pageant wagon and processional, or portable, staging were used. The pageant wagon (in Spain called a *carros*) was a platform on wheels, something like our modern parade float (see Figures 2.8 and 2.9). It was a portable playing area with a hut, or **tiring-house**, on top for the actors, which could also serve as a scenic background or acting area. No one is certain of the wagons' dimensions, but they had to move through the narrow streets of medieval towns. The wagons stopped for performances at a number of places and may have been used individually or in groups.

The audience stood around the wagons to watch, so the actors were very close to the audience, just as they were on the fixed stage. The flexible playing space encouraged vigorous action (especially by the Devil, who was booed and hissed energetically by audiences); episodic, loose-knit plot

structure; and some sort of scenic element to fix locale. *The Crucifixion Play*, one of thirty-two surviving plays of the English Wakefield cycle (c. 1375), is based on Biblical scenes of Christ's torture at the hands of soldiers, followed by his death on the cross. The cycle requires continuous action from the scourging of Christ to his raising on the cross to his death.

The Elizabethan Theatre

By the late sixteenth century, permanent structures were being built in England and on the continent to house a new kind of theatrical entertainment, one that was losing its ceremonial and festive qualities and focusing more on plays as imitations of human events, that is, Shakespeare's "mirror held up to Nature." In 1576, James Burbage built London's first theatre, naming it simply "The Theatre." It was an open-air structure that adopted features from various places of entertainment: innyards, pageant wagons, banquet halls, fixed platforms, and portable booth-stages.

FIGURE 2.10

An enlargement of a theatre labeled "The Globe" from the engraving by J. C. Visscher, c. 1616.

Shakespeare's Globe

In 1599, Richard Burbage, James' son and leading actor, and associates built the Globe Theatre, which became a showcase for Shakespeare's talents as actor and playwright. The most famous of all Elizabethan theatres, the Globe was an open-air building with a platform stage in the middle surrounded on three sides by open standing room (see Figure 2.10). This space was surrounded in turn by a large enclosed balcony topped by one or two smaller roofed galleries. The stage was backed by a multilevel facade as part of the superstructure, called the tiring-house. On the stage level were places for hiding and discovering people and objects, highly influenced by the variety of medieval platform stages with their many huts or mansions. A roof jutting out above the stage platform was supported by two columns; the underside of the roof, called "the heavens," was painted with moons, stars, and planets. After paying an admission fee, the audience stood around the stage or — for an additional charge — sat in the galleries or private boxes. Like the medieval audience, they were never far from the performers.

With little scenery and few properties, the Elizabethan theatre encouraged both playwright and actor to create unlimited illusions, transporting the audience from Juliet's tomb in one play to a raging storm at sea in another.

Elizabethan Theatres and Reconstructions

The De Witt drawing of the *Swan Theatre* in London dates from about 1596; it is the first picture we have of the interior of an Elizabethan theatre. In *The Globe Restored* (1968), C. Walter Hodges describes the Elizabethan theatre as self-contained, adjustable, and independent of any surroundings other than its audience.

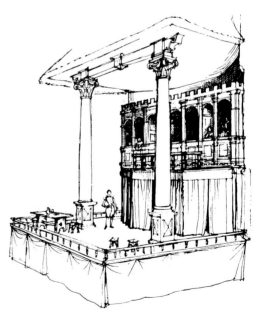

It is generally agreed that the *tiring-house* (the area around and within the house wall at the back of the stage as shown in Hodges' drawing) was divided from the stage by hangings of some sort, usually curtains opening in the middle.

The Shakespeare Theatre at the Folger, Washington, D.C., is a 253-seat modified indoor Elizabethan reconstruction opened in 1970 as part of the Folger Shakespeare Library. Its proscenium-thrust stage provides a neutral facade and a flexible, multilevel playing space, and its auditorium utilizes modern seating surrounded above by a gallery on three sides.

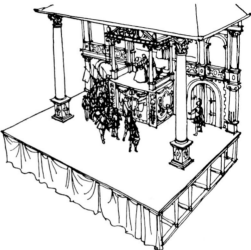

The *inner stage* or *discovery space* is thought to be a small, recessed area with curtains in the tiring-house wall. Hodges shows a discovery area surrounded by curtains. The permanent upper level or upper stage is a characteristic feature of the Elizabethan stage; it was used for scenes such as the balcony scene in *Romeo and Juliet*. Hodges' reconstruction of the inner and upper stages brings them forward into the main acting area.

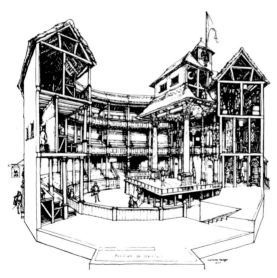

Hodges' detailed reconstruction of the *Globe Playhouse* (1599–1613) shows the building's superstructure, with galleries, yard, and railed stage. Notice the trapdoor in the stage, stage doors, curtained inner and upper stages, tiring-house (as backstage area with workrooms and storage areas), hut with machines, "the heavens," and playhouse flag.

41

William Shakespeare

William Shakespeare (1564–1616) was an Elizabethan playwright of unsurpassed achievement. Born in Stratford-on-Avon, he received a grammar-school education and married a twenty-six-year-old woman when he was eighteen. He became the father of three children, Susanna and twins Judith and Hamnet.

Few other facts about Shakespeare's life have been established. By 1587–1588 he had moved to London, where he remained until 1611, except for occasional visits to his Stratford home. He appears to have found work almost at once in the London theatre as an actor and a writer. By 1592 he was regarded as a promising playwright; by 1594 he had won the patronage of the Earl of Southampton for two poems, *Venus and Adonis* and *The Rape of Lucrece*.

In 1594–1595 he joined James Burbage's theatrical company, The Lord Chamberlain's Men, as an actor and a playwright; later he became a company shareholder and part owner of the Globe and Blackfriars theatres. He wrote some thirty-seven plays for this company, suiting them to the talents of the great tragic actor Richard Burbage and other members of the troupe. Near the end of his life he retired to Stratford as a well-to-do country gentleman. Shakespeare wrote sonnets, tragedies, comedies, history plays, and tragicomedies, including some of the greatest plays written in English: *Hamlet, King Lear, The Tempest, Macbeth,* and *Othello.*

Theatrical Influences

The Elizabethan theatre, like that of Greece and medieval Europe, was a festive theatre depicting cosmic drama that touched all people: peasant, artist, and noble. Its architecture, as we shall see, affected the structure of the plays written for it. Yet it all happened so long ago. Why do we study these ancient modes of theatre, whose traditions are often so hard to trace? Do they really tell us anything about our own theatre buildings and stages? Are they related to the buildings and performance spaces that we think of as being so modern?

The answer is yes, and you will agree next time you see a Mardi Gras or mummers' float (see Figure 2.9) or an open-air theatre designed for summer productions of Shakespeare (see Figure 2.11). In large parks, plays with historical themes are performed outdoors for audiences looking for family entertainment; touring groups travel widely to college campuses with portable stages, costumes, and properties to present plays about current themes. And street theatre performers — aided by puppets, mimes, musicians, loudspeakers, and colorful displays — trumpet political and social messages with the spectacle and passion of a medieval pageant.

FIGURE 2.11

The Oregon Shakespearean Festival Theatre is a modern reconstruction similar to The Fortune Theatre of Shakespeare's London, which was built in 1599. Although the seating and lighting facilities are modern, the stage and tiring-house are patterned after the earlier theatre.

The Proscenium Theatre

The proscenium theatre dates from the Italian Renaissance of the early seventeenth century. The Farnese Theatre built in 1618 at Parma was one of the early proscenium theatres (see Figure 2.12). An ornamental facade framed the stage and separated the audience from the actors and scene.

The development of the proscenium arch, framing the stage and masking its inner workings, brought innovative scenery techniques. Renaissance architects painted perspective scenery on large canvas pieces placed on a *raked*, or slanted, stage. In the seventeenth century, an architect named Giambattista Aleotti created a new system for changing scenery with movable, two-dimensional wings painted in perspective. This method, now called a wing-in-groove system (because grooves were placed in the stage floor to hold the scenery), replaced the raked stage.

Most of the theatres built in the Western world over the last 350 years are proscenium theatres. The concern of scenic designers working within this *picture-frame stage* was to use perspective scenery (see Figure 2.13) and

FIGURE 2.12

The Farnese Theatre in Parma, Italy, was one of the earliest to have a permanent proscenium arch. Our modern proscenium theatre with perspective scenery had its origins in Italy. Between 1500 and 1650, a typical theatre eventually developed with an auditorium, painted scenery, proscenium, curtain, and musicians' pit. Spectacle, illusion, and entertainment were its primary purpose.

FIGURE 2.13

The principles of perspective painting were introduced to theatrical scene design in the sixteenth century. Perspective scenery was painted to create the illusion of large streets or town squares, with houses, churches, roofs, doorways, arches, and balconies, all designed to appear exactly as they would seem to a person at a single point. This kind of painted background was intended to give a sense of depth to the scene. In his book Architettura, *Sebastiano Serlio (1475–1554) explained the construction and painting of scenery for* comedy, *including the houses, tavern, and church shown in the drawing.*

mobile scenic pieces to achieve the effect of life being lived within the picture frame. The result was literally to frame the actors so that an audience, sitting in an enclosed, darkened space, could observe the actors in their setting. Playgoers were confined to the tiered galleries and to the orchestra or pit, as the ground-level seats were called.

Recent Proscenium Theatres

As audiences grew larger and playhouses became more profitable, the auditoriums of public theatres increased steadily in size. And as the auditoriums expanded, theatre architects added boxes for the affluent and cheap seats in the galleries for the less well-off. In the nineteenth century the proscenium opening was enlarged to exploit the pictorial possibilities of the stage space. The auditorium was made shallower so that the audience was drawn closer to the stage, where they could see the actors' expressions and the details of their environment.

Today our proscenium theatres (many built in the late 1800s) contain a framed *stage* with scenery, machines, and lighting equipment; an *auditorium* (possibly with balconies) seating 500 to 600 or more; and *auxiliary rooms*, including foyers, workrooms, dressing rooms, and storage space.

The function of the proscenium theatre is to create illusion. In this complex, technicians, designers, directors, playwrights, and actors collaborate to create make-believe worlds. For instance, the **box set** of Anton Chekhov's *The Cherry Orchard* (1904) contains the world of the play — Madame Ranevskaya's drawing room on her bankrupt estate in rural Russia at the turn of the century (see Figure 2.14).

In the proscenium theatre, the stage is usually hidden by a curtain until it is time for the play's world to be "discovered" by the audience (see Figure 2.15). Staging, scenery, lighting, and production style all work together to suggest that inside the proscenium arch is a self-contained world. The room may look like a typical living room. The street, garden, factory, or railway station may resemble places the audience would know. But in the proscenium theatre, the audience is intentionally kept at a distance. They are primarily onlookers or witnesses to an event.

FIGURE 2.14

A box set. Constantin Stanislavsky's setting for the 1904 Moscow Art Theatre production of The Cherry Orchard *includes box set (with ceiling), details of a recognizable room (notice the dog), and morning light coming through the windows as essential details.*

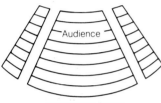

Proscenium Stage

FIGURE 2.15

The Eisenhower Theatre, a proscenium theatre, at the John F. Kennedy Center for the Performing Arts in Washington, D.C. The audience is seated before the closed curtain.

FIGURE 2.16

The thrust stage at the Stratford (Ontario) Festival Theatre has a permanent facade or background resembling Shakespeare's theatre (see page 41). In contrast, the Guthrie Theater in Minneapolis is a proscenium-thrust stage utilizing changeable, perspective scenery as background for the actor (see page 7).

Thrust, or Open, Stages

Variations of the proscenium theatre often display features from Elizabethan inn-theatres and open stages. Today's thrust, or open, stage is an example (see Figure 2.16). Thrust stages were largely designed to utilize perspective scenery without distancing the actor physically and psychologically from the audience. The idea here, as in many open, postwar theatres, was to minimize the separation of actor and audience created by the proscenium arch and the recessed stage. The actor literally performs on a platform that thrusts into the audience, and audiences have a keen sense of the actor's presence in direct communication with them, sharing the text and the world of the play.

The Eastern Theatre

Until this century, the theatrical traditions of Eastern cultures have been curiously removed from the West. The Japanese Noh theatre, developed in the late fourteenth and unchanged since the seventeenth century, has only recently influenced Western directors and actors. Unlike Western drama, it is highly stylized and depends heavily on music and mime.

FIGURE 2.17

FIGURE 2.17

The Noh stage is a square, polished cedar platform open on three sides; it has a temple roof and a back wall with a painted pine tree. In this photo the National Theatre of Japan performs for a modern audience. The musicians and chorus surround the principal actor (shite) on two sides; the audience is seated in front and to the left of the stage.

The Japanese Noh Stage

The stage is situated in a corner of a building at the audience's right hand. A temple roof rises above the stage floor, which is divided into two areas: the stage proper (*butai*) and the bridge (*hashigakari*). All elements on this stage, including the four columns supporting the roof, have names and significance during performance. (See Figure 2.17.)

The stage proper is divided into three areas: The largest is about eighteen feet square and marked off by four pillars and roof; at the rear of the stage are the musicians — a flute player and two or three drummers; and to the left of the main area sits the six-to-ten-member chorus. The stage's two entrances are the bridge, a railed gangway that leads from the dressing room to the stage and is used for all important entrances, and the "hurry door." Only three feet high, the hurry door is used by minor characters, musicians, chorus, and stage assistants. Three small pine trees in front of the bridge symbolize heaven, earth, and humanity. Another pine tree, symbolizing the play's earthly setting, is painted on the center wall behind the musicians. This wall forms the scenic background for all Noh performances.

FIGURE 2.18

The ancient craft of mask-making for the Noh theatre has been handed down from one generation of artists to the next. The masks are made of wood and painted. The purity and simplicity of the Noh mask reflect the highly formal theatrical tradition of which it is a part.

The Performers

Like the stage, all features of a Noh performance are carefully controlled and fixed by tradition. The principal character (*shite*) is usually an aristocrat, lady, or supernatural being. The actor playing this character performs facing the column at the downstage (nearest the audience) right corner. The downstage left column is associated with the secondary character (*waki*).

The conventions of performance are handed down from one generation of actors (all male) to the next. Every movement of the hands and feet and every vocal intonation follow a set rule. The orchestra supplies a musical setting and controls the timing of the action. The chorus sings the actor's lines while he is dancing, and narrates many of the play's events. Song and dialogue outline circumstances.

Some Noh actors wear painted wooden masks (see Figure 2.18) that designate basic types: men, women, aged people, deities, monsters, spirits. The silk costumes and headdresses are rich in color and design.

Japanese Kabuki Theatre

By about 1600 the Noh theatre was replaced in popular taste, first by the Bunraku puppet theatre and then Kabuki. Whereas Noh largely remained the theatre of the court and nobility, Kabuki — which originated in Edo,

FIGURE 2.19

The theatrical excitement and commercialism of this modern Kabuki performance are illustrated by the painted scenery, elaborate costumes, musicians, and the onnagata in a climactic pose atop a giant bell.

Kyoto, and Osaka, and was less formal and distant—had more popular appeal. The modern Kabuki stage is a rare combination of the old and the new, of thrust and proscenium type stages. (See Figure 2.19.)

The Kabuki Stage

The Kabuki stage covers the entire front of the theatre and is approached by a ramp, called a *hanamichi*, or "flower way," which is a raised narrow platform connecting the rear of the auditorium with the stage proper. The performers (all male) make dramatic entrances and exits on this runway. Occasionally, they perform short scenes on the *hanamichi* as well, literally in the middle of the audience.

The proscenium stage is long (some as long as ninety feet) but has a relatively low opening. Visible musicians (usually seated stage left) generally accompany the stage action. Kabuki plays originally required a full day in performance but today are about five hours long. They deal with vendettas, revenge, adventure, and romance, featuring elaborate and beautiful scenic effects, including a revolving stage that was developed in Japan before it was used in the West.

FIGURE 2.20
Bertolt Brecht's production of The Caucasian Chalk Circle *at the Theater am Schiffbauerdamm, East Berlin, in 1954 shows the influence of Eastern theatre. In the photo, Grusha journeys with the child to the mountains. On a bare stage she mimes her long journey before a simple white curtain with pine trees in the center.*

The Performers

Like Noh actors, Kabuki actors are trained from childhood in singing, dancing, acting, and feats of physical dexterity. Kabuki roles are divided into such basic types as brave and loyal men, villains, comic roles, children, and women's roles. Male actors who play women's parts are called *onnagata*. They are particularly skillful in their ability to imitate feminine sensibilities through stylized gestures and attitudes.

The Kabuki actor does not use a mask but instead boldly patterned makeup—a white base with designs of red, black, brown, or blue. The makeup symbolizes the character and describes the role. The *onnagata* use only white makeup along with false eyebrows and rouging to shape the mouth and at the corners of the eyes. Each role has its conventional costume, based on historical dress and often weighing as much as fifty pounds.

The Kabuki actor's performance is always highly theatrical, colorful, and larger than life. Since he does not sing, he is often assisted by a narrator and chorus. The narrator may set the scene, speak dialogue, recite passages, and even comment on the action.

These Eastern nonillusionistic conventions have greatly influenced Western writers and directors like Bertolt Brecht, as we shall see in his play *The Caucasian Chalk Circle*. (See Figure 2.20.)

Chikamatsu Monzaemon (1653–1724)

Born into a provincial samurai (warrior) family in the seventeenth century, Chikamatsu became the most important Japanese playwright since the great period of Noh drama 300 years earlier. When he was thirty, Chikamatsu began writing for the Bunraku puppet theatre; he also wrote for the Kabuki theatre, and many of his puppet plays were later adapted for Kabuki.

Chikamatsu wrote both history and domestic plays — loosely constructed stories about the nobility featuring military pageantry, supernatural beings, battles, suicides, beheadings, and many kinds of violent deeds, all rendered through choreographed movements. His domestic plays featured unhappy lovers driven to suicide. Every play was characterized by the beauty of Chikamatsu's poetry.

A prolific writer, Chikamatsu has been compared by Western critics to William Shakespeare and Christopher Marlowe for the power of his verse and the sweep of his social canvas. His best-known plays in the West are *The Battles of Coxinga* (1715) (his most popular work); *The Love Suicides at Sonezaki* (1703); *The Courier for Hell* (1711); and *The Love Suicides at Amijima* (1721).

Eastern Theatre in the West

In recent years, Western scholars, directors, and actors have become interested in several Eastern theatrical practices: minimal staging; revolving stage; fixed conventions of movement, style, and dress; symbolic properties, dress, and masks; and visible musicians and stage assistants. In addition, the main forms of Eastern theatre — the Beijing Opera (China); Noh theatre, Bunraku or puppet theatre, and Kabuki theatre (Japan); shadow puppets (Malaysia); Balinese dance theatre (Bali); and Kathakali dancers (India) — have influenced Western producer-directors such as Edward Gordon Craig, William Butler Yeats, Vsevelod Meyerhold, Antonin Artaud, Bertolt Brecht, Jerzy Grotowski, Ariane Mnouchkine (Figure 2.21), Harold Prince (Figure 2.22), and Peter Schumann.

Summary

In Western and Eastern theatre, traditional spaces are divided into stage and auditorium. Beginning with ritual performances in early societies, the theatrical space has always been special — a privileged place, to paraphrase

FIGURE 2.21

Shakespeare's Richard II, *as directed by Ariane Mnouchkine for her celebrated company, the Théâtre du Soleil, 1981, was visually modeled on the grand theatrical styles of the Kabuki and Noh theatres. Designer Jean-Claude Barriera's costumes are a mix of Japanese and English period dress. Here, actors stand in classical Japanese poses, clad in layered clothing, cutaway kimonos, belted sashes, and heavily lined makeup.*

FIGURE 2.22

Kabuki costumes, like the one worn by this principal actor in Pacific Overtures, *are made of layers of richly embroidered, hand-painted kimonos. This 1975 elaborate Broadway musical was directed by Harold Prince, with lyrics by Stephen Sondheim and dazzling costumes by Florence Klotz.*

anthropologist Mircea Eliade, where spectators perceive the revelation of a reality separate from that of their daily lives. Those making theatre have traditionally sought out a place — a hillside, a street, a marketplace, a building — to engage audiences in the experience of seeing life imitated by performers. Over the centuries those places have been ritual dancing circles, stone amphitheatres, church naves and choir lofts, fixed platforms and movable wagons in open spaces, and complex thrust and proscenium stages in enclosed buildings. In all cases inflexible conventions eventually developed regarding the relation of spectator to performer. These conventions are played with, violated, even turned upside down, as many contemporary theatre practitioners attempt to engage audiences directly by breaking the established molds of actor–audience relationships.

Questions for Study

1. What are the two essential components of theatrical space?

2. In what sense are *enactment, imitation,* and *seasonal rites* forerunners of today's theatre?

3. What are the essential features of the ancient Greek theatre?

4. In what sense is the medieval European theatre a *festival theatre*?

5. How are the medieval theatre's *fixed* and *processional* stages related to our own theatre practices?

6. How did the features of Shakespeare's stage influence his use of space in *Hamlet*?

7. What are the principal features of the proscenium theatre?

8. How are the acting and audience spaces related in proscenium theatres?

9. How does the modern proscenium-thrust stage, or open stage, combine features of the Elizabethan theatre and of the picture-frame stage?

10. What are the fixed traditions of the Japanese Noh theatre and Kabuki theatre?

11. Modern directors are interested in Eastern theatre because it does not attempt to create an illusion of life being lived before us. How does Noh or Kabuki staging differ from the Western realistic theatre of Anton Chekhov or Tennessee Williams?

12. How have the physical relationships between actor and audience changed throughout theatrical history?

13. Describe the types of theatres found on your campus.

14. Plays to Read: *The Crucifixion Play* (Wakefield) and Shakespeare's *Hamlet*.

15. Suggested Reading: Joseph Campbell with Bill Moyers, *The Power of Myth* (New York: Doubleday, 1988).

The elimination of the stage–auditorium dichotomy is not the important thing — that simply creates a bare laboratory situation, an appropriate area for investigation. The essential concern is finding the proper spectator–actor relationship for each type of performance and embodying the decision in physical arrangements.
JERZY GROTOWSKI, *TOWARDS A POOR THEATRE*[1]

Modern efforts to find new kinds of theatrical space have created different ways of seeing theatre. Over the past two decades Jerzy Grotowski in Poland, Ariane Mnouchkine in Paris, Peter Schumann in Vermont, and Peter Brook from Africa to Avignon in France, have rearranged theatrical space to bring audiences and actors closer together. As audiences, we are part of the staged action, seeing both as spectators and as participants.

Chapter 3

The Seeing Place: Nontraditional Spaces

One way of thinking about nontraditional (or alternative) theatrical spaces is to consider what Carlos Castaneda says about special places in *The Teachings of Don Juan: A Yaqui Way of Knowledge* (1968). Having been instructed by his teacher to find a special place by using his eyes, Castaneda explores the porch of Don Juan's house, searching for a "personal" spot where he can sit down. After many hours, he senses the correct place and settles into it, shaping and filling it. In recent years, there have been similar approaches to Castaneda's experience with space in the creation of alternative or environmental performance spaces. Polish director Jerzy Grotowski describes the essential concern as "finding the proper spectator–actor relationship for each type of performance and embodying the decision in physical arrangements."

We find historical precedents for performing theatre in strange places and in unusual buildings in the performances of wandering minstrels and mimes and in the processional stages of the Middle Ages. The great populist theatre of the Italian Renaissance, the **commedia dell'arte** companies, also performed in nontraditional spaces. They were professional itinerant players who often improvised their stages (and performances) on wagons or on temporary stages in marketplaces, town fairs, and banquet halls.

All theatre people who have performed singly or in groups wherever an audience could be gathered around them are background to the modern avant-garde creation of environmental theatre, associated in particular with the Vietnam War era in the United States, though international in practice.

By definition, environmental theatre rejects conventional seating and arranges the audience as part of the playing space. Each member of the audience seeks out and finds a space as special and particular as that occupied by the actors. Like the actors, the spectators also become part of what is seen and done; they are both seeing and seen. In contrast, traditional theatres with proscenium and thrust stages arrange the audience *before* a stage, where we see and hear at a comfortable remove.

Forerunners: Meyerhold, Reinhardt, Copeau

In modern Russia, Germany, and France, such leaders as the inventive Vsevelod Meyerhold (1874–c. 1940), Max Reinhardt (1873–1943), and Jacques Copeau (1879–1949) developed unorthodox production methods. They are the chief forerunners of today's many experiments in nontraditional performance. In the 1930s the Russian director Meyerhold, rejecting the proscenium arch as too confining for his actors, removed the front curtain, footlights, and proscenium. He had stagehands change properties and scenery in full view of audiences, and actors perform on trapezes, slides, and ramps to arouse exhilarating feelings in both performers and audiences.

Max Reinhardt explored vast acting areas, such as circus arenas, to stage *Oedipus the King* (1910) in Berlin's Circus Schumann, which he thought of as a people's theatre, or his "theatre of the five thousand." He dreamed of a theatre on the scale of classical Greek and Roman theatres to be used for spectacles and mass audiences. In 1920, he created his most famous spectacle (*Everyman*) in the square before the Salzburg Cathedral.

French director Jacques Copeau, another opponent of the proscenium arch, converted a hall into the Théâtre du Vieux Colombier in Paris in 1913 and developed a *unit setting*, a single stage environment for all productions. The forestage was brought forward from an inner proscenium, and a set of asbestos curtains moved on rods to effect rapid changes of locale. Copeau used only a few pieces of essential furniture and set pieces, similar to Elizabethan practices, in his approach to minimal staging (see Figure 3.1).

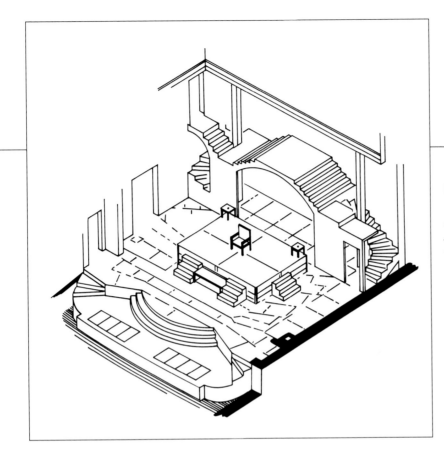

FIGURE 3.1
The unit setting or "single locale" visualized by Jacques Copeau for the new stage at the Théâtre du Vieux Colombier, Paris. Its neutral space, many levels, and minimal scenic pieces are reminiscent of the Elizabethan stage.

During the last forty years some theatre directors and designers have looked for new theatrical spaces in warehouses, lofts, and halls. They reshaped *all* of the space available to audience and actor, seeking to bring the audience into direct contact with the actor, and to make it a more obvious part of the theatrical event.

This chapter is a brief discussion of three nontraditional approaches to the use of theatrical space: the Polish Laboratory Theatre, the Théâtre du Soleil, and the Bread and Puppet Theatre.

The Polish Laboratory Theatre

Grotowski's Poor Theatre

When Jerzy Grotowski founded the Polish Laboratory Theatre in 1959, he set out to answer the question: What is theatre? Grotowski evolved a concept that he called poor theatre. For him, theatre's essentials are the actor and the audience in a bare space. He found that theatre could happen

Jerzy Grotowski

Jerzy Grotowski (b. 1933) is founder and director of the Polish Laboratory Theatre, an experimental company located in Wroclaw. Not a theatre in the usual sense, the company became an institute for research into theatre art in general and the actor's art in particular. In addition, the laboratory also undertook performances for audiences as well as instruction of actors, producers, students (many of them foreigners), and people from other fields. The plays performed were based on Polish and international classics. In the 1960s and '70s Grotowski's productions of Stanislaw Wyspianski's *Akropolis*, Shakespeare's *Hamlet*, Marlowe's *Dr. Faustus*, and Calderón's *The Constant Prince* attracted worldwide attention. His closest collaborators were actor Ryszard Cieslak and literary adviser Ludwik Flaszen. He wrote about his methods in *Towards a Poor Theatre* (1968).

After 1970, Grotowski disbanded his company to explore human creativity outside the theatre (he called these projects para-theatre). He intended to lead participants back to elemental connections between themselves and the natural world by exposure to basic myths, dancing, playing, bathing, and the elements of fire, earth, air, and water. In 1975 the event called *Holiday* took place in a forest, where participants in a pure ritualized experience were encouraged to rediscover the roots of theatre and themselves.

In 1984, Grotowski started a new phase of work called objective drama, consisting of performance fragments examining the "roots of theatre" common to all cultures. He has since divided his time between the United States and Italy working with a team of international performers.

without costumes, scenery, makeup, stage lighting, and sound effects; all it needed was the actor and audience in live communion in a special place. Grotowski writes:

> I propose poverty in theatre. We have resigned from the stage-and-auditorium plant: for each production, a new space is designed for the actors and spectators. . . . The essential concern is finding the proper spectator–actor relationship for each type of performance and embodying the decision in physical arrangements.[2]

Environments

In his production of *Akropolis* (1962), the actors built structures among the spectators, subjecting them to a sense of congested space (see Figures 3.2 and 3.3). In *Dr. Faustus* (1963), the entire space became a monastery dining

FIGURE 3.2

The theatrical space at the beginning of the performance of Akropolis. *Note that the wire struts above the audience are empty.*

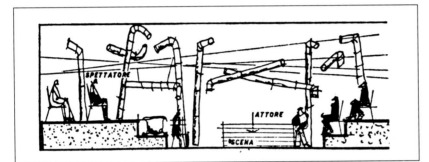

FIGURE 3.3

The theatrical space at the end of Akropolis. *The actors have disappeared, leaving the stovepipes hanging from the wire struts as gruesome reminders of the events in the concentration camps.*

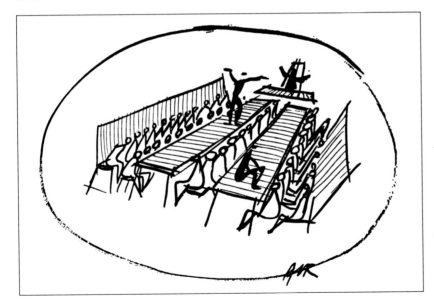

FIGURE 3.4

A view of the scenic action for Grotowski's production of Dr. Faustus, *based on the Elizabethan text by Christopher Marlowe. One hour before his death, Faustus offers a last supper to his friends (the audience) seated at the refectory tables. The theatrical space has been converted into a monastery dining hall.*

hall, and the spectators were guests at a banquet during which Faustus offered them entertaining episodes from his life. In *The Constant Prince* (1965), the audience was separated from the actors by a high fence. They looked down on the actors like medical students watching a surgical operation. (See Figures 3.4 and 3.5.)

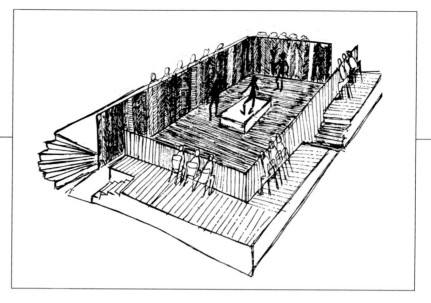

FIGURE 3.5

A view of the scenic action for The Constant Prince, *based on the seventeenth-century Spanish text by Pedro Calderón de la Barca. The audience, seated behind a barrier, looks down on a forbidden act. Their positioning suggests a surgical operating theatre or a bullring.*

Holy Theatre

Within the whole space, Grotowski creates what he calls holy theatre: The performance is a semireligious act in which the actor, prepared by years of training and discipline, undergoes a psychospiritual experience. Grotowski sets about to engage the audience in this act, and thus to engage both actor and audience in a deeper understanding of personal and social truths.

Akropolis

In *Akropolis*, Grotowski adapted a text written by Polish playwright Stanislaw Wyspianski in 1904. In the original, statues and paintings in Cracow Cathedral come to life on the eve of Easter Sunday. The statues re-enact scenes from the Old Testament and antiquity. But Grotowski shifted the action to an extermination camp, Auschwitz, in wartime Poland. In the new setting he contrasted the Western ideal of human dignity with the human degradation of a death camp.

The Setting *Akropolis* takes place in a large room. (See Figure 3.6.) Spectators are seated on platforms, and passageways for the actors are created between the platforms. Wire struts are strung across the ceiling. In the middle of the room is a large, boxlike platform for the actors. Rusty pieces of metal are heaped on top of the box: stovepipes, a wheelbarrow, a bathtub, nails, hammers. With these objects the actors build a civilization of gas chambers. They wear a version of a camp uniform — ragged shirts and trousers, heavy wooden shoes, and anonymous berets.

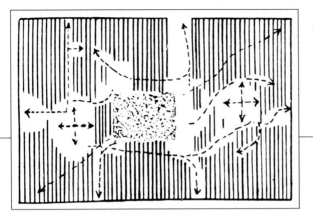

FIGURE 3.6
The diagram shows Grotowski's use of space for Akropolis. The lines with arrows indicate the actors' movements and areas of action; the straight lines show audience areas. The central playing space is a boxlike "mansion" where pipes are assembled and into which the actors disappear at the end of the performance.

FIGURE 3.7
This photo depicts a "dialogue between two monuments." The metal stovepipe and human legs with boots make a visual statement about the way human beings can be treated as objects. This is one of many statements in the performance about the effects of inhumanity throughout our history. The actor is Zbigniew Cynkutis.

FIGURE 3.8
The character Esau (played by Ryszard Cieslak) sings of the freedom of a hunter's life while enmeshed in the wire struts.

The Action Grotowski juxtaposes Biblical and Homeric scenes and heroes against the grotesque reality of the modern death camp (see Figures 3.7 and 3.8). The love of Paris and Helen, for instance, is played out between two men to the accompaniment of the laughter of the assembled

Richard Schechner

Richard Schechner (b. 1934) is an American director, writer, and teacher. With the Performance Group, which he founded in 1967, he produced and directed *Dionysus in 69* (1968–69), *Makbeth* (1969), *Commune* (1970), *The Tooth of Crime* (1973), *Mother Courage and Her Children* (1974), *The Marilyn Project* (1975), *Oedipus* (1977), and *Cops* (1978). The group disbanded in 1980. Author of *Public Domain* (1969), *Environmental Theater* (1973), *The End of Humanism* (1982) and *Between Theater & Anthropology* (1985), Schechner teaches at the Tisch School of the Arts, New York University. His writings on environmental theatre in the '70s changed our ways of thinking about theatre spaces.

prisoners; Jacob's bride is a stovepipe with a rag for a veil. *Akropolis* ends with a procession around the box in the center of the room led by a Singer carrying the headless corpse of the Savior. Grotowski describes it:

> The procession evokes the religious crowds of the Middle Ages, the flagellants, the haunting beggars. . . . The procession reaches the end of its peregrination. The Singer lets out a pious yell, opens a hole in the box, and crawls into it, dragging after him the corpse of the Savior. The inmates follow him one by one, singing fanatically. . . . When the last of the condemned men has disappeared, the lid of the box slams shut. The silence is very sudden; then after a while a calm, matter-of-fact voice is heard. It says simply, "They are gone, and the smoke rises in spirals." The joyful delirium has found its fulfillment in the crematorium. The end.[3]

Grotowski's poor theatre returns us to the essentials of theatre: actor, audience, space.

Environmental Performance Groups

Much of the work of Julian Beck and Judith Malina (the Living Theatre), Jerzy Grotowski (the Polish Laboratory Theatre), Peter Brook (International Centre for Theatre Research), Ariane Mnouchkine (Théâtre du Soleil), and Peter Schumann (the Bread and Puppet Theatre) is labeled *environmental theatre*. Writing about environmental production as a particular way of creating and experiencing theatre, Richard Schechner says: "The

FIGURE 3.9

Pentheus announcing his presence in Dionysus in 69. *The space designed by
Michael Kirby and Jerry N. Rojo is populated with platforms and towers.
There is no clearly defined stage; the spectators sit just about anywhere.
The action goes on around and among them. In this scene the actor as Pentheus
speaks from the tower through the bullhorn seen in the photo, announcing,
"I am Pentheus, son of Echion and Agave, and King of Thebes."*

thing about environmental theatre space is not just a matter of how you
end up using space. It is an attitude. *Start with all the space there is and then
decide what to use, what not to use, and how to use what you use.*"[4]

Schechner founded the Performance Group, disbanded in the late
1970s, in a garage at 33 Wooster Street, New York City. Like the Polish
Laboratory Theatre, the Performance Group ordinarily used the same
space for each new production, but constructed a different environment in
it. The group's first work was *Dionysus in 69*, performed in 1968–69; it was
based on Euripides' *The Bacchae*, a play about the seduction and death of
Pentheus at the instigation of the god **Dionysus**. The space within the
Performance Garage was roughly fifty feet by thirty-five feet in extent and
twenty feet high. For *Dionysus in 69*, there were two dominant towers and
a central area marked by black rubber mats. The audience arranged themselves on the carpeted floor, the platforms, and the towers, and the actors
moved among them horizontally on the floor and platforms, and vertically
on the towers (see Figure 3.9).

Environmental Theatre — A Perspective

THE LIVING THEATRE

The oldest of the collective groups creating environmental theatre began in 1948 in a cellar on New York's Wooster Street. Judith Malina and Julian Beck were the foremost gurus of the '60s **Off-Off-Broadway** groups. Their zeal and talents were directed toward encouraging a nonviolent revolution to overhaul society and to creating a performance style to confront that society (the United States).

In 1959, in a converted space on 14th Street in New York, Malina and Beck produced Jack Gelber's *The Connection*, a disturbing play about heroin addicts. The addicts' environment, of which the audience was a part, was naturalistically reproduced, as was the junkies' lifestyle.

After an encounter with the U.S. Internal Revenue Service, which led to prison sentences for tax evasion, the Living Theatre became a nomadic group traveling throughout Europe and South America. They performed outside traditional theatres in streets, prisons, even bars, provoking audience riots and confrontations with civil authorities.

In 1984, after an absence of fourteen years, the Living Theatre returned to New York with four productions, including Brecht's *Antigone*. Although still politically confrontational, these works marked a turning away from street encounters toward performances within identifiable theatres. Julian Beck, who died in 1985, once said that "art opens perception and changes our vision. I think without art we would all remain blind to reality. We go to the theatre to study ourselves. The theatre excites the imagination, and it also enters into the spirit. . . ."[5]

The Living Theatre's 1963 production of Kenneth Brown's *The Brig* recreated the repetition and senseless routine of a day in a Marine prison camp, of which the audience was a part.

Actors form a living totem pole in one of many theatrical rites that composed *Paradise Now: The Revolution of Cultures* (1968). The piece was one of the first to incorporate nudity (of the actors and — sometimes — the audience) as an integral part of the performance.

THE PERFORMANCE GROUP.
Based on Euripides' *The Bacchae, Dionysus in 69* became a paradigm of environmental theatre production in the early '70s. In the birth ritual the God Dionysus is born through the collective efforts of the actors who, as chorus, represent society. A birth- ritual canal is formed by the line of bodies, and the actor who plays Dionysus is pushed through and born as the god.

THÉÂTRE DU SOLEIL.
Théâtre du Soleil production of Shakespeare's *Richard II* staged in the munitions factory in Paris in 1981.

INTERNATIONAL CENTRE FOR THEATRE RESEARCH. *The Mahabharata*, a nine-hour drama adapted from the epic Sanskrit (Indian) novel, was initially staged in France by Peter Brook, head of the Paris-based International Centre for Theatre Research. Brook, celebrated English director for more than three decades, brought the production to America on international tour in 1987–88. The initial 1985 staging in a rock quarry near Avignon is shown here.

Dionysus' birth and Pentheus' seduction and death took place on the black mats. After Pentheus was killed, the women in the company rushed into the audience, each telling her part in the murder simultaneously. At the play's end, weather permitting, the large overhead garage door at the end of the room was opened and all the performers marched out into Wooster Street, often followed by the audience in a kind of impromptu ritual procession.

Performance Style

As we see from the descriptions of the Polish Laboratory Theatre's work and *Dionysus in 69*, environmental theatre requires a different attitude toward performance, text, action, and the division between actors and audience. The script for *Dionysus in 69* was not written, in the usual sense, by a playwright, but was developed in rehearsals by the company as a whole. The group reduced Euripides' play from 1300 lines to 600; actors wrote some of their own dialogue; and Euripides' story took on new meaning — it became an enactment of rituals of birth and death. The actors and the audience are not separated from each other by architecture or scenery — they are both contained within a whole space. Moreover, the style of performance draws them together visually, physically, and psychically. In *Dionysus in 69* the actors, for example, implored audiences to help murder Pentheus.

Théâtre du Soleil

Another group having impact on environmental production, especially in Europe, is the Théâtre du Soleil ("Theatre of the Sun"), founded in Paris in 1964 by Ariane Mnouchkine and a group of politically committed individuals.

In the 1960s the Théâtre du Soleil modeled itself on an egalitarian commune: They arrived at artistic decisions through democratic

▼▼▼

Ariane Mnouchkine

Of the French directors who have come to prominence since 1965, Ariane Mnouchkine (b. 1940) has become one of the most important. She founded the Théâtre du Soleil, a commune composed of about forty members, in the '60s. Until 1968 they performed in the Cirque d'Hiver, creating a considerable stir with productions of Shakespeare's *A Midsummer Night's Dream* and Arnold Wesker's *The Kitchen*.

In 1970 the company moved to an abandoned munitions factory just outside Paris (the Cartoucherie), where they have since produced internationally celebrated environmental productions of *1789* (in 1971) and *1793* (in 1972), treatments of the early years of the French Revolution that argued that the revolution was more concerned with property than with social injustice. *The Age of Gold* (1975) dealt with various aspects of materialism, and Molière's *Don Juan* (1978) with sexual values. The group recently staged Shakespeare's *Richard II* and *Henry IV, Part 1* in Paris and *Twelfth Night* at the Avignon Festival (France). They appeared at the 1984 Los Angeles Olympic Arts Festival. The company is one of France's finest.

participation and divided the theatre's profits equally among themselves. The company challenged traditional modes of theatrical presentation in its attempts to create a populist theatre, using improvisation as well as techniques from mime, *commedia*, Chinese opera, Japanese Noh and Kabuki, and circus clowning. Audiences moved from platform to platform to keep up with the play's action or sat around the edge or even in the center of a large pit.

Starting in 1967, with productions of Arnold Wesker's *The Kitchen* and a controversial adaptation of *A Midsummer Night's Dream* that anticipated Peter Brook's legendary 1970 production for the Royal Shakespeare Company, Mnouchkine's company attracted considerable international attention. The company was acclaimed for its radical environmental staging techniques and its explosive politicizing of dramatic materials. Their productions grew out of discussion, group study, improvisations with all members of the group sharing in the research, writing, staging, design, and construction. Their commitment to left-wing political beliefs and to creating vibrant "performance texts" out of the whole cloth of French history resulted in *1789*, then *1793*, and finally *The Age of Gold* (see Figures 3.10–3.11). In environmental spaces that directly engaged audiences, these performances dealt with theatre as revolution, historical data, and contemporary social facts; improvised stage action and audience participation; and spectacle and ritual.

FIGURE 3.10

Théâtre du Soleil's 1793, *produced in Vincennes in 1972 at the Cartoucherie (a former munitions factory). This view of the performance shows actors on raised platforms and audience seated in a center pit as well as on a balcony (left).*

FIGURE 3.11

The environmental production of The Age of Gold (L'Age d'Or), *1975, by the Paris-based company, Théâtre du Soleil. The centerpiece of the design was a ten-foot-high cruciform ridge covered with matting. Audiences became part of the action, participating in the story of society's exploitation and oppression of classes. Here, the central character, Abdallah-Harlequin, an immigrant worker in* commedia *mask, declaims standing in the middle of the audience.*

Théâtre du Soleil came to symbolize, along with the Living Theatre and the Bread and Puppet Theatre, the best that political theatre had to offer anywhere in the world.

But as political fervor waned worldwide in the late 1970s, along with the Vietnam War, groups like these either went out of existence (as did the Performance Group) or, like Théâtre du Soleil, became appreciated largely for their prodigious artistic experimentations, which overshadowed any

FIGURE 3.12

Théâtre du Soleil production of Shakespeare's Rich-ard II, *staged in a munitions factory in 1981.*

FIGURE 3.13

The Bread and Puppet Theatre performs The Same Boat: The Passion of Chico Mendes *in an open town space as part of the 1990 "Earth Day" celebration. The masked actors, the band, and the larger-than-life-size puppets are now traditional features of a Bread and Puppet production.*

"environmental" trendiness or political and sociological messages contained in their works. Théâtre du Soleil's Asian-inspired Shakespearean productions have further challenged contemporary notions of theatrical presentation (see Figure 3.12).

The Bread and Puppet Theatre

Peter Schumann founded the Bread and Puppet Theatre in New York in 1961. Today, the group makes its home in Glover, Vermont. Unlike many radical theatres that grew out of the social and political unrest of the 1960s in America, the Bread and Puppet Theatre flourishes today. Schumann's group does not attempt to create an environment but performs in almost any situation: streets, fields, gyms, churches, and sometimes theatres. Developed from Biblical and legendary sources and using both actors and

Peter Schumann

Peter Schumann (b. 1934 in Silesia) moved from Germany to the United States in 1961 and two years later founded the Bread and Puppet Theatre in New York City.

Until he was ten, the Schumann family lived in a village near Breslau, renamed Wroclaw at the end of World War II when this part of Germany was incorporated into Poland. In late 1944, the family fled barely ahead of the Soviet army and survived on his mother's baked rye sourdough bread until they reached Schleswig-Holstein. The twin themes of family and survival in Schumann's work stem from this period. In 1956, he met his American wife in Munich, and they emigrated to the United States in 1961 where their artistic collaboration began with the creation and performances of street pageants, anti-Vietnam War parades, productions based on religious themes, and summer workshops with giant puppets.

In 1970, Schumann was invited to take up residency at Goddard College in Plainfield, Vermont, and "practice puppetry." Living now in Glover, Vermont, Schumann has assembled a small troupe of puppeteers and designers. Each August the troupe performs in a grassed-over gravel pit with actors on five- or six-foot stilts, strolling jazz bands, rope walkers, and fire jugglers. Sourdough rye bread that Schumann has baked is passed among audiences.

Schumann's pageants are always about life and death, good and evil. His work with puppets reflects a traditionalism that harks back to Indian effigies, Japanese Bunraku and Noh theatre, and to the masks of African and Alaskan shamans. Mistrusting the power of words, Schumann uses puppets to simplify and caricature the horror of modern living in a time of potential global annihilation. His aim is to bring a spiritual reaction into the lives of ordinary spectators. In a Bread and Puppet performance, the stories are simple, the giant puppets riveting, and the tempo majestically slow. Schumann is best known for his antiwar pieces dating from 1965: *Fire, The Gray Lady Cantata, The Stations of the Cross,* and *A Man Says Goodbye to His Mother.*

larger-than-life-size puppets, Bread and Puppet plays advocate the virtues of love, charity, and humility.

The group takes its name from two constant elements of their work: puppets and bread. At the start of a Bread and Puppet performance, loaves of bread are passed among the spectators. Each person breaks off a piece and hands the rest to the next person, who does the same. When everyone has tasted bread, in an act of communion, the performance begins. Thus the audience participates in an instantly recognizable ritual: sharing the staff of life, a symbol of humanity's most basic need.

Like itinerant groups of past ages, Schumann brings theatre to the people by going out into the streets with processions made up of tin-horn bands, gigantic puppets manipulated by actors (they are similar in style to the Bunraku puppets of the Asian theatre), masked actors, and short plays on contemporary, though universal, themes dealing with the poor, hungry, meek, and victimized (see Figure 3.13).

Summary

Nontraditional theatre, like many of the environmental groups and productions we have considered here, describes modern efforts to rethink, reshape, and re-create the theatrical experience for actors *and* audiences. As Grotowski tells us, the experiment to discover the "proper spectator–actor relationship" takes place in a bare space where each type of performance requires its own special "physical arrangements." Grotowski has worked in a large room, Schechner in a garage, Mnouchkine in a warehouse, and Schumann in fields and streets.

Environmental theatre, as this type of nontraditional performance was called in the 1960s, rejects conventional seating and arranges the audience as part of the playing space. Each member of the audience seeks out and finds a space as special and particular as that occupied by the actors. Like the actors, the spectators become part of what is seen and done; they are both seeing and seen. In contrast, traditional theatre arranges the audience *before* a stage, where they see and hear at a comfortable remove.

Questions for Study

1. How does Jerzy Grotowski define "poor theatre"?

2. Why is the work of the Polish Laboratory Theatre important?

3. What are the social and moral objectives of Grotowski's Laboratory Theatre?

4. How does Grotowski's production of *Akropolis* portray these objectives?

5. What is *environmental theatre*?

6. What seating arrangements are used in environmental productions?

7. What was the original environment for Peter Brook's *The Mahabharata*?

8. What is the actor–audience relationship in the Performance Garage's production of *Dionysus in 69*? Study the photograph to arrive at your answer.

9. Describe the relationship between politics and environmental theatre events. Use as your examples the Théâtre du Soleil and the Living Theatre.

10. What are the distinct elements of a Bread and Puppet performance?

11. What solutions have environmental directors arrived at to discover the proper actor–audience relationship for each production?

12. Are there any created or "found" spaces used for theatrical productions on your campus or in your community? If so, describe them.

13. *Plays to Read*: María Irene Fornés, *Fefu and Her Friends: A Play* (New York: Performing Arts Journal Publication, 1990). Fornés has written an "environmental performance text." Part One situates the audience in the theatre's auditorium to observe Fefu's living room. Part Two takes place in four locations: a lawn, study, bedroom, kitchen. The audience is divided into four groups and each scene is repeated four times until the audience has seen all four. They return to the auditorium in Part Three to observe the play's ending.

14. *Suggested Reading*: Jerzy Grotowski's *Towards a Poor Theatre* (1968), Richard Schechner's *Environmental Theatre* (1973), and Judith Malina's *Diaries (1947–1957)* (1984).

The playwright envisions the play's world, its
people, environment, objects, relationships,
emotions, attitudes, and events. Playwriting
is a creative act that enlarges our understanding of
human experience and enriches our appreciation
of life.

Chapter 4

The Image Makers: The Playwright

Who fills the theatrical space? Who is seen in the space? What methods and materials are used to create the stage environment, what a famous designer called "the machine for acting"? In theatre we continually encounter the idea of building. Actors speak of building a character. Technicians build the set and costumers build costumes. The director often "blocks" the play. The word *playwright* is formed in the same way as *wheelwright* and *shipwright*: It means "playbuilder." Theatre is the creative collaborative effort of all these builders; the whole is greater than the sum of its parts. The American scene designer Robert Edmond Jones (1887–1954) referred to this wholeness when he said, "All art in the theatre should be not descriptive, but evocative." The efforts of many creative talents using various methods and materials evoke an imaginary world, but the initial artist is most often the playwright. In the next five chapters we consider the working methods of *playwrights, directors, actors, designers,* and *producers.*

The Playwright

A Personal Vision

The playwright writes a play to express some aspect of reality, some emotions and feelings connected with all of humanity, some measure of experience, some vision or conviction about the world. Like any artist, the playwright shapes a personal vision into an organized, meaningful whole. Thus a script is more than words on a page—it is the playwright's *blueprint* of a special kind of experience, created to appeal as much to

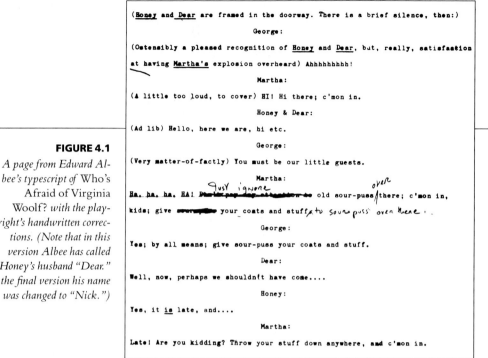

FIGURE 4.1

A page from Edward Albee's typescript of Who's Afraid of Virginia Woolf? *with the playwright's handwritten corrections. (Note that in this version Albee has called Honey's husband "Dear." In the final version his name was changed to "Nick.")*

the eye as to the ear. All in all, playwriting is the search for the truth of human experience as the playwright perceives it.

Playwrights such as Henrik Ibsen write plays to expose truths about the realities of social injustice. Other playwrights, like Bertolt Brecht, have political statements to make about people and governments. These writers use the theatre as a vehicle for a message or ideology. Other writers turn their personal experiences, wishes, and dreams into drama. For American playwright Adrienne Kennedy, writing is an outlet for psychological confusion and questions stemming from childhood. Other writers, like Eugene Ionesco, ridicule the conventions of theatre and certain kinds of human behavior to persuade us to see the world differently.

The Playwright's Beginnings

The playwright creates on paper an image or sense of life being lived before us. The playwright's script is of major importance because it is the usual starting point for the theatrical production (see Figure 4.1).

Playwrights start with an idea, theme, dream, image, or notes and work out an action; or begin with an unusual character or a real person and develop an action around that character; or start with a situation based on

Sam Shepard

Sam Shepard (b. 1943) began his theatrical career as a bit actor. Since 1964 he has dominated avant-garde theatre in New York and London, exploring contemporary American myths among the refuse of our junk culture. His characters are Americans we all know, but his situations are often unfamiliar and jarring. Recipient of the Off-Off-Broadway (*Village Voice*) Obie Award for distinguished playwriting on eight separate occasions, Shepard was awarded the 1979 Pulitzer Prize for *Buried Child*. Among his other well-known plays are *Cowboys* (1964); *Chicago* (1965); *Red Cross* and *La Turista* (1967); *Operation Sidewinder* (1970); *The Tooth of Crime* (1972); *Angel City* and *Curse of the Starving Class* (1976); *True West* (1980); *Fool for Love* (1982); and *A Lie of the Mind* (1987).

Shepard has also acted in such films as *Days of Heaven, The Right Stuff, Country,* and *Crimes of the Heart,* and wrote the screenplay for *Far North* and for *Paris, Texas,* which won the 1984 Cannes Film Festival award for best film.

In 1984 he shared some of his thoughts on playwriting with a magazine interviewer: "I feel like there are territories within us that are totally unknown. Huge, mysterious, and dangerous territories. We think we know ourselves, when we really know only this little bitty part. We have this social person that we present to each other. We have all these galaxies inside of us. And if we don't enter those in art . . . whether it's playwriting, or painting, or music, or whatever, then I don't understand the point in doing anything."[2]

---

a personal experience, their reading, or an anecdote. Other writers working with groups evolve scenarios with actors and arrange a final script from the group's improvisations, situations, dialogue, and movement. Some write from scenarios or plot summaries; others write from outline, crisis scene, images, dreams, myth, or imagined environment.

Bertolt Brecht usually worked from a story outline, which he called *the draft plan.* Next, he summarized the story's social and political ideas before developing scenes based on the outline. Sam Shepard writes by hand in a notebook first. Then he rewrites the script on his typewriter. He wrote literally a dozen different versions of *Fool for Love* (1982), but the first five pages remained the same in each version. Marsha Norman, author of *'Night, Mother* (1983), uses a personal computer; after spending a long evening in the theatre making script revisions with the director, she'll return home and type the changes into her computer in the early morning hours. Some playwrights claim their characters talk to them and develop themselves; others claim they hear the play's voices and sounds in their heads. Some playwrights speak lines out loud before writing them down, or work from visions of their characters moving and talking.

The Plays of Sam Shepard

Question: So, why are you writing plays?
Answer: I have to. I have a mission (*Shepard laughs*). No, I don't know why I do it. Why not?³

Curse of the Starving Class deals with a family — father Weston (Will Marchetti), son Wesley with lamb (Paul Richard Connell), and daughter Ella (Kathy Baker) — starved, not for class status, but for selfhood, belonging, and distinctiveness as individuals. Performed by the Magic Theatre, San Francisco, 1982, and directed by its artistic director, John Lion, who called Shepard "the inkblot of the '80s."⁴

True West, performed at the Magic Theatre, San Francisco, 1980, and directed by Robert Woodruff. Two brothers, Lee the drifter (Jim Haynie) and Austin the successful Hollywood screenwriter (Peter Coyote), clash in their efforts to define who they are in a world where the old myths have been used up and the new myths of our pop culture are unsatisfactory.

Buried Child, Theatre de Lys, New York, 1978. Dodge (Richard Hamilton) collapses among the carrot tops as Tilden (Tom Noonan) and Shelly (Mary McDonell) watch.

The Tooth of Crime (1972) pits a burned-out rock star (Hoss) against an arrogant young contender (Crow) for Shepard's views of competition and aggression in American life. In this 1985 production directed by Sharon Ott and Richard E. T. White for the Berkeley Repertory Theatre, Crow (Howard Swain) was conceived as a nihilistic punk rocker destined to topple the aging hippie singer Hoss (Charles Dean).

The Playwright's Function

In the theatre the playwright is an anomaly. Though playwrights win Pulitzer Prizes and Nobel awards, they are both central and peripheral to the production. In the privacy of the home or studio, the playwright puts paper in the typewriter or turns on the computer and constructs an imaginary world. As the creative imagination takes over, people, events, conflicts, words, and whole speeches resound in the writer's inner eye and ear. The script belongs to the playwright but once this original creative act — this *blueprint* for performance — is completed and handed over to director, designers, and actors, the playwright in one sense becomes peripheral to the final process. In the harrowing process of transforming the manuscript into a living performance, the writer takes a backseat in the rehearsal hall only to emerge a success or a failure on opening night. One exception is the playwright who also directs his or her own work, such as Bertolt Brecht, Samuel Beckett, or María Irene Fornés. They remain central to the production process. Others, like Shakespeare and Molière, have not only been part owners of their companies but have also been actors in their plays. In order to prolong the run of *Small Craft Warnings* in 1972, Tennessee Williams, by no means a professional actor, took the role of narrator in his play and his performance was critically acclaimed.

But in the modern rehearsal hall, playwrights usually take a backseat to their collaborators. Huddled in a back row with a legal pad in hand, their job is to note awkward lines and words that don't ring true, to rewrite speeches and even whole scenes when directors find difficulties in making sense of the action or need a few more seconds for an actor to make an entrance.

The playwright's independence also makes him or her an anomaly in the theatre. Like novelists, playwrights usually create alone, though there are exceptions. Their material, even for a political writer like Bertolt Brecht, is personal. The example, Grusha in *The Caucasian Chalk Circle* is a personal creation and a political statement on the human instinct for survival. We look to playwrights to give us insights into the world around us — to provide fresh perspectives and new visions. To do this, they reach inside themselves, in a private act, and pull forth intensely personal feelings, perceptions, and situations to construct the public world of the play.

Where do playwrights come from? What are their origins? Their backgrounds? Though drama departments offer courses in playwriting, no mastery of technique has ever made a writer. Playwrights have come from every conceivable background: acting, literature, gag-writing, teaching, housewifery, politics, medicine, and so on. Lillian Hellman worked as a reader for a literary agent before writing *The Children's Hour*. Tennessee Williams wandered the United States writing poems, short stories, one-acts, and his first full-length play, *Battle of Angels*. Aeschylus was a soldier, Terence a slave, Shakespeare an actor, Luigi Pirandello a teacher, Anton Chekhov a doctor, and Caryl Churchill a housewife. Among playwrights, there is no common denominator other than the exercise of the creative imagination in dialogue form — the conversion of dreams, fears, thoughts, and inner voices into a concrete, visible world that expands our horizons.

Aspects of Playwriting

The tools of the playwright's craft are plot, character, and language. These are also familiar to us as the novelist's tools, and, like novels, plays are studied as literature in the classroom and read for pleasure. Though plays are an arrangement of words on a page (as dialogue), the play-as-text is incomplete. It attains its finished form only in performance on the stage. That is why we call the playscript a blueprint for performance. To look at several lines of dialogue without actors, scenic space, lights, and costumes is to be convinced of the "incompleteness" of a script. The following lines of *Waiting for Godot* strike us as wholly incomplete without the production elements:

ESTRAGON: He should be here.
VLADIMIR: He didn't say for sure he'd come.
ESTRAGON: And if he doesn't come?
VLADIMIR: We'll come back to-morrow.
ESTRAGON: And then the day after to-morrow.
VLADIMIR: Possibly.
ESTRAGON: And so on. (Act I)

August Wilson

August Wilson (b. 1945), born in Pittsburgh, has had four plays produced on Broadway: *Ma Rainey's Black Bottom* (1984), *Fences* (1987), *Joe Turner's Come and Gone* (1988), and *The Piano Lesson* (1990). He has won two Pulitzer Prizes (for *Fences* and *The Piano Lesson*).

At nineteen Wilson left home to become a writer; he supported himself as a cook and stock clerk; in his spare time he read voraciously in the public library. Writing became his means of responding to changing race relations in America and to the violence erupting within the black community. In 1968, he co-founded Pittsburgh's Black Horizons Theatre and secured a production of his first play, *Black Bart and the Sacred Hills*, in St. Paul, Minnesota, where he has lived since 1977. In St. Paul, Wilson was hired as a scriptwriter for the Science Museum of Minnesota, which had a theatre company attached to the museum. In 1981, after several rejections of other scripts, a draft of *Ma Rainey's Black Bottom* was accepted by the Eugene O'Neill Theatre Center's National Playwrights Conference in Waterford, Connecticut, and Wilson's career was launched.

Many of Wilson's plays had their world premieres at the Yale Repertory Theatre, including *Ma Rainey's Black Bottom* (1984), *Fences* (1985), *Joe Turner's Come and Gone* (1986), *The Piano Lesson* (1987), and *Two Trains Running* (1990).

Wilson's major plays, set in different decades of twentieth-century America, are a series in progress. He is writing a history of black America, probing what he perceives to be the crucial opposition in black culture between those who celebrate black Americans' African roots and those who deny that historical reality.

Despite the dialogue's bare bones quality, the playscript is most often the basis for the production that becomes the play's complete realization.

The playwright "builds" that foundation with plot, character, and language. A story is told with characters, physical action, and dialogue. But, the building does not begin until the playwright conceives a whole event with *conflict* (the clashing of personal and social forces) and then develops a series of related events to resolve that conflict in new and unusual ways. The conflict and events must be compelling. Some are bold and unusual — such as Sophocles' Oedipus unwittingly chasing his own identity through a plague-ridden city, or Shakespeare's Hamlet avenging his father's murder at the invitation of a ghost. Some are seemingly ordinary, as in domestic situations depicted in modern realistic plays. But, Blanche DuBois' encounter with her brother-in-law in a New Orleans tenement becomes life-threatening in Tennessee Williams' *A Streetcar Named Desire* (1947), and Troy Maxson destroys his domestic tranquility through his need to control his son and assert his manhood in August Wilson's *Fences* (1987).

Playwrights conceptualize events — hear and see them in the mind's eye — for they are to be enacted and must hold the audience's attention. *Performability* is the key to the success of the playwright's story and dialogue. Whether the story is told in a straightforward manner (linear, point-to-point storytelling) or arranged as a series of nonlinear or discontinuous scenes, audiences respond to powerful and sustained dramatic impact. But that impact must be based on the dramatization of events with believable persons that audiences can put together in some sort of meaningful and satisfying fashion.

In the playwright's so-called bag of tools, plot — what Aristotle called "the soul" of drama — requires compression, economy, and intensity. Romeo and Juliet meet, marry, and die within a "two-hour traffic upon the stage." Though plots may encompass many years, the events are compressed so that the story is introduced, told, and resolved within a reasonable amount of time. The intensity of emotions, changed fortunes, and unexpected happenings accounts for our interest in the story and its outcome.

To sustain our interest, the playwright's characters must be believable, rich, and complex. We may never meet a Hamlet, but his dilemma and responses are credible and far more complex and intriguing than events in our daily lives. **Characters**, according to Tennessee Williams, add the mystery and confusion of living to plays.

> My chief aim in playwriting is the creation of character. I have always had a deep feeling for the mystery in life, and essentially my plays have been an effort to explore the beauty and meaning in the confusion of living.[5]

Plot and character are two of the playwright's means of conveying the confusion and mystery of life. Language is the playwright's third essential tool. As dialogue, it must be speakable, actable, and stageable. As justification for the pain he causes his family, Troy Maxson speaks of his plight as a black man in a predominantly white society:

> . . . you born with two strikes on you before you come to the plate. You got to guard it closely . . . always looking for the curve-ball on the inside corner. You can't afford to let none get past you. You can't afford a call strike. If you going down . . . you going down swinging. (2,i)[6]

Women Playwrights: Emerging Voices and Perspectives

Women playwrights are emerging in growing numbers to provide significant contributions to the contemporary theatre. These are five among many. While Lillian Hellman and Lorraine Hansberry were singular voices for many years, the feminist movement and regional theatres have provided avenues for women writers both here and abroad.

Lorraine Hansberry (1930–1965) is best known for *A Raisin in the Sun* (1959), which ran on Broadway for 530 performances and then was made into a film. She was the youngest American playwright, the first black writer, and only the fifth woman to win the New York Drama Critics' Award for the Best Play of the Year. Of playwriting, Hansberry said in 1962: "Plays are better written because one *must*, even if people think that you are being either artsy-craftsy or a plain liar if you say so. One result of this is that I usually don't say it any more, I just write — at my own dismally slow (and, yes, heart-breaking and maddening) commercially disinterested pace and choice of subject matter. . . ."[7]

Lillian Hellman (1905–1984) was produced success-
fully on Broadway for almost thirty years. Best
known for *The Children's Hour, The Little Foxes,* and
Toys in the Attic, Hellman pioneered as a woman in
the tough commercialism of the Broadway theatre.
She has said of the theatre: "The manuscript, the
words on the page, was what you started with and
what you have left. The production is of great importance, has given the play the only life it will
know, but it is gone, in the end, and the pages are
the only wall against which to throw the future or
measure the past."[8]

María Irene Fornés (b.
1930) emerged in the
mid-'60s as a writer, director, and designer. Pro-
duced **Off-Broadway**, her
plays include *Promenade*
(1965), *Fefu and Her
Friends* (1977), and *Mud*
(1984). Of women play-
wrights she says: ". . . We
have to reconcile our-
selves to the idea that the
protagonist of a play can
be a woman and that it is
natural for a woman to
write a play where the
protagonist is a woman.
Man is not the center of
life. And it is natural
when this fact reflects
itself in the work of
women."[9]

Caryl Churchill (b. 1938) is a British writer associated with the Joint Stock Theatre Company, the Royal Court Theatre, and the Royal Shakespeare Company. She is best known in this country for *Cloud 9* (1979), *Top Girls* (1980), *Fen* (1983), and *Serious Money* (1987), produced Off-Broadway to critical acclaim. Churchill has said: "I believe in the magic of theater, but I think it's important to realize that there is nothing magical about the work process behind it. I spend ages researching my plays and sitting alone writing them."[10] *Softcops*, written in 1984 for the Royal Shakespeare Company, examines the way social institutions use discipline and punishment to force people to conform to accepted patterns of behavior.

Marsha Norman (b. 1940), one of many emerging women writers of the past decade, grew up in Louisville, Kentucky, of fundamentalist parents and was encouraged in her writing by Jon Jory, artistic director of Actors Theatre of Louisville. *Getting Out*, about a young woman being released from prison, was first produced there and then became an Off-Broadway success in 1979. In 1983, she won the Pulitzer Prize for *'Night, Mother*, about a determined young woman's suicide. In trying to explain the increasing numbers of women playwrights in the American theatre, she says, "Plays require active central characters. Until women could see themselves as active, they could not really write for the theater. We are the central characters in our lives. That awareness had to come to a whole group before women could write about it. . . ."[11]

Wilson's language is graphic, active, filled with gesture, emotion, and metaphor that convey the essence of Troy's plight and understanding of his situation in life.

In *Fences*, Troy Maxson speaks an ethnic dialect highly charged with feelings, gestures, and baseball images. Wilson's character swings his favorite baseball bat against a rag ball and delivers pronouncements on life in a manner that is at once actable and stageable. No baseball diamond is required to convey Troy's philosophy of life as he stands in his front yard in reduced circumstances and swings the bat against defensive thoughts and lost dreams.

The Playwright and the Industry

Since the Greek festivals in ancient Athens, **producers** have clamored for new and better plays from playwrights. Today, hundreds of producers and literary agents are anxious to discover new authors and new scripts. To do so, they employ a cadre of "readers" to find the exceptional manuscript: the new David Mamet or the undiscovered Marsha Norman. International Creative Management (ICM) is one of the largest literary agencies in New York, representing Arthur Miller and others. For years, Tennessee Williams was represented by Audrey Wood who guided him through the most successful part of his career. The agent and the producer are two essential connections for the playwright's success. Moreover, some writers develop working relationships with directors; for example, Arthur Miller and Tennessee Williams with Elia Kazan, Edward Albee and Samuel Beckett with Alan Schneider, and August Wilson with Lloyd Richards.

For the successful Broadway playwright, the rewards are staggering, including television, film, and publishing contracts, and interviews in glamorous magazines. Prestigious awards are also forthcoming as indicators of success: the Pulitzer Prize, the Drama Critics' Circle Award, the Antoinette Perry "Tony" Awards, and for some, even Nobel Prizes for Literature. Luigi Pirandello and Samuel Beckett both received Nobel awards.

In many respects, playwrights are the most celebrated of the theatre's artists because audiences are aware that they sit in the presence of the writer's world. We listen to and experience a personal vision that makes us laugh and cry. The public may revere the actor—a Dustin Hoffman or a Meryl Streep—but the actor's creativity usually begins with the playwright's creation: the characters, situations, environment, and original world of conflicts, feelings, and choices.

In one sense, playwriting is only one facet of the theatre profession and the theatrical machine—the industry. In another sense, it transcends both because when the curtain comes down on a production, there still remain the playwright's words, ideas, characters, and fictions. As Lillian Hellman, creator of *The Little Foxes*, said: "The manuscript, the words on the page, was what you started with and what you have left" after the production is over. Whereas we might not have an opportunity to see a production of *A Streetcar Named Desire* or *Fences*, we can read the playwright's published script and partake of the playwright's creative act, incomplete though it is.

Summary

Because the whole theatrical process usually begins with the script, the playwright is one of the theatre's most important collaborative artists. The playwright creates the play's world—its events, people, and meaning—on paper.

The director interprets the playwright's text in the theatre's three-dimensional space, giving it shape, sound, rhythm, images, and action. Audiences experience the play through the director's eyes, ears, emotions, and intellect, so the modern director has become in many instances as distinct a force in the theatre as the playwright.

Questions for Study

1. What does the word *playwright* mean in its most literal sense?

2. What does designer Robert Edmond Jones mean when he refers to the theatre as "evocative"?

3. What are some of the ways a play takes shape in a playwright's imagination?

4. What is the playwright's function as a collaborator in the theatrical process?

5. What are the playwright's tools for creating a fictional world?

6. What is dialogue?

7. What does Tennessee Williams mean when he refers to the "confusion of living"?

8. How and why have recent women writers placed "women" at the center of their plays?

9. What is the function of a literary agent?

10. *Plays to Read*: Wilson's *Fences*, Shepard's *Buried Child*, Hellman's *The Little Foxes*.

11. *Suggested Reading*: David Mamet, *Writing in Restaurants* (New York: Viking Penguin, Inc., 1986); Arthur Miller, *Timebends: A Life* (New York: Grove Press, 1987); *In Their Own Words — Contemporary American Playwrights*, ed. David Savran (New York: Theatre Communications Group, 1988).

The theater of the future, if it is to hold us, will have to shake off a belief it has held only a relatively short time — the belief that it is showing us "a real room with real people." For the theatre's role is to present life not in its literal exactness but rather through some kind of poetic vision, metaphor, image — the mirror held up as *'twere* to nature.[1]
ALAN SCHNEIDER

The director, in collaboration with the playwright and with the help of many others, creates the performance in the theatre's space for us to see and hear.

Chapter 5

Background

In the 1860s in Europe, the practice of a single person guiding all aspects of the production process began to take hold. Before that time, leading actors, theatre managers, and sometimes playwrights "staged" the play, thereby setting actors' movements, dictating financial matters, and making decisions on casting, costumes, and scenery. During the first half of the nineteenth century, actor-managers (following the tradition of James Burbage in England and Molière in France) resembled the modern director in some respects. Nevertheless, the actor-manager was first of all an actor and considered the production from the perspective of the role he was playing. David Garrick (1717–1779) was one of England's successful actor-managers. Although the theatre between 1750 and 1850 was immensely popular in Europe, most actor-managers — Garrick was an exception — maintained inferior artistic standards in their pursuit of large box office receipts.

This general condition in the theatre began to worry a growing number of theatre people, who re-examined the production process. With the formation in 1866 of Duke George II of Saxe-Meiningen's company in Germany (known as the Meiningen Players), the director in the modern sense of the term began to emerge. The Duke's efforts to define the director's role were followed by those of André Antoine in France and Constantin Stanislavsky in Russia. Under their influence, the modern stage director's identity took shape in Europe: someone who understood all theatre arts and devoted full energies to combining them into a unified, artistic whole.

The Image Makers: The Director and the "New" Collaborators

Duke of Saxe-Meiningen — George II

Duke of Saxe-Meiningen, George II (1826–1914), transformed the Duchy of Meiningen's court theatre into an example of scenic historical accuracy and lifelike acting. As producer-director, the Duke designed all costumes, scenery, and properties for historically authentic style, and worked for **ensemble acting**. The Duke was assisted by Ludwig Chronegk (1837–1891), an actor responsible for supervising and rehearsing the company. The Meiningen Players were noted throughout Europe for their crowd scenes, in which each member of the crowd had individual traits and specific lines. In rehearsals the actors were divided into small groups, each under the charge of an experienced actor. This practice was in keeping with the company's rule against actors being stars, and was the beginning of the new movement in 1874 toward unified production under the director's control. Saxe-Meiningen's example of the *single creative authority* in charge of the total production influenced Antoine and Stanislavsky.

The Director's Role

The director collaborates with playwright, actors, designers, and technicians to create on stage a carefully selected vision of life — a special mirror. Alan Schneider described the *theatre's* role from a director's viewpoint as presenting life, not in its literal exactness, but through some kind of poetic vision, metaphor, or image — the mirror held up to nature. The director has several roles in the theatre ranging from the mundane, like attending to publicity and box office details, to the imaginative discovery and creative interpretation of the playwright's text.

Although each director has his or her own way of working creatively in the theatre, in general three types of directors have evolved over the years. On the first day, one type of director gives a speech to the cast on what the play is about and describes the approach that will be taken to interpreting the text. Actors, directors, and designers are often treated as "servants" to the director's concept and expected to deliver the "look" and "meaning" of the play's world as specified by the director. Another type of director reverses this approach and becomes the servant or coordinator of a group of actors, thereby limiting his or her own vision to the suggestions, criticisms, and encouragements of the group.

The third type of director functions as a guide, or helmsman, who senses at the outset the direction that the production will take but proceeds in rehearsals to provoke and stimulate the actors. This director creates an atmosphere in which actors dig, probe, and investigate the whole fabric of

The "Creative" Director

Ariane Mnouchkine, founding director of the *Théâtre du Soleil*, removed Shakespeare's plays from traditional Western trappings. *Richard II* relies on Kabuki traditions of setting, costumes, props, makeup, and movement.

Top right, Peter Brook, an innovative force for over twenty-five years, filled the "empty space" of the stage with circus tricks and techniques borrowed from puppet theatre and the English music hall for his 1970 production of Shakespeare's *A Midsummer Night's Dream.*

Left and bottom right, The Mahabharata at the Bouffes du Nord Théâtre in Paris, 1986, directed by Peter Brook. The natural quarry has been replaced by a conventional theatre—but one left unrepaired after a fire years ago. The floor is simple clay, the walls disfigured. Brook's actors create their story with simple props and stylized gestures.

Top, JoAnne Akalaitis ignored Beckett's stage directions and set the action of *Endgame* in a subway station littered with debris. This 1984 American Repertory Theatre production was defended by artistic director Robert Brustein: "To insist on strict adherence to each parenthesis of the published text . . . threatens to turn the theatre into a waxworks."

Bottom, in the 1988 Arena Stage production of *The Cherry Orchard,* Rumanian-born director Lucian Pintilie collaborated with designers Radu and Miruna Boruzescu to transform the arena space into a pastoral scene of great beauty and isolation. Actress Lex Manson (left) as Madame Ranevskaya reexperiences the estate.

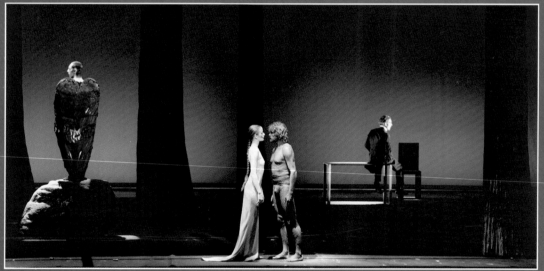

Robert Wilson admits to an affinity with the formality of Japanese theatre and its notions of movement, time, and emotion. His twelve-hour opera, *the CIVIL warS: a tree is best measured when it is down*, presents images of overwhelming beauty to bridge the disjunction between story, sound, silence, and space. *Top,* Lincoln sings: "From flowered fields/ Abundance yields . . . " Design and lighting by Robert Wilson, with Tom Kamm and Jennifer Tipton.

Bottom, the temptation scene from *The Forest* (West Berlin, 1988). Stark visual images of a man and woman against a backdrop of nature—giant trees and a brilliantly feathered bird—depict the temptation of the hero (Enkidu) by the seductress. Based loosely on the ancient *Epic of Gilgamesh, The Forest* tells the old story of humanity's loss of innocence in the march toward civilization. Robert Wilson's principal collaborators were David Byrne, Heiner Muller, and Darryl Pinckney.

André Antoine

André Antoine (1858–1943) was producer-director of the Théâtre Libre, or Free Theatre, in France. Beginning as a part-time actor, Antoine founded in 1887 a theatre and a naturalistic production style that became world-famous. The Théâtre Libre was a subscription theatre, one open only to members, and therefore exempt from censorship. It became a showcase for new plays (Ibsen's *Ghosts* was one) and new production techniques. Seeking authentic detail, Antoine tried to reproduce exact environments. In one play he hung real beef carcasses on stage. In an effort to stage "real" life, Antoine developed three important principles: realistic environments, ensemble acting, and the director's authority.

the play. Rehearsals are used to search out ("to harrow" in the original sense of the word *rehearse*), to listen, and to yield to suggestions. The "directional conception" is what Alan Schneider refers to as the director's poetic vision and it precedes the first day's work. Nevertheless, the "sense of direction" only crystallizes into a consistent stage image at the very end of the process.

The director's question, unlike the critic's, does not deal so much with "What's the event about?" as with questions about the event's *potential*. This is the reason a director chooses one sort of theatrical material over another — because of its potential. It is this realization of a play's or event's potential that motivates directors to find space, actors, and forms of expression. The director, like the hunter or the explorer, intuits that a potential exists within a work (or text) and yet explores the unknown with a sense of expectation and discovery and with a deepening commitment to leading the team. Try to imagine the potential of an untried script called *A Streetcar Named Desire* and the excitement of its first director, Elia Kazan, struggling to find the direction of what he called the **spine** (or the **throughline**) of the play's main action. In his notebook, he defined the play's spine as the "last gasp" of a dying civilization: "This little twisted, pathetic, confused bit of light and culture . . . snuffed out by the crude forces of violence, insensibility and vulgarity which exist in our South — and this cry is the play."[2]

Consider a director like Peter Brook who sets out, over a number of years, to explore an ancient Hindu epic, *The Mahabharata*; Brook's nine-hour theatrical realization presents humanity's greatest dilemma: human beings caught up in the conflict of divine versus demonic forces. The story of this 1985 theatre epic is essentially a quest for morality: how to find one's

Constantin Stanislavsky

Constantin Stanislavsky (1863–1938) was producer-director-actor and co-founder of the Moscow Art Theatre (see Figure 6.3). As a director, Stanislavsky aimed for ensemble acting and the absence of stars; he established such directional methods as intensive study of the play before rehearsals began, the actor's careful attention to detail, and re-creation of the play's milieu after visiting locales or doing extensive research. The Moscow Art Theatre's reputation was made with Anton Chekhov's plays depicting the monotonous and frustrating life of the rural landowning class.

Stanislavsky is remembered most for his efforts to perfect a truthful method of acting. His published writings in English — *My Life in Art* (1924), *An Actor Prepares* (1936), *Building a Character* (1949), and *Creating a Role* (1961) — provide a record of the "Stanislavsky System" as it evolved.

way in an age of destruction regardless of epoch, culture, or society. As director, Brook — with the assistance of collaborators, including writers and actors — himself created a theatrical epic out of an ancient, sacred poem of Hindu origins. With *A Streetcar Named Desire*, Elia Kazan *interpreted* Tennessee Williams' text. They are both directors creating a "mirror" that is held up to our nature in its many forms, varieties, and expressions.

Auditions and Casting

Basically, a director has six responsibilities: (1) selecting or creating a script, especially in college and university productions; (2) deciding on the text's interpretation and the "look" and configuration of the stage space; (3) casting actors in the various parts; (4) working with other theatre artists to plan and execute the production; (5) rehearsing the actors; and (6) coordinating all elements into the final stage performance. Nevertheless, none of the director's process is cut and dried. It is as variable as the names, faces, and talents of the team players.

Casting is matching an actor to a role. During auditions the director looks for actors whose physical appearance, personality, and acting style flesh out the director's idea of the characters. In college and university theatres, audition or tryout procedures are more or less standardized. Copies of the play are made available and notices of auditions posted. The director holds private interviews or general tryouts, or a combination of the two. The director usually asks actors to come prepared to illustrate their acting range by performing selections from plays of their own choosing, or provides material at the audition for them to read aloud.

Alan Schneider

Alan Schneider (1917–1984) was born Abram Leopoldovich Schneider in Kharkov, Russia, the son of medical students. The Schneiders escaped to the United States during the Russian Revolution and settled in Maryland. Educated at Johns Hopkins University and Cornell University, Alan Schneider taught at Catholic University in Washington, D.C. In 1944, he made his acting debut on Broadway in a Maxwell Anderson play. His first work as a director was at Arena Stage in Washington, D.C., where he began the pattern of his distinguished directing career: alternating between professional regional and Broadway theatres.

The turning point in his career was the 1956 American premiere of *Waiting for Godot* (see Figure 5.1). Bringing Samuel Beckett's plays to the public's attention became a life-long crusade for Schneider. He directed the American premieres of Beckett's *Krapp's Last Tape, Happy Days, Endgame, Not I,* and *Rockaby.* On Broadway he directed the original productions of Edward Albee's *Who's Afraid of Virginia Woolf?, Tiny Alice,* and *A Delicate Balance.* Amid this flurry of activity he became for four years the head of the Juilliard Theatre Center in New York. At the time of his death he was artistic director of the Acting Company.

Few American directors have been so consistently involved with plays of quality and significance. Few have worked with so many seminal playwrights of our time.

Beginning with the leads, the director narrows the choices for each part and calls back a final group. This group reads together from the play to be produced so that the director can visualize the actors together. It is important to see how they relate to one another, how they work together, and how they complement one another in physical appearance and in vocal and emotional quality. Once the director decides on the desired ensemble effect, there is a further elimination process, the casting notice is posted, and rehearsals begin.

The Director and the Actor

At the most basic level, the director helps the actor to find the character's inner life and to project this life vocally and visually to the audience. One basic approach still used by some directors is to preplan the actors' movements, and, like a photographer composing a group photograph, arrange the actors in the stage space to show their physical and psychological relationships. The director's emphasis here is on where the people are in *space.* Like a photographer, this director composes pictures with actors on

FIGURE 5.1

The 1956 Broadway premiere of Waiting for Godot *(directed by Herbert Berghof) with Kurt Kasznar as Pozzo, E. G. Marshall as Vladimir, Bert Lahr as Estragon, and Alvin Epstein as Lucky.*

stage to show relationships, emotions, and attitudes, to convey truths about human relationships, and to tell the playwright's story.

The first three or four rehearsals are used to *block* the play. In blocking rehearsals, the director goes through each scene line by line, working with the actors on when to come in, where to stand or sit, on what lines to move. As they go through the actions, the actors write down the directions and **stage business** (specific actions, such as answering a telephone or turning on a table lamp) in their scripts.

As we have seen, directors vary a great deal in their approach to beginning rehearsals. Some give full directions immediately; others leave much of the detail to be worked out later as the actors try out their lines and reactions to one another. Almost any director makes adjustments in later rehearsals as director and actors discover better ways of moving and reacting and generally shaping the script into a meaningful performance.

A second basic approach, which most modern directors favor, is the *collaborative approach*. This organic method involves director and actors working together in rehearsals to develop movement, gestures, character relationships, stage images, and line interpretations. Rather than entering the rehearsal period with entirely preset ideas, the director watches, listens, suggests, and selects as the actors rehearse the play. The methods of German playwright and director Bertolt Brecht (1898–1956) have been described in this way:

> During rehearsals Bertolt Brecht sits in the auditorium. His work as a director is unobtrusive. When he intervenes it is almost unnoticeable and always in the "direction of flow." He never interrupts, not even with suggestions for im-

FIGURE 5.2

Actors improvise movement in Hair *(the 1967 "American tribal love-rock musical" directed by Tom O'Horgan on Broadway). Improvisation is primarily a rehearsal tool and not a performance technique. How much improvisation is used in rehearsal depends on the director's skill with it and on the actors' needs. Viola Spolin's* Improvisation for the Theatre *(1963) is a good book about this approach to freeing the actor from inhibitions.*

provement. You do not get the impression that he wants to get the actors to "present some of his ideas"; they are not his instruments.

Instead he searches, together with the actors, for the story which the play tells, and helps each actor to his strength. His work with the actors may be compared to the efforts of a child to direct straws with a twig from a puddle into the river itself, so that they may float.

Brecht is not one of those directors who knows everything better than the actors. He adopts towards the play an attitude of "know-nothingism"; he waits. You get the impression that Brecht does not know his own play, not a single sentence. And he does not want to know what is written, but rather how the written text is to be shown by the actor on the stage. If an actor asks: "Should I stand up at this point?", the reply is often typically Brecht: "I don't know." Brecht really does not know; he only discovers during the rehearsal.[3]

The importance of the rehearsal process is to discover a unity, rhythm, and meaning for the production. At some point in the rehearsal period, the director sets the performance by selecting from what has evolved in rehearsals. In this second approach, improvisation or game playing is often an important director's tool.

Improvisation can free the actors' imaginations and bodies for spontaneous story telling. Often the director uses improvisations early in rehearsals to spark the cast's imagination, behavior, reactions, and mood as they begin to work together. In later rehearsals, improvisations can increase concentration, discover dramatic action and character relationships, and develop good working relations among actors (see Figure 5.2).

The modern director uses other tools to stimulate the actors' imaginations so that they will give life to their roles. The director's *ground plan*

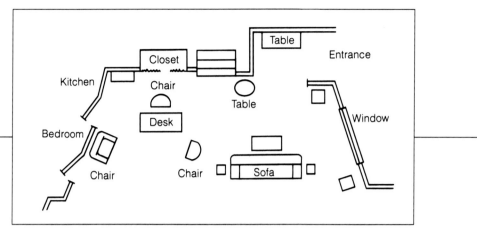

FIGURE 5.3

The ground plan. Director and designer work out the play's environment, noting where the doorways, windows, steps, levels, walls, and furniture are. These are then outlined in tape on the stage floor so the actor can visualize the environment in rehearsals.

defines the space limitations for the story, such as obstacles of furniture, doors, stairs, and so on (see Figure 5.3). As the director physically arranges the actors in the ground plan, they discover physical relationships with other characters and come to understand the play's action. As the actors move about the stage, they discover gestures that further illustrate character and emotion. As the director and actors add story-telling details of gesture and speech, the characters' emotional truth is illustrated visually and vocally and the living quality of the play is communicated.

Assistants

To prepare a play within a three- to ten-week rehearsal period, the modern director needs assistants. The *assistant director* attends production meetings, coaches actors, and rehearses special or problem scenes. The *stage manager* compiles the promptbook (a copy of the play with directions for performance; see Figure 5.4); records stage business, blocking, lighting, sound, and other cues; makes the rehearsal schedule; takes notes during rehearsals; coordinates rehearsals; and runs the show after it has opened.

The Director as Creative Artist

As a creative artist, the director serves the playwright by translating the script as faithfully as possible into theatrical form. Elia Kazan interpreted Arthur Miller's and Tennessee Williams' plays on Broadway. Samuel Beckett often directed his own plays. Mike Nichols searches for what he calls the "Event"—the truthful moment or series of moments—that will illuminate the author's meaning, that will reveal "real people living their lives."

Elia Kazan

Elia Kazan (b. 1909 in Istanbul, Turkey) was educated at Williams College and Yale University. He was a member of the Group Theatre and acted in their productions of Clifford Odets' *Waiting for Lefty, Paradise Lost,* and *Golden Boy.*

He is best known today for his direction of plays by Tennessee Williams and Arthur Miller: *A Streetcar Named Desire* (1947), *Death of a Salesman* (1949), *Camino Real* (1953), *Cat on a Hot Tin Roof* (1955), and *Sweet Bird of Youth* (1959). Kazan also directed the films of *A Streetcar Named Desire, On the Waterfront,* and *East of Eden.*

Along with designer Jo Mielziner, Kazan established selected realism as the dominant American theatrical style during the 1950s. The style combined acting of intense psychological truth with simplified but realistic scenery. Marlon Brando as Stanley Kowalski embodied the style of acting for which Kazan's productions were famous (see Figure 1.1, page 11).

LYUBOV ANDREYEVNA. Cut down the cherry orchard? My dear, excuse me, but you don't understand. If, in the entire province, there is a single remarkable place, it's our cherry orchard.

LOPAKHIN. It's remarkable only because it's big. In fact, it bears only once in two years, and even then there's nothing you can do with cherries; there's no market for them.

GAYEV. But even in the encyclopedia they talk about our cherry orchard.

LOPAKHIN. (Consulting his watch.) There's no other way. If you don't decide, the cherry orchard, the whole estate, will be sold at auction on the twenty-second of August. Make up your mind. There is no other solution. None. Absolutely none.

FIRS. In the old days forty or fifty years ago, they picked the cherries; they dried, soaked and marinated them, and made them into jam. And sometimes . . .

GAYEV. Firs, be quiet.

FIRS. Sometimes they used to send the dried cherries by the cartload to Moscow, and Kharkov . . . and that made piles of money. And the cherries then were sweet, juicy, and the smell . . . they knew how to do it . . . they had a recipe.

LYUBOV ANDREYEVNA. Well, what is the recipe?

FIRS. It's forgotten; nobody remembers.

PISHCHIK. And what about Paris? How was it? Did you eat frogs?

LYUBOV ANDREYEVNA. I ate crocodiles.

PISHCHIK. Incredible!

LOPAKHIN. So far there've been only landlords and peasants in the country, but now summer residents are moving in. Today every village, even the most insignificant, is surrounded by summer homes. In twenty years very likely the summer residents will be enormously multiplied. All they do now, of course, is drink tea on their front porches but maybe one day each will cultivate his own acre, and then the cherry orchard will become a happy, rich, and productive place.

GAYEV. (Indignant.) Ridiculous. (Enter Varya and Yasha.)

FIGURE 5.4

The stage manager's notes for the 1989 production of Chekhov's The Cherry Orchard, *directed by David Hammond, for PlayMakers Repertory Company, Chapel Hill, N.C., have been entered on this page of the production promptbook. The stage manager keeps this record of the director's notes for performance.*

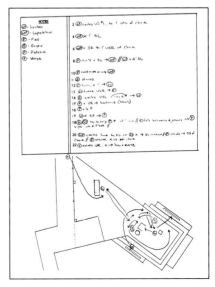

Peter Brook

Peter Brook (b. 1925) is a British director and founder of the International Centre for Theatre Research in Paris. He was born in London, educated at Oxford University, and began his directing career in the 1940s. As co-director of England's Royal Shakespeare Company (RSC) from 1962 to 1971, he directed acclaimed productions of *King Lear, The Tempest, Marat/Sade,* and *A Midsummer Night's Dream*. His activities with the Centre include *Orghast* for the Shiraz Festival at Persepolis (Iran), a central African tour, and *The Ik* (based on Colin Turnbull's book *The Mountain People*), which toured London and America. He directed the 1963 *The Lord of the Flies* film, and wrote an influential book on theatre, *The Empty Space* (1968).

Known for his radical adaptations of familiar plays, Brook enjoys an enormous international reputation. His version of *A Midsummer Night's Dream* is not about the romantic fairies and haunted woodlands that Shakespeare imagined. It is an exploration of love performed in a white boxlike set with actors on trapezes and in "mod" clothing and circus costumes (see page 23).

Since founding the Centre, Brook has experimented with actor training and developing new scripts from ideas taken from myths, anthropology, and fables, producing such international successes as *Conference of the Birds, The Cherry Orchard, La Tragédie de Carmen,* and *The Mahabharata.*

More recently, directors, taking cues from such great experimental directors as Meyerhold and Brecht, fashion the script into a wholly new and directorially original work of art. In this role, the director alters the play — changes the period represented, cuts the text, rearranges the scenes — and practically takes over the role of author. In his re-creation of Shakespeare's *A Midsummer Night's Dream* for the Royal Shakespeare Company in 1970, director Peter Brook worked in this way. (See the color photo essay on creative directors.)

The "New" Collaborators

Among the newest directors, Martha Clarke and Robert Wilson have their roots in a nonnarrative theatrical tradition beginning with the Living Theatre, the Performance Group, Meredith Monk's dance pieces, and the Mabou Mines. Their work has its inception in images and sounds, not in a verbal text. For this reason (among many) their work differs from other contemporary directors, such as Elia Kazan, Alan Schneider, and Lloyd

Martha Clarke

Martha Clarke (b. 1944) entered the theatre through dance training at the Juilliard School (New York City), and as a member of Anna Sokolow's dance company and later the Pilobolus Dance Theatre. The New York-based Music Theatre Group funded Clarke to develop her own theatrical form. The result was a series of increasingly complex works resulting in *The Garden of Earthly Delights* (1984) and *Vienna: Lusthaus* (1986). Her recent *Endangered Species* (1990) links the lives and fates of men, women, and nature.

Richards. Their theatre pieces grow out of intense collaboration with different types of theatrical artists — including designers, composers, dancers, and singers.

Martha Clarke, a dancer turned theatrical creator, is celebrated as the creator of *The Garden of Earthly Delights* (1984) and *Vienna: Lusthaus* (1986). Working in collaboration with dancers, musicians, designers, actors, and singers, she collects and connects hundreds of imagistic fragments for a theatre piece. First, she asks singers and dancers to move to music, re-creating fragmentary scenes. Later in the collaborative process among the various artists, Clarke superimposes other parts on these early scenes, which may in turn suggest other scenes.

If the pieces connect, she then weaves them into the fabric of the total work that is shaped and reshaped in six months or more of rehearsal, but may last only sixty minutes in performance. Of her process she says: "I'm a very instinctive person and I feel my way around like someone blindfolded in the attic. I stumble the piece into shape and often don't get a vision until late in the process. Then I take out my scissors and my paste and in the very last moments before a first preview it falls together."[4]

The Garden of Earthly Delights, Clarke's 1984 interpretation of painter Hieronymus Bosch's fifteenth-century triptych, gained international attention (see Figure 5.5). This one-hour evocation of the Garden of Eden and the netherworld — inhabited by ten dancers and musicians who at times were earthbound and at others celestially somersaulted through the air on cables — opened in New York City and subsequently toured the United States and Europe.

Clarke's theatre pieces, in which she is the prime creator, are not narrations of a story line but are ultimately expressions of her subconscious. They link the points between inspiration and a volatile inner emotional life. *Vienna: Lusthaus* is made up of forty-four fragments depicting turn-

FIGURE 5.5

The Garden of Earthly Delights, a theatre piece created in 1984 by Martha Clarke, uses actors-dancers in contrasting stark and playful images to evoke the events of the "Garden of Eden."

of-the-century Vienna and pairing eroticism and death. Clarke sees lust and death as corrosive powers undermining social order.

Commenting upon her collaborative process, she says:

> . . . If you watched a rehearsal of mine, you would see that nine-tenths of it is in such disarray. I flounder. . . . I'm foggy a lot of the time. And the actors and dancers have to search as much as I do. We're all children dropped on another planet at the beginning of this process and, tentatively, hand-in-hand, we find our way through this mire to whatever. The day-by-day process couldn't be more collaborative.[5]

Robert Wilson (b. 1941) is author, designer, and director of nearly one hundred theatre, opera, dance, film, and video works. He is best known for such innovative productions as *Einstein on the Beach* (a 1976 opera with composer Philip Glass), *the CIVIL warS: a tree is best measured when it is down* (a 1985 opera with playwright Heiner Müller), and *The Forest* (a 1988 production with author Heiner Müller and composer David Byrne).

Wilson's work is rooted in what he calls the "visual book." He says: "I'm not a writer of words. . . . I usually find a form before I have content. Before I've gathered material, I have a form. Once I have a form, it's a question of how to fill in the form."[6] He then proceeds in workshops and rehearsals to structure time and episodes, to imagine landscapes, and to add themes and references (see Figure 5.6).

FIGURE 5.6

A scene from Robert Wilson's A Letter to Queen Victoria *(1975). Wilson juxtaposes images from the past and present against a background of nonsensical language. The actress, dressed as Queen Victoria, produces a prolonged scream forecasting the explosion of the Victorian's ordered universe. In the background elegantly attired people "chitter chatter" oblivious to the collapse of civilization as they know it.*

Describing his workshop/rehearsal period, Wilson uses the analogy of cooking a meal:

> . . . I've said many times it's like making a dinner. The four of us here at this table are now going to make a dinner. Well, I know I can make a salad, and that's about it. You can make coffee. But maybe he knows how to make pasta, and she knows how to make something else, and then we have this dinner based on what we can do. So Heiner Müller [writer] can do one thing and Darryl Pinckney [writer] can do another, and David Byrne [composer] can do another, and maybe they're all very different, with different aesthetics, different viewpoints. But we make a work together. We have to try to figure out how we can take these different people and make this meal. And then we offer it.[7]

Unlike the stage tradition of the director who carefully interprets the playwright's world for audiences, the "new" collaborators, like Martha Clarke and Robert Wilson, develop their own visionary statements with other artists. Referred to as a "theatre of visions," these works *are* the staging with live performers of the maker's vision of a new theatrical reality. In this theatre of visions, there is no concern for verbal analysis, no concern for plausibility, no question of conveying information or of generating meaning. Of ultimate importance is imparting an artistically created vision together with a sense of its significance and visual excitement.

FIGURE 5.7

The archery contest in Peter Brook's 1986 production of the epic Sanskrit (Indian) work, The Mahabharata, *brought on tour to the United States in 1987–1988.*

Summary

Emerging in the nineteenth century, the theatre director is one of the most recent additions to the list of principal theatre artists. Before the director became part of theatre, leading actors, theatre managers, and sometimes playwrights set the actor's movements, dictated production elements, and took care of financial matters. Nineteenth-century technological advances made stage machinery and lighting more complex; changing social, aesthetic, and political thought so altered the theatre's subjects, characters, and staging that a *coordinating specialist* became necessary.

Whereas the playwright creates the play's world—its events, people, and meaning—on paper, the modern director, with other artists, interprets the playwright's vision in the theatre's three-dimensional space, giving it shape, sound, rhythm, images, activity, and unity. Audiences experience the play largely through the director's imagination—eyes, ears, emotions, and intellect—so the modern director has become as distinct a force in the theatre as the playwright. Since the ancient Greek festivals, the actors' role in the theatre has been more predictable and defined, though acting styles and training have changed throughout theatrical history as we will see in the next chapter.

Questions for Study

1. What is the artistic role of the director in the theatre?

2. What are the director's responsibilities? Name *six* major ones.

3. Why were the Duke of Saxe-Meiningen, André Antoine, and Constantin Stanislavsky "pioneering" directors?

4. In what ways are auditions important for a director?

5. What does a director look for in casting a play?

6. What is meant by the play's *spine*?

7. How is *improvisation* often a helpful rehearsal tool for director and actor?

8. What are the functions of the *assistant director* and the *stage manager*?

9. What is the director's *ground plan*?

10. What information is given in a Samuel French Publishers' acting edition of a play? Bring several editions to class for illustration.

11. What is a director's *promptbook*?

12. Give examples of the director's wide range of creative possibilities in staging a performance.

13. Describe the work of the contemporary theatre's "new" collaborators.

14. *Plays to Read*: Tennessee Williams' *A Streetcar Named Desire*.

15. *Suggested Reading: Peter Brook's Production of William Shakespeare's A Midsummer Night's Dream for the Royal Shakespeare Company*. Complete and authorized acting edition, edited with interview by Glenn Loney (Chicago: Dramatic Publishing Company, 1974). Arthur Bartow, *The Director's Voice: Interviews* (New York: Theatre Communications Group, 1989). Elia Kazan, *A Life* (New York: Alfred A. Knopf, 1988). Alan Schneider, *Entrances: An American Director's Journey* (New York: Viking Penguin, 1986).

Acting is the belief and technique by which the actor brings human presence into the theatre. Theatre is, after all, the art human beings make out of themselves. It doesn't require scenery, costumes, or lighting. It does not even require a play text. It requires only people acting and people watching them act.

Chapter 6

The Image Makers: The Actor

We discovered in earlier chapters the modern trend to reduce the theatrical experience to essentials. Grotowski's "poor theatre" and Samuel Beckett's minimalist theatre are perhaps the most widely publicized examples of this trend today. However, in the American theatre, the trend has its roots in the 1938 Broadway production of Thornton Wilder's *Our Town*. Director Jed Harris took Wilder's straightforward play about recognizable townspeople in Grover's Corner, U.S.A., and placed the actors on a bare stage framed simply by the theatre's back wall (see Figure 6.1). Virtually no scenery was used, costumes were muted, and hand properties were minimal. Even stage furniture was done away with. The actors told the story using only those properties, such as chairs and umbrellas, that they could move on and off stage for themselves. But there was one essential element of the theatrical experience that remained in this revolutionary production: *the actor*.

Not only could the actor not be dispensed with (as Grotowski told us again thirty years later), but Harris' approach to staging placed even greater responsibility on the actor. For over thirty years, actors have re-created *Our Town* following the original stage directions, and they have discovered that a new experience occurs for actor and audience when the stage has minimal scenery or properties. When the only object of the audience's focus is the actor, the modern audience *rediscovers* the actor's presence and art. In this chapter we investigate what acting is all about.

FIGURE 6.1

Minimal staging. This photo from the 1938 New York production of Our Town *shows the back wall of the theatre. The photo reveals two essential theatrical elements: stage space and actors.*

The Astonishing Art

Acting does not begin with performing on stage before an audience. It begins with the process of observation — with the eyes and ears, with sensitivity, selection, and memory of what the actor has seen, heard, and felt over a lifetime.

The body, voice, emotions, and the mind are the actor's tools. They must be flexible, disciplined, and expressive to communicate a wide range of attitudes, traits, emotions, and situations. They must be prepared to simulate an Oedipus, Hamlet, or a Blanche DuBois. In training and rehearsals, the actor works to understand the body and voice: how to control them; how to release psychological tensions and blocks that inhibit them; how to increase powers of imagination, observation, and concentration; and how to integrate them with the demands of the script and the director. In using these tools, the actor combines an inner belief in the role with external performance techniques. Successful acting combines belief and technique to create a sense of life taking place on stage as if for the first time.

English actor Ralph Richardson (1902–1984) commented on the acting process:

> Acting is to some extent a controlled dream. In one part of your consciousness it really and truly is happening. But, of course, to make it true to the audience all the time, the actor must, at any rate some of the time, believe himself that it is really true. But in my experience this layer of absolute reality is a comparatively small one. The rest of it is technique, as I say, of being very careful that the thing is really accurate, completely clear, completely as laid down beforehand. In every performance you're trying to find a better way to do it, and what you're re-shaping, the little experiments, may be very small indeed, and quite unnoticed by your fellow actors; but they are working all the time. Therefore three or four layers of consciousness are at work during the time one is giving a performance.[2]

Internal belief and *external technique* are fundamental aspects of stage acting. Although over the years the two tasks have been separated for reasons of analysis, the successful actor aims to integrate them into a perfect alignment that, in performance, makes acting an astonishing art.

The Actor's Reality

Reduced to its simplest terms, the actor's goal is to tell the character's *situation* and the play's story as effectively as possible. The actor works in rehearsals to behave as a person would in the situation existing among the play's characters. The actor must concentrate on the character's behavior in this context — not on the performance or the audience.

The actor comes to believe in what he or she is doing on stage regardless of the underlying reasons for the actions. To understand better the actor's reality (and stage reality), let us compare the situation in a play with that in an event on the sports field. Like baseball, for example, a play has its own rules and regulations, the set dimensions of the playing area, and a set number of persons on the field. The interactions among the players are real, vital, and intense. For the playing time, the field is the players' whole universe. The game, like a play, has its own reality that is frequently "more real" and vibrant than everyday reality. Likewise, the actor is given a story, a character, relationships, actions, and environs. The play sets the number of persons; the director and designers set the dimensions of the playing area. The play has its own reality that the actor finds in the exploration of the play's life and in the character's emotions and needs.

The Actor's Training

Throughout stage history, actors have used both external technique and internal belief to create their staged reality. Technique and belief are the fundamentals of their training. Sometimes, however, one has been favored over the other.

Great Moments of Acting

Given 2,500 years of theatrical history, the names of great actors illuminating particular roles are legion. The list of great actors of the modern theatre includes such names as Sarah Bernhardt, Eleanora Duse, John Barrymore, Judith Anderson, Ethel Barrymore, John Gielgud, Eva Le Gallienne, Jean-Louis Barrault, Laurette Taylor, Ralph Richardson, and Laurence Olivier. Such legendary performances as Laurette Taylor's Amanda Wingfield, Laurence Olivier's Hamlet, or Jessica Tandy's Blanche DuBois grow out of rigorous training, keen sensitivity, vivid dramatic imagination, and an intelligence equal to the demands of text, director, and stage.

Director Peter Brook describes unforgettable moments in an actor's performance as "a flash of insight that comes from the confrontation of the performer's hidden world and the hidden world of character. . . . For theatre to be seen at its most alive, there has to be a very, very exact balance between the living personality of the performer and the second personality, which is that of the character."[3] Great acting is a seamless integration of the actor's personality and the character in the context of the given circumstances of the play.

This photo essay illustrates unforgettable moments from four plays discussed in this book. They capture a single moment in the work of great actors in the modern theatre whose names have become synonymous with certain roles: Jessica Tandy with Williams' Blanche DuBois, Bert Lahr with Beckett's Estragon, Irene Worth with Chekhov's Madame Ranevskaya, and James Earl Jones with Wilson's Troy Maxson.

JESSICA TANDY (b. 1909) as Blanche DuBois in the 1947 Broadway production of *A Streetcar Named Desire* with Marlon Brando as Stanley Kowalski and Kim Hunter as Stella in the background.

Tandy played Blanche, one of the longest and most exacting roles on record, for over two years on Broadway, establishing her as one of America's leading actresses. Critic Brooks Atkinson said of her performance: "She acts a magnificent part magnificently. . . . She plays it with an insight as vibrant and pitiless as Mr. Williams' writing, for she catches on the wing the terror, bogus refinement, and intellectual alertness and the madness that can hardly be distinguished from logic and fastidiousness."

With her husband Hume Cronyn, Tandy formed a distinguished stage partnership. They have appeared together on Broadway, at The Guthrie Theater, and at Stratford Ontario's Shakespeare Festival. Most notable has been their work together in *The Fourposter* (1951), *The Gin Game* (1979), and *Foxfire* (1982). Most recently, Tandy starred on Broadway as Amanda Wingfield in Williams' *The Glass Menagerie* (1984) and recreated the role of Miss Daisy in the film version of Alfred Uhry's play *Driving Miss Daisy* (1989) for which she won an "Oscar" Award for Best Actress. During her distinguished stage career she won three Antoinette Perry ("Tony") awards as Best Actress for *A Streetcar Named Desire*, *The Gin Game*, and *Foxfire*.

IRENE WORTH (b. 1916) as Madame Ranevskaya, one of the great Chekhov roles from *The Cherry Orchard*, in the 1977 New York Shakespeare Festival production, directed by Andrei Serban at Lincoln Center. Worth has had an extraordinary career on American and British stages in plays by Chekhov, Henrik Ibsen, Edward Albee, Lillian Hellman, Tennessee Williams, and Samuel Beckett, to name only a few. Her work has spanned two continents and included appearances on Broadway, the Edinburgh Festival, London's West End, the Royal Shakespeare Company, the Chichester Festival, Stratford Ontario's Shakespeare Festival, and The Public Theatre. She created the role of Celia Coplestone in T. S. Eliot's *The Cocktail Party* (1949), starred in Lillian Hellman's *Toys in the Attic* (1960), played Goneril in Peter Brook's production of *King Lear* (1962), and performed Winnie in *Happy Days* (1979), directed by Andrei Serban, all to vast critical acclaim.

In an interview with the *New York Times* (February 5, 1976), she talked about the actor's art, which her own work epitomizes: "You know what a salmon does when it goes upstream? It feels about for the point of maximum energy in the water, the point where the water whirls round and round and generates a terrific centrifugal force. It looks for that point, and it finds it, and the water quadruples the salmon's own natural strength, and then it can jump. That's what an actor has to do with the text. The point of maximum energy is always there, but it takes finding."

BERT LAHR (1895–1967) as Estragon (right) in Beckett's *Waiting for Godot*. Beginning his stage career as a stand-up vaudeville comic, Lahr moved on to Broadway musical comedy, became identified with the role of the Cowardly Lion in the film *The Wizard of Oz* (1939), and closed his career as a distinguished actor best remembered in the United States for his performance as Gogo (Estragon) in Beckett's existential masterpiece.

Lahr created the role in the American premiere of Beckett's play in Miami, 1956, directed by Alan Schneider, continuing on Broadway later that same year (directed by Herbert Berghof) with E. G. Marshall as Vladimir, Kurt Kasznar as Pozzo, and Alvin Epstein as Lucky. These productions are described in *Notes on a Cowardly Lion* (1969), a perceptive biography by his son, John Lahr, a notable theatre critic.

As Estragon, Lahr was unfailing in his instincts to be clear, simple, and to the point. Audiences waited in vain for hints of the famous "cowardly lion," but Lahr refused to retread familiar ground. His warmth and common humanity extended across the footlights and caught up audiences in a shared experience. British critic Kenneth Tynan put it this way: "Mr. Lahr's beleaguered simpleton [Estragon], a draughts-player lost in a universe of chess, is one of the noblest performances I have ever seen."

JAMES EARL JONES (b. 1931 in Arkabutla, Michigan) was educated at The University of Michigan, Ann Arbor, and studied acting in the late 1950s with Lee Strasberg and with the American Theatre Wing in New York City. He made his Broadway debut as an understudy in *The Egghead* (1957) and his London debut in *Paul Robeson* (1978), a one-man show.

Jones has performed a variety of stage and film roles. He has been seen as Othello, Claudius (in *Hamlet*), Macbeth, and King Lear with the New York Shakespeare Festival Theatre; as Jack Jefferson in *The Great White Hope* with Arena Stage in Washington, D.C., and again on Broadway in 1968; and as Troy Maxson (in *Fences*) with the Yale Repertory Theatre in 1985. *Fences* moved to Broadway in 1987. Jones won the Antoinette Perry ("Tony") Award for Best Actor in 1969 for *The Great White Hope* and the American Academy of Arts and Letters Medal for Spoken Language in 1981.

He has appeared in such major films as *Dr. Strangelove* (1964), *The Great White Hope* (1970), and *The Hunt for Red October* (1990) and as the voice of Darth Vader in *Star Wars* (1977), *The Empire Strikes Back* (1980), and in *Return of the Jedi* (1983).

The central character, Troy Maxson, in August Wilson's *Fences* has been described as the best role of James Earl Jones's career. His performance as Troy was called "mountainous," "magnificent," "towering." One critic called it one of Jones's "most powerful and riveting performances, rising to brilliant outbursts of anguish and irony." Director Lloyd Richards described Jones's performance as the Maxson family patriarch as the "life force that at once nurtures and stunts the characters who share his blood. . . ."

FIGURE 6.2

Garrick's Macbeth, *which he played in a contemporary military uniform. He was famous for the dagger scene; his contemporaries praised him for his ability to project the fact that he was "seeing" the dagger before him. It has been said that Garrick's "face was a language."*

External Technique

External technique (or external acting) is that activity by which one person imitates another. The mimetic actor chooses to imitate or illustrate outwardly the character's behavior. He or she approaches a role through a deep and passionate study of human behavior *in all its outward forms*, with an eye toward reproducing them in a disciplined and sensitive way.

The English actor David Garrick (1717–1779) approached acting as an imitation of life—he called acting *mimical behavior* (see Figure 6.2). To prepare for the role of King Lear, for example, he studied the appearance and behavior of a friend who had been driven mad by his child's death. By his accurate reproduction of such behavior on stage, Garrick introduced what some have called *naturalistic acting* into the English theatre. He believed that the actor could produce emotions by a convincing imitation and skilled projection of those emotions being imitated. He did not believe that the actor should experience anger or sadness or joy to project these emotions to an audience. The following words are ascribed to him: ". . . that a man was incapable of becoming an actor who was not absolutely independent of circumstances calculated to excite emotion, adding that for his own part he could speak to a post with the same feelings and expression as to the loveliest Juliet under the heaven."[4] His contemporaries wrote that on occasion he would delight them in relaxed moments with his face alone, without any outward motivation or any inward feeling of personal emotion. In this external or purely technical approach, actors, like Garrick, aim for a calculated *presentation* of a character's life on stage.

Many actors, in England and elsewhere, have followed Garrick's approach. Richard Boleslavski, one of Stanislavsky's students, wrote a classic book for the beginning actor called *Acting: The First Six Lessons* (1933) in which he sums up the importance of mimetic behavior for the actor. He says that just as children must crawl before they run, so beginning actors must be capable of observation and mimicry before they can project emotional experience onstage.

English actor John Gielgud (b. 1904) — counted among the three greatest actors of his generation (Laurence Olivier and Ralph Richardson are the others) — says of his early days in the theatre that he slavishly imitated other actors:

> I imitated all the actors I admired when I was young, particularly Claude Rains, who was my teacher at dramatic school. I admired him very much. I remember seeing him play Dubedat in *The Doctor's Dilemma*, especially his death scene, in which he wore a rich dressing gown and hung his hands — made up very white — over the arms of his wheelchair. And then I understudied him. I also understudied Noel Coward, whom I felt I had to imitate because he was so individual in his style. I followed him in *The Vortex* and, naturally, the only way to say the lines was to say them as near to the way he said them as possible because they suited his style. It was, after all, written by him for him. Of course, it got me into some rather mannered habits. . . . [And Komisarjevsky, the Russian director] was an enormous influence in teaching me not to act from outside, not to seize on obvious, showy effects and histrionics, not so much to exhibit myself as to be within myself trying to impersonate a character who is not aware of the audience, to try to absorb the atmosphere of the play and the background of the character, to build it outward so that it came to life naturally. . . .[5]

Modern actors, such as Gielgud, strive to simulate the character, to walk, talk, and look like the king or beggar they are playing. But they also reach into the subtleties of the character's psychology and wholly embody the role, filling it with breath, blood, desires, and emotions so that we believe the actor when he says in Hamlet's words: "The time is out of joint. Oh, cursed spite/That ever I was born to set it right!" We forget that we are watching a working actor and become absorbed in the life and trials of Hamlet, the character.

Internal Belief

For many years, European and American actors were trained in the theatre itself. A young man or woman who showed ability would be hired to play small parts in a provincial stock company. The older actors would coach the young person, prescribing voice and body exercises that had been handed down for generations. This kind of external training developed a voice capable of being heard in large theatres, exaggerated gestures, and skill in speaking verse and Shakespeare. If actors showed talent, they would be given longer parts and eventually invited to join the company.

When realism came into fashion late in the nineteenth century, this "large" style of acting began to seem exaggerated and unconvincing. As the stage came to be thought of not as a symbolic world — a place that symbolized the universe the audience lived in (such as Shakespeare's "'Globe" theatre) — but as a recognizable place with a reality that corresponded to what ordinary people observed with their own senses, scenic design, stage decor, and acting styles changed. The play's world — the environment and characters — were to be represented as directly and as lifelike as possible. A middle-class street, house, and living room represented on a stage were to look like middle-class streets, houses, and living rooms outside the theatre. Actors were to be dressed like the middle-class businessmen or menial laborers that they were playing and that the audience encountered outside the theatre. So, too, the actor was called upon to set aside declamation and artificial gestures for the speech, walk, and behavior of such a person outside the theatre and to become a living *representation* of a recognizable character. To capture on stage and before an audience this sense of life being lived as it actually is, new methods for training actors had to be developed.

Stanislavsky's "Method"

Constantin Stanislavsky, the Russian actor-director, set about in the 1900s developing a systematic approach to training actors *to work from the inside outward* (see Figure 6.3). Today, his premises, developed over a lifetime, are accepted as the point of departure for most contemporary thinking about

FIGURE 6.3

Stanislavsky as Gaev, Madame Ranevskaya's brother, in the 1904 Moscow Art Theatre production of Chekhov's The Cherry Orchard.

acting. The essence of Stanislavsky's achievement (and lasting influence) was that he laid the basis for a psychological understanding of acting and fused it with a deep sense of drama as aesthetic truth. "The fundamental aim of our art," Stanislavsky wrote in *An Actor Prepares*, "is the creation of [the] inner life of the human spirit and its expression in artistic form." To arrive at this truth, which had been lost in the theatre, Stanislavsky proposed that actors understand how men and women actually behave physically and psychologically. Stanislavsky's approach asked the actor to study and experience subjective emotions and feelings and to manifest them to audiences by physical and vocal means. He also stressed that personal truth in acting had to be balanced by attention to the *text*, to imaginative realities outside the actor's immediate experience. The actor was called upon to enter "the world of the play" as a whole, not just to attend to his or her part. Over the years, Stanislavsky developed a means of training actors (later called in America "the Method") whereby they would not only create

Lee Strasberg

Lee Strasberg (1901–1982), one of the best-known acting teachers in America, transformed Stanislavsky's system of acting into an American "Method."

In 1947, members of the Group Theatre — a pre-World War II acting ensemble founded in 1931, that included Elia Kazan, Harold Clurman, Cheryl Crawford, and Stella Adler — started the Actors Studio (located today at 432 West 44th Street in New York) as a workshop for professional actors to concentrate on acting problems away from the pressures of the commercial theatre. Strasberg assumed leadership of the Studio in 1951. As a teacher and acting theorist, he revolutionized American acting, producing such remarkable performers as Marlon Brando, Marilyn Monroe, Julie Harris, Paul Newman, Geraldine Page, Shelley Winters, Ellen Burstyn, and Al Pacino.

The methods of the Studio derived from Stanislavsky were tailored by Strasberg for plays of American realism. He demanded great discipline of his actors, as well as great depths of character relationships and inner truthfulness. He once explained his approach in this way:

> The human being who acts is the human being who lives. That is a terrifying circumstance. Essentially the actor acts a fiction, a dream; in life the stimuli to which we respond are always real. The actor must constantly respond to stimuli that are imaginary. And yet this must happen not only just as it happens in life, but actually more fully and more expressively. Although the actor can do things in life quite easily, when he has to do the same thing on the stage under fictitious conditions he has difficulty because he is not equipped as a human being merely to play-act at imitating life. He must somehow believe. He must somehow be able to convince himself of the rightness of what he is doing in order to do things fully on the stage.[6]

a subjective reality of their own — an inner truth of feeling and experience — but would also represent the "outer" truth of the character's reality in the surrounding world of the play. Speaking of the "external" acting that he had seen and abhorred in his time, Stanislavsky said that "the difference between my art and that is the difference between 'seeming and being.'"[7]

What distinguished Stanislavsky's theory of actor-training was the emphasis on the purpose and objectives of human behavior. For Stanislavsky, stage acting rested on the actor's discovery of the purpose and objectives of his or her character and the successful "playing" of those goals.

Stanislavsky developed rehearsal methods by which the actor would "live life" onstage. He developed a set of exercises and principles designed to help the actor call on personal feelings and experiences, along with the

FIGURE 6.4

Actor James Earl Jones as Othello in the 1964 New York Shakespeare Festival Theatre production, Delacorte Theatre. Jones, who studied with Lee Strasberg, won a Tony Award as the boxer in The Great White Hope *(1968). He played Othello on Broadway in 1981 to Christopher Plummer's Iago.*

body and the voice, in the creation of the role. This aspect of his training was called the "psychotechnique." Through the development of self-discipline, observation, relaxation, and total concentration, his actors learned to recall emotions from their own lives that were analogous to those experienced by the characters they played. What mattered to Stanislavsky was the *actor's truth*: What the actor feels and experiences internally expresses itself in what the character says and how the character reacts to given circumstances. Actors learned to experience what their characters experienced *as if* it were actually happening to them (see Figure 6.4). Stanislavsky called this "the magic if" by which the actor thinks, "If I were in Othello's situation, what would I do?" Not "If I were Othello, what would I do?" By "becoming" a person in the character's situation, the actor could give a performance that became a real experience, not merely the imitation of a fiction.

Subtext

The actor's job is to portray the many levels of what the play's character and situation are about. For example, the character may be saying one thing while thinking or feeling the opposite. Stanislavsky called this real, underlying meaning of the line the subtext. For Stanislavsky, the actor's preparation involved understanding the text and the subtext, or hidden level, as well.

In *Othello*, Iago speaks volumes of subtext when he insists that he is "honest Iago." The actor must speak the text the playwright has written; conveying the subtext is the actor's main contribution, demonstrating his or her insight and sensitivity into the character's motives and the play's meaning.

Subtext has been defined as a movement against or away from the *literal* statement of the character's purposes or intentions. It is the actor's job to show the pressures — outer and inner — that are being put on the character by the play's situation.

In Anton Chekhov's *The Three Sisters* (1901), Tusenbach, the youngest sister's fiancé, is telling Irina goodbye because he is going immediately to fight a duel that he cannot win. She knows something is wrong, but not what is literally happening. Their farewell speech shows Chekhov's mastery of subtext. All of the anxiety and pain of parting suffuses talk of their present relationship, trivialities, and future plans.

> TUSENBACH: My dear, I'll be back in a moment.
> IRINA: Where are you going?
> TUSENBACH: I must slip back to the town, and then . . . I want to see some of my colleagues off.
> IRINA: It's not true . . . Nikolai, why are you so absent-minded today? [*A pause.*] What happened outside the theatre last night?
> TUSENBACH: [*with a movement of impatience*]. I'll be back in an

hour. . . . I'll be back with you again. [*Kisses her hands.*] My treasure! . . . [*Gazes into her eyes.*] It's five years since I first began to love you, and still I can't get used to it, and you seem more beautiful every day. What wonderful, lovely hair! What marvellous eyes! I'll take you away tomorrow. We'll work, we'll be rich, my dreams will come to life again. And you'll be happy! But — there's only one 'but,' only one — you don't love me!

IRINA: I can't help that! I'll be your wife, I'll be loyal and obedient to you, but I can't love you. . . . What's to be done? [*Weeps.*] I've never loved anyone in my life. Oh, I've had such dreams about being in love! I've been dreaming about it for ever so long, day and night . . . but somehow my soul seems like an expensive piano which someone has locked up and the key's got lost. [*A pause.*] Your eyes are so restless.

TUSENBACH: I was awake all night. Not that there's anything to be afraid of in my life, nothing threatening. . . . Only the thought of that lost key torments me and keeps me awake. Say something to me. . . . [*A pause.*] Say something!

IRINA: What? What am I to say? What?

TUSENBACH: Anything.

IRINA: Don't, my dear, don't. . . . [*A pause.*]

TUSENBACH: Such trifles, such silly little things sometimes become so important suddenly, for no apparent reason! You laugh at them, just as you always have done, you still regard them as trifles, and yet you suddenly find they're in control, and you haven't the power to stop them. But don't let us talk about all that! Really, I feel quite elated. I feel as if I was seeing those fir-trees and maples and birches for the first time in my life. They all seem to be looking at me with a sort of inquisitive look and waiting for something. What beautiful trees — and how beautiful, when you think of it, life ought to be with trees like these!

[*Shouts of 'Ah-oo! Heigh-ho!' are heard.*]

I must go, it's time. . . . Look at that dead tree, it's all dried-up, but it's still swaying in the wind along with the others. And in the same way, it seems to me that, if I die, I shall still have a share in life some-

how or other. Goodbye, my dear. . . . [*Kisses her hands.*] Your papers, the ones you gave me, are on my desk, under the calendar.
IRINA: I'm coming with you.
TUSENBACH: [*alarmed*]. No, no! [*Goes off quickly, then stops in the avenue.*] Irina!
IRINA: What?
TUSENBACH: [*not knowing what to say*]. I didn't have any coffee this morning. Will you tell them to get some ready for me? [*Goes off quickly.*]

The nonverbal layer of meaning is what Stanislavsky called *subtext*; Anton Chekhov proved a master at writing dialogue that vibrated with hidden meanings and emotions. In this scene from *The Three Sisters*, Chekhov avoids the obvious farewell, such as Romeo and Juliet's famous "Parting is such sweet sorrow/That I shall say good night till it be tomorrow" (2, iii). Chekhov's characters disguise their terror (Tusenbach knows he will be killed in the duel) and anxieties (Irina is aware that some dimension in their relationship has changed). Their "farewell" scene is an expression of triviality, hope, unrequited love, desperation, inarticulateness, and discovery of the world's beauty. Tusenbach's final words to his fiancée asking for coffee are his means of masking his distress and pain over his loss — of hope, love, and life.

Recalling Emotions

How does the actor induce emotion at the moment of performance night after night? One of the first methods developed by Stanislavsky was "emotional recall" or "affective memory," in which the actor recalled a situation in his or her own life to stimulate an emotional display that corresponded with the playwright's intention. Julie Harris (b. 1925) tells us that she conjures up something in her own life that produces tears when she is called upon to cry.

Not only will the actor think of something sad (for example, a relative's death or something connected with the sad event), but the actor will try to re-create in the mind's eye all of the surrounding circumstances, the sensory

FIGURE 6.5

Uta Hagen as Blanche DuBois. She succeeded Jessica Tandy on Broadway in the role in A Streetcar Named Desire *in 1948.*

and emotional details that were part of the experience. Actress Uta Hagen (b. 1919; see Figure 6.5) writes of her work on the role of Tennessee Williams' heroine, Blanche DuBois:

> Suppose I am going to work on the part of Blanche DuBois in *A Streetcar Named Desire*. I have to hunt for an understanding of — and an identification with — the character's main needs: a need for perfection (and always *when* and *how* have I needed these things); a romantic need for beauty; a desire for gentleness, tenderness, delicacy, elegance, decorum; a need to be loved and protected; a strong sensual need; a need for delusion when things go wrong, etc.
>
> If I return to my cliché image of myself — the earthy, frank, gusty child of nature — I'm in trouble and there will be an enormous distance between Blanche and myself. If, on the other hand, I remember myself preparing for an evening at the opera (bathing and oiling and perfuming my body, soothing my skin, brushing my hair until it shines, artfully applying makeup until the little creases are hidden and my eyes look larger and I feel younger, spending hours over a silky elegant wardrobe, and a day over the meal I will serve before the opera, setting out my freshest linen, my best crystal and polished silver among dainty flowers); if I recall how I weep over a lovely poem by Rilke or Donne or Browning, how my flesh tingles when I hear Schubert chamber music, how tender I feel at a soft twilight, how I respond to someone

pulling out a chair for me at the table or opening a car door for me or offering me their arm for a walk in the park — *then* I am beginning to find within myself realities connected with Blanche DuBois' needs.

I was not raised on an elegant plantation like Belle Reve, nor have I lived in Laurel, Mississippi, *but* I have visited elegant mansions in the East, I have seen many photographs of Faulkner country and estates, I have toured some of the South, and from a conglomerate of these experiences I can now make *my* Belle Reve and start to build a reality for my life there before the play's beginning.

Unfortunately, I have never been in New Orleans or the French Quarter, but I have read a great deal, seen many films and newsreels. I have even related the French Quarter of New Orleans, in a way, to a little section of the Left Bank in Paris where I once lived to make it real to myself.

The Kowalski apartment itself, which is dictated for me by the playwright, the designer and the director, must, nevertheless, be made real to me by substitutions from my own life. It is *I* who must make the sense of cramped space, the lack of privacy, the disorder and sleaziness, the empty beer cans and stale cigarette butts, the harsh street noises all move in on me chaotically and frighteningly. Each object or thing that I see or come in contact with must be made particular so that it will serve the new me and bring about the psychological and sensory experiences necessary to animate my actions.[8]

Many actors like Uta Hagen and Julie Harris build an emotion in sympathy with the character's situation through the substitution of remembered sensory and emotional details. But the actor does not stop there. In the theatre the emotional impact must be produced night after night with precise timing, on cue, and with a minimum of conscious thought.

Physical and Vocal Training

The Actor's Body

Modern movement training provides actors with a wide range of physical choices in the creation of character. It is not simply a matter of physically demonstrating a pompous valet or a nervous debutante. In movement training ("stage movement" is now an old-fashioned term), the emphasis is on developing the actor's body as a more open, responsive, physical

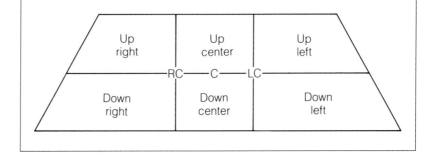
instrument by first eliminating unnecessary tensions and mannerisms. Movement training today is not the imposition of arbitrary positions or alignments, as it was when young actors copied the gestures of the leading actor. Rather, it is more a matter of sensitizing actors to the variety of possibilities of human movement *as an expressive signal* of character and intentions.

In recent years movement training in the United States has changed in two fundamental ways. First, the influence of psychology has given insight into the actor's inner world and consequently how that world may be expressed through the body's motion. Second, numerous approaches to movement or physical training from many different cultures and traditions have entered our classrooms and rehearsal halls and have had an enormous impact on actor training over the last decade. They range from techniques in martial arts, yoga, juggling and circus arts, stage combat, and mask training to Feldenkrais and the Alexander techniques. Our best movement teachers are familiar with and work through one or more of these approaches.

Today's movement teacher is, above all, an acting teacher who chooses to work through the body. Our best teachers have found ways to train actors to make fresh choices — for movement grows from the urge to move as an expression of something that, until one critical moment, is hidden. The violent encounter between Stanley Kowalski and Blanche DuBois in *A Streetcar Named Desire* is an expression of Stanley's pent-up hostility and fear of his sister-in-law. He chooses a physical encounter — a fight and sexual assault — to express his fear and rage at this intruder who has so disrupted his household and violated his sense of masculine authority.

Truly expressive stage movement, even combat like the duel in *Hamlet*, begins with the character's inner needs. When those needs are well understood, it is always possible to create physical realities that are compelling — like Laurence Olivier's grotesque Richard III (Shakespeare) or James Earl Jones' Troy Maxson (in *Fences*) whose physical stance is that of an aging athlete whose age and race have denied him an opportunity to play professional baseball (see page 116).

To be convincing, the actor's movements must *embody* the character's attitudes or needs. In performance, all physical and vocal choices must serve those needs.

The Actor's Voice

The voice is our means of communicating to others, presenting ourselves, expressing our personality, thoughts, and feelings. The function of the actor's speech, like our own, is to communicate needs. For example, if we are speaking trivialities, it is not the *triviality* that is important, it is the *need* to speak it that matters. Therefore, however ordinary, stylized, or heightened (as in poetry) stage language is, when the actor speaks lines from the dramatic text, he or she must root those lines in the *need* to speak in a particular fashion and in particular words.[9]

Voice training today happens only in relation to the whole acting process and involves the actor's entire being — the physical and the psychological. Vocal exercises practiced in the classroom are, therefore, aimed at "freeing" the voice. These exercises involve relaxation, breathing, and increased muscularity of lips and tongue. These are followed by particular exercises on texts that stretch the voice, making it more responsive to the demands of the character.

The primary objective in voice training is to open up the possibilities of the voice — its energy, its instinctive responses to what the actor has to say. Correcting one's speech (a regional accent, for example) is not as important in voice training today as it once was. The aim of vocal exercises is to keep the essential *truth* of the actor's own voice, yet make it large and malleable enough for projecting feelings to a large auditorium or modulating to the intimacy of a television studio. To get this balance between the size of the voice and its malleability, vocal work involves both technique and imagination. Unlike the singer whose "sound" is the message, the actor's voice is an extension of the person. Its possibilities are as complex as the actor's persona. Because actors deal with *words* that come off a printed page, they have continually to find ways to make those words their own. Voice training aims at establishing an ongoing process for the actor to become as sensitive as possible to the physical make-up of the voice in relation to the body (breath, diaphragm, ribs, head, neck). The goal is to merge techniques learned in voice exercises with the actor's imagination to communicate the character's needs through the words of the text. Hamlet's instructions to the Players on the use of the voice and the body, "Suit the action to the word, the word to the action . . . ," are still appropriate to the actor's training.

Rehearsals and Performance

This task of creating an emotional impact through the careful reconstruction of one's life experience and then relating those emotions to the character and the situation is carried out in rehearsals, which may last from three to ten weeks. The work of rehearsals is to condition the actor's responses so that during performance, emotions flow from the actor's concentration on the material—the character's situation and objectives.

In rehearsals the actor works with the director and other actors to find the role and to "set" movement and interpretation. Not until dress rehearsal, as a rule, is an actor able to work with a complete set of properties, settings, costumes, makeup, and stage lighting. However, special rehearsal clothes and properties, like fans, keys, and walking sticks, are provided if they are significantly different from ordinary dress and handheld objects.

On each night of the play's run, the actor re-creates the character's situation for the audience. Everything the actor has set or memorized in rehearsals—objectives, mannerisms, vocal intonations, movements—stays (or should stay) much the same. But the actor's creativity continues within the boundaries set in rehearsal: This is the actor's art. Each performance requires the actor to give fresh life to the character's situation, feelings, responses, desires, goals—to concentrate anew on the character's speech, behavior, and theatrical effectiveness.

British actor Ian McKellen (b. 1939) expressed his views on his profession thus: "At its most rewarding, acting involves an intense combination of intellect, imagination, and hard work, belying the popular distorted image of dressing-up, booming voices, and shrieking exhibitionism."[10]

Summary

The actor brings living human presence to the stage. The audience observes and is engaged in the actor's thinking, planning, working, and living the life of the character in a play. And the actor must be seen to do all of these things not in the context of the theatre, but in the situation shared with the other actors onstage—within the world of the play. The actor must be continually redefining relationships with other characters, and must be seen as striving to achieve some goal or objective within the play's situation. The search for new depths of character and creative energy to keep the performance fresh and alive continues night after night.

Questions for Study

1. Study the photo of *Our Town* on page 110. How is the stage stripped down to essentials?

2. Where does the actor's art begin?

3. What is the actor's *external technique*? Think of an example.

4. What is a character's *situation*? What is Hamlet's situation? What is Blanche DuBois' situation?

5. What is *subtext*?

6. What are the objectives of movement and voice training for the actor?

7. The following terms were used by Stanislavsky: "the magic if," "psychotechnique," character's "objective," "emotional recall." What does each mean?

8. What do we mean when we talk about "the Method" of acting?

9. What is the Actors Studio?

10. What is the purpose of a *dress rehearsal*?

11. Select a scene from *A Streetcar Named Desire* in which Blanche DuBois appears. What is her objective in the scene? What is her objective for the entire play?

12. Memorize Hamlet's speech (3, iii, 73–96) and play it to an imaginary Claudius. What was your objective in the speech?

13. What do we mean when we say that "acting is the art of human presence"?

14. According to Peter Brook, what constitutes an "unforgettable moment" in an actor's performance?

15. Select one of the actors discussed in the photo essay "Great Moments of Acting" and study that actor's background in the theatre and special accomplishments. Write an essay in which you describe that actor's understanding of the acting process.

16. *Plays to Read*: Thornton Wilder's *Our Town*, Anton Chekhov's *The Three Sisters*.

17. *Suggested Reading*: Lee Strasberg's famous entry on "acting" in *Encyclopaedia Britannica* (included in editions printed since 1957). For an understanding of the realities of the acting profession in America today, read Robert Cohen, *Acting Professionally: Raw Facts about Careers in Acting*, 4th ed. (Mountain View, CA: Mayfield, 1990).

18. *Suggested Writings and Biographies*: Laurence Olivier, *Confessions of an Actor: An Autobiography* (1982); Jean Benedetti, *Stanislavsky: A Biography* (1990).

Theatre artists — actors, directors, and designers — create the play onstage in concrete visual terms. Designers of scenery, costumes, sound, and lighting realize the playwright's intentions graphically, aurally, and visually in the theatrical space.

Chapter 7

The Image Makers: The Designers

Designers collaborate with the director to focus the audience's attention on the actor in a special environment: the stage. Designers shape and fill the stage space. They create the actor's environment and make the play's world *visible* and *interesting* to us. Sometimes one person (the **scenographer**) designs scenery, lighting, and costumes. But since scene, costume, light, and sound design are essentially four different arts, we will look at each of them separately.

The Scene Designer

Background

The scene (or stage) designer became part of the American theatre over a hundred years ago. The designer's nineteenth-century counterpart was the resident *scenic artist*, who painted the large pieces of scenery for the theatre manager. Scenery's main function in those days was to give the actor a painted background and to indicate time and place. Scenic studios staffed with specialized artists were even set up to turn out scenery on demand. Many of these studios conducted a large mail-order business for standard backdrops and scenic pieces. By the turn of the century, realism had come into the theatre and the job of making the stage look real became more complex.

Theatre in the late nineteenth century was dominated by a naturalistic philosophy that proclaimed life could be explained by the forces of environment, heredity, economics, society, and

Appia and Craig

Adolphe Appia (1862–1928) and Edward Gordon Craig (1872–1966) built the theoretical foundations of modern expressionistic theatrical practice. For the Swiss-born Appia, *artistic unity* was the basic goal of theatrical production. He disliked the contradiction in the three-dimensional actor performing before painted two-dimensional scenery, and he advocated the replacement of flat settings with steps, ramps, and platforms. He thought the role of lighting was to fuse all visual elements into a unified whole. His *Music and Stage Setting* (1899) and *The Work of Living Art* (1921) are the basic source books for modern stage-lighting practices.

Gordon Craig was born into an English theatrical family (he was the son of actress Ellen Terry and architect and scenic designer Edward Godwin) and began his career as an actor in Henry Irving's company. The 1902 exhibit of his work as a stage designer and the publication of his *The Art of the Theatre* in 1905 created controversy throughout Europe; indeed, his entire theatrical life was a storm of controversy. He thought of theatre as an independent art that welded action, words, line, color, and rhythm into an artistic whole created by the single, autonomous artist. Many of his ideas on simplified decor, three-dimensional settings, moving scenery, and directional lighting prevailed in the new stagecraft that emerged after World War I.

the psyche. This being the case, theatre had to present these forces as carefully and effectively as possible. If environment (including economic factors) really did govern people's lives, then it needed to be shown as they actually saw it. The responsibility for creating this stage environment shifted from the playwright and scene painter to the designer. The demands of stage realism called for the stage to look almost photographically like the actual place where the play's action takes place.

Realism has been the dominant convention of the theatre in our time. However, many new and exciting movements in the modern theatre have come about as reactions to this direct representation of reality, which pretends that the stage is not a stage but someone's actual living room and that the audience (seated in a dark auditorium) is really not there beyond the invisible "fourth wall," observing the play. Leaders of many new theatre movements have argued that the stage living room and box set were themselves unnatural; they set about pioneering a special kind of theatrical reality for the stage (see Figure 2.14 on page 46).

Before World War I in Europe, Adolphe Appia and Edward Gordon Craig became self-proclaimed prophets of a new movement in theatre design and lighting. They were concerned with creating mood and atmosphere, opening up the stage for movement, and unifying visual ideas; they

FIGURE 7.1

One model for Edward Gordon Craig's famous setting of Hamlet *for the 1912 Moscow Art Theatre production. Note how the huge white screens dwarf the human figure; Craig designed these screens to be sufficiently mobile so that the appearance of the scene could be changed without closing the front curtain. Unfortunately they did not function with the efficiency he had envisioned.*

assaulted the illusion of stage realism and led the way to a rethinking of theatrical design (see Figure 7.1). In his *Music and Stage Setting* (1899), Appia called for theatrical art to be expressive. And today, in the same spirit, many modern set designers have extended the traditional media of wood, canvas, and paint to include steel, plastics, projected images, pipes, ramps, light, platforms, and steps to *express* the play's atmosphere and imaginative life instead of attempting to *reproduce* the details of its time and place realistically.

Appia and Craig influenced the young American designers of the 1920s, Robert Edmond Jones, Lee Simonson, and Norman Bel Geddes, who dedicated themselves to bringing the new stagecraft to Broadway. Two generations of American scene designers have followed their lead. Prominent among them are Jo Mielziner, who designed *Death of a Salesman, A Streetcar Named Desire,* and *The King and I*; Boris Aronson, the designer of *Cabaret, Company,* and *Pacific Overtures*; Oliver Smith, designer of *Brigadoon, The Sound of Music,* and *Plaza Suite*; and Ming Cho Lee, designer of *Hair, for colored girls who have considered suicide/when the rainbow is enuf,* and *K2.*

Ming Cho Lee

Ming Cho Lee (born 1930 in Shanghai and educated at Occidental College and UCLA) designed his first Broadway show, O'Neill's *Moon for the Misbegotten*, in 1962. Since then, he has designed settings for Broadway, Off-Broadway, regional theatres, opera, and dance.

Speaking of his methods, Lee said: "I generally read the script once just to get an impact from which I will try to form some kind of visual concept. . . . I always design for the total play and let the specifics fit in. The total play demands some kind of expression through materials, and this is something I always first ask a director. . . . And then, I would make the choice as to whether it is a realistic play that requires very literal settings or if it's a play that requires a nonliteral approach and essentially you present it on a platform — you create a framework on which to hang your visual statement."[1]

The Designer's Training

Sixty years ago the designer, like the actor, was trained in stock and repertory theatres. The scenic artist, with only a rough knowledge of theatrical settings, was concerned almost solely with painting. Design training consisted of an apprenticeship in a scenic studio. With the emergence of the director as artistic coordinator, the concept of the stage designer as a collaborative, interpretive artist with responsibility for all visual and technical elements developed as well. In the 1920s, universities became the training ground for the new theatre artists — the scene, costume, and lighting designers.

Designing for the Theatre

Scene designers use one of five basic methods to design stage settings: (1) Start with a real room or place, select from it, change the dimensions, and reshape it for a particular stage. (2) Start with the actors and the play's most important events and then add platforms, shapes, and voids around them. (3) Start with the play's mood and find the lines, shapes, and colors that will reflect it. (4) Design the scene as an idea or metaphor — in the 1920s, the expressionists in Germany sought to reflect the nightmarish outlook of the disturbed mind in their stage settings (see Figure 7.2). (5) Organize the entire space, including actor and audience, as environment. The environmentalist begins with the notion that the production

FIGURE 7.2

The skeleton scene of the 1922 New York production of German playwright Georg Kaiser's From Morn to Midnight *is a good example of expressionist design and production style, which stressed imaginative lighting (a tree has been transformed into a human skeleton), symbolic decor on an almost empty stage, and the distortion of natural appearances. Notice how the actor is dwarfed by the huge projection. The setting was designed by Lee Simonson.*

will both develop from and totally take place in a given space. There is no effort to create an illusion or imitation; rather, the performer and audience, space and materials, exist as what they are: people, ramps, platforms, ladders, stairs, mazes.

The design process can take months. The designer usually begins by studying the script in much the same way as the director, visualizing details of place, movement, and objects in space. The designer asks certain basic questions about the script's requirements: Where does the play take place? What is the play's historical period? How does the play proceed in time and seasons? What kinds of movements do the characters make? What elements from life are essential parts of the play's world? What is the play's spatial relationship to the audience? Is it close up or far away? Are the play and the audience in the same space? How are character relationships expressed in the space? How much playing space is needed? Is the action to be violent or sedate? What is the play's mood? How many exits, properties, and essential pieces of furniture are needed? What is the director's concept?

As the designer visualizes the space, details are established in *sketches*, a *ground plan*, and a *model*. Sketches (or rough pencil drawings) are made in the early period when both the director and the designer are visualizing the stage floor and theatrical space. When their ideas have reached some degree of concreteness, they confer and agree on the ground plan: shape, entrances, exits, and major scenic elements, including color.

Modern Stage Designs

Jo Mielziner (1901–1976) pioneered, along with director Elia Kazan, "selective realism" in scenic design. Of his type of design Mielziner said: ". . . If you eliminate nonessentials, you've got to be . . . sure that the things you do put in are awfully good. They've got to be twice as good, because they stand alone to make a comment. . . . I got to feel that even realistic plays didn't need realistic settings necessarily."[2]

In the final scene of *A Streetcar Named Desire* (1947) Stanley Kowalski's friends play poker while Blanche DuBois is taken away to an asylum. In the foreground are the selected realistic details of Mielziner's setting: living spaces, beds, tables, and chairs.

For Arthur Miller's *Death of a Salesman* (1949), Mielziner designed the salesman's house on several levels (kitchen, sons' bedroom, porch, and forestage). The actors' movements with area lighting were the only scene-change devices. The large backdrop upstage was painted to show tenement buildings looming over Willy Loman's house in the play's present time. When lighted from the rear, the buildings washed out to be replaced with projections of trees with leaves. The leaves indicated the pleasant atmosphere of Willy's remembered past with its bright sunshine and cheerful ambience.

The Berliner Ensemble's 1949 production of Brecht's *Mother Courage and Her Children* in East Berlin was originally designed by Teo Otto (see Figure 7.5). In this final scene, Mother Courage's wagon is the main set piece, which actress Helene Weigel as Courage, alone in the harness, pulls toward yet another war.

Bertolt Brecht's favorite designers — Teo Otto, Caspar Neher, and Karl von Appen — did not create illusions of real places but provided background materials (projections on a rear cyclorama, placards, signs, and set pieces, like Courage's wagon) that commented on the play's historical period and the characters' socioeconomic circumstances. The *setting* itself (the theatrical space) was used to make the dramatic action and individuals appear strange or unfamiliar because it resembled little that was familiar in our daily lives. Brecht did not disguise the fact that all was taking place in a theatre under exposed lighting instruments, creating "white light," and before an audience.

Oedipus the King, designed and directed by Svoboda at the Smetana Theatre, Prague, 1963. The setting was a vast flight of stairs, starting in the orchestra pit and reaching almost out of sight. The stairs were punctuated by platforms that thrust out from the stairs themselves. The actor playing Oedipus appears on a platform (stage right). "At the end Oedipus was left alone. Virtually all the flat levels disappeared. He climbed an endless staircase, into sharp counterlighting. . . ."

Josef Svoboda (b. 1920), chief designer at Prague's National Theatre in Czechoslovakia, is Europe's most celebrated scenographer, making highly imaginative use of an array of contemporary technologies, including computerized slide and film projections, laser beams, moving platforms, plastics, and netting. His use of surfaces to project images around the actor, creating what he calls "dramatic space" as "psycho-plastic," is his trademark. "The goal of the designer," Svoboda has said, "can no longer be a description of a copy of actuality, but the creation of its multidimensional model."[3]

The elevations for this rock and ice face resembled a government geological survey map. Fifty-thousand board feet of plastic foam was used to build the wall over a wooden frame armature. Finishing touches included an oil fog mist and nightly avalanche of snow from a theatrical-supply house.

Designer Ming Cho Lee's (see box, page 138) spectacular setting for *K2* by Patrick Meyers was a sheer ice wall representing K2, the world's second-highest mountain. In the play two climbers are trapped on the icy ledge just below the summit. *K2* opened in 1982 at Arena Stage, Washington, D.C., before going to Broadway.

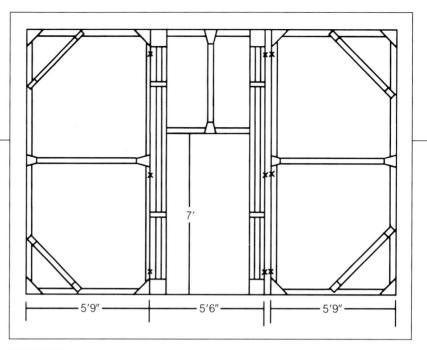

FIGURE 7.3

A designer's elevation is a two-dimensional drawing that shows no perspective. The elevation for the unit of scenery shows overall dimensions, as well as the dimensions of a door.

The designer also researches the play's historical period, background, and style, including architecture, furniture, and decor. Over the next several weeks, sketches, color *renderings* (watercolor paintings of the stage with scenery), and a model follow until the director and designer have arrived at the look and details of the setting. The designer then drafts plans, front elevations (two-dimensional drawings outlining the object as it appears to the eye; see Figure 7.3), and paint elevations (Figure 7.4) to give to the technical director or shop foreman, who converts them into technical drawings, showing how the scenic pieces are to be constructed, their dimensions, and materials. Scenery is basically two- or three-dimensional, framed or unframed. It is built from these drawings and moved onto the stage at the appointed time. (This effort is commonly called "put-in.") The technical drawings detail the profile and outer dimensions of all scenic elements, showing where and how they function, and the order in which they will appear onstage.

Scenery must be strong, portable, and dependable. As we look at a set, we are usually not aware of types of scenery, how it fits together, how it is moved about during scene changes — unless the moving is done for theatrical effect (see Figure 7.5).

FIGURE 7.4

The scene painter — in nonprofessional theatres usually the designer — is a specialized artist who paints the scenery following painter's elevations and a model provided by the designer. Conjoined with lighting, the scene painter's art provides onstage color, perspective, depth, shape, and texture.

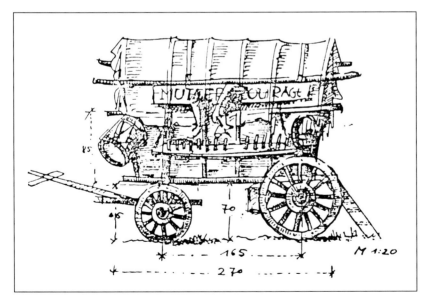

FIGURE 7.5

For the East Berlin production of Mother Courage and Her Children *at the Deutsches Theater in 1949, Brecht used the set model devised by Teo Otto for the 1941 Zurich production. The wagon and movable screens were the main set pieces of the design.*

The Costume Designer

Costume design has been compared by American designer Patricia Zipprodt to a car trip in which unpredictables of life pop up — unavailable fabric, the inadequate budget, the temperamental actor. The designer, like the car's driver, is in a constant state of problem solving.

The Costume

Costumes include all the character's garments and accessories (purse, cane, jewelry, handkerchief), all items related to hairdressing, and everything associated with face and body makeup, including masks.

Costumes tell us many things about the characters and about the nature, mood, and style of the play. They are visual signals adding color, style, and meaning to the play's environment. Costumes establish period, social class, economic status, occupation, age, geography, weather, and time of day. They help to clarify the relationships and relative importance of various characters. Ornament, line, and color can tie together members of a family, group, faction, or party. Changes in costume can indicate alteration in relationships among characters or in a character's psychological outlook. Similarities or contrasts in costumes can show sympathetic or antagonistic relationships. Hamlet's black costume, for instance, is contrasted with the bright colors worn by the court and speaks eloquently of his altered attitude toward the court. Designer Lucinda Ballard's costumes for *A Streetcar Named Desire* (see Figure 7.6) express Blanche DuBois' self-image of Southern gentility. Jessica Tandy's costume for Blanche's evening with Mitch includes tasteful summer dress, pearls, hat, gloves, pocketbook, bracelet, and bouquet (see Figure 1.2).

The Design Conference

Scene and costume designers work with the director to make visible the world in which the play's characters live. They explore verbally and with rough sketches the many different approaches and ideas that might bring

FIGURE 7.6

One of designer Lucinda Ballard's costumes created for the 1947 Broadway production of A Streetcar Named Desire. *This is Blanche DuBois's famous party costume. Tennessee Williams described the dress as a "somewhat soiled and crumpled white satin evening gown and a pair of scuffed silver slippers with brilliants set in the heels." Stanley describes the dress to Blanche as a "worn-out Mardi Gras outfit."*

As Blanche, betrayed by Stanley and Mitch, places a rhinestone tiara on her head, she drinks to imaginary "admirers." The costume was completed with rhinestone tiara, bracelet, and faded corsage.

the script into dramatic focus onstage. Designers supplement visually the director's concepts, and, in so doing, often inspire the director to a new way of thinking about the play. Award-winning designer Theoni V. Aldredge has said: "The costumes are there to serve a producer's vision, a director's viewpoint, and an actor's comfort."

Like the director and the scene designer, the costume designer begins by studying the script and taking note of the story, mood, characterization, visual effects, colors, atmosphere, geography, period, and season. Then the designer asks the practical questions: What is the costume budget? How many costumes (including changes) and accessories are needed? What actors have been cast? What stage actions, such as fighting, will affect the construction or wear of the costumes?

COSTUME RESOURCES

Years ago, the actor, director, or person in charge of stage wardrobe was responsible for costumes. But in the last sixty years, the new stagecraft has required costume designers trained in the visual arts to select and control these visual elements with far more attention to detail. Costume design has become an industry. Professional designers work in film, fashion, theatre, opera, television, dance, commercials, and extravaganzas (ice shows, nightclubs, circuses, and dance revues). Many people are involved in costume research and in sketching, choosing fabric, cutting, fitting, sewing, and making accessories. The large costume houses, such as the Costume Collection (New York), Western Costume Company (Hollywood), Costume World (Pompano Beach, Florida), Eaves-Brooks Costume Company (New York), buy stage costumes from closing shows, build costumes on demand, and rent garments to regional, community, and university theatres. A visit to their vast warehouses to select costumes for a play in production is not only an exciting adventure in itself, but also serves as a tour through the history of theatre design.

The overall plan of the production is worked out in design conferences. The costume designer brings sketches, color plates, costume charts, accessory lists, and fabric swatches to these meetings to make his or her visual concept clear to the director and scene designer. The designer must be specific to avoid later misunderstandings and costly last-minute changes.

Sometimes a brilliant costume design develops through trial and error. While designing the costumes for the Broadway production of the musical *Pippin* (1972), Patricia Zipprodt and director Bob Fosse had difficulty deciding on the right look for the strolling players (see Figure 7.7). With music and lyrics by Stephen Schwartz, the musical is performed by a group of actors costumed as some kind of theatrical caravan, who relate the story of Charlemagne's eldest son, Pippin, an idealist journeying through courts, battles, and love's intrigues. The script said, "Enter strolling players of an indeterminate period." Zipprodt remembers:

> Now, to me, this meant exactly nothing. I did a lot of sketches, which everybody seemed to like. On the day I was supposed to present finished sketches, time ran short. Instead of fully coloring the costumes of the strolling players as was planned and expected, I just painted beige and off-white washes so that Fosse could read the sketches more easily. I put the whole group of 14 or 15 in front of him and was just about to apologize for not getting the color done when he said, "That's just brilliant, exactly the colors they should be. How clever of you." The minute he said it, I knew he was right.[4]

But more often, the selection is made only after numerous alternatives have been explored.

FIGURE 7.7
Patricia Zipprodt's off-white and beige costumes for the strolling players in the original New York production of the musical Pippin *(1972).*

Costume Construction

After approving the sketches and plans, the director turns full attention to rehearsals, and the costume designer arranges for purchase, rental, or construction of costumes and schedules fitting dates with the actors. If the costumes are being constructed in the theatre's shop (as is most often the case in college and resident theatre productions), actors are measured, patterns cut, garments constructed, dyeing and painting of fabric done, and accessories built or purchased. After several fittings with the actors, the costumes are ready for the *dress parade*, during which designer and director examine the costumes on the actors before the dress rehearsal begins.

To accomplish this work, the designer may have an assistant designer, shop supervisor, cutters, drapers, seamstresses, crew head, and crew to cut, sew, dye, and make hats, footwear, and wigs. Often in small costume shops this personnel will double up on the responsibilities.

Dress Rehearsal

The dress parade and rehearsal (where the costumes, masks, and makeup are worn onstage in front of scenery and under lights) usually take place a week before opening night. It is not unusual to discover that a costume is inappropriate, or that a color doesn't work under the lights or against the scenery. In this event, the designer may redesign the garment, select another fabric or color (or both), and have the costume reconstructed or dyed almost overnight and ready for the next rehearsal or opening performance.

Patricia Zipprodt

Patricia Zipprodt, American costume designer, studied at Wellesley College and the Fashion Institute of Technology (New York). She has designed costumes for regional theatres (see Figure 7.8), as well as many Broadway musicals and plays, including *Sunday in the Park with George* (with Ann Hould-Ward), *Brighton Beach Memoirs, The Glass Menagerie, Fiddler on the Roof, Cabaret, Zorba, 1776, The Little Foxes, Plaza Suite, Pippin, Chicago,* and *Cat on a Hot Tin Roof.* She has won nine Drama Desk Awards and has been nominated for the Tony Award ten times, winning three. She has also designed costumes for opera, dance, and film: the Metropolitan Opera's acclaimed *Tannhäuser* and *The Barber of Seville,* Jerome Robbins' ballets *Les Noces* and *Dybbuk Variations,* and such films as *The Graduate* and *1776.* She teaches at Brandeis University.

FIGURE 7.8

Patricia Zipprodt's elaborate period costumes for Molière's Don Juan *in the 1981 Guthrie Theatre production, directed by Richard Foreman.*

Theoni V. Aldredge

Theoni V. Aldredge, one of theatre's most gifted and respected designers, has produced a total of 1,000 costumes and designed costumes for five hit musicals that ran simultaneously on Broadway: *A Chorus Line*, *42nd Street*, *Dreamgirls*, *La Cage aux Folles*, and *The Rink*. She begins her creative process by studying the characters and the cast of any given production: "To me, good design is design you're not aware of. It must exist as part of the whole — as an aspect of characterization. Also, a designer must be flexible and extremely patient. . . . A performance will suffer if an actor doesn't love his costume, and it's your job to make him love it."

For *A Chorus Line* (1975), essentially the story of a Broadway audition, Aldredge closely observed the personalities of the dancers and singers and the outfits they wore to rehearsals. Of this long-running musical, conceived and directed by Michael Bennett, and produced by Joseph Papp for the New York Shakespeare Festival, she has said: "I took millions of snapshots of what the kids came in wearing, and adapted what they had on for my costumes. I didn't depart too much, because it's what made each of them so unique. The only real transformation came with the golden chorus line at the end of the show, which, incidentally, Michael had wanted to be a red chorus line. But I felt red was too definite a color. I thought it should be a fantasy number. I told him it ought to be the color of champagne — of celebration — and that's what we did."[5] (See Figure 7.9.)

FIGURE 7.9

The final musical number of A Chorus Line *(1975), conceived by Michael Bennett and costumed by Theoni V. Aldredge.*

Wardrobe Personnel

Once costumes and accessories are finished, the costumes leave the shop and usually a new group (the wardrobe crew) takes charge of them during dress rehearsals and performances. Their responsibility is to mend, iron, clean, and generally maintain the costumes for the play's run. Although in the professional theatre there is a clear-cut division between these two groups, in college, university, and regional theatres the construction and wardrobe crews may be many of the same people.

The wardrobe supervisor (sometimes called the wardrobe master or mistress) or crew head makes a list of the costumes and accessories worn by each actor before dress rehearsals begin. These lists are used by crew members and actors to check that each costume is complete. The wardrobe "running" crew helps each actor dress and is responsible for the costumes before, during, and after each performance. Wardrobe routines are established during the dress rehearsal period and are followed during the production. The crew is also responsible for "striking" the costumes when the production closes: Costumes are cleaned, laundered, and placed in storage along with accessories, such as hats, wigs, shoes, and jewelry.

Makeup

Makeup enhances the actor and completes the costume. It is essential to the actor's visibility. In a large theatre, distance and lighting can make an actor's features without makeup colorless and indistinct. And makeup, like the costume, helps the actor reveal character by giving physical clues to personality, age, background, race, health, environment.

Makeup is classified as *straight* and *character*. Straight makeup highlights an actor's normal features and coloring for distinctness and visibility. Character makeup transforms the actor's features to reveal age or attitude. Noses, wrinkles, eyelashes, jawlines, eyepouches, eyebrows, teeth, hair, and beards can be added to change the actor's appearance. Character (sometimes called *illustrative*) makeup can make a young actor look older, can give the actor playing Cyrano his huge, bulbous nose, and can transform Laurence Olivier into Othello the Moor. When misused, makeup can destroy the actor's characterization by giving an external look that conflicts

In the ancient Asian and Greek theatres, actors used a white-lead makeup with heavy accents or they used masks. Today, basic makeup consists of a foundation and color shadings to prevent the actor from looking "washed out" beneath the glare of the stage lights. Pancake makeup has replaced the traditional greasepaint, or oil-base makeup, as the foundation for the actor's basic skin color. Cake makeup — less messy and more flexible than greasepaint — comes in small plastic cases (as does everyday makeup) and is applied with a damp sponge. Color shadings with rouge, lipstick, liners, mascara, and powder are applied with pencils and brushes. A well-equipped makeup kit (which can be purchased inexpensively from theatrical-supply houses) includes the standard foundations and shading colors plus synthetic hair, glue, solvents, wax, and hair whiteners.

with the character's inner life. The actor must know, then, the basis of makeup as an art and how to work with hair and wigs.

Most frequently, makeup is designed and applied by the actor (especially in the professional theatre), although in fantasy productions, such as the musical *Cats*, makeup and wigs may be designed by someone else. (See color insert following page 158.)

How does the actor make up? There is no substitute for practice with a basic makeup kit; every actor comes to know his or her face in a new way as soon as practice begins. Each face is different, catching and reflecting light in a different way. Each character presents a new set of challenges in which pancake makeup, rouge, liners, mascara, false eyelashes, wigs, facial hair (usually made from crepe wool), nose putty, and various prosthetic materials for aging, scarring, and disfiguring the skin's appearance are used to accent the character's expressions and attitudes. For this reason, actors should apply their own makeup, since actors know best the expressions, lines, and shadows their characters use.

Masks

In the early theatre, masks had many uses. They enlarged the actor's facial features so that the character's image would be apparent at great distance. The Greek masks expressed basic emotions: grief, anger, horror, sadness, pity. But most important for us today, the masked actor created an altogether different *presence* onstage than the actor without a mask. Although a masked actor may lose something in subtlety of expression, the presence the actor creates can be stately, heroic, awesome, or mysterious; the actor

FIGURE 7.10

The commedia dell'arte *mask. All characters in Italian* commedia, *with the exception of the young lovers, wore masks. Unlike classical masks and those of China and Japan,* commedia *masks did not express any particular emotion like joy or sorrow. Instead, they gave a permanent expression to the character, such as cunning or avarice. The mask's expressiveness varied with the angle from which it was seen. Pantalone, one of the chief* commedia *characters, was a miserly merchant. His mask, brown with a hooked nose, gray, sparse moustache, and a pointed white beard, represented a permanent expression of crafty greed.*

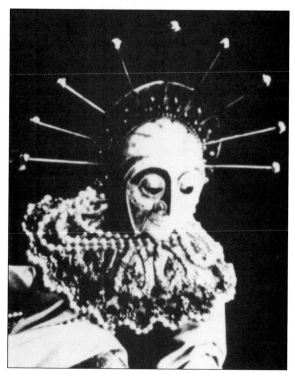

FIGURE 7.11

The mask-headdress of the governor's wife designed by Tanya Moiseiwitch for Brecht's The Caucasian Chalk Circle *reflects light and lends her awesome stature in the 1965 Guthrie Theater production in Minneapolis.*

FIGURE 7.12

A modern commedia *mask designed for Théâtre du Soleil's production of* L'Age d'Or *(1975). Here, the immigrant worker Abdallah-Harlequin finds a place to sleep in a flophouse jammed with sleeping bodies; his action is entirely mimed.*

may move the audience simply by standing onstage and reflecting light. Nor is the masked actor totally deprived of the facial subtlety available to the actor whose facial muscles move and change expression. By changing the mask's position (if the mask is made with this effect in mind), by angling the head and catching the light, different emotional responses can be evoked.

Mask-making is an ancient art dating from early cultures where masks were objects of fear; they were thought to have supernatural powers. Masks were used in the Greek and Roman theatres, by the *commedia dell'arte* in Renaissance Italy (see Figure 7.10), in Japanese Noh, and in the modern theatre (Figures 7.11 and 7.12). In addition to an artful exterior, a mask must be comfortable, strong, light, and molded to the contours of the actor's face. Today, in college and regional theatres, the costume designer makes the masks as part of the costume, designing for color, durability, and expressiveness.

The Lighting Designer

Light affects what we see, how we see, how we feel, and even how we hear. It is essential to the modern stage's theatrical effectiveness. It is also one of the most powerful tools the director has to control the audience's focus of attention and to enhance their understanding.

Artificial lighting (first candles and then gas) had been used to illuminate the stage since the seventeenth century, but by 1879 the invention of electric light had transformed overall possibilities for design in the theatre. It made possible complete control of a range of intensities and colors; it could be used flexibly to light or darken different areas of the stage; it provided a source of mood and atmosphere for the actor.

Swiss designer Adolphe Appia (see page 136) understood the artistic possibilities of light in the theatre. In *Music and Stage Setting* he argued that light should be the guiding principle of all design. He believed that light could unify or bring into harmony all production elements, including two- and three-dimensional objects, living and inanimate people, shapes, and things. Appia established light as an artistic medium for the theatre designer.

The Art of Light

Designer Jean Rosenthal defined lighting design as "the imposing of quality on the scarcely visible air through which objects and people are seen." One rule of lighting maintains that *visibility* and *ambience* (the surrounding atmosphere) must be inherent to the total theatrical design, including scenery and costumes. The light designer's tools, other than the instruments themselves, are *form* (the shape of the lighting's pattern), *color* (the lighting's mood achieved by filters — thin, transparent sheets of colored plastic, gelatin, or glass, or by varying degrees of intensity, or by both), and *movement* (the changes of form and color by means of dimmers, switchboards, and computerized control consoles located in the light booth). (See Figures 7.13–7.18.)

FIGURE 7.13

The Fresnel, named for the Fresnel lens, concentrates very bright light over a controllable, large area, beyond which brightness fades rapidly to near black with no discernible edge. This instrument is used whenever blending between areas is important, or when sharp edges of light would be distracting. The light beam can be further controlled and shaped by using a set of shutters (called "barn doors") placed on the instrument's front. The Fresnel is not well suited for positions over the audience that point toward the stage unless some illumination of the audience is acceptable.

FIGURE 7.14

The focusing scoop does not have a lens. Often used instead of strip lights to light cycloramas or backdrops.

FIGURE 7.15

The ellipsoidal reflector spotlight, the most commonly used instrument for any "throw" (or the distance from the light to the object to be illuminated) when a fine control and versatility of the light pattern is important. The new design is compact for use in small theatres with low ceilings. The edges of the light pattern of a well-focused ellipsoid (or "Leko") are sharp, but the instrument may deliberately be kept slightly out of focus to facilitate blending between areas. The beam of light, which is normally circular, can be decreased in size by using an iris or changed by using shutters.

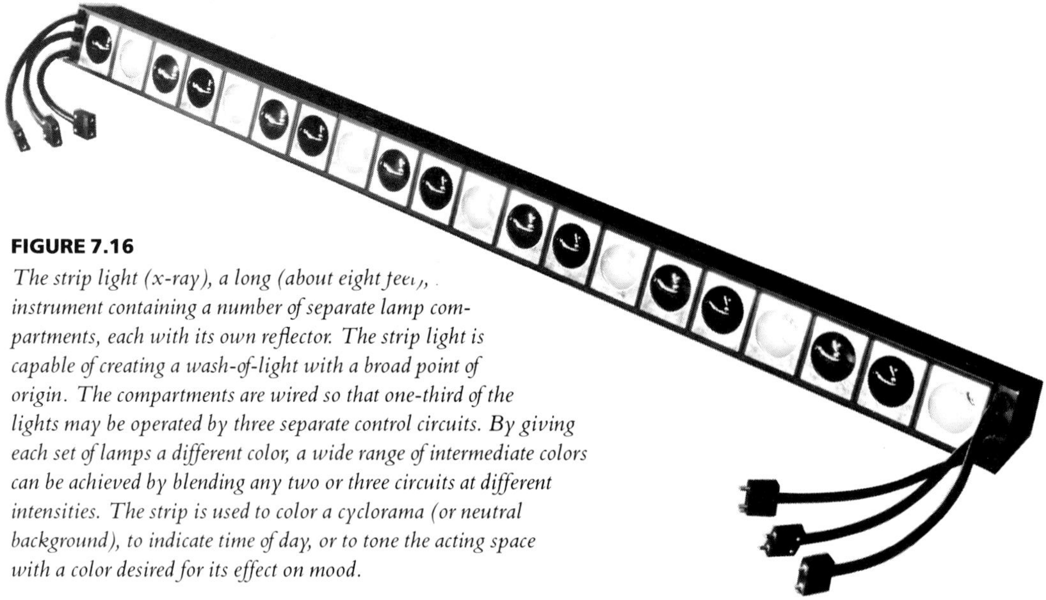

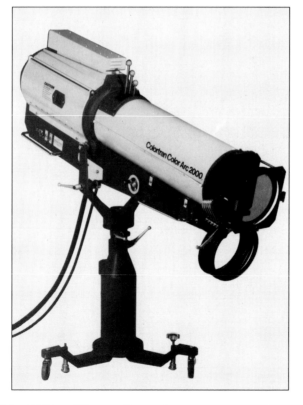

FIGURE 7.16

The strip light (x-ray), a long (about eight feet), instrument containing a number of separate lamp compartments, each with its own reflector. The strip light is capable of creating a wash-of-light with a broad point of origin. The compartments are wired so that one-third of the lights may be operated by three separate control circuits. By giving each set of lamps a different color, a wide range of intermediate colors can be achieved by blending any two or three circuits at different intensities. The strip is used to color a cyclorama (or neutral background), to indicate time of day, or to tone the acting space with a color desired for its effect on mood.

FIGURE 7.17

The follow spot. An expected part of the lighting scheme for most American musicals, this blatantly theatrical instrument is used to hold the attention of the audience on a point of interest, such as a leading singer or dancer. Ice shows and other extravaganzas also make use of follow spots; their moving pools of light are bright, compact, and enhance mood and create an ever-changing environment.

Makeup and Wigs for Cats

Designers John Napier and Paul Huntley designed the makeup and wigs for the long-running musical *Cats* (1981), based on poet T. S. Eliot's *Old Possum's Book of Practical Cats*. With music by Andrew Lloyd Webber, who is also the composer for the successful musicals *Jesus Christ Superstar*, *Evita*, *Joseph and the Amazing Technicolor Dreamcoat*, and *The Phantom of the Opera*, *Cats* was directed by Trevor Nunn, with lighting by David Hersey.

Also known in the United States for his designs for *Nicholas Nickleby* (seen on Broadway and television), John Napier is a major designer for England's Royal Shakespeare Company, the National Theatre, and for shows on London's West End. He designed the setting, costumes, and makeup for the lavish five-million-dollar New York production of *Cats*. At Broadway's Winter Garden Theatre Napier created a spectacular city dump upon which thirty-two cats howl, prowl, sing, and dance. Scenically, the stage was one huge piece of junk sculpture—a paradise for streetwise city cats roaming among the flotsam and jetsam of urban life: cereal boxes, used automobile tires, rusty cars, license plates, discarded cans, boxes, and trash of all varieties. Napier also designed the costumes and makeup for the "cats." American designer Paul Huntley designed and constructed the extraordinary yak wigs for the New York production, which became Broadway's first *bona fide* hit of the 1982-83 season, winning seven Tony Awards, including Best Musical.

This photo series illustrates the transformation of actors through the use of costumes, makeup, and wigs into the celebrated cats of the musical.

The makeup table with all accessories, including makeup pots, brushes, and wigs on stands, spread out in preparation for the actors to begin the arduous process of changing themselves into their feline characters.

Top left, Reed Jones sits in costume at the makeup table, watching his assistant tighten and adjust his wig for the character Skimbleshanks. The railroad cat in charge of the sleeping car express, Skimbleshanks appears on stage in puffs of locomotive steam.

Top right, Jones applies final touches to his makeup.

Bottom left, Christine Langner looking into the mirror as she applies final touches to her makeup as Rumpelteazer, Eliot's notoriously efficient cat-burglar (portrayed as a female in this production).

Bottom right, a makeup assistant fits one of Paul Huntley's wigs on Christine Langner.

Langner's costume is now complete. After a final look at the makeup and wig, she goes on stage to perform two roles: Etcetera and Rumpelteazer.

Top, Terence V. Mann as Rum Tum Tugger, Eliot's curious cat, in full costume, makeup, and wig.

Bottom left, Timothy Scott as the magical Mr. Mistoffelees, the conjuring cat, in heavily lined white makeup and skin-tight black, sequined costume of the magician's trade.

Bottom right, Betty Buckley as Grizabella, the Glamour Cat, in bedraggled wig and costume, including a coat of rabbit fur in shades of gray, emphasizing her declining health and beauty. Grizabella's song, "Memory," became the hit song of the show and Buckley won the Tony award for Best Supporting Actress in a Musical.

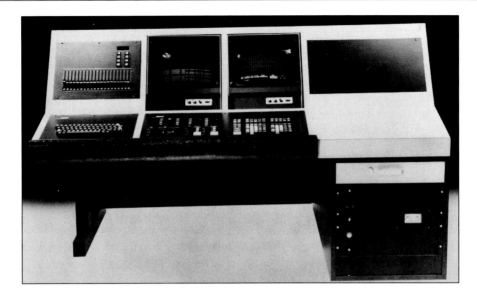

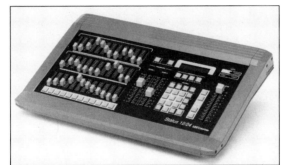

FIGURE 7.18

Various state-of-the-art computerized memory lighting control consoles. The small, portable boards are used on Broadway, road show tours, rental houses, college campuses, and even in permanent installations. The large permanent consoles are sometimes preferred in performing arts centers where portability is not a factor. All of the new memory lighting control boards use computer programs; store lighting cues; provide dimming, power distribution, and security; and display all photometric data for designers and electricians.

Jennifer Tipton

Jennifer Tipton (b. 1937), born in Columbus, Ohio, graduated from Cornell University in physics, studied dance at the Martha Graham school, and began her career as a lighting designer with the Paul Taylor Dance Company, having studied with Thomas Skelton.

Since the late '60s, she has worked consistently as a lighting designer for regional theatres, dance companies, and on Broadway. In 1974, she began working with Joseph Papp and the New York Shakespeare Festival. She won the Drama Desk Award in 1976 for lighting Ntozake Shange's *For Colored Girls Who Have Considered Suicide/When the Rainbow is Enuf* and the Antoinette Perry "Tony" Award for *The Cherry Orchard* at Lincoln Center in 1977. She designed Robert Wilson's *CIVIL warS* at the American Repertory Theatre (see the color essay, The "Creative" Director, and Figure 7.19). In 1989, she again received the Drama Desk Award for lighting *Jerome Robbins' Broadway, Long Day's Journey into Night,* and *Waiting for Godot.* Tipton's use of light is characterized by "textured and sculptured space" and by use of a palette based on white. She has summarized the essence of the lighting designer's art: "While 99.9 percent of an audience is not aware of light, 100 percent is affected by it."

Plotting and Cueing

The lighting designer reads the script and confers with the scene designer and director. The basic questions to be answered are: What degree of reality does the director want to suggest? Where are the important scenes placed within the set? What restrictions are there? What forms, moods, color patterns, and movements does the play require? Are special effects needed?

With answers to these questions, the designer sketches out a preliminary *light plot,* starting with a simple sketch of the stage and theatre building as it would be seen from directly above. On this basic plan the designer marks the location of the lighting instruments that will be needed, including type, size, wattage, its wiring and connection to an appropriate dimmer or computer circuit. There are no set rules that any particular instrument may or may not be used in any location. The only limitations in light design are those imposed by the director, by the physical nature of the theatre, by the theatre's available technology, and by safety.

The designer's finished lighting plot (see page 163) shows: (1) the location of each lighting instrument to be used; (2) the type of instrument, wattage, and color filter; (3) the general area to be lighted by the instrument; (4) circuitry necessary to operate the instruments; (5) any other details necessary for the electrical operation of the lighting. For example,

FIGURE 7.19

Stage lighting controls what we see. Jennifer Tipton's lighting for the 1977 production of Agamemnon *at the Vivian Beaumont Theater, Lincoln Center, New York, creates a somber atmosphere while calling attention to the bodies of Agamemnon and Cassandra lying before the palace doors.*

if a wall fixture is needed onstage so that an actor can turn on a light, the position of this fixture is shown on the light plot.

After the instruments are hung, angled, focused, and circuited, the designer is ready to cue the show. A written cue sheet (or chart of the control board indicating instrument settings and color with each cue numbered and keyed to the script) may be provided in advance to the crew at the control board, or a series of rehearsals may be called during which the designer asks for various intensities of light and makes changes until satisfied. For each change of stage lighting (or light cue), a notation is made that tells how to set the control board and at what point in the stage action to change the lighting's intensity or color. If it is a computerized control console, then it is programmed with cues for the entire show. All of this is done in consultation with the director.

Successful stage lighting complements and unifies the whole without calling attention to itself. It contributes to the play's interpretation with visibility and ambience — controlling what we see and the way we see it (see Figure 7.19).

The Sound Designer

Sound effects have always been a part of the theatre event. In earliest times, music (pipes, drums, lyres), choral chanting, and actors' voices provided the chief sound effects. Until the use of disc recordings in the 1950s, all sound effects in the theatre were produced live offstage; many — such as bells, door slams, and gunfire — still are. In Elizabethan times, "thunder machines" (a series of wooden troughs for cannonballs to rumble down) were invented to simulate tremendous storms, such as the one required in *King Lear*; cannons were fired to convince audiences of fierce battles taking place. Today, advances in sound technology have brought a new artist into the theatre: *the sound designer.*

The Working Designer

PlayMakers Repertory Company, a member of the League of Resident Theatres, performs on a thrust stage designed by Desmond Heeley. For the 1989 production of Chekhov's *The Cherry Orchard*, scenic and costume designer Bill Clarke constructed two set models for the two acts of this production.

The rear and upper levels of the stage were masked with multiple doors and neutral window shades that could be raised and lowered. The thrust stage, itself a neutral playing space, became with different furniture and properties at once a living room, dining room, riverbank, roadway through woods, and so forth.

Designer Bill Clarke's costume rendering for Madame Ranevskaya's Act One traveling costume. The dress is silk with cut-velvet coat in burgundy with burnt-ostrich feathers as trim, fur-lined sleeves and muff; the black hat is velvet with peacock feathers.

Sheriden Thomas as Madame Ranevskaya in Act One.

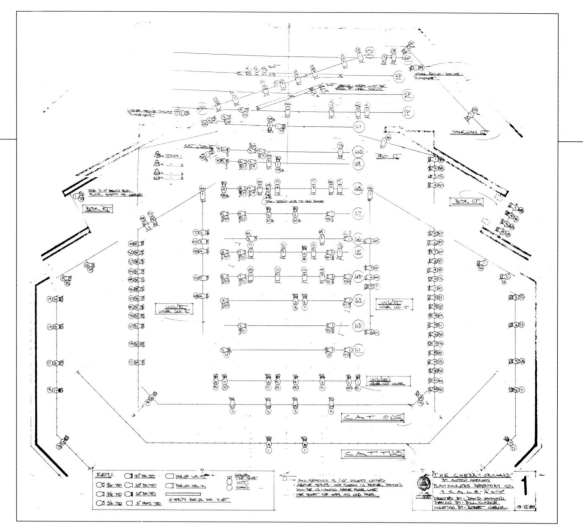

Lighting by Robert Wierzel. The light plot by designer Robert Wierzel for *The Cherry Orchard* illustrates the positioning of 250 instruments around three sides of the thrust stage, as well as the back-lighting behind the doorways and the overhead chandelier.

Designer Bill Clarke's set
model for Act One of *The
Cherry Orchard*.

Act One of *The Cherry Orchard*: The arrival of Madame Ranevskaya and her companions after an absence of five years.

Designer Bill Clarke's set model for Act Two of *The Cherry Orchard*. The scene is of the party with dining room table, chairs, and chandelier.

Act Two of *The Cherry Orchard*: The house is open, window shades are raised, and the chandelier indicates that it is late.

Theatres today have the capability for both live and recorded sound. Whatever the source or quality of the sound, the sound designer and technicians are responsible for it: mood music, sounds of nature (bird calls, crickets chirping), telephones and doorbells ringing (usually produced with electrical buzzers), gunshots, abstract sounds, rain and thunder, airplanes and trains passing overhead or in the distance, even military bands marching offstage, as Chekhov requires at the end of *The Three Sisters*.

In consultation with the director, the sound designer plots the effects required by the script (and often added to by the director). The technology available to the sound designer includes tape recorders and playback units, microphones and turntables, mixers and amplifiers, speaker systems of high quality and versatility placed throughout the auditorium, a patch bay (a means of connecting tapes and microphones to any outlet), and a control console. Like the lighting designer, the sound designer develops a cue sheet indicating the placement of each sound in the script, the equipment involved, sound levels, control, and timing of sound modulations.

Just as in our daily lives, sound in the theatre enhances mood, style, atmosphere, and even sense of locale.

Summary

Theatre artists — actors, directors, designers — create the play onstage in *concrete visual and aural terms*. They translate the playwright's words and concepts into a living evocation whose parts are acting, costume, scenery, light, and sound — a visual and aural representation of what occurs in the script. The job of the designer or designers is to convert the stage space into the world of the play. The designer transforms what director Peter Brook refers to as the "empty space" into theatre's special world. Central to the play's world is the actor, and all good stage design enhances the actor's presence in the space. Moreover, all design elements (scenery, costumes, properties, makeup, masks, lighting, and sound) must serve the play's dramatic action — developing, visualizing, and enriching it — without distracting the audience.

Questions for Study

1. What are five methods used by scene designers to design stage settings?

2. How does a designer study a script?

3. How did Appia and Craig pioneer as scenic artists?

4. Why are *ground plans, models,* and *renderings* important in the design process?

5. What is the *technical director's* job?

6. What is a *costume*?

7. How does a costume establish aspects of character, social class, age, weather?

8. What is a design conference? Why is it important?

9. How does the costume designer study a script? What questions do costume designers ask about the script?

10. Why is the dress rehearsal important for designers and directors?

11. What is the function of stage makeup?

12. What is the difference between *straight* and *character* makeup?

13. Why are masks effective onstage?

14. What are the light designer's tools?

15. What is a light plot?

16. What is the function of sound effects in the modern theatre? Give some examples.

17. How do scenery, costume, lighting, and sound enhance the actors' work?

18. *Suggested Reading: Theatre Crafts,* the leading magazine on American design and technology.

The producer is responsible for financing the production, for hiring and firing the artistic and managerial personnel. The producer is frequently all things to all people: money machine, tyrant, boss, mediator, friend, enemy, gambler, investor, consultant. In a word, the producer's job is to present the play.

Chapter 8

The Image Makers: The Producer

Thus far we have been discussing the special contributions of the theatre's *artists* — playwrights, actors, directors, designers — to this highly complex collaborative art form.

The producer is that anomalous person who in the highly competitive and risky business of theatre deals with plays, investors, artists, theatre owners, trade unions, agents, contracts, taxes, rentals, deficits, and grosses. The producer is rarely an artist but rather an astute business person with creative judgment who knows the demands of the commercial or nonprofit theatre. In answer to the question "What exactly do you do?", producer Cheryl Crawford said: "I find a good play or musical, I find the money required to give it the best physical form on a stage, I find the people to give it life, I find a theatre and try to fill it."[1]

The Broadway Producer

There are thirty-seven Broadway theatres at the present time (see Figure 8.1), sixteen and a half of which are owned by the Shubert Organization of major New York producers. Because of the high cost of producing on Broadway — over $6 million for a musical; $1 million for a dramatic play — many Broadway producers are seasoned veterans and are collaborating more frequently with one another in their producing efforts. Four major Broadway producers joined forces to bring the Royal Shakespeare Company's *Nicholas Nickleby* to New York: James M. Nederlander, the Shubert Organization, Elizabeth I. McCann,

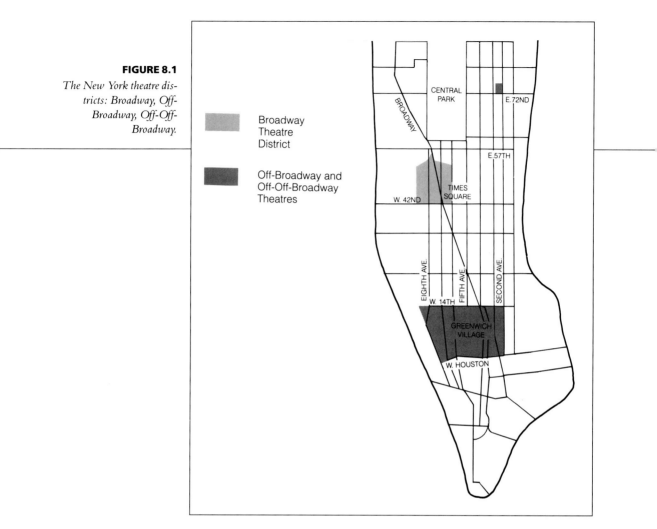

Broadway
Theatre
District

Off-Broadway and
Off-Off-Broadway
Theatres

and Nelle Nugent. As the costs of producing on Broadway continue to skyrocket (*Jerome Robbins' Broadway* cost $8.8 million in 1989), the pattern of producers commingling their know-how and assets has become a trend of the '80s and '90s. General managers, accountants, and lawyers assist them with the business of financing a Broadway play from option to opening.

Why is theatre, and especially the commercial Broadway theatre, so costly? Analysts agree that theatre is a service business in which most of the cost of the product is labor. As wages rise with general living standards across the country, most businesses turn to machines or technology rather than to people to blunt the cost of inflation. However, in the theatre, the opportunities for saving labor costs are limited. It takes just as long for actors to bewail the death of Hamlet as it did in Shakespeare's day and just

> "I function in the commercial world, I have to live in the commercial world, I have to finance the productions I do — not by writing a check on what Mr. Ziegfeld left me because he knew I was coming, but by going out and hustling to get the money to produce plays on Broadway. . . ."[2]
>
> **Alexander H. Cohen, producer**

as long to design Madame Ranevskaya's living room as it did in Chekhov's. Moreover, unlike the film industry, the multimillion-dollar production cannot be put in a "can" and distributed for tens of thousands of showings in moviehouses to dilute the original costs.

The Broadway Option

Once a play is finished, the playwright usually sends it to an *agent* who contacts the producers and options the play for a commission. The *option* — a payment advanced against royalties to the playwright — is the starting point on that long road to opening night. It is an agreement that grants producers the right to produce a play within a specified period of time and place in exchange for a fee paid to the writer. The amount paid, the length of the option, what the money buys are all negotiable.

Another approach to getting a play produced is to send the script directly to a regional theatre or university theatre department in the hope that the play interests a director. University, regional, and Off-Broadway theatres produce new plays, and many Broadway hits are first seen elsewhere, particularly in the professional regional theatres. For example, August Wilson's *Fences* was produced at the Yale Repertory Theatre, a professional regional theatre, before transferring to Broadway.

All plays produced on Broadway by an American author are optioned by producers under the Dramatists Guild contract. There are separate contracts for musicals, dramatic productions, stock tryouts, and collaborations; the Dramatists Guild's is a minimum basic contract.

When a commercial producer options, or buys, the exclusive rights to a play for a Broadway production, the playwright then is asked to rewrite parts of the script during rehearsals, out-of-town tryouts, and previews. Tryouts and previews are the testing ground for commercial productions. On the basis of critical notices and audience response during this period, the play is reworked and sometimes completely rewritten before the official New York opening. There is enormous pressure on the playwright to satisfy various interest groups, including director and producer.

The initial option usually lasts for one year from the date of delivery of the completed play. There are permissions for extending the option (if a star is unavailable for six months, for example, or if there is a wait of four to six months to get into a choice Broadway theatre), but that can be expensive.

In 1938, producer-director Jed Harris used an unusual strategy to open *Our Town* on Broadway. Convinced that Thornton Wilder's play could not open in just any theatre, but not wanting to extend the option, Harris gambled on a suitable theatre becoming available once the show had opened. He opened the play in a theatre that was available for only one week, reasoning that if the play was a success, another theatre would materialize. And so it did: When the play proved to be a hit, the favored Morosco theatre magically became available.

The producer enters into comparable arrangements with the director, actors, and designers. In addition, the producer most likely will be concerned with potential foreign productions, cast albums, television, video and film rights, and touring companies.

Since producing a Broadway show is an expensive, high-risk investment, the producer usually seeks assistance from co-producers and associate producers in raising the money and in handling other business details. Backers, or "angels," are sought to invest in the show in the full knowledge that they can lose their total investment.

The Associations and Craft Unions

The Broadway producer deals with a variety of organizations. The League of American Theatres and Producers (located at 226 West 47th Street), an association of producers and theatre owners, was founded in 1930 to oversee the common interests and welfare of theatre owners, lessees, operators, and producers. The League's primary function is to act as bargaining representatives for theatre owners and producers with the many unions and associations, ranging from ticket sellers to press agents.

Contracts Negotiated by the League of American Theatres and Producers

- ▼ Theatre Protective Union, Local No. 1, IATSE: basic theatre house crews, including electricians, curtain, carpenters, property people.
- ▼ Treasurers and Ticket Sellers Union, Local No. 751: all box office personnel involved in ticket selling.
- ▼ Legitimate Theatre Employees Union, Local No. B-183: all ushers, doormen, ticket takers.
- ▼ Theatre, Amusement and Cultural Building Service Employees, Local No. 54: custodians, cleaners, matrons, and the like.
- ▼ International Union of Operating Engineers (affiliated with the AFL-CIO), Local No. 30: employees involved in operation and maintenance of heating and air-conditioning systems.
- ▼ Mail and Telephone Order Clerks Union Local B-751: all mail clerks and telephone operators employed by theatres.
- ▼ Actors' Equity Association: actors, stage managers, singers, dancers.
- ▼ Theatrical Wardrobe Attendants Union, Local No. 764: wardrobe supervisors, assistants, and dressers.
- ▼ The Society of Stage Directors and Choreographers: directors and choreographers.
- ▼ The Dramatists Guild Minimum Basic Production Contract: authors.
- ▼ The **United Scenic Artists**, Local No. 829: set, lighting, costume designers and assistants.
- ▼ Associated Musicians of Greater New York, Local No. 802, American Federation of Musicians: musicians.
- ▼ Association of Theatrical Press Agents and Managers, No. 18032: press agents, house and company managers.

Casting

General, "open" casting calls (announced in such trade journals as *Variety* and *Backstage*) are conducted by the stage manager and casting director (if one is used). Once a small group of finalists has been selected, they are brought before the director, author, and producer. The director makes the final casting decisions, but the author also has cast approval. The producer does the hiring.

Actors' Equity Association has three basic contracts for actors, singers, dancers, and stage managers: a standard minimum contract for principal actors (at most a Broadway star may make $15,000 a week); a standard minimum contract for chorus; and a standard run–of–play contract. (All of

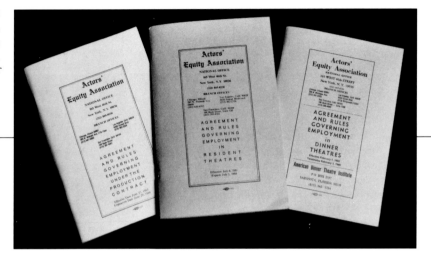

these are spelled out in the *Actors' Equity Rules Handbook*; see Figure 8.2.) Once assembled for rehearsals, the cast elects a deputy to represent Equity members in dealing with the producer over any breach of agreements or other employment terms. Chorus singers and dancers have separate deputies.

The Agent

When asked "What does an agent do?", Audrey Wood, possibly the most famous playwrights' agent of the last forty years, answered as a character in Arthur Kopit's play *End of the World* (1984): "This is a question I am asked all the time. In *theory*, an agent is supposed to find her client *work*! Now, while this has certainly been *known* to happen, fortunately, for all concerned, we do much, much more."

An agent, whether for playwright or actor, acts on behalf of that artist to find theatre, film, television, commercials, and publishing contracts. For a fee, the agent looks after the livelihood of the artist, negotiates contracts and royalties, and writes checks. The agent is as much a part of the artist's professional life and success in the commercial theatre as the director or producer, because it is through the agent that the actor or playwright is seen and heard by directors and producers. As the artist's lifeline into the commercial theatre, the agent is frequently friend, mentor, counselor, parent, psychiatrist, and investment broker.

Preview or Out-of-Town Tryout

Until recently, almost every Broadway show had a trial run in New Haven, Boston, or Philadelphia before its New York opening. The purpose was to

Broadway's "Hottest" Property: The Musical

American musical theatre has evolved as a distinctive Broadway product, though the British are competing heavily today with such imports as *Les Misérables* and *The Phantom of the Opera*.

In its beginnings, musical comedy was popular entertainment whose main ingredients were beautiful chorus "girls," popular music and dance numbers, and stand-up comedians. In 1928, *Showboat* by Jerome Kern and Oscar Hammerstein II gave birth to musicals with coherent story lines. The need for strong directors and choreographers was a consequence of integrating story, music, lyrics, and dance. The prestige and influence of the director-choreographer (Michael Bennett, Jerome Robbins, and Tommy Tune) contributed to the "concept musical" in which a staging device or personal imprint takes precedence over the narrative. *A Chorus Line* and *Grand Hotel* are but two examples.

The Broadway musical, budgeted today at over $6 million with costs rising, remains the producer's greatest challenge and the commercial theatre's greatest attraction for audiences.

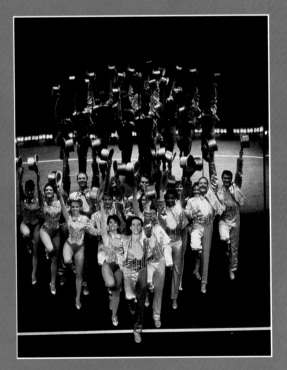

A Chorus Line, conceived, directed, and choreographed by Michael Bennett, opened on April 15, 1975. Broadway's longest-running musical, it ran for 6,104 performances, closing in 1990.

Top, Jerome Robbins' Broadway, a retrospective of numbers from twenty musicals from Robbins' long career on Broadway, opened in 1989.

Bottom, the finale. In the show's final number, characters representing Robbins' fabulous Broadway career include Peter Pan in flight, from the musical version of J.M. Barrie's story for children.

Top left, Les Misérables was imported from London's West End in 1987. Directed by Trevor Nunn and designed by John Bury, the musical retells the story of Victor Hugo's novel.

Top right, The Phantom of the Opera, an Andrew Lloyd Webber creation, directed by Harold Prince, opened on Broadway in 1988 while still running in London's West End.

Bottom left, Meet Me in St. Louis, based upon the popular movie, opened on Broadway in 1989. One of the most appealing production numbers in the show was the famous trolley car song.

Top, City of Angels, with book by Larry Gelbart and music by Cy Coleman, tells the story of a young Hollywood screenwriter's rise to fame and fortune. The innovative staging device lets us see the detective story as it is created by the writer (in film noire) side by side with the ups and downs of his real-life career.

Bottom, Grand Hotel opened in 1989 with direction and choreography by Tommy Tune. The musical, set in Berlin's grandest hotel, depicts multiple stories of love and "hearts of gold" amidst the decadence of Berlin in the 1920s.

Audrey Wood

Playwrights' agent Audrey Wood (1905–1985) helped define the American theatre by representing and guiding the careers of Tennessee Williams, William Inge, Robert Anderson, Clifford Odets, Carson McCullers, Preston Jones, Arthur Kopit, and many others.

Wood discovered Tennessee Williams through his entry in a playwriting contest sponsored by the Group Theatre. It took her eight years to sell the script of *The Glass Menagerie*, but when she did, it launched Williams' international career. When "her" playwrights were young and struggling, she found them jobs and grants and often loaned them money herself. She was known for her extraordinary devotion to her clients and was tireless in her calls on their behalf to producers and influential people. Moreover, she was the first agent in the American theatre to be given billing on the bottom of the program: "Mr. Williams' Representative — Audrey Wood." In her autobiography, *Represented By Audrey Wood* (1981), she said: "The theater is a venture (one hesitates to call it a business) built on equal parts faith, energy and hard work — all tied together with massive injections of nerve."[3]

get audience response and to fix script and casting problems before subjecting the production to the scrutiny of Broadway critics. Today, out-of-town tryouts as they were conceived in the past are so expensive that producers are trying new options: one is the Broadway preview (of one to three weeks); another is transferring directly onto Broadway a play or musical that has had a successful debut in a regional theatre (*A Chorus Line, Big River, Ain't Misbehavin'*); or transferring directly the successful commercial London production (*Cats, Les Misérables, The Phantom of the Opera*); or opening on campus in a university theatre with commercial producers and moving the production onto Broadway from there (*Broadway Bound, The Circle, A Few Good Men*).

The pre-Broadway production, like the preview, brings the show into its permanent theatre, avoiding the expenses of the road, and provides a period of time for Broadway audiences to respond to the show and generate word-of-mouth publicity before its official opening.

The Broadway Opening and After

Those late opening-night parties at Sardi's restaurant where everyone connected with the show waits to learn the critics' verdict are legendary. Will the show have a run or won't it? Tension mounts while a group of people wait to learn their fate. Usually the show's press agent or publicity manager reports the television critics' views or brings the newspapers in around midnight.

The morning after the opening, there is a customary meeting among the producer, press agent, and general or company manager (and sometimes an attorney). If the show has received rave reviews, like Andrew Lloyd Webber's *The Phantom of the Opera* (1988) or *Jerome Robbins' Broadway* (1989), the job of planning advertising expenses is an easy one. If the reviews are "pans," the decision to close is equally easy. However, if the reviews are mixed, decisions are difficult. There's always a chance that the show can make it, but figuring out how much money to spend to try to keep it running until expenses can be made is tricky.

Neither is it an easy decision to close a show if the possibility exists of developing business at a later date. So many jobs, from electricians' to actors', depend on this decision. Advance sales to theatre parties have to be weighed against current box office sales. Generally, when a show is panned, it has little chance of making its costs, much less returns on investments.

The National Touring Company

If the show is a hit in New York, a touring company is financed through guarantees from the various theatres where it will appear. A smash hit in New York can gross $350,000 to $800,000 a week in Seattle, Pittsburgh, Detroit, Los Angeles, Philadelphia, and Toronto. During December 1989, the highest-grossing national companies were all musicals with stars.

Producing Off-Broadway

Once a haven from the strictures of Broadway commercial contracts and unions, **Off-Broadway** is now a smaller, somewhat less expensive version of its parent. There is a League of Off-Broadway Theatres and Producers; the Dramatists Guild and Actors' Equity have developed Off-Broadway contracts, which apply to the smaller theatres (299 seats) and the smaller box office potential.

SHOWBILL™

THEATRE DE LYS

sam shepard's
buried child

THEATRE DE LYS

121 Christopher Street   WA 4-8782

WILLIAM   BURRY   RICHARD   ROSITA
DONNELL   FREDRIK   HUMPHREY   SARNOFF

present

SAM SHEPARD'S

BURIED CHILD

A "Theatre For The New City" Production

Directed by
ROBERT WOODRUFF

Set by   *Lighting by*   *Costumes by*
JONATHAN PUTNAM   JOHN P. DODD   JESS GOLDSTEIN

with

JACQUELINE BROOKES   RICHARD HAMILTON

CHRISTOPHER McCANN   MARY McDONNELL   TOM NOONAN

JAY SANDERS   BILL WILEY

Presented By Special Arrangement With Lucille Lortel Productions

The Producers wish to express their appreciation to Theatre Devedopment Fund
for its support of the production

FIGURE 8.3

Playbill of Sam Shepard's Buried Child, *produced
Off-Broadway at the Theatre de Lys in 1978.*

At one time it was said that producing Off-Broadway was unlike any-thing else in the world since contractual arrangements were so loosely defined.

However, Off-Broadway today mirrors the larger enterprise. It all be-gins when the producer options the play, or *property*. The producer pays for the right to produce it Off-Broadway. As soon as the play is presented before paying audiences, the producer makes a weekly payment of an agreed-upon fee to the author. This fee is directly related to gross weekly box office receipts (the author's percentage is anywhere from 5 percent to 7½ percent).

Co-producers and associate producers also appear on the Off-Broad-way scene (see Figure 8.3), since money, regardless of the sum, is always required. A *co-producer* enters into a joint venture (or *limited partnership*, as it is called) to assist the producer in raising money for the production: now a minimum of $350,000 for a musical and $325,000 for a nonmusical. Why use a co-producer? A certain amount of "front money," or risk capital, is needed immediately to pay for the option, printing scripts, making payments to lawyers and general managers, and to pay for a backers' audition, where potential investors are invited to sample the play. This audition is key to money-raising. The author gives the storyline, scenes from the script are presented, musical numbers are sung, and major investors from all areas of the business world are often forthcoming. *Associate producers* also join up for a percentage (1 percent) to get others to invest in the show, and they get billing credits for their efforts.

Once the money is reasonably assured, the producer proceeds to rent a theatre and hire a director, stage manager, actors, designers, press agent, advertising agency, general manager (who oversees the budget and takes care of all financial transactions), accountant, and lawyer. For a musical, additional personnel — musicians, arrangers, choreographers, dancers, and singers — are needed.

Today there is little difference, other than scale and amount of investment, between producing on and off Broadway. The language is the same, contracts similar, key personnel identical, and risks ever present.

Producing in the Nonprofit Regional Theatre

In **regional theatres** — sometimes referred to as **resident theatres** or companies — a person called an executive producer, producing director, or general manager (the titles vary from theatre to theatre) deals with a board of directors or trustees, corporations, foundations, federal and state agencies, patrons, and subscribers.

While Broadway remains the mecca for American commercial theatre, both commercial and nonprofit professional theatres have proliferated beyond Broadway and throughout the United States. Just as Off-Off-Broadway provides alternative performance spaces for nonprofit groups in New York, so the regional theatre movement, beginning in the '50s, has established a network of nonprofit professional theatres across the country. They have formed a national alliance as the League of Resident Theatres (LORT), which negotiates contracts with all theatre unions, including

Actors' Equity, and establishes the general contract under which all non-profit professional regional theatres operate. It is unusual to find a major city that does not have one or more professional resident theatres, although the majority are clustered in the Northeast (see Figure 8.4).

The terms *resident* and *regional* have been used interchangeably to describe nonprofit professional theatres located outside New York City. Today, there are over sixty theatres in fifty-one cities with operating budgets ranging from $200,000 to more than $9 million. They produce over 600 productions yearly to audiences of 14,000,000. Most perform seasons of from five to ten months, generally to subscription audiences. Many have touring programs. Others have outreach programs for audiences of all ages, which are models for community-wide social organizations. And they all offer opportunities for writers and actors that are unavailable within Manhattan.

Writers have found that the regional theatres have an inherent mandate to develop new works; because New York productions boast prohibitive staging costs, astronomical ticket prices ($45 to $55 for a single Saturday night ticket), and mercurial critics, writers increasingly prefer to have their works initially produced by regional companies. There, during a guaranteed four- to six-week run, writers have time to make changes without the threat of closing notices being posted on opening night. Regional theatres have developed such writers as August Wilson, Wendy Wasserstein, David Hwang, Christopher Durang, David Rabe, Terrence McNally, Marsha Norman, Sam Shepard, Beth Henley, and David Mamet, among others. In 1985, even an established playwright like Arthur Miller eschewed Broadway and unveiled *The Archbishop's Ceiling* at the Long Wharf Theatre in New Haven, Connecticut.

Moreover, New York has its own resident theatres, not unlike regional theatres elsewhere. Circle Repertory Company, for example, has nurtured writer Lanford Wilson for over a decade. The Manhattan Theatre Club, Playwrights Horizons, the American Place Theater, La Mama ETC (Experimental Theatre Club), the Negro Ensemble Company, and the New York Shakespeare Festival at the Public Theater have all provided stages for the talents of writers Tina Howe, Samm-Art Williams, Wendy Wasserstein, Charles Fuller, A. R. Gurney, Jr., Christopher Durang, David Rabe, John Ford Noonan, and David Hwang.

Theatre	City	Artistic Director
Actors Theatre of Louisville	Louisville	Jon Jory
Alley Theatre	Houston	Gregory Boyd
Alliance Theatre Company	Atlanta	Kenny Leon
American Conservatory Theatre	San Francisco	Ed Hastings
American Repertory Theatre	Boston	Robert Brustein
Arena Stage	Washington, D.C.	Zelda Fichandler
Berkeley Repertory Theatre	Berkeley	Sharon Ott
Center Stage	Baltimore	Stan Wojewodski
Dallas Theatre Center	Dallas	Ken Bryant
Denver Center Theatre	Denver	Donovan Marley
GeVa Theatre	Rochester	Howard J. Millman
Goodman Theatre	Chicago	Robert Falls
Guthrie Theatre	Minneapolis	Garland Wright
Hartford Stage Company	Hartford	Mark Lamos
Indiana Repertory Theatre	Indianapolis	Tom Haas
La Jolla Playhouse	San Diego	Des McAnuff
Lincoln Center Theatre	New York City	Gregory Mosher
Long Wharf Theatre	New Haven	Arvin Brown
Manhattan Theatre Club	New York City	Lynne Meadow
Mark Taper Forum	Los Angeles	Gordon Davidson
McCarter Theatre Company	Princeton	Emily Mann
Milwaukee Repertory Theatre	Milwaukee	John Dillon
Missouri Repertory Theatre	Kansas City	George Keathley
New York Shakespeare Festival Theatre	New York City	Joseph Papp
Old Globe Theatre	San Diego	Jack O'Brien
Oregon Shakespeare Festival	Ashland	Jerry Turner
PlayMakers Repertory Company	Chapel Hill	David Hammond
Repertory Theatre of St. Louis	St. Louis	Steven Woolf
Seattle Repertory Theatre	Seattle	Daniel Sullivan
Shakespeare Theatre at the Folger	Washington, D.C.	Michael Kahn
South Coast Repertory	Cosa Mesa	David Emmes
Studio Arena Theatre	Buffalo	David Frank
Syracuse Stage	Syracuse	Arthur Storch
Trinity Repertory Company	Providence	Richard Jenkins
Williamstown Theatre Festival	Williamstown	Peter Hunt
Yale Repertory Theatre	New Haven	Lloyd Richards

The producer's job in the resident theatres is both similar to and different from the Broadway producer's job. He or she deals with Actors' Equity through the special LORT contract; in the New York, Boston, Chicago, and Los Angeles areas, some even deal with craft unions. However, the *regional theatre producer* produces not a single play, but a season spanning eight to eleven months. The producer consults with the theatre's *artistic director* (the director in charge of choosing the plays, company, designers) to plan a season of six to ten plays, usually including both classical and modern works (Shakespeare, O'Neill, Miller, and Williams are favorites), musicals, sometimes lesser-known European works, and new American plays. The artistic director usually stages two or more plays within each season, hiring other directors to complete the season, while the producer develops a projected budget to cover all contingencies:

▾ artistic salaries and fees

▾ administrative salaries and costs

▾ travel (for casting and artists)

▾ marketing and development costs

▾ production expenses

▾ equipment, facilities maintenance, and services

In this milieu, producing is precarious. Although there is usually continuity of administrative and artistic leadership within regional theatres, no continuous financial support system exists from season to season, though some theatres have developed endowment funds to offset annual operating costs. The regional theatres and their producers depend on a delicate balance of federal and state dollars (now dwindling), private foundation and corporation money, and subscribers' dollars. The producer must at all times juggle the season's budgeted expenses against real and projected income. Although most theatres hire permanent administrative staff and artistic leadership, they have not yet been able to fund a resident company for the entire season, as do Britain, France, and West Germany. At best, a small core of actors remains year after year, playing a broad variety of roles.

Zelda Fichandler

Zelda Fichandler, producing director of Arena Stage, Washington, D.C., and newly appointed artistic director of The Acting Company, discusses the distinction between a producer and a manager:

> How do you define the difference between a producer and a manager? Well, in my way of thinking (and I'm like the Red Queen, when I use words they mean exactly what I mean them to mean — no more, no less) in my way of thinking, as the Red Queen, they don't belong in the same category, they're two different functions. The producer does what the title says. He or she leads out, leads forth, leads through. The producer is the total organizing human being who generates the impulse from the organization: what direction is it going to take? When is it necessary to move in another direction? The style of the work; are you going to do only new works? Are you going to do only female playwrights between the ages of forty and forty-five? Are you going to do only dead playwrights? Who can come to rehearsals? Are you going to increase your deficit and say "To hell with it, let's see what happens?" Are you going to cut costs? Are you going to have two theatres? Which twin has the Toni? — all of the big questions. The manager, it seems to me, has a very important function. But the manager works within the compass design, works within the full circle to manage whatever area. We're lousy with managers — we've got a box office manager, a house manager, a theatre manager, a production manager. A manager is an executor of the design set by somebody else, in my view. . . .[4]

They are allied with other performers who are hired for a season to play five or six different roles while in residence with the company. The artists themselves often support the theatre by accepting minimal salaries until they grow tired and move on into commercials, film, television, and the commercial theatre. New actors replace them and the cycle begins again. This talent drain is wearing as well as discouraging. But despite the lack of permanent funding and resident companies the regional theatre movement is strong.

One way a number of producers have chosen to counterbalance the deficit budget that can result in a theatre's closing has been to re-establish connections with the New York commercial theatre. In the last decade, Broadway has been enlivened by shows that established themselves first with regional audiences (a variation on the out-of-town tryout) and then moving with added capital (and co-producers) onto Broadway. A short list includes: *A Chorus Line* and *The Pirates of Penzance* from the New York

FIGURE 8.5

Director Zelda Fichandler discusses a scene from Anton Chekhov's The Three Sisters *with actor Charles Janasz during rehearsals for a production at Arena Stage in Washington, D.C.*

Shakespeare Festival Theatre (or the Public Theater), *The Gin Game* from Actors Theatre in Louisville, *Ma Rainey's Black Bottom* and *A Walk in the Woods* from the Yale Repertory Theatre, *Children of a Lesser God* from the Mark Taper Forum in Los Angeles, *American Buffalo* from the Long Wharf Theatre in New Haven, *Glengarry Glen Ross* and *Hurlyburly* from the Goodman Theatre in Chicago.

Broadway producer Alexander H. Cohen has said that the commercial and nonprofit theatre share something in common: *"What's good succeeds."* If the material is good—if it addresses the nature of our society—then it will succeed in either the commercial or nonprofit theatre, or in both, as the case may be. There's a great deal of trial and error in choosing material and producing it. But finally the dross sinks beneath its own undistinguished weight and the meaningful, imaginative, and exciting continue on our stages. Out of the commercial and nonprofit theatres, and out of producers' visionary risk taking, have come such American classics as *A Streetcar Named Desire, Death of a Salesman, Who's Afraid of Virginia Woolf?, A Chorus Line,* and *Buried Child.*

Summary

The producer's job, as the name implies, is to produce. However, many business people are attracted to "show biz" and to producing for a variety of reasons, most of them the wrong ones: the glamour of associating with Broadway and "stars"; the get-rich-quick dream of an overnight hit.

But producing means making a lot of difficult, educated decisions about people and money, and carrying them out. It is not for the dilettante or faint of heart. Producing is frequently painful because it can mean firing your favorite actor, director, or designer who turns out not to be right for the show. A producer has to have the personality and experience to influence people, raise money, hire, fire, mediate disputes, encourage and assist people to work together and to get along, to option wisely, sell expediently, hold hands and soothe bruised egos, comfort the sick, and to be all things to all people. All important is the ability to extract money from investors. In a word, to produce the show.

Questions for Study

1. What is the producer's job in the commercial Broadway theatre?

2. Who works directly with the producer?

3. What is the Dramatists Guild contract? Why is it important?

4. What is an *option*?

5. Name some of the major New York producers.

6. What are the current costs of a Broadway musical? A dramatic play?

7. What is an "angel"?

8. What is the League of American Theatres and Producers?

9. Name some of the unions that operate within the commercial theatre.

10. What is Actors' Equity Association and whom does it represent?

11. What is an "open" casting call?

12. Where are casting calls for the commercial theatre usually posted or announced?

13. What are the three basic contracts used by Actors' Equity Association?

14. What is the job of an Equity "deputy"?

15. What is the function of an agent for an actor or playwright?

16. What is the purpose of an out-of-town tryout?

17. What is a preview performance?

18. What is a national touring company?

19. What is Off-Broadway? Off-Off-Broadway?

20. How does producing Off-Broadway differ from Broadway?

21. What is a regional theatre?

22. What is a nonprofit or not-for-profit theatre?

23. What regional theatre is located near your campus?

24. *Suggested Reading*: Profile of Audrey Wood by Tennessee Williams in *Esquire* magazine (December 1962); Cheryl Crawford, *One Naked Individual: My Fifty Years in the Theatre* (Indianapolis: Bobbs-Merrill, 1977); William Goldman, *The Season: A Candid Look at Broadway* (New York: Harcourt, Brace and World, 1969); Revised Edition (New York: Limelight Editions, 1984).

P laywrights use different dramatic forms to express their understanding of human experience. Tragedy and comedy are the forms most familiar to us, but there are many other ways to classify plays and to label the playwright's vision — the way he or she *perceives* life in theatrical terms. A study of drama's changing forms is also a study of the playwright's changing perception of the world.

Chapter 9

Drama's Perspectives and Forms

O ver the centuries, playwrights have developed ways of imitating behavior in different dramatic forms and styles. Drama's forms change as societies and perceptions of the world change. This is what Peter Brook means when he says that every theatrical form, once born, is mortal.[1] Dramatic forms, or as Bertolt Brecht called them, "special mirrors," fall into many categories. The main ones are *tragedy, comedy, tragicomedy, melodrama,* and *farce.* In the twentieth century, two more significant forms have been devised, the *epic* and the *absurd.*

Drama's essential forms are ways of *seeing* human experience. The words *tragedy, comedy,* and *tragicomedy* are not so much ways of classifying plays by their endings as ways of talking about the playwright's vision of experience — of the way he or she perceives life. They furnish clues about how the play is to be taken or understood by audiences. Is the play a serious statement about, say, the relationship between men and women? Does it despair at the possibilities of mutual understanding? Or does it hold such attempts up to ridicule? Or does it explore humanity's unchanging existential situation?

Tragedy

It is not altogether simpleminded to say that a tragedy is a play with an unhappy ending. Tragedy, the first of the great dramatic forms in Western drama, makes a special statement about human fallibility.

FIGURE 9.1
The Royal Shakespeare Company production of The Greeks *in London, 1979. In* Part One: The War *(from* The Trojan Women*), left to right, are Deirdra Morris as Polyxena, Eliza Ward as Queen Hecuba, and Diana Berriman as a chorus member.*

The Tragic Vision

The writer's tragic vision of experience conceives of people as both vulnerable and invincible, as capable of abject defeat and transcendent greatness. Tragedies like *Oedipus the King, The Trojan Women, Hamlet, Ghosts,* and *A Streetcar Named Desire* show the world's injustice, evil, and pain. Tragic heroes, in an exercise of free will, pit themselves against forces represented by other characters, by their own inner drives, or by their physical environment. We witness their suffering, their inevitable defeat, and, sometimes, their personal triumph in the face of defeat. (See Figure 9.1.) The trials of the hero give meaning to the pain and paradox of our humanity.

Some tragedies are concerned with seeking meaning and justice in an ordered world, others with humanity's helpless protest against an irrational one. In both kinds, the hero, alone and willful, asserts his or her intellect and energy against the ultimate mysteries of an imperfect world.

Tragic Realization

The realization (a **recognition** or **anagnorisis**) that follows the hero's efforts usually takes one of two directions: that, despite suffering and calamity, a world order and eternal laws exist and people can learn from suffering; or that human acts and suffering in an indifferent, capricious, or

DIFFERENCES BETWEEN TRAGEDY AND COMEDY

TRAGEDY	COMEDY	TRAGEDY	COMEDY
Individual	Society	Terror	Euphoria
Metaphysical	Social	Unhappiness	Happiness
Death	Endurance	Irremediable	Remediable
Error	Folly	Decay	Growth
Suffering	Joy	Destruction	Continuation
Pain	Pleasure	Defeat	Survival
Life-denying	Procreative	Extreme	Moderation
Separation	Union/ Reunion	Inflexible	Flexible

mechanical universe are futile, but at the same time that the hero's protests against the nature of existence are to be celebrated. In *Oedipus the King* and *A Streetcar Named Desire* we find examples of these two kinds of tragic realization.

Aristotle on Tragedy

Aristotle spoke of tragedy as "an imitation of an action . . . concerning the fall of a man whose character is good (though not pre-eminently just or virtuous) . . . whose misfortune is brought about not by vice or depravity but by some error or frailty . . . with incidents arousing pity and fear, wherewith to accomplish the catharsis of these emotions."[2]

Aristotle and the Greek playwrights depicted tragedy's action as an imitation of a noble hero experiencing a downfall and tragedy's subjects as suffering and death. The heroes of ancient tragedies were usually aristocrats, to show that even the great among us are subject to the fate of the human condition. In modern plays, the hero's averageness speaks to us of kinship in adversity. Whether the hero is aristocratic or ordinary, his or her actions are influenced by the writer's tragic view of life, which centers on the need to give meaning to our fate despite the fact that we are doomed to failure and defeat.

Comedy

In the eighteenth century, Horace Walpole said: "The world is a comedy to those that think, a tragedy to those that feel." In comedy the playwright examines the social world, social values, and people as social beings. Frequently, comic action shows the social disorder created by an eccentric

TARTUFFE

▼▼

Tartuffe (1664) is Molière's comedy about a hypocrite. Tartuffe disguises himself as a cleric, and his apparent piety ingratiates him with the credulous merchant Orgon and his mother, Madame Pernelle. As the play begins, Tartuffe has taken over Orgon's house. Both Orgon and his mother believe that Tartuffe's pious example will be good for the family. But everyone else in the family, including the outspoken servant Dorine, is perceptive enough to see throughTartuffe.

Despite the protests of his brother-in-law Cléante and his son Damis, Orgon determines that his daughter Marianne, who is in love with Valère, will marry Tartuffe. When Orgon's wife Elmire begs Tartuffe to refuse Marianne's hand, he tries to seduce her. Damis, who has overheard, denounces Tartuffe. Orgon banishes his son rather than his guest and signs over his property to Tartuffe.

Elmire then plots to expose the hypocrite. She persuades Orgon to conceal himself under a table while she encourages Tartuffe's advances. Orgon's eyes are opened, but it is too late. The impostor realizes he has been discovered and turns Orgon's family out of the house. Then he reports to the authorities that Orgon has a strongbox containing seditious papers and contrives to have Orgon arrested. But, by the king's order, the arresting officer takes Tartuffe to prison instead.

The play ends with Damis reconciled to his father, Orgon reconciled with his family, and Valère and Marianne engaged.

FIGURE 9.2

Tartuffe pretends to be a person of utmost piety to Elmire, Orgon's wife, while plotting to seduce her and to take her husband's property. John Wood is Tartuffe and Tammy Grimes is Elmire in the 1977 Circle-in-the-Square production (New York), directed by Stephen Porter.

Molière

Molière (Jean Baptiste Poquelin, 1622–1673), French playwright-actor-manager, was the son of Louis XIV's upholsterer. Poquelin spent his early years close to the court and received a gentleman's education. He joined a theatrical troupe in 1643 and became a professional actor with the stage name Molière. Molière helped to found the Illustre Théâtre Company in Paris, which soon failed, and spent twelve years touring the French provinces as an itinerant actor and company playwright. He returned to Paris to become the foremost writer and comedian of his time. Within thirteen years (1659–1673), he wrote and acted in *Tartuffe, The Misanthrope, The Doctor in Spite of Himself, The Miser,* and *The Imaginary Invalid.* Written during France's golden age, Molière's comedies balance follies of eccentric and devious humanity against society's reasonable good sense.

character who deviates from reasonable values like sensibility, good nature, flexibility, moderation, tolerance, and social intelligence. Deviation is sharply ridiculed in comedy because it threatens to destroy revered social structures such as marriage and the family.

The writer of comedy calls for sanity, reason, and moderation in human behavior so that society can function for the well-being and happiness of its members. In comedy, society survives the threat posed by inflexible or antisocial behavior. In Molière's *Tartuffe* (see Figure 9.2), the title character's greed is revealed and Orgon's family is returned to a normal, domestic existence at the play's end. For the seventeenth-century French playwright, as for some of his contemporary American counterparts, the well-being of the family unit is a measure of the well-being of the society as a whole.

At the end of almost any comedy, the life force is ordinarily celebrated in a wedding, a dance, or a banquet symbolizing the harmony and reconciliation of opposing forces: young and old, flexible and inflexible, reasonable and unreasonable. These social ceremonies allow us to see that good sense wins the day in comedy and that humanity endures in the vital, the flexible, and the reasonable.

Tragicomedy

Tragicomedy, as its name implies, is a mixed dramatic form. Up to the end of the seventeenth century in Europe, it was defined as a mixture of tragedy, which went from good fortune to bad, and comedy, which reversed

Chekhov's most critically acclaimed work during his lifetime was first produced at the Moscow Art Theatre in 1901 with Olga Knipper as Masha, Constantin Stanislavsky as Colonel Vershinin, and Vsevelod Meyerhold as Baron Tusenbach.

In a garrison town in rural Russia, the cultured Prozorov sisters think longingly of the excitement of Moscow, which they left eleven years ago. Olga, the oldest, is constantly exhausted by her work as a schoolteacher; Masha, married at eighteen to a man she considered an intellectual giant, bitterly realizes that he is merely a pedant; Irina, the youngest, dreams of a romantic future and rejects the sincere love of Lieutenant Tusenbach and the advances of Captain Solyony. Their brother, Andrey, an unambitious man, courts Natasha, the daughter of a local family. Into this circle comes Lieutenant Colonel Vershinin. Like Masha, he is unhappily married. They are immediately attracted to one another.

The Prozorovs and their friends recognize the frustration of their lives, but hope in some vague future keeps their spirits high. For the sisters it is a dream of returning someday to Moscow. The atmosphere changes when Andrey marries Natasha. The sisters' immediate prospects of returning to Moscow are dashed. Irina tries to find relief in her job in the telegraph office. Natasha takes control of the household, and as time goes on the sisters are moved about in the house to make room for her two children. Andrey takes refuge in gambling and mortgages the house that he and his sisters own jointly.

News that the garrison is to be transferred brings depressing prospects for the future. Irina decides to marry Tusenbach, an unattractive but gentle man, who resigns his army commission in the hope of finding more meaningful work. As Masha and Vershinin, who have become open lovers, bid each other goodbye, and the regiment prepares to leave, word comes that Tusenbach has been killed by Solyony in a duel over Irina. The sisters cling to one another for consolation. As the military band strikes up, the gaiety of the music inspires them to hope that there is a new life in store for them in another "millennium."

the order from bad fortune to good. Tragicomedy combined serious and comic incidents as well as the styles, subject matter, and language proper to tragedy and to comedy, and it also mixed characters from all stations of life. The *ending* (up until the nineteenth century) was its principal feature: Tragicomedies were serious and potentially tragic plays with happy endings, or at least with averted catastrophes.

The term *modern tragicomedy* is used to designate plays with mixed moods in which the endings are neither exclusively tragic nor comic, happy nor unhappy. The great Russian playwright Anton Chekhov (1860–1904) wrote plays of mixed moods in which he described the lives of "quiet desperation" of ordinary people in rural Russia around the turn of the century: provincial gentry, writers, professors, doctors, farmers, servants, teachers, government officials, and garrisoned military. What they had in common, finally, was their survival.

Chekhov's most frequently revived major play, *The Three Sisters* (1901), tells of the provincial lives of the Prozorov family: three sisters (Olga, Masha, and Irina), their brother (Andrey), his wife (Natasha), their lovers,

FIGURE 9.3
The Three Sisters, *with Kim Stanley as Masha, Shirley Knight as Irina, and Geraldine Page as Olga in the 1964 Actors Studio Theatre production, directed by Lee Strasberg, at Broadway's Morosco Theatre.*

a brother-in-law, and military friends. The play's only action in the traditional sense is the departure of a military regiment from a small town after an interval of several years. For four acts the sisters dream of escape to Moscow from the dull routine of their lives. But, unlike the regiment, they are unable to move on to new places and experiences (see Figure 9.3).

As we scrutinize the seriocomic quality of Chekhov's play, a theme emerges: *the value of surviving in the face of social change*. The three sisters are emotionally adrift in a society whose institutions supply avenues of change only for the soldier, the upstart, and the entrepreneur. The weak and ineffectual, like the three sisters (and these women *are* products of their time), are locked into a way of life that is neither emotionally nor intellectually rewarding. The most Chekhov's people can do is *endure* the stultifying marriage, the routine job, and the tyrannical sister-in-law. But they survive. With no prescription for the future, Masha says only that "We've got to live."

Modern Tragicomedy

Samuel Beckett subtitles *Waiting for Godot* (see Figure 9.4) a "tragicomedy" though it is also an enduring absurdist play of modern times. In this play, two tramps entertain themselves with comic routines while they wait in a

Samuel Beckett

Samuel Beckett (1906–1989) was an expatriate Irishman living in France. Beckett grew up near Dublin and attended Trinity College, where he received two degrees in literature and began a teaching career. In the 1930s Beckett left his teaching position, traveled in Europe, published his first book *(More Pricks Than Kicks)*, and wrote poetry in French. During World War II he worked with the French Resistance and barely escaped capture by the Nazis.

Since 1953 Beckett wrote some thirty theatrical pieces, including radio plays, mime sketches, monologues, and four full-length plays *(Waiting for Godot, Endgame, Krapp's Last Tape, Happy Days)*. *Endgame*, like *Waiting for Godot*, is a modern classic.

Recently, Beckett's plays became minimal. *Come and Go* (1965) is a 3-minute play, *Breath* (1966) is a 30-second play, *Rockaby* (1980) is a 15-minute play, and *Not I* (1973) consisted of eight pages of text. With these brief pieces Beckett constructed a theatrical image of how we come and go on this earth, briefly filling a void with our bodies and voices and then disappear into darkness without a trace.

FIGURE 9.4

Samuel Beckett's tramps, Vladimir and Estragon, entertain themselves by searching for a missing boot. Although Godot has not kept his appointment with them, the tree has grown leaves between the first and second acts. With Godot's absence and the tree's growth, Beckett juxtaposes despair with hope, loss with gain. The photo is from the 1961 Paris revival of Waiting for Godot *directed by Jean-Marie Serreau with Lucien Raimbourg as Vladimir and Etienne Berg as Estragon. The tree was designed by sculptor Alberto Giacometti.*

sparse landscape adorned by a single tree for someone named Godot to arrive. But Godot never comes. As they react to this situation, humor and energy are mixed with anguish and despair. In the modern form of tragicomedy, playwrights show people laughing at their anxieties and life's contradictions with little effect on their situations. Beckett's Vladimir summarizes the form when he says, "The essential doesn't change."

Sam Shepard's *Buried Child* and August Wilson's *Fences* are more recent tragicomedies. Although principal characters die in both plays, the writers affirm humanity's endurance — despite anguish and loss — among little potential for social or personal change.

Melodrama

Another mixed form, melodrama, derives its name from the Greek word for music, *melos*. It is a combination of music and drama in which the spoken word is used against a musical background. Jean Jacques Rousseau, who introduced the term's modern use in 1772, applied it to his *Pygmalion*, a *scène lyrique* in which words and music were linked in the action.

The term became widely used in the nineteenth century to describe a play without music but having a serious action usually caused by the villainy of an unsympathetic character. Melodrama's characters are clearly divided — either sympathetic or unsympathetic — and the villain's destruction brings about the happy resolution. Melodrama usually shows a main character in circumstances that threaten death or ruin from which he or she is rescued at the last possible moment. Like a film's musical score, incidental music heightens the mood of impending disaster. The term *melodrama* is most often applied to such nineteenth-century plays as *Uncle Tom's Cabin* (1852), based on Harriet Beecher Stowe's novel, and Dion Boucicault's *The Octoroon* (1859). Today, we apply the term to such diverse plays as Lillian Hellman's *The Little Foxes* (1938), Lorraine Hansberry's *A Raisin in the Sun* (1959), and such suspenseful thrillers as Ira Levin's *Death Trap* (1978).

The melodramatic view of life sees human beings as whole, not divided; enduring outer conflicts, not inner ones, in a generally hostile world; and sees these conflicts resulting in victory or defeat as they are pressed to

The Little Foxes, written by Lillian Hellman in 1938–39, is a quintessential melodrama. The play takes place in the American South in 1900 and concerns the wealthy Hubbards, a prosperous family eager to parlay their success as merchants and bankers into vast industrial wealth. "To bring the machines to the cotton, and not the cotton to the machines," as Ben Hubbard says. Regina Hubbard Gibbons is the powerful villainess of the play that demonstrates the corrosive consequences of money and lust.

To compete with her brothers, Oscar and Ben, Regina must persuade her dying husband, Horace Gibbons, to invest one-third interest in their get-rich-quick scheme. Because of a heart condition, Horace has been in a Baltimore hospital; Regina sends their daughter Alexandra to bring him home so that Regina can invest his Union Pacific bonds in the scheme. Horace arrives but refuses to advance the money. Her brothers tell Regina they will go elsewhere for another business partner, although they would prefer not bringing in an outsider. When the brothers learn from Leo — Ben's son who works in the bank that holds Horace's bonds — that the bonds could be "borrowed" from the bank strongbox without fear of discovery, they take the bonds and tell Regina she's out of the deal. Learning of the theft, Regina blackmails her brothers into giving her 75 percent interest in the venture for her unauthorized "investment." Their alternative is jail. When Horace discovers the bonds are missing

and learns of his wife's manipulations, he reverses her victory by saying he will claim that he loaned the bonds to his brothers-in-law. Regina's scathing attack on Horace brings on his fatal heart attack. Because his death will eliminate her problems and make her rich, she stands immobile while he pleads with her for his medicine. She watches his desperate but futile struggle to climb the stairs to reach his medicine. With her husband's death, the bonds now belong to Regina and she is once again victorious. Alexandra, who suspects Regina's complicity in her father's death, voices her disgust and leaves home, but this is only a minor shadow on the bright horizon of Regina's future.

Hellman's episodes turn on theft, blackmail, sudden and unexpected shifts of fortune, unrelenting greed, and major changes in the balance of power in the Hubbard money game. The play's characters range from the genteel Birdie Hubbard and naive Alexandra to the "little foxes that spoil the vines" — the vicious and manipulative Regina, Ben, and Oscar Hubbard. Hellman does not attempt to deepen our understanding of society or of human values. Rather she shows evil in conflict with evil and the good and decent as merely impotent onlookers. But the fascination with Regina's manipulations and her victory over her pernicious brothers stimulate audiences into applauding her resourcefulness and withholding moral judgment before her wit, glamour, and cunning.

extreme conclusions. Melodrama's characters win or lose in the conflict. The endings are clear-cut and extreme. There are no complex and ambiguous resolutions, as when Hamlet wins in losing. Replying to critics complaining about her melodramatic plots, Lillian Hellman said: "If you believe, as the Greeks did, that man is at the mercy of the gods, then you write tragedy. The end is inevitable from the beginning. But if you believe that man can solve his own problems and is at nobody's mercy, then you will probably write melodrama."[3]

Melodrama oversimplifies, exaggerates, and contrives experience. In short, melodrama is the dramatic form that expresses the truth of the

Noises Off (1982) by British playwright Michael Frayn is a farce about farce. It ridicules the many clichés of the genre within the format of a play-within-a-play. Act I is the final dress rehearsal by a provincial touring company of *Nothing On*. The typical confusions of farce result from actors who can't remember their lines, their entrances, and their stage business. Plates of sardines, doors, and telephones add to the actor's difficulties. Frayn heaps onto his play-within-a-play a melee of stock characters — cheery housekeeper, incompetent burglar, unexpected lovers, outraged wife, harried husband — who stampede in and out of the many doors. The stage clichés of the farce *Nothing On* (*Noises Off*, Act I) are repeated in the backstage confusion of relationships (Act II). Act III takes place at the same time as the second Act, only this time we see Act II from the front of the theatre; there are even further actorly mishaps and temper tantrums.

Frayn's farcical contrivances are further compounded by the onstage versus the backstage view of life. The director of *Nothing On* summarizes the improbable confusions of the genre: ". . . That's what it's all about. Doors and sardines. Getting on — getting off. Getting the sardines on — getting the sardines off. That's farce. That's the theatre. That's life."

human condition as we perceive it most of the time. We have our victories, and our "accidents" or failures are attributable to external factors.

Farce

Farce is best described as comedy of situation. In farce, pies in the face, beatings, mistaken identities, slips on the banana peel — exaggerated physical activities growing out of situations — are substituted for comedy's traditional concern for social values. The writer of farce presents life as mechanical, aggressive, and coincidental, and entertains us with seemingly endless variations on a single situation. A typical farce situation is the bedroom crowded with concealed lovers as the cuckolded husband or deceived wife arrives on the scene.

The "psychology of farce," as Eric Bentley calls it, is that special opportunity for the fulfillment of our unmentionable wishes without taking responsibility for our actions or suffering the guilt.[4] Farce as a dramatic form gives us a fantasy world of violence (without harm), adultery (without consequences), brutality (without reprisal), and aggression (without risk). Today we enjoy farce in the films of Charlie Chaplin, W. C. Fields, the Marx Brothers, Woody Allen, Chevy Chase, Eddie Murphy, and Richard Pryor; and in the plays of Georges Feydeau (see Figure 9.5), Neil Simon, and Michael Frayn. Farce has also been an element of some of the world's great comedies, including those of Shakespeare, Molière, and Chekhov.

FIGURE 9.5

In farce's familiar situation, the hero seduces the wife only to have their affair almost discovered by her husband who, by chance, is meeting his mistress at the same hotel. Louis Jourdan is the lover and Patricia Elliott the wife in the Circle-in-the-Square's 1978 production in New York of Georges Feydeau's 13 Rue de L'Amour.

Adaptations

Nicholas Nickleby, Les Misérables, and *The Grapes of Wrath* are enormously successful examples of another play form: *the adaptation.* The current explosion of interest in adaptations in contemporary French, English, Russian, and American theatres is not related to the availability of new plays but to a desire of theatre companies to create their own texts. (See Figure 9.6.)

Dickens' novels, with their wealth of dramatic incident and social detail, have been prime properties for adaptation. Many theatrical adaptations (not counting films and television) have been made of *A Christmas Carol, The Pickwick Papers, A Tale of Two Cities, David Copperfield, Great Expectations, Nicholas Nickleby,* and *Little Dorrit.* In France, novels by Jack London, Voltaire, Honoré de Balzac, Gustave Flaubert, and Marguerite Duras have found their way onto the stages of both established and experimental theatres.

How is a dramatic adaptation created and how does it work theatrically? An adaptation is largely the result of the director's concept and the actors' work. As French director Antoine Vitez says: "The theatre is *someone* who takes his material wherever he finds it — even things not made for the stage — and puts them on stage. Or, rather, stages them."[5] In the process of adaptation, director and actors emerge as primary creators. What matters is not what the author meant the text to say but how the director reads and stages it.

FIGURE 9.6

The Life and Adventures of Nicholas Nickleby, *a Dickens novel written in 1838–39, has been one of the most popular stage adaptations of a novel in modern times. Adapted for the Royal Shakespeare Company by David Edgar and directed by Trevor Nunn and John Caird, Nicholas Nickleby became the RSC's greatest success since Peter Brook's* A Midsummer Night's Dream. *The daring concept involved forty-two actors in a production that ran more than eight and a half hours. Even more so than Dickens' novel, the RSC production conjured up the seaminess, and violence of Victorian England, with its extremes of cruelty and compassion, wealth and poverty, corruption and innocence. In this photo, Smike (David Threlfall), left, struggles to communicate to his friend Nicholas (Roger Rees) against the noises of Victorian London, as provided by the actors at left.*

One method of adapting novels to the stage is to retain the novel's narrative voice (with actors as narrators), substituting storytellers for characters. The aim is to blend narrative techniques (descriptions, comments, interior monologues) with dramatic ones (one character speaking directly to another). In some cases, social documents relevant to the action are read aloud. In others, adaptations seem *to objectify* the act of reading. For instance, the action begins at one side of the stage and moves to the other, then recommences—like turning the pages of a novel. Descriptions are also included in what is spoken. Sometimes actions simply give voice to both descriptions and conversations, including the phrases "he said" or "she said."

The Grapes of Wrath was commissioned by the Steppenwolf Theatre Company, Chicago, and adapted by the group's writer-director Frank Galati in 1988. Concentrating on the place and time of Steinbeck's novel, Galati traces a stage action that tells an epic story about dislocation as the Joads move across country (on a bare stage) in the play's most significant stage prop, the heavily laden Hudson Super Six truck (reminiscent of the canteen wagon in Brecht's *Mother Courage and Her Children*), and propelled in time by ballad music played on a guitar.

As the novel's adaptor for a thirty-five member cast, Galati worked with the essential elements of the novel. He concentrated on Steinbeck's

▼▼▼

The Grapes of Wrath was first published by John Steinbeck in 1939 and was awarded the Pulitzer Prize in 1940. The novel chronicles the troubled journey of the Joad family, displaced from their Oklahoma farm by the dust bowl disaster in the mid-1930s to the migrant labor camps of California. John Ford's classic 1940 film starred Henry Fonda as Tom Joad.

The novel (and the stage adaptation) follows the Joads: their exodus from Oklahoma, their wanderings in the Southwest, and their trials in the "promised" land — California. The spine of the novel follows the growth and discovery of its commonplace though heroic figures (Ma and Pa Joad, Tom Joad, Rose of Sharon, Jim Casy, and to some degree, Uncle John). At the novel's end, Tom's friend Casy has sacrificed his life in a labor dispute with management and the police; Rose of Sharon becomes a mother but loses her child and feeds another from her breast;

Ma refuses to be "wiped out" ("We're the people — we go on"); and Tom's rage over Casy's death and the possibility that he has killed a policeman force him to leave the family to join an undefined movement committed to social struggle. He becomes our common hero fighting for human rights. He promises his mother at the novel's end: "Wherever they's a fight so hungry people can eat, I'll be there. Wherever they's a cop beating up a guy, I'll be there."

The Grapes of Wrath is a compelling, realistic treatise on the plight and nobility of ordinary laborers. It is also a bitter commentary on the human costs of industrial "progress" and the radicalization of an individual by social injustice. Centrally concerned with issues of social and economic justice, it is regarded as one of the most important American novels to emerge from the Great Depression.

language, the journey of the characters, and their strength of spirit in great adversity. Galati also reasoned that Steinbeck's story applies to our own time when so many are homeless and dispossessed and when the hope for the salvation of the world lies with the human heart.

One challenge in adapting the 500-page novel to the stage was how to find an appropriate setting for the Joads' epic saga. After much research into the writings and photographs of the era, an abstract version of the plowed, barren earth was created for the stage out of "corrugated sheet metal and old wood." Sections of the stage floor opened up to permit real fire, rain, and water for the nine scenes. A piece of barbed wire represents a fence, a gate represents a ranch, a huge wall with doors becomes the solid interior of a barn. The Joads' authentic '30s truck carries twelve people and their belongings in full view of the audience.

Galati paces Steinbeck's story for a two-and-a-half hour dramatic production. He eliminated most of the novel's "general chapters," using songs, music, and some narrative as transitions to trace the family's journey from Oklahoma to California. Galati wrote no dialogue of his own but used Steinbeck's words to create the play's dialogue and to tell the story of an epic adventure in which adversity follows adversity but the human spirit endures.

The Grapes of Wrath

The Steppenwolf Theatre Company presented the world premiere of *The Grapes of Wrath* in 1988 in Chicago. John Steinbeck's famous novel was adapted and directed by Frank Galati for the ensemble. The 35-member company presented the world premiere of the stage adaptation first in Chicago, then at the La Jolla Playhouse, California, and again at The National Theatre of Great Britain before bringing the production to Broadway where Frank Galati was awarded a "Tony" Award for Best Play of the 1989 season.

Gary Sinise as Tom Joad and Terry Kinney as his friend Jim Casy discuss their bleak future at the start of their journey away from the Oklahoma dustbowl and toward the migrant labor camps of California.

Tom and Ma Joad (Gary Sinise and Lois Smith) join in an evening of country dancing to fiddles and guitars.

The Joad family and friends drive through the night along Route 66 toward the "promised land" of California. Gary Sinise as Tom Joad drives the truck, which moves about the stage; the converted Hudson is the play's most important scenic element made of authentic parts from 1930s vehicles. Sally Murphy (above) is Rose of Sharon.

Ma Joad (Lois Smith) and the pregnant Rose of Sharon (Sally Murphy) endure the sweltering heat and their homeless condition as they take shelter in barns and warehouses along their route to California.

The Joad family, having arrived in California, are questioned by a foreman before being admitted inside the wire fence as hired laborers to work the fields. Set designer, Kevin Rigdon, used old wood planks and corrugated sheet metal to suggest barren earth and cultivated fields with furrows. In this scene, a piece of a barbed-wire gate represents the entranceway to the ranch — to work, food, and shelter.

Lois Smith as Ma Joad holds her son Tom (Gary Sinise) in their farewell scene at the play's end. After the death of his friend Casy and his futile struggle with police and camp guards, Tom must abandon the family for their welfare and to save his life.

Epic Theatre

Bertolt Brecht, the director and playwright who has probably had more influence on our postwar theatre than any other theatrical artist, reacted against Western traditions of the **well-made play** and the proscenium theatre of pictorial illusion. Over a lifetime, he adapted methods from Erwin Piscator (who pioneered the docudrama for German working class audiences in the '20s), Chinese opera, Noh drama, chronicle history plays, English music-hall routines, and films to create "epic" theatre.

Episodic and Narrative Theatre

When Brecht spoke of *epic* theatre, he was thinking of drama as *episodic* and *narrative*: as a sequence of incidents or events narrated without artificial

Bertolt Brecht

Bertolt Brecht (1898–1956) was born in Augsburg, Germany, where he spent his early years. In 1918, while studying medicine at Munich University, he was called up for military service as a medical orderly. He began writing poems about the horrors of war. His first play, *Baal* (1918), dates from this period.

After World War I, Brecht drifted as a student into the bohemian world of theatre and literature, singing his poetry in Munich taverns and coffeehouses. By 1921, Brecht had seriously entered the theatre world as a reviewer and playwright. During the 1920s in Berlin, Brecht became a Marxist, wrote plays, and solidified his theories of epic theatre. *The Threepenny Opera* (1928) — produced in collaboration with the composer Kurt Weill — was an overnight success and made both Brecht and Weill famous. (See Figure 9.7.)

With the rise of the Nazi movement, many German artists and intellectuals left Germany. Brecht and his family fled in 1933, first to Sweden, and then to the United States, where he lived until 1947. In October of 1947, Brecht was subpoenaed to appear before the House Un-American Activities Committee to testify on the "Communist infiltration" of the motion-picture industry. He left the United States the day following his testimony, eventually settling in East Berlin, where he founded the Berliner Ensemble. This great theatre company continues to perform his works at the Theater am Schiffbauerdamm, where he first produced *The Threepenny Opera*. Brecht's greatest plays date from his years of exile (1933–1948): *The Good Person of Setzuan, Mother Courage and Her Children, Galileo*, and *The Caucasian Chalk Circle*.

restrictions as to time, place, or formal plot. Its structure was more like that of a narrative poem than of a well-made play.

Because Brecht wanted to represent historical process in the theatre and have it judged critically by audiences, he departed from many theatrical traditions. First, he thought of the stage as a platform on which political and social issues could be debated. And he rejected the idea that a play should be "well made," reminding us that history does not end but moves on from episode to episode. Why should plays do otherwise? Brecht's plays therefore were a series of loosely knit scenes, each complete in itself. The effect was achieved through the juxtaposition of contrasting *episodes*. The nonliterary elements of production — music, acting style, lighting, and moving scenery — also retained their separate identities. His epic play is, therefore, *historical, narrative, episodic*, and highly theatrical. It treats humans as social beings in their economic, social, and political milieus.

Brecht's characters are both individuals and collective beings. This type of characterization dates to the morality plays of the late Middle Ages,

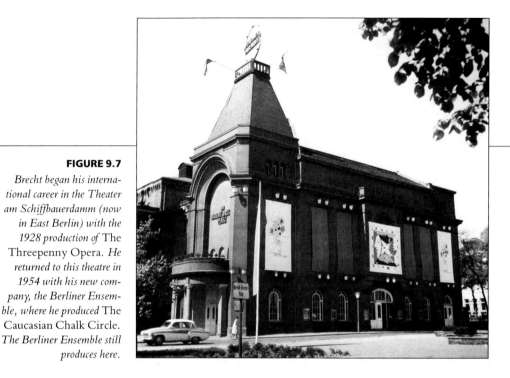

FIGURE 9.7

Brecht began his international career in the Theater am Schiffbauerdamm (now in East Berlin) with the 1928 production of The Threepenny Opera. *He returned to this theatre in 1954 with his new company, the Berliner Ensemble, where he produced* The Caucasian Chalk Circle. *The Berliner Ensemble still produces here.*

where "Everyman" is both a recognizable individual and a representative of all human beings.

In Brecht's plays, character emerges from the individual's social function and changes with that function. In keeping with the idea that the theatre is a platform to discuss political and social issues, theatrical language is discursive and polemical.

Epic Acting as Eyewitness Account

Early in his career Brecht admonished actors not to regard themselves as impersonating or becoming characters so much as *narrating* the actions of people in a particular time, place, and situation. The model he used to demonstrate this approach was the behavior of an eyewitness to a traffic accident.

In retelling the event, eyewitnesses clearly differentiate between themselves and the victim, although they may reconstruct the victim's reactions and gestures. So, too, Brecht argued, actors clearly differentiate between themselves as actors and the characters in the play. The eyewitness never *becomes* the victim. He further explained:

> It is comparatively easy to set up a basic model for epic theatre. For practical
> experiments I usually picked as my example of completely simple "natural"
> epic theatre an incident such as can be seen at any street corner; an eyewitness

FIGURE 9.8

Bertolt Brecht's The Good Woman of Setzuan, *directed by Andrei Serban with music by Elizabeth Swados, was staged by the American Repertory Theatre, Cambridge, in their 1986–1987 season. Like Brecht's* The Caucasian Chalk Circle, *this play combines a non-illusionistic performance style with the statement that it is hard for human beings to reconcile our instincts for goodness with the necessity for economic survival.*

demonstrating to a collection of people how a traffic accident took place. The bystanders may not have observed what happened, or they may simply not agree with him, may "see things a different way": the point is that the demonstrator acts the behavior of driver or victim or both in such a way that the bystanders are able to form an opinion about the accident.[7]

In Brecht's theatre, the actor did not "become" the character as in the Stanislavsky approach to acting; rather, actors "demonstrated" the characters' attitudes while retaining freedom to comment on the actions of the person whose behavior they were displaying. This device of the actor as eyewitness to the plays' events was also part of Brecht's efforts to *distance* or *alienate* the audience emotionally from what was happening on stage.

The Alienation Effect

Brecht called this jarring of the audience out of its sympathetic feelings for what is happening on stage his **alienation effect** (sometimes called A-effect or *Verfremdungseffekt*). He wanted to prevent the audience's empathetic "willing suspension of disbelief," to force them to look at everything in a fresh light, and, above all, to think. Brecht wanted audiences to absorb his social criticism and to carry new insights out of the theatre into their own lives (see Figures 9.8 and 9.9).

Brecht was certainly aware of the entertainment value of theatre. For Brecht, pleasure in the theatre came from observing accounts of past situations, discovering new truths, and enlarging upon an understanding of the present. What he opposed was a theatre solely of **catharsis**, where the audience lost its critical detachment by identifying emotionally with the characters. All of the epic devices — music, scenery, lighting, placards, projections, acting style — reminded audiences that they were in a theatre, that the stage was a stage and not someone's living room.

Absurdist Theatre

In 1961 Martin Esslin, a British critic, wrote a book called *The Theatre of the Absurd* about trends in the post-World War II theatre. He used the label to describe new theatrical ways of looking at existence.

Absurdist writers, like Eugene Ionesco and Samuel Beckett, made their breakthrough in dramatic form by *presenting*, without comment or moral judgment, situations showing life's irrationality. The common factors in the absurdist plays of Ionesco, Beckett, and others are unrecognizable plots, mechanical characters, situations resembling dreams and nightmares, and incoherent dialogue. The absurdist does not tell a story or discuss social problems. Instead, the writer presents in concrete stage images, such as two tramps waiting for a person who never shows up, *a sense of being* in an absurd universe.

The Absurd

Absurdist playwrights begin with the premise that our world is *absurd*, meaning irrational, incongruous, and senseless. Albert Camus (1913–1960)—a French philosopher, novelist, and playwright—diagnosed the human condition as absurd in *The Myth of Sisyphus*.

> A world that can be explained even with bad reasons is a familiar world. But, on the other hand, in a universe suddenly divested of illusions and lights, man

Eugene Ionesco

Eugene Ionesco (b. 1912) is a Rumanian-born former schoolteacher and refugee from Nazism who lives in France. Forty years ago he puzzled and outraged audiences with plays about bald sopranos, octogenarian suicides, homicidal professors, and human rhinoceroses as metaphors for the world's absurdity. Today, *The Bald Soprano*, *The Chairs*, *The Lesson*, and *Rhinoceros* are modern classics.

Since *The Bald Soprano* was first produced in Paris at the Théâtre de Noctambules in 1950, Ionesco has written over thirty plays in addition to journals, essays, and children's stories. Ionesco says that his theatre expresses the malaise of contemporary life, language's failure to bring people closer together, the strangeness of existence, and a parodic reflection of the world. Breaking with the theatre of psychological realism, Ionesco pioneered a form of theatre closer to our dreams and nightmares.

feels an alien, a stranger. His exile is without remedy since he is deprived of the memory of a lost home or the hope of a promised land. This divorce between man and his life, the actor and his setting, is properly the feeling of absurdity.[8]

Ionesco defined *absurd* as "anything without a goal . . . when man is cut off from his religious or metaphysical roots, he is lost; all his struggles become senseless, futile and oppressive."[9] The meaning of Ionesco's plays *is* simply what happens on stage. The old man and old woman in *The Chairs* (1952) gradually fill the stage with an increasing number of empty chairs. They address absent people in the chairs. At the play's end, the two old people leave the message of their life's meaning to be delivered by an orator, and jump out of windows to their deaths. The orator addresses the empty chairs, but he is a deaf-mute and cannot make a coherent statement. The subject of Ionesco's play is conveyed by the empty chairs themselves — the emptiness of the world.

Ionesco subtitled his first play, *The Bald Soprano* (1949), "the tragedy of language." In it, he was one of the first to confront the absurdity of the universe with new dramatic techniques. This farce, like many of his early plays, demonstrates the emptiness of middle-class life in a world devoid of significant problems (see excerpt on pages 210–211).

In more recent plays, Ionesco's concerns about middle-class conformity have a more political cutting edge. In *Rhinoceros*, written in 1958, Ionesco's hero, Berenger, is an individual in a world of conformists. Ionesco's political concern is with people who are brutalized by dogma (in this case,

The "Bobby Watson" exchange from Ionesco's *The Bald Soprano* (1950) presents aural and visual images showing the banality of middle-class suburban life. Mr. and Mrs. Smith, seated in their middle-class English living room discussing their middle-class English dinner, engage in conversation about Bobby Watson.

> *Another moment of silence. The clock strikes seven times. Silence. The clock strikes three times. Silence. The clock doesn't strike.*

MR. SMITH: [*still reading his paper*]: Tsk, it says here that Bobby Watson died.

MRS. SMITH: My God, the poor man! When did he die?

MR. SMITH: Why do you pretend to be astonished? You know very well that he's been dead these past two years. Surely you remember that we attended his funeral a year and a half ago.

MRS. SMITH: Oh yes, of course I do remember. I remembered it right away, but I don't understand why you yourself were so surprised to see it in the paper.

MR. SMITH: It wasn't in the paper. It's been three years since his death was announced. I remembered it through an association of ideas.

MRS. SMITH: What a pity! He was so well preserved.

MR. SMITH: He was the handsomest corpse in Great Britain. He didn't look his age. Poor Bobby, he'd been dead for four years and he was still warm. A veritable living corpse. And how cheerful he was!

MRS. SMITH: Poor Bobby.

MR. SMITH: Which poor Bobby do you mean?

MRS. SMITH: It is his wife that I mean. She is called Bobby too, Bobby Watson. Since they both had the same name, you could never tell one from the other when you saw them together. It was only after his death that you could really tell which was which. And there are still people today who confuse her with the deceased and offer their condolences to him. Do you know her?

MR. SMITH: I only met her once, by chance, at Bobby's burial.

MRS. SMITH: I've never seen her. Is she pretty?

MR. SMITH: She has regular features and yet one cannot say that she is pretty. She is too big and stout. Her features are not regular but still one can say that she is very pretty. She is a little too small and too thin. She's a voice teacher.

> [*The clock strikes five times. A long silence.*]

MRS. SMITH: And when do they plan to be married, those two?

MR. SMITH: Next spring, at the latest.

The maid dominates the scene with the Smiths, the Martins, and the fire chief. The photo is from the original Paris production at Théâtre des Noctambules, 1950, directed by Nicholas Bataille.

MRS. SMITH: We shall have to go to their wedding, I suppose.

MR. SMITH: We shall have to give them a wedding present. I wonder what?

MRS. SMITH: Why don't we give them one of the seven silver salvers that were given us for our wedding and which have never been of any use to us? [*Silence*]

MRS. SMITH: How sad for her to be left a widow so young.

MR. SMITH: Fortunately, they had no children.

MRS. SMITH: That was all they needed! Children! Poor woman, how could she have managed!

MR. SMITH: She's still young. She might very well remarry. She looks so well in mourning.

MRS. SMITH: But who would take care of the children? You know very well that they have a boy and a girl. What are their names?

MR. SMITH: Bobby and Bobby like their parents. Bobby Watson's uncle, old Bobby Watson, is a rich man and very fond of the boy. He might very well pay for Bobby's education.

MRS. SMITH: That would be proper. And Bobby Watson's aunt, old Bobby Watson, might very well, in her turn, pay for the education of Bobby Watson, Bobby Watson's daughter. That way Bobby, Bobby Watson's mother, could remarry. Has she anyone in mind?

MR. SMITH: Yes, a cousin of Bobby Watson's.

MRS. SMITH: Who? Bobby Watson?

MR. SMITH: Which Bobby Watson do you mean?

MRS. SMITH: Why, Bobby Watson, the son of old Bobby Watson, the late Bobby Watson's other uncle.

MR. SMITH: No, it's not that one, it's someone else. It's Bobby Watson, the son of old Bobby Watson, the late Bobby Watson's aunt.

MRS. SMITH: Are you referring to Bobby Watson the commercial traveler?

MR. SMITH: All the Bobby Watsons are commercial travelers.

MRS. SMITH: What a difficult trade! However, they do well at it.

MR. SMITH: Yes, when there's no competition.

MRS. SMITH: And when is there no competition?

MR. SMITH: On Tuesdays, Thursdays, and Tuesdays.

MRS. SMITH: Ah! Three days a week? And what does Bobby Watson do on those days?

MR. SMITH: He rests, he sleeps.

MRS. SMITH: But why doesn't he work those three days if there's no competition?

MR. SMITH: I don't know everything. I can't answer all your idiotic questions! . . . [10]

A new production of The Bald Soprano *by Eugene Ionesco with the Smiths, the Martins, the Maid, and the Fire Chief. Produced by the American Repertory Theatre, Cambridge, 1989–1990 season.*

fascism) and changed by it into beasts. The rhinoceros, with its thick hide and small brain, is Ionesco's brilliant analogue for the herd mentality. Berenger emerges as a lonely but authentic hero, for he resists the physical and moral conformity that overwhelms his world and his loved ones. Like other Ionesco heroes, he represents a genuine assertion of personal value in a world dominated by nationalism, bureaucracy, and "groupthink."

His more recent plays, such as *Exit the King* (1962), *Macbett* (1972), *Man With Bags* (1975), and *Scene* (1982), are parables on human evil, the will to power, and the inevitability of death.

Summary

Drama's forms are the organization of the playwright's vision of and statement about the world. Tragedy, comedy, tragicomedy, melodrama, farce, epic, and absurdist drama are ways of labeling the playwright's view of the world's substance, shape, and meaning so that we can understand the world's form and substance as the playwright does. Dramatic form is conveyed to us in the theatre through numerous means: endings, situations, character awareness, social ceremonies, mood, wish fulfillment, episodes, narration, language, and staged images.

However, there is a larger dramatic pattern that has the potential for becoming living words and actions. We call this pattern for "doing" or "becoming" *drama*. It all begins with the imitation of human events, speech, and behavior.

Questions for Study

1. Tragedy is the name of one dramatic form. Can you name six others?

2. What terms do we use to describe a playwright's vision of his or her world?

3. What was Aristotle's understanding of tragedy?

4. How does the hero of modern tragedy differ from Oedipus or Hamlet?

5. What are comedy's subjects?

6. How does tragicomedy combine elements of both comedy and tragedy?

7. What is the origin of the word *melodrama*?

8. What different kinds of melodrama are found today on television?

9. How does farce fulfill our darkest wishes?

10. Can you describe the farce situation in a recent play, film, or TV series that you have seen?

11. Why are many theatre companies interested in adapting nondramatic materials for the stage?

12. What methods are used to create an *adaptation*?

13. How was *The Grapes of Wrath* adapted for the stage?

14. What is *epic theatre*?

15. What is meant by Brecht's "alienation effect"?

16. In what ways does *The Caucasian Chalk Circle* demonstrate Brecht's concept of epic theatre?

17. How does the playwright Eugene Ionesco define *absurd*?

18. How does Ionesco present life's absurd quality in *The Bald Soprano* without debating or discussing it?

19. *Plays to Read*: *Tartuffe* by Molière, *The Three Sisters* by Chekhov, *The Little Foxes* by Hellman, and *The Bald Soprano* by Ionesco.

20. *Suggested Reading*: Leon Rubin, *The Nicholas Nickleby Story: The Making of the Historic Royal Shakespeare Company Production* (London: Heinemann, 1981).

21. *Suggested Biography*: Ronald Hayman, *Brecht: A Biography* (New York: Oxford University Press, 1983).

To read drama, the printed page of a script, is to experience much of the playwright's art. Drama has the potential for becoming human speech, action, sound, and movement. Different types of play structures and dramatic conventions help playwrights shape their materials into potential theatrical experiences for us to share.

Drama, the playwright's art, takes its name from the Greek verb *dran*, meaning "to do" or "to act." Drama is most often defined as a pattern of words and actions having the potential for "doing" or becoming living words and actions.

On the printed page drama is mainly *dialogue* — words arranged in sequence to be spoken by actors. Stage dialogue can be similar to the dialogue we speak in conversation with friends. In some cases, as with Shakespeare's blank verse or the complex verse forms of the Greek plays, dialogue is more formal. But stage dialogue differs from ordinary conversation in one important way: The playwright creates it and the actor speaks it. *Performability* is the link between the playwright's words and the actor's speech.

Let us begin to think about drama as a way of seeing by discussing *play*, with which it shares similar features.

Structures of Seeing

Imitation

Play as Imitation

Children at play are a kind of amateur playwright as they imitate reality through playing such games as "space invaders," "school," and "hospital." Children play to entertain themselves, to imitate adult behavior, and to help fit themselves into an unfamiliar world. In play, children try out and learn roles they will experience in their adult lives. In their imitations they develop what the American psychiatrist Eric Berne calls *lifescripts*.

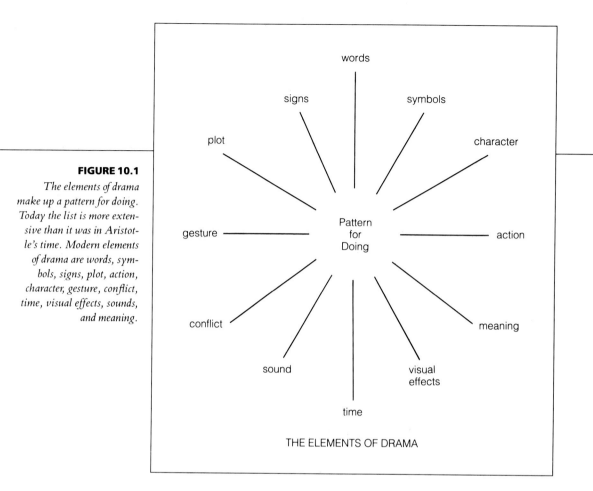

FIGURE 10.1

The elements of drama make up a pattern for doing. Today the list is more extensive than it was in Aristotle's time. Modern elements of drama are words, symbols, signs, plot, action, character, gesture, conflict, time, visual effects, sounds, and meaning.

words

signs   symbols

plot   character

gesture — Pattern for Doing — action

conflict   meaning

sound   visual effects

time

THE ELEMENTS OF DRAMA

What do we mean by *imitation*, especially imitation at the psychological level? In *Play, Dreams and Imitation in Childhood* (1962), French psychologist Jean Piaget shows that we tend to imitate through play those things that arouse ambivalent emotions within us. We do this to handle the fears those things evoke because of their strangeness. We imitate the unknown as a way of mastering and gaining dominance over it. Children, adults of primitive societies, and artists all use imitation and for many of the same reasons.

So imitation is a process by which we confront and transform our fears of the strange and unknown by becoming one with them. Every drama is an imitation that confronts the mystery of human behavior. It does so concretely through *the living presence* of the actor, who is both a real person and a fictional character. The great British actor Laurence Olivier once remarked, "Acting is an almost childish wish. . . . Pretend to be somebody else. . . . Let's pretend—I suppose that's the original impulse of acting. . . ."[2]

Drama as Imitation

As we have seen, play and drama have much in common. The child playing firefighter or the actor playing *Hamlet* must start with a scenario or script, or imagined situation, character, dialogue, and locale. Both play and drama entertain. They contribute to a sense of well-being and to an understanding of ourselves and others. They have their own fixed rules. Most important, they *imitate human events*.

In the fourth century B.C. the Greek philosopher Aristotle (384–322) described drama as *mimesis* — the imitation of human beings in action. In his *Poetics* (c. 335–323), he showed that the playwright used certain devices to turn written material into human action: plot, character, language, ideas, music, and visual elements. From our modern perspective, we could add time and space to Aristotle's list of dramatic elements (Figure 10.1).

The Elements of Drama

Drama's chief elements are still often modeled on Aristotle's criteria, beginning with plot, character, and language. *Plot* is an arranged sequence of events or incidents usually having a beginning, middle, and end. These incidents spring from an action or motive. *Character* includes the physiological and psychological makeup of the persons in the play. *Language* is the spoken word, including symbols and signs. The play's *meaning* is its underlying idea — its general and particular truths about experience. Today we frequently use the word *theme* or message when we talk about a play's meaning. A play may have more than one basic theme. *Macbeth*, for example, is a play about crime and punishment, but it is also about the destructive effects of power and ambition on the psyche.

Aristotle used the word *spectacle* to take in all visual and aural elements: costumes, settings, music, and singing. In the modern theatre, we add stage lighting and sound technology to this list.

The modern idea of a play's *time* refers not to *actual time* — the length of the performance — but to *symbolic time*, which is integral to the play's structure and may be spread out over hours, days, or years. *Hamlet* takes about four hours to perform, although the story covers many months. In Henrik

Ibsen's *Ghosts* we are asked to believe that the incidents take place in a little more than twenty-four hours.

Action is a crucial element of drama. Aristotle did not use *action* to refer to those external deeds, incidents, situations, and events we tend to associate with a play's plot. He likened the relationship of action and drama to that of the soul and the body. He saw action as the source of the play's inner meaning, a spirit that moves through the play, holding all its elements together in a meaningful way.

American scholar Francis Fergusson defines action as "the focus or aim of psychic life from which the events, in that situation, result."[3] The source of the play's outward deeds, action embodies all the physical, psychological, and spiritual gestures and motivations that result in the visible behavior of the characters. The action of Oedipus in Sophocles' play occurs on two levels. On one level, Oedipus' action is to find the killer of Laius, the former Theban king, and to purify the city of plague by punishing the guilty person. During his investigation of the plague's cause, Oedipus discovers that he is the guilty man, that he unwittingly killed his father and married his mother. On another, deeper level, the action of *Oedipus the King* is really a man's efforts *to know himself*. In short, action is the play's all-encompassing purpose.

Over the centuries, playwrights have developed different ways of using dramatic forms, structures, and styles to mirror the changing intellectual and emotional life of their cultures. The play's structure is the playwright's way of organizing the dramatic material into a coherent whole.

Play Structure

In Western drama, plot and action are based on a central *conflict* and organized usually in the following progression: confrontation–crisis–climax–resolution. This generalization is true for plays written by William Shakespeare, Henrik Ibsen, or Sam Shepard. The way the playwright varies this pattern determines the play's structure. In general, plays have been organized in three basic ways: *climactic, episodic,* and *situational.* Entirely new structures, such as "happenings," "talking pieces," and "synthetic fragments" have recently been devised.

Henrik Ibsen

Henrik Ibsen (1828–1906), Norwegian playwright, is considered by many to be the most influential playwright since Shakespeare. Finding his early plays (celebrating his country's past glories) poorly received, Ibsen immigrated to Italy. There he wrote *Brand* (1865), a symbolic tragedy in verse, which brought him immediate fame. For twenty-seven years he remained with his family in self-imposed exile in Rome, Dresden, and Munich, writing such plays as *A Doll's House, Ghosts, An Enemy of the People, The Wild Duck,* and *Hedda Gabler.* These plays changed the direction of the nineteenth-century theatre. In 1891 he returned to Norway, and in 1899 completed *When We Dead Awaken,* the play that James Joyce considered his finest. He died there in 1906.

Called the father of modern drama, Ibsen wrote plays dealing with problems of contemporary life, particularly those of the individual caught in a repressive society. Although his social doctrines, radical and shocking in his own day, are no longer revolutionary, his portraits of humanity are timeless.

GHOSTS

Ghosts, written by Henrik Ibsen in 1881, is the story of the Alving family. Mrs. Alving, widow of the admired and respected Captain Alving, has been living alone on her husband's estate with her maid Regina, carrying on her husband's philanthropic projects. Her son, Oswald, has returned from Paris for the dedication of an orphanage she has built.

The play opens with a conversation between the carpenter Jacob Engstrand and Regina, his supposed daughter. He tries to convince the girl to do her duty to her father and become the "hostess" of a sailors' hostel, which he plans to open with his savings. Regina refuses; she hopes for a more genteel life. Pastor Manders, a longtime friend of the family, arrives to dedicate the orphanage. He and Oswald heatedly discuss new moral codes. Oswald goes into the dining room, where sounds of his advances to Regina are heard. Mrs. Alving remarks that the "ghosts" of the past have risen to haunt her.

In Act II, Mrs. Alving explains that Regina is actually Captain Alving's daughter by a serving girl, and that his upstanding reputation has been falsely derived from her own good works. At the end of Act II the orphanage burns to the ground as a result of Engstrand's carelessness.

In Act III, it is revealed that Manders' fear of scandal has led him to bribe Engstrand. (Engstrand has convinced Manders that the pastor started the fire himself.) Engstrand goes off with Regina to open the sailors' "home." Oswald confesses that he suffers from syphilis inherited from his father—another ghost. Mrs. Alving promises to give him a deadly drug should he become insane as the disease progresses. As the play ends, Oswald's mind disintegrates under a final seizure, and Mrs. Alving must decide whether to administer the drug as she has promised or to let her son live as a helpless invalid. The curtain falls as she tries to decide.

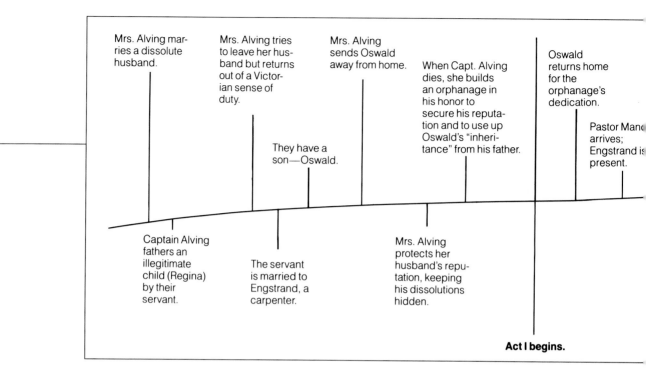

FIGURE 10.2

Climactic play structure. Ghosts, *like the classical plays* Oedipus the King *and* The Trojan Women, *begins late in the story, near the crisis and climax. All the events of the story's past (to the left of the first vertical line) occur before the play begins and are revealed in exposition. Each act of Ibsen's play ends with a climax, building to the highest point of tension: Oswald's collapse. Since a climactic plot begins late in the story, the period of time covered is usually limited. The classical play usually covers a few hours.* Ghosts *begins in the afternoon and ends at sunrise the following day.*

Climactic Play Structure

Found in classical and modern plays, climactic structure confines the character's activities and intensifies the pressures on the characters until they are forced into irreversible acts — the **climax**. As the action develops, the characters' range of choices is reduced. In many cases, they are aware that their choices are being limited and that they are being moved toward a crisis and turning point. Climactic structure is a *cause-to-effect* arrangement of incidents ending in a climax and quick resolution.

Mrs. Alving in Ibsen's *Ghosts* (1881) is progressively shown that the "ghosts" of her past are the cause of the present situation. Her son looks like his father; like his father, he makes advances to the serving girl; he also carries his father's moral corruption within him as a physical disease; and Mrs. Alving is conditioned to do what society dictates is proper and dutiful. Mrs. Alving has two alternatives at the play's end: to kill her terminally ill son or not. (See Figures 10.2 and 10.3.) She must choose *one.*

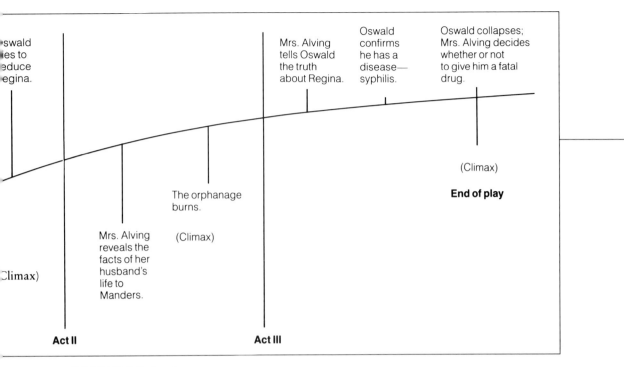

Oswald
tries to
seduce
Regina.

Mrs. Alving
tells Oswald
the truth
about Regina.

Oswald
confirms
he has a
disease—
syphilis.

Oswald collapses;
Mrs. Alving decides
whether or not
to give him a fatal
drug.

The orphanage
burns.

(Climax)

(Climax)

End of play

Mrs. Alving
reveals the
facts of her
husband's
life to
Manders.

(Climax)

(Climax)

Act II

Act III

FIGURE 10.3 (below)

In climactic drama the characters are confined within time and space. Ghosts has five characters and takes place in Mrs. Alving's living room. As the pressures of the past go to work in the present, the choices the characters have open to them become limited. An explosive confrontation becomes inevitable. Here Mrs. Alving (Margaret Tyzack) learns the truth from Oswald (Nicholas Pennell) about his terminal disease in the 1977 Stratford Festival Theatre production of Ghosts.

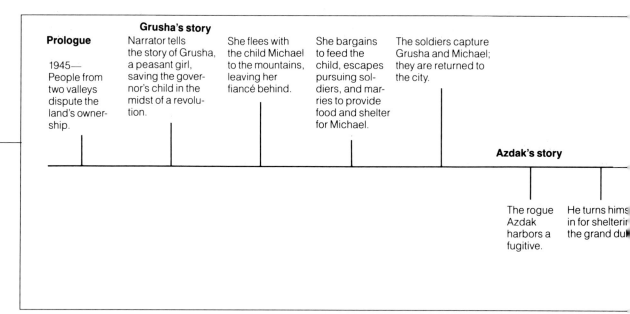

Prologue

1945—
People from two valleys dispute the land's ownership.

Grusha's story

Narrator tells the story of Grusha, a peasant girl, saving the governor's child in the midst of a revolution.

She flees with the child Michael to the mountains, leaving her fiancé behind.

She bargains to feed the child, escapes pursuing soldiers, and marries to provide food and shelter for Michael.

The soldiers capture Grusha and Michael; they are returned to the city.

Azdak's story

The rogue Azdak harbors a fugitive.

He turns hims in for shelterir the grand du

Episodic Play Structure

Episodic play structure, found in medieval plays and the work of William Shakespeare, Bertolt Brecht, and Edward Bond, traces the characters through a *journey* of sorts to a final action and to an understanding of what the journey meant. It can always take a new turn. In Shakespeare's plays, people are not forced immediately into unmaneuverable positions. Possibilities of action are usually open to them until the very end. Events do not accumulate to confine the characters because the play encompasses large amounts of time and distance. *Hamlet* takes place over several years and countries. And the expanding plot takes in a variety of events. In this loose structure, characters are not caught in circumstances but pass through them, as Grusha does in Brecht's *The Caucasian Chalk Circle*[4] (see Figures 10.4 and 10.5).

Situational Play Structure

In absurdist plays of the 1950s, *situation* shapes the play, not plot or arrangement of incidents. It takes the place of the journey or the pressurized events. For example, two tramps wait for a person named Godot who never arrives (*Waiting for Godot*); a husband and wife talk in meaningless clichés as they go about their daily routines (in Eugene Ionesco's *The Bald Soprano*).

The situation has its own inner rhythms, which are like the basic rhythms of life: day, night, day; hunger, thirst, hunger; spring, summer, winter. Although the situation usually remains unchanged, these rhythms move in a cycle.

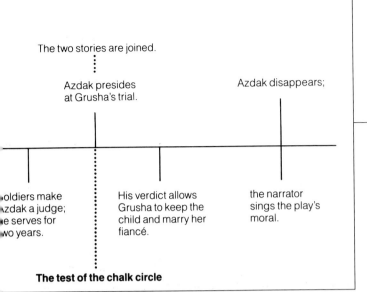

The two stories are joined.
⋮

Azdak presides
at Grusha's trial.

Azdak disappears;

◦oldiers make
◦zdak a judge;
◦e serves for
◦wo years.

His verdict allows
Grusha to keep the
child and marry her
fiancé.

the narrator
sings the play's
moral.

The test of the chalk circle

FIGURE 10.4

Episodic play structure begins early in the story and involves many characters and events. Place and event do not confine the characters; instead, the plot expands to include a variety of events and activities. Brecht's Caucasian Chalk Circle *is made up of two stories, Grusha's and Azdak's. The expanding plot moves in a linear fashion, telling the two seemingly unrelated stories until Brecht combines them in the chalk-circle test to make his point about decent people caught in the injustices of a corrupt political system.*

FIGURE 10.5

Azdak the judge, played by Ernst Busch, in a 1954 production of The Caucasian Chalk Circle *by the Berliner Ensemble, in East Berlin.*

THE CAUCASIAN CHALK CIRCLE

The Caucasian Chalk Circle, written by German playwright Bertolt Brecht in 1944–45, begins in 1945 with two Soviet villages disputing the ownership of a fertile valley.

Before they decide the issue, a singer entertains them with a Chinese parable, the story of the chalk circle. The scene changes to a Georgian city being overthrown by a nobles' revolt. The governor is killed, and his wife abandons their son Michael in order to escape. Grusha, a peasant girl, rescues the child and flees to the mountains. In order to give the child a name and status, she marries a peasant whom she believes is near death. When the revolt ends, the governor's wife sends soldiers to get the child. The scene

shifts again, to the story of Azdak, a rogue made village judge by the rebellious soldiers. He is corrupt and prepares to judge the case of Grusha versus the governor's wife for possession of Michael. He uses the test of the chalk circle to identify the child's true mother, but reverses the outcome: The child is given to Grusha because she will *not* engage in the tug-of-war that is supposed to end in the child's being pulled out of the circle by maternal affection. He also decrees Grusha a divorce so that she can return to her soldier fiancé, Simon. Brecht's moral is that things — children, wagons, valleys — should go to those who serve them best.

THE BALD SOPRANO

The Bald Soprano (produced at the Théâtre de Noctambules, Paris, 1950) is Ionesco's "antiplay" that dramatizes the absurdity of human existence. In 1948, while taking a course in conversational English, Ionesco conceived the idea of using many of the practice sentences to create a theatre piece.

Mr. and Mrs. Smith talk in clichés about the trivia of everyday life. The meaninglessness of their existence is caricatured in dialogue in which each member of a large family, living and dead, regardless of age or sex, is called Bobby Watson. Mr. and Mrs. Martin enter. They converse as strangers but gradually discover that

they are both from Manchester, that they arrived in London at the same time, that they live in the same house, sleep in the same bed, and are parents of the same child. The Martins and the Smiths exchange banalities, a clock strikes erratically, and the doorbell rings by itself. A fire chief arrives. Although in a hurry to extinguish all fires in the city, he launches into long-winded, pointless anecdotes. After he leaves, the two couples talk in clichés until language breaks down into basic sounds. The end of the play completes a circle: The Martins replace the Smiths and speak the same lines that opened the play.

In *The Bald Soprano* (1949), Ionesco introduces a fire chief and the Martins into Mr. and Mrs. Smith's typical middle-class English living room. After a series of absurd events, the dialogue crescendos into nonsensical babbling. The words stop abruptly and the play begins again. This time Mr. and Mrs. Martin are seated as the Smiths were at the play's beginning, and they repeat the Smiths' lines from the first scene. With this repetition, Ionesco demonstrates the interchangeability of middle-class lives. (See Figures 10.6 and 10.7. For more on Ionesco, see page 209.)

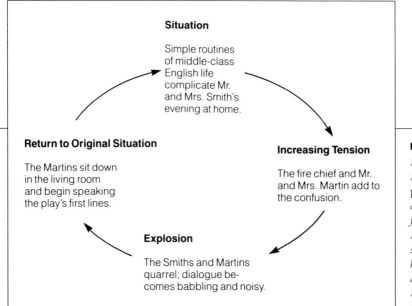

Situation

Simple routines
of middle-class
English life
complicate Mr.
and Mrs. Smith's
evening at home.

Return to Original Situation

The Martins sit down
in the living room
and begin speaking
the play's first lines.

Increasing Tension

The fire chief and Mr.
and Mrs. Martin add to
the confusion.

Explosion

The Smiths and Martins
quarrel; dialogue be-
comes babbling and noisy.

FIGURE 10.6

Situational play structure in Ionesco's The Bald So-
prano. *The "theatre of the absurd" emerged in Europe following World War II. Absurdist plays convey a sense of alienation, of people having lost their bearings in an illogical or ridiculous world. Situational play structure mirrors this world view.*

FIGURE 10.7

Ionesco's middle-class English couple, Mr. and Mrs. Smith, discuss dinner, the newspaper, and Bobby Watson in the original 1950 Paris production of The Bald Soprano.

Drama's Conventions

Over the years, playwrights have worked out different dramatic structures to convey different ideas about experience. In addition, they have worked out dramatic conventions, ground rules, to set plot and character in motion. A **convention** is an agreed-upon method of quickly getting something across to an audience. Just as we have social conventions in life to help us meet strangers or answer the telephone, so the playwright has conventions to solve problems, pass along information, develop plot and action, and create interest and suspense. These shortcuts make it possible for the playwright to give information and to present experiences that in life would require weeks or even years, to tell two stories at once, and to complicate the stage action without confusing the audience. What follows is a discussion of seven *dramatic conventions*: exposition, point of attack, complication, crisis, resolution, double plots, and the play-within-the-play.

Exposition

In a play's opening scene we are frequently given certain information about what is going on, what has happened in the past, and who is to be seen. This is one type of *exposition*. In Euripides' *The Trojan Women* (415 B.C.) a prologue, which gives the essential exposition, is spoken by the sea god, Poseidon, and Athene, the goddess defender of Troy. First, Poseidon describes the treachery of the Greeks' use of the Trojan horse to gain entry into the city of Troy, the city's collapse, and the fate of its defenders. Athene describes how the Greeks defiled her altars in Troy. Second, the exposition then shifts to the human level. Troy's Queen Hecuba describes the physical and mental suffering of the Trojan people. Following this background information, the action begins; we learn one by one the fate of the women and the death sentence assigned to Hector's young son, Astyanax.

In contrast to the formal exposition of Greek plays, some modern plays begin with a telephone ringing; the person answering—for instance, a maid or butler in drawing-room comedy—gives the background information by talking to an unseen party about the family, its plans, and conflicts.

The Trojan Women, written by Euripides and produced in 415 B.C. at the Theatre of Dionysus, Athens, is the third (and only surviving) play in his trilogy about Troy — its destruction, the death of its defenders, and the enslavement of its women. (See Figure 10.8.)

In a prologue we witness the sea god Poseidon agree to aid Athene — goddess defender of Troy — in her revenge: To teach them to respect all gods, he will destroy the Greeks on their victorious voyage home.

Amid the ruins of Troy, Queen Hecuba (wife of Troy's dead King Priam and mother of Hector, the chief Trojan warrior slain in battle), describes her physical and mental suffering. She calls on the chorus (the captive women) to lament Troy's fate. Talthybius, the Greek messenger, arrives the first of four times to announce decisions made by the Greek generals about the women. Eventually, Talthybius announces that Cassandra goes to Agamemnon, Andromache to Achilles'

son, Helen to Menelaus, and Queen Hecuba to Odysseus. These scenes are further complicated by the trial of Helen of Troy and the execution of Hector's young son. On his third entrance Talthybius brings the child's body carried on Hector's shield. Hecuba pronounces his funeral oration and the body is carried off on the shield for burial.

Talthybius' last entrance ends the waiting period and all suspense. Troy is set afire and the captives are ordered to the ships. Hecuba tries to run into the flames, but Talthybius stops her because she is "Odysseus' property."

In Euripides' universe, gods are as vengeful and irrational as human beings. It is a universe without order; therefore, the spectacle of the human dilemma is pitiable but without moral or ethical meaning. A line in the play sums up his vision: "The man who sacks cities is a fool; he makes temples and tombs, the shrines of the dead, a desert, and then perishes himself."

FIGURE 10.8

The Greeks *presented by the Royal Shakespeare Company in London, 1979. In the foreground is Billie Whitelaw as Andromache; in the background Eliza Ward as Hecuba holds the child Astyanax, in* Part One: The War *(from* The Trojan Women*). The production was directed by John Barton and designed by John Napier.*

In most cases, plays begin with informational exchanges of dialogue. *Macbeth* begins ominously with the three witches in thunder and lightning against a background of battle. They are planning their next meeting "when the battle's lost and won," after which they'll meet Macbeth on the heath. The implication is that no good will come of this meeting.

Contemporary drama presents less information of this kind. Instead of asking who these people are and what is going to happen next, we usually ask: "What's going on now?"

Point of Attack

The moment early in the play when the story is taken up is the *point of attack*. In *The Trojan Women*, the point of attack comes when Hecuba describes her suffering and calls on the chorus (the captive women) to lament the destruction of Troy and to mourn being sent to Greece as slaves. In *Macbeth*, the point of attack grows out of the victorious battle reports to King Duncan who, learning of the death of the traitorous Thane of Cawdor, rewards Macbeth with that title. In the very next scene Macbeth encounters the witches, who greet him with many prophesies, including the title "Thane of Cawdor."

Complication, Crisis, Climax

The middle of a play is made up of *complications*—new information introduced by new characters, unexpected events, or newly disclosed facts. Macbeth's encounter with the witches is the beginning of many violent complications. In *Ghosts*, Mrs. Alving overhears Oswald seducing Regina, who is the child of her husband and a servant with whom he had an affair and is therefore Oswald's half-sister. Mrs. Alving must deal with this complication.

A play's complications usually develop into a *crisis*, or turning point of the action. In fact, plays like *Ghosts* and *Hamlet* may have several crises. The crisis is an event that makes the resolution of the play's conflict inevitable. In *Macbeth*, the crisis is the murder of King Duncan by the Macbeths. They have killed an anointed king and a universal bloodbath will follow

The last of Shakespeare's four great tragedies (along with *Hamlet, Othello,* and *King Lear*), *Macbeth* (1606) was written when his creative powers were at their highest. Macbeth, King Duncan's noble warlord, hears witches prophesy that greatness will be his — that he will be king someday (see Figure 10.9).

When his wife, Lady Macbeth, learns of the witches' prophecy, her imagination — over-charged with ambition — conceives the King's assassination. While he sleeps in their castle, the Macbeths murder Duncan, engendering a seemingly endless series of murders to conceal their original crime and to thwart other pretenders to the throne.

As the play progresses, the disintegrating effects of evil work on a once noble man and his wife. Macbeth's crimes distort his judgment; he is terrified by hallucinations of the ghosts of his victims, symbolizing a warning of retribution to come. He becomes increasingly isolated from his followers and his wife, whose guilty conscience eventually leads her to suicide. Pessimism and despair take hold of Macbeth as he contemplates his inevitable punishment. Only in the end does he revive a part of his former self, as he duels his rival (Macduff) to a certain death.

This story of crime and punishment illustrates the destructive effects of power and ambition on the human psyche. Macbeth's self-awareness endows the action with its tragic dimension: Feeling responsibility for the moral chaos he has created, he explores life's meaning in **soliloquies** that transcend his particular dilemma.

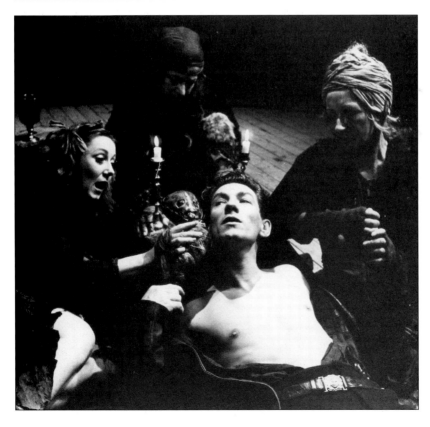

FIGURE 10.9

The witches entice Macbeth (Ian McKellen) with voo-doo dolls, as they paint symbols on his body in the Royal Shakespeare Company production of Macbeth *(1976), directed by Trevor Nunn:*

MACBETH: Speak, if you can. What are you?

1. WITCH: All hail, Macbeth! Hail to thee, Thane of Glamis!
2. WITCH: All hail, Macbeth! Hail to thee, Thane of Cawdor!
3. WITCH: All hail, Macbeth, that shalt be King hereafter!

FIGURE 10.10

The 1966 New York Shakespeare Festival production of Macbeth *at the Delacorte Theatre in Central Park, featuring James Earl Jones in the title role.*

until the murderers are punished and the rightful heir restored to the throne. Even at this point of crisis Macbeth knows that all great Neptune's ocean will never wash them clean again. (See Figure 10.10.)

A play usually ends when the conflict is resolved in the *climax*, or highest point of intensity, and any loose strands of action are then tied off. When Hector's son, the heir to Troy, is sentenced to die and carried off to be executed, the highest moment of the play's intensity has been reached. The consignment of the women to the Greek generals is almost anticlimactic because — without a male to procreate the tribe — Troy has no hope for a future generation.

Macbeth's climax is the appearance of the murdered Banquo's ghost at the banquet table — further evidence of Macbeth's ongoing bloody deeds and his unquiet conscience. After the ghost's appearance, forces turn against Macbeth leading him finally to fight his rival Macduff; this secondary climax results in Macbeth's death and the restoration of the rightful heir to Duncan's throne.

Resolution

The resolution usually restores balance and satisfies the audience's expectations. The captive Trojan women are marched away to board the Greek ships; the Macbeths have paid for their crimes with their lives, and Duncan's son is to be crowned king of Scotland. In *A Streetcar Named Desire*, Blanche is taken to an asylum and the Kowalski household settles back into its routines of poker, beer, and Saturday-night bowling. The absurdist play

FIGURE 10.11
The secondary plot resolved. Hamlet stands above the wounded Laertes near the end of the duel. Laertes' death concludes the story of his family. Albert Finney as Hamlet watches Simon Ward as Laertes in the 1976 production at London's National Theatre, directed by Peter Hall.

usually completes a cycle in its resolution, suggesting that the events of the play will repeat themselves over and over again. Some plays end with unanswered questions — for example, will Mrs. Alving give Oswald the fatal drug, or won't she? — to stimulate the audience to think about what kind of choice each would make in a similar situation. Whatever the case, the resolution brings a sense of completed or suspended action, of conflicts resolved in probable ways, and of promises fulfilled.

Other dramatic conventions relate past and present events and behavior. **Simultaneous plots** and the *play-within-the-play* are two important conventions used by Renaissance and modern playwrights.

Simultaneous or Double Plots

The Elizabethans used **double plots** (or **subplots**) to represent life's variety and complexity. Two stories are told concurrently; the lives of one group of characters affect the lives of the other group. *Hamlet*, for instance, is the story of two families: Hamlet-Claudius-Gertrude, Laertes-Polonius-Ophelia. The secondary plot or subplot is always resolved before the main plot to maintain a sense of priority. Laertes dies before Hamlet in the duel resolving that family's story (see Figure 10.11).

The Play-Within-the-Play

The play-within-the-play was used by Shakespeare and is still a common plot device, most notably in the work of such modern writers as Bertolt Brecht, Peter Weiss, Tom Stoppard, and Luigi Pirandello (see Figure 10.12). In *Hamlet*, the play-within-the-play (called *The Murder of Gonzago*) is used in what is now thought of as a highly traditional way. The strolling

Pirandello's "six characters" make their mysterious appearance in the play-within-the-play. Six Characters in Search of an Author *was directed by Liviu Ciulei for Arena Stage, Washington, D.C.*

players re-create a second play on stage about the murder of Hamlet's father; Claudius' reaction to it gives Hamlet proof of the King's guilt.

Brecht's *Caucasian Chalk Circle* is almost in its entirety a play-within-the-play. The singer-narrator links the outer play (the settling of the farmers' dispute) with the inner one (the stories of Grusha, Azdak, and the chalk-circle test). The long inner play manifests a kind of collective wisdom that has practical applications in an actual dispute over ownership of property (the outer play).

Recent playwrights use the play-within-the-play in a more complex way than even Brecht, to demonstrate that *life is like theatre*, and vice versa. In his celebrated masterpiece *Marat/Sade* (*The Persecution and Assassination of Jean-Paul Marat as Performed by the Inmates of the Asylum of Charenton under the Direction of the Marquis de Sade*), written in 1964, Peter Weiss (1916–1982) used the play-within-the-play convention to suggest that our contemporary world is a madhouse. Set in 1808, *Marat/Sade* depicts the production of a play by the inmates of an insane asylum in Charenton, France. Their text, about the events surrounding the death of political revolutionary Jean-Paul Marat fifteen years earlier, has been composed by the Marquis de Sade, who is also director, fellow actor, and fellow inmate. (See pages 268–270.)

Weiss uses two time frames: (1) the events of 1793 — the historical setting of de Sade's play about the French Revolution — that culminate in the assassination of Marat, and (2) the "present" of 1808, when de Sade and his

FIGURE 10.13

Calling, *a happening by Allan Kaprow, was performed in New York City in 1965. It involved an orchestration of cars converging at prearranged points to pick up passengers, wrapping someone in aluminum foil to sit motionless on the back seat of a parked car, and two girls wrapped in muslin to be taken to the information booth at Grand Central Station. The photo shows the two muslin-covered girls, one standing and one seated at lower left corner, unwrapping themselves. They leave the train station and telephone certain numbers. A name is asked for and the person at the other end clicks off.*

mentally deranged cast are staging their play. The madhouse world of Charenton mirrors the violence and irrationality of our modern world. And the play-within-the-play forces us to compare the manner in which conflicting political ideologies resolve their differences: then, with the guillotine, and now, with nuclear weapons.

New Play Structures

Happenings

Happenings, one of several new trends in the American theatre in the early 1960s, were an attempt to break down barriers between the arts, as well as between performers and their audiences. American painter Allan Kaprow (b. 1927) became interested in creating environments of artworks as an exhibit (that is, using the entire space, not just the artworks on display) to give persons attending the exhibit something to do to involve them with the art. (See Figure 10.13.)

The name *happening* resulted from Kaprow's use of the word in his presentation called *18 Happenings in 6 Parts* (1959). It soon became a label for task-oriented events in which chance and improvisation played a large part. The aim of the happening was to permit participants to engage in a

Spalding Gray

Spalding Gray is a theatre creator, performer, and teacher. A graduate of Emerson College, he came to New York in 1967, where he performed in Off-Broadway plays. He worked for brief periods with the Alley Theatre in Houston and with Joseph Chaikin's Open Theatre before joining Richard Schechner's Performance Group in 1969. There he played in Sam Shepard's *The Tooth of Crime* and in Bertolt Brecht's *Mother Courage*. In 1975, he and Elizabeth LeCompte, along with other former members of the Performance Group, formed the Wooster Group.

For the Wooster Group, Gray composed and/or performed in *Sakonnet Point, Rumstick Road, Nayatt School, Point Judith,* and *Route 1 & 9*. The first three are known as *The Trilogy: Three Places in Rhode Island*, based on Gray's life. He also created a series of monologues, or talking pieces, with the Wooster Group, including *Swimming to Cambodia* (1983), a monologue about that country, Thailand, Hollywood, and his participation as an actor in the film *The Killing Fields*. He played the narrator in the 1988 Broadway production of Thornton Wilder's *Our Town*.

Gray has taught in the Experimental Theatre Wing of New York University's School of Drama and has led many workshops there and in India and Europe. As with the Wooster Group work and his monologues, the emphasis of his workshops for both children and adults is autobiographical; participants are encouraged to develop material and theatrical metaphors from their own lives. Since 1979, he has toured America and Europe with his autobiographical storytelling.

task, usually related to urban society, to encourage them to perceive the world's complexity in a new way.

Most happenings failed to engage our sense of theatre, and they declined in popularity in the late 1960s. However, they did contribute to greater reliance in the theatre on improvisation, use of whole space as environment, and a new actor–audience relationship.

Talking Pieces

Solo performances have a long stage history. Most recently in the mainstream of the American theatre we have seen Julie Harris as the Belle of Amherst (Emily Dickinson), Pat Carroll as Gertrude Stein, Zoe Caldwell as Lillian Hellman, and Robert Morse as Truman Capote. However, solo performances have also been a part of our contemporary avant-garde, as evidenced in the work of Spalding Gray and others.

In the late 1970s, the inflationary economy and the lack of large social and political issues resulted in the disbanding of many of the American theatrical collectives that had gathered momentum in the '60s over issues like the Vietnam War. Many performers, such as Spalding Gray, who had worked for a time with Richard Schechner's Performance Group in New York, turned to creating a new kind of theatre piece for the solo performer (and also for small casts). Gray's pieces, developed for performance by him, have been called "talking pieces," even "epic monologues." They represent a new and interesting dramatic structure, as well as theatre event.

Gray improvised his memories, free associations, and ideas of childhood, family relationships, and private emotions to create an open narrative of personal actions.[5] Using properties bought at Woolworth's, a tape recorder, old family photograph albums, slide projections, and phonograph records, he worked before small audiences that included director Elizabeth LeCompte of the Wooster Group, giving shape to his autobiographical sketches. The text as it developed was talked through with the director and audiences in what Gray calls "an act of public memory." Once satisfied with the final product, Gray "set" the text. Because of these improvisational methods, Gray refers to the pieces as "poetic journalism" or as "talking pieces"—a series of simple actions using free associations as building blocks to create a series of images like personal, living Rorschachs.

Gray's series of monologues, or talking pieces, include *Sex and Death to the Age 14; A Personal History of the American Theatre; Booze, Cars and College Girls;* and *Terrors of Pleasure.* Even in the trilogy *Three Places in Rhode Island,* the monologue remains a foundation stone. *Rumstick Road* opens with a monologue in which Gray discusses his acting career, his mother's psychiatric treatment, her Christian Science faith, her illness from cancer, and her eventual suicide.

Samuel Beckett's *Rockaby* as Monodrama

Since the original production of *Waiting for Godot* in 1953, Samuel Beckett has been a major influence on experimentalists looking for ways to introduce into the theatre intuitive events, talking pieces, interior monologues,

W = *Woman in chair.*
V = *Her recorded voice.*

Fade up on W in rocking chair facing front downstage slightly off centre audience left.

Long pause.

W: More.

    Pause. Rock and voice together.

V: till in the end
    the day came
    in the end came
    close of a long day
    when she said
    to herself
    whom else
    time she stopped
    time she stopped
    going to and fro
    all eyes
    all sides
    high and low
    for another
    another like herself
    another creature like herself
    a little like
    going to and fro
    all eyes
    all sides
    high and low
    for another
    till in the end
    close of a long day
    to herself
    whom else
    time she stopped
    time she stopped
    going to and fro
    all eyes
    all sides
    high and low
    for another

    another living soul
    one other living soul
    going to and fro
    all eyes like herself
    all sides
    high and low
    for another
    another like herself
    a little like
    going to and fro
    till in the end
    close of a long day
    to herself
    whom else
    time she stopped
    going to and fro
    time she stopped
    time she stopped

    Together: echo of "time she stopped," coming to rest of rock, faint fade of light.

    Long pause.

W: More.

    Pause. Rock and voice together.

V: so in the end
    close of a long day
    went back in
    in the end went back in
    saying to herself
    whom else
    time she stopped
    time she stopped
    going to and fro
    time she went and sat
    at her window
    quiet at her window
    facing other windows
    so in the end
    close of a long day
    in the end went and sat
    went back in and sat

at her window
let up the blind and sat
quiet at her window
only window
facing other windows
other only windows
all eyes
all sides
high and low
for another
at her window
another like herself
a little like
another living soul
one other living soul
at her window
gone in like herself
gone back in
in the end
close of a long day
saying to herself
whom else
time she stopped
time she stopped
going to and fro
time she went and sat
at her window
quiet at her window
only window
facing other windows
other only windows
all eyes
all sides
high and low
for another
another like herself
a little like
another living soul
one other living soul

Together: echo of "living soul,"
coming to rest of rock, faint fade
of light.

Long pause.

W: More.

Pause. Rock and voice together.

V: till in the end
the day came
in the end came
close of a long day
sitting at her window
quiet at her window
only window
facing other windows
other only windows
all blinds down
never one up
hers alone up
till the day came
in the end came
close of a long day
sitting at her window
quiet at her window
all eyes
all sides
high and low
for a blind up
one blind up
no more
never mind a face
behind the pane
famished eyes
like hers
to see
be seen
no
a blind up
like hers
a little like
one blind up no more
another creature there
somewhere there
behind the pane
another living soul
one other living soul

till the day came
in the end came
close of a long day
when she said
to herself
whom else
time she stopped
time she stopped
sitting at her window
quiet at her window
only window
facing other windows
other only windows
all eyes
all sides
high and low
time she stopped
time she stopped

Together: echo of "time she stopped,"
coming to rest of rock, faint fade
of light.

Long pause.

W: More.

Pause. Rock and voice together.

V: so in the end
close of a long day
went down
in the end went down
down the steep stair
let down the blind and down
right down
into the old rocker
mother rocker
where mother sat
all the years
all in black
best black
sat and rocked
rocked
till her end came

in the end came
off her head they said
gone off her head
but harmless
no harm in her
dead one day
no
night
dead one night
in the rocker
in her best black
head fallen
and the rocker rocking
rocking away
so in the end
close of a long day
went down
in the end went down
down the steep stair
let down the blind and down
right down
into the old rocker
those arms at last
and rocked
rocked
with closed eyes
closing eyes
she so long all eyes
famished eyes
all sides
high and low
to and fro
at her window
to see
be seen
till in the end
close of a long day
to herself
whom else
time she stopped
let down the blind and stopped
time she went down

down the steep stair
time she went right down
was her own other
own other living soul
so in the end
close of a long day
went down
down the steep stair
let down the blind and down
right down
into the old rocker
and rocked
rocked
saying to herself

no
done with that
the rocker
those arms at last
saying to the rocker
rock her off
stop her eyes
fuck life
stop her eyes
rock her off
rock her off

*Together: echo of "rock her off," coming to
rest of rock, slow fade out.*

NOTES

Light
Subdued on chair. Rest of stage dark. Subdued spot on face constant throughout, unaffected by successive fades. Either wide enough to include narrow limits of rock or concentrated on face when still or at mid-rock. Then throughout speech face slightly swaying in and out of light. Opening fade-up: first spot on face alone. Long pause. Then light on chair. Final fade-out: first chair. Long pause with spot on face alone. Head slowly sinks, comes to rest. Fade out spot.

W
Prematurely old. Unkempt grey hair. Huge eyes in white expressionless face. White hands holding ends of armrests.

Eyes
Now closed, now open in unblinking gaze. About equal proportions section 1, increasingly closed 2 and 3, closed for good halfway through 4.

Costume
Black lacy high-necked evening gown. Long sleeves. Jet sequins to glitter when rocking. Incongruous frivolous headdress set askew with extravagant trimmings to catch light when rocking.

Attitude
Completely still till fade-out of chair. Then in light of spot head slowly inclined.

Chair
Pale wood highly polished to gleam when rocking. Footrest. Vertical back. Rounded inward curving arms to suggest embrace.

Rock
Slight. Slow. Controlled mechanically without assistance from W.

Voice
Lines in italics spoken by W with V a little softer each time. W's "More" a little softer each time. Towards end of section 4, say from "saying to herself" on, voice gradually softer.[6]

FIGURE 10.14

Billie Whitelaw as the woman in the rocking chair in Samuel Beckett's Rock- aby, *directed by Alan Schneider, at the Samuel Beckett Theater, New York, 1984.*

and minimal staging. To do so required new dramatic forms, conventions, and performance techniques. Cause-to-effect plots, soliloquies, and formal exposition were no longer adequate.

Beckett's **monologues** and narrative voices in his novels and plays, together with his minimal staging (an old man, a table, and a tape recorder; a woman buried in a mound of dirt: two lips speaking; a woman in a rocking chair), influenced the work of Lee Breuer, Sam Shepard, Spalding Gray, and others. The aim of the convention (let us call it *monodrama*) is the same as that of the stream-of-consciousness novel: to present the conscious and unconscious thought processes of the narrator. To take us into the character's or speaker's consciousness in the theatre, playwrights (follow- ing Beckett's lead) have introduced electronic amplification, sound tracks, holograms, and voice-overs.

Rockaby, written in 1980, was interpreted for New York audiences in 1984 by British actress Billie Whitelaw (see Figure 10.14) and directed by Alan Schneider. *Rockaby* is a fifteen-minute monodrama in which a woman, seated in a rocking chair, rocks herself into the grave. The actress speaks only one word ("more") four times. The single word is separated by a litany of other words recorded on tape by the actress. The words on tape represent the final thrashings of the woman's consciousness. As death comes, she ceases rocking. A single stage light picks out the actress' face; her eyes are closed. Then the darkness is total.

With no scenery, one actor, few words, and scant movement, Beckett makes us feel the weight of the solitary, seemingly endless night of living. Death comes as a release — a happy ending.

Theatre of Visions

In 1976 critic Bonnie Marranca coined the label "The Theatre of Images" to describe the works of American writer-director-designer-producers Robert Wilson and Lee Breuer. Revolting against words and "old-fashioned" verbal texts, these innovators independently created theatre events dominated by visual and aural images. Since the early 1970s, their avant-garde experiments have evolved in form and structure to resemble the painter's collage. Absent are climactic drama's cause-to-effect relationships of action, plot, and character. In their place we find actors juxtaposed with holographic shapes, sounds, and sculpted images that develop as large-scale performances requiring more than a few hours to complete. This new mixture of creative sources (sound, music, light, technology, text) ultimately raises the same issues as more traditional theatre: questions of humanity's relationship to society, to environment, and to itself.

Robert Wilson A student of architecture and painting, Robert Wilson creates living pictures on stage with sounds, sculptured forms, music, and visual images that require many hours to experience. (One of his productions, *Ka Mountain*, lasted seven days.) His *A Letter for Queen Victoria*, which appeared briefly on Broadway in 1974, is composed of bits and pieces of overheard conversations, clichés, newspaper blurbs, colors, spot announcements, television images, and film clips. One theme of the piece was American imperialism, but instead of discussing the topic, Wilson simply projects *images* of it: In Act II, pilots talk about faraway lands against a background of sounds of gunfire and bomb blasts.

One of Wilson's boldest ventures is the opera *the CIVIL warS: a tree is best measured when it is down* (1984), a collaborative work involving East German playwright Heiner Müller, American composer Philip Glass, and others. Although Wilson first thought of the work as an exploration of the American Civil War and the Industrial Revolution, as he continued to

Robert Wilson

Born in 1941, Robert Wilson created the Byrd Hoffman Foundation to work with autistic children, as well as performers of all ages, on developing a new kind of theatre. The results were unusually long performances — five to seven hours — intended to provoke contemplation rather than to tell a story.

Wilson's productions "assemble" actors, sounds, music, light, and shadow to comment on American society and cultural myths. They are known as much for their length and complexity as for their unique titles:

▾ *The Life and Times of Joseph Stalin*
▾ *Einstein on the Beach*
▾ *The Life and Times of Sigmund Freud*
▾ *Death Destruction and Detroit*
▾ *I was Sitting on My Patio This Guy Appeared I Thought I Was Hallucinating*
▾ *The Golden Windows*
▾ *The Knee Plays*

His epic productions stretch the audience's attention in an attempt to alter perceptual awareness of people, places, and things. Wilson has said of his work: "Most theatre that we see today is thought about in terms of the word, the text. . . . And that's not the case with my work. In my theatre, what we see is as important as what we hear. What we see does not have to relate to what we hear. They can be independent."[7]

develop his themes he expanded his vision to include all "civil struggles" that have existed throughout history, from mythological Greece to the distant future. With haunting, violent images of the American Civil War at its center, its recurrent theme is destruction and death contrasted with the importance of civilization and the value of life.

Wilson's theatre of visions combines architectural landscapes, striking verbal and musical images, long physical and verbal pauses that exaggerate our sense of time passing, and incongruous characters (including astronauts, Robert E. Lee, and Dorothy and the Tin Man of Oz). Literally towering above them all is Abraham Lincoln, a sixteen-foot-tall figure formed by a singer suspended in a harness and wearing a long black coat — the "tree" that is best measured when cut down.

Lee Breuer   One of the founders of the Mabou Mines Ensemble in 1970, Breuer as writer-director disregards the conventional uses of plot, dialogue, setting, time, and character in favor of an open-ended form. The

Lee Breuer

Lee Breuer (b. 1937) first worked in theatre with the San Francisco Actors' Workshop, and in 1963 he began his own experimental company. During a five-year period in Europe, where he studied the work of the Berliner Ensemble in East Germany and Jerzy Grotowski in Poland, he directed Brecht's *Mother Courage and Her Children* and Beckett's *Play* in Paris. In 1970 he brought the company of *Play* to New York as the Mabou Mines (named for a mining town in Nova Scotia), and continued to act as their artistic director until 1976, when the group became a "theatre collaborative."

In addition to writing the company's three animations, Breuer has directed other Mines productions: *Mabou Mines Performs Samuel Beckett* (1975), which included his adaptation of *The Lost Ones*, and *A Prelude to Death in Venice* (1979). He choreographed *The Saint and the Football Players* for the American Dance Festival, and directed Wedekind's *Lulu* for the American Repertory Theatre (1980), and Shakespeare's *The Tempest* (1981) and his own *Hajj* (1983) for the New York Shakespeare Festival. His epic collage *Gospel at Colonus* (1984) combines classical Greek tragedy with black gospel music in a jubilant assertion of the need for rebirth. *The Warrior Ant* (1988) mixes Bunraku puppets, musical bands, and singers/narrators whispering the story of the ant as cultural hero: the little ant who tries to get a better deal for other ants in his society. *Lear* (1990), an adaptation of *King Lear*, puts a woman in the title role as the classic mother figure confronting the crucial issues facing modern women: Can they have love *and* power?

idea of life passages, made fashionable by Gail Sheehy and other writers, is substituted for plot; monologue for dialogue; personal space for setting. Memory controls dramatic time, and a chorus takes the place of individual characters in conflict. But unlike the Greek chorus that gives information and emotional response to the events of the play, Breuer's chorus serves as an individual voice.

Between 1970 and 1978, Breuer wrote three animations: *The Red Horse, The B. Beaver,* and *The Shaggy Dog.* They are called *animations,* as in cartoons, because the principal characters are animals with human personalities. The animals are Breuer's "mask"—a way of distancing himself (and his audience) from the material. Like storytellers of old, the animals tell their personal histories. They delight in word play—verbal and visual puns—but they do not engage in traditional stage dialogue.

Actors take turns enacting events from the animal's life rather than imitating them, helped by electronic music, films, photographs, puppets, sculpted space, and movement. As in Asian theatre, voices are separated from the characters.

Theatre for a High-Tech World

Robert Wilson and Lee Breuer have forged a new kind of theatre for the 21st century, manipulating technology to create experiences for audiences that they cannot find in any other medium.

The Knee Plays. Originally intended as an interlude between the fifteen scenes of *the CIVIL warS* (and also used again in *The Forest*), *The Knee Plays*, created by Robert Wilson in 1984, consists of thirteen vignettes running about ninety minutes in performance. With music and lyrics by David Byrne (of The Talking Heads), the company of nine dancers creates a cascade of imagery — visual, aural, verbal, and choreographic — focusing on "a tree of life." Using square modules, puppets, and masks, they tell a story dealing with the life cycle through history, beginning with the tree of life and proceeding through the American Civil War.

The Forest. Scene from the 1988 American premiere of Robert Wilson's *The Forest* (with music by David Byrne) based on *The Epic of Gilgamesh* and produced at the Brooklyn Academy of Music. Enkidu (right, actor Howie Seago), the story's hero, confronts images of civilization's history: hunter, whore, slave, priest, scholar, and godhead. Wilson's production takes Enkidu on a journey through the history of civilization from primitive times up through the nineteenth-century industrial revolution and the end of the "modern" world.

Einstein on the Beach. Originally produced in 1976 for two sold-out performances at the Metropolitan Opera House, New York City, *Einstein on the Beach* is a collaboration between Robert Wilson and composer Philip Glass. The five-hour production dealt with contradictions implicit in the genius Albert Einstein and his legacy to our world. On the one hand, Einstein produced evolutionary new understandings of the universe, an impulse toward pacifism and love of music; on the other hand, the prospect of nuclear holocaust. Wilson's staging established contrasting images (with actors, lighting, costumes, props, and sculpted forms) of Einstein's legacy to our times.

In *Hajj* (1983), Ruth Maleczech confronts images of herself at her vanity table in the Mabou Mines production. An example of new theatre's high technology, *holography* is a special photographic technique in which lasers are used to record highly realistic images of three-dimensional objects; the photographic record is called a *hologram*. When illuminated by a laser beam, the hologram produces images that are exact replicas of the original three-dimensional object.

This collage of visual images, music, sound, and actor reconstructs a mental journey among past memories and present responses. *Hajj* is Breuer's effort to objectify how the artist makes art out of images and ideas from the past and the present.

FIGURE 10.15

JoAnne Akalaitis and Linda Hartinian sing Rose the Puppet's thoughts as she reads in her high-tech bathroom in Lee Breuer's Shaggy Dog Animation, *1978.*

In *The Shaggy Dog Animation* (Figure 10.15), performed at the Public Theater in 1978, the narrative voice belongs to a dog named Rose, visualized as a human puppet. A love story of Rose and John, dog and master, woman and man, it follows an almost classical narrative line: The heroine, Rose, comes to know the truth about herself by going through a series of meaningful experiences. Rose the dog (read also *person*), chained in an emotional relationship with her master, finds a new freedom and develops a feminist consciousness. As the story progresses, it makes fun of the traditions of Western love: ecstasy, illusion, pain, disillusion, sentimentality, and silliness.

Slick and stylish, *Shaggy Dog* is controlled by sound and light technicians. The glossy setting is decorated with gadgetry of a technological society: illuminated radio dial as scenic background, shaggy white carpeting, and chrome-plated dollhouse furniture. The clichés of romance are filtered through the language and sounds of the mass media: disc jockeys, movies, sound tracks, popular songs, and other elements of our pop culture.

Hajj, written and directed by Breuer in 1983 at the Public Theater, is an hour-long "performance poem" in which a woman (Ruth Maleczech) sits at a vanity table, looks into multiple mirrors, and sees not only her reflection but also her past, projected on large screens by closed-circuit video

This nine-member "theatre collaborative" based in New York has dispensed with a leader, artistic director, and group aesthetic. A leading avant-garde company, it is a model of experimentalism in writing, acting, directing, production, technology, and collaboration. Some of the founders still work with the current group: Lee Breuer, JoAnne Akalaitis, and Ruth Maleczech. Today, most of the company works inside *and* outside the group on other projects.

Breuer calls the company a "producing collective." The group sits around a table amid rehearsal rubble of empty coffee cups and unfinished models and talks about the current project. The conversation focuses on acting and media techniques. Frequently starting with a text, such as Beckett's *Company* (a novella), the group spends about four months investigating holograms, laser beams, and solid forms to try to create images of another person, another body, in the performance space with the actor. Their work mixes a strong narrative thread with the high technology of videotapes and sound systems.

cameras and prerecorded tapes. This pilgrimage into the mind shows how art is made out of present reflections and past memories.

Lee Breuer is a critic of our popular culture, recycling its clichés so that we see and hear them for what they are: a parody of our humanity. But, like Sam Shepard, Breuer is also an optimist. He believes that, like Rose the dog, we can liberate ourselves from false value systems and relationships and become authentic individuals.

Summary

Drama is a special way of imitating human behavior and events. Just as children imitate adults as a way of mastering the strangeness of the world around them, so playwrights create dramatic blueprints representing physical and psychological experience to give shape and meaning to their world as they see it.

Drama comes from the Greek *dran*, meaning "to do" or "to act." From our modern perspective, it defines an art form having the potential for placing *action* before us in a performance space. That action, which the actor brings before us, takes many forms depending on the playwright's attitudes and interpretations of experience. For 2,500 years, the major play structures have been climactic, episodic, and situational, and drama's conventions have been fairly consistent, relying on exposition, crisis, climax, and resolution to convey the play's meaning to audiences. But in a world of high technology and ambivalent meanings, writers and directors have tried different methods to create verbal and visual texts that speak to audiences familiar with computer graphics, sophisticated electronic sound systems, video equipment, and spectacular holographic effects. Almost in ironic juxtaposition to the elaborate technology being brought into the theatre space is the minimalist art of Samuel Beckett. Imagistic texts, both *elaborate* and *minimal*, by Robert Wilson and Samuel Beckett, have articulated in performance the difficulties of what it means to be a human being in the world of the last quarter of the twentieth century. Like the texts themselves, *language* for the theatre has its own special techniques and ways of communicating to audiences.

Questions for Study

1. What is *dialogue*?

2. What similarities are there between children at play and theatre?

3. What is *mimesis*?

4. What is the difference between a play's *actual time* and its *symbolic time*?

5. What are the basic differences between *climactic, episodic,* and *situational* play structure? Give examples of each.

6. What is a dramatic *convention*?

7. Why is *exposition* an important playwright's tool? Give some examples of exposition.

8. Why does *complication* often follow the *point of attack*?

9. How are *crisis* and *climax* related?

10. What does an audience expect at a play's *resolution* or ending?

11. What is the function of a *double plot*?

12. Describe the double plot in *Hamlet*.

13. *The Murder of Gonzago*, as performed by the strolling players in *Hamlet*, is an example of a play-within-the-play. What is the function of this "inner" play?

14. Describe Brecht's variation on the play-within-the-play convention in *The Caucasian Chalk Circle*.

15. How has Peter Weiss further complicated the play-within-the-play convention?

16. What are "happenings"?

17. What are "talking pieces"?

18. What is *monodrama*? Describe Beckett's *Rockaby* as monodrama.

19. In what ways do the theatre of Robert Wilson and of Lee Breuer reflect a high-tech world?

20. *Plays to Read*: Bertolt Brecht's *The Caucasian Chalk Circle* and Peter Weiss' *Marat/Sade* to study two different uses of the play-within-the-play convention; *The Shaggy Dog Animation* by Lee Breuer in *Animations: A Trilogy for Mabou Mines*, introduction by Bonnie Marranca (New York: Performing Arts Journal Publications, 1979); *Swimming to Cambodia* by Spalding Gray (New York: Theatre Communications Group, 1985).

Like other stage elements, theatre's language is special and complex. It organizes our perceptions of what is taking place before us, forcing us into self-discovery or radical changes of attitude. Language in the theatre communicates meaning and activity to us in many ways — verbal and nonverbal. Theatre's language is a way of seeing that engages our eyes, ears, and minds.

Chapter 11

Theatre Language

I n theatre we see and hear a story being lived before us with the intensity of a traveler experiencing new worlds for the first time. Playwrights, directors, designers, and actors use a special *language* to organize our perceptions of it, one that is both *visual* and *aural*.

Language in the theatre is both like and unlike the way people talk in real life. First, it is the playwright's means for expressing what characters experience, and for developing plot and action. Unlike conversation in real life, actors speak highly selective words supported by highly selective gestures. Hamlet's soliloquies, some of the most beautiful verse written in English for the theatre, express his feelings and thoughts in blank verse. This unusual and eloquent language is acceptable to us because it has its own reality, consonant with a world other than our own.

Theatre language, then, is the language of the characters and of the stage world and expresses the life of the play. Language spoken by actors as characters expresses ideas and feelings, revealing the consciousness of the characters; it makes their decisions to act dramatically meaningful.

We are so used to equating language (and communication) with words that we must constantly remind ourselves that in the theatre the *word* is what Peter Brook called "a small visible portion of a gigantic unseen formation."[2] Words in the theatre are enhanced by nonverbal language: for example, gestures, costumes, sounds, and light express moods, intentions, and meanings.

Others have also remarked that one characteristic of theatre language is that words have their source in gesture. To repeat George Steiner's statement about this: "Drama is language

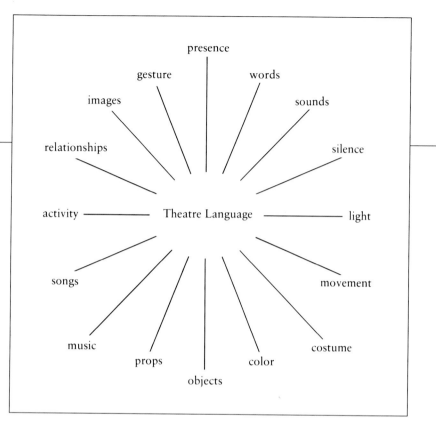

FIGURE 11.1

Theatre language, like our ways of communicating in real life, has both verbal and nonverbal characteristics. Language for the theatre is carefully selected by the playwright, actors, director, and designers. For this reason, it can be divided into the many different ways that meaning is communicated to an audience. The diagram lists sixteen ways of communicating the characters' experience, the plot and action, and the stage's living reality.

presence

gesture   words

images   sounds

relationships   silence

activity —— Theatre Language —— light

songs   movement

music   costume

props   color

objects

under such high pressure of feeling the words carry a necessary and immediate connotation of gesture. . . ."[3] Theatre language expresses not only the characters' thoughts, attitudes, and intentions, but also the *presence* of human beings in a living world. For this reason, Figure 11.1 includes along with words many other facets of theatre language.

It has been argued that the language we use for communication in real life is also multifaceted and theatrical: Our clothes are costumes, we speak words and make gestures, we carry props (bookbags or smoking pipes), we wear makeup, and we are affected by the environment's sounds and silences. Although this is true, there is an important difference between language in the theatre and in life. In the theatre, language (both verbal and nonverbal) is selected and controlled. It shapes the action. Much more must happen through conversation in the theatre than in ordinary life. Our conversations with friends are often random, purposeless, except on formal occasions. But language in the theatre is carefully arranged by playwright, actor, director, and designer in a meaningful pattern that can be repeated night after night.

Let us examine the verbal and nonverbal characteristics of theatre language.

Verbal and Nonverbal

On the page of a script, words are signs and symbols with the potential for making something happen in the theatre. When spoken by an actor, they communicate to other actors and to the audience. Besides words, other kinds of signals make up the theatre's language: sound, light, shape, movement, silence, activity, inactivity, gesture, color, music, song, objects, costumes, props, and visual images.

In communication theory, a *sign* has a direct physical relationship to the thing it represents — to its referent. Thunder is a sign of rain: It has a real physical connection with changes in the atmosphere. *Symbols* differ from signs in that they have an arbitrary connection to their referents. The American flag, for example, is a symbol of our country, and many people associate everything good in America with the flag that represents it. But during the Vietnam War, some people associated the flag with everything wrong with America (see Figure 11.2). When they wore motorcycle helmets or clothing painted with the flag, they revised its meaning. This was possible because its meaning was arbitrary — it was a symbol, not a sign. Today, the use and abuse of the American flag have become issues of legal debate, further emphasizing the flag's symbolism.

In the theatre, both verbal and nonverbal symbols and signs are used to enhance our perception of the actors' living presence. In Anton Chekhov's *The Cherry Orchard* (1904), the orchard (usually located offstage) is a verbal

symbol variously interpreted as the passing of the old way of life and/or of the coming of a new social order. Characters refer to the orchard as a family treasure, a local tradition, a beautiful object, and the means of saving the estate from auction. The orchard is symbolic of the ways Chekhov's characters deal with or fail to deal with life's demands. The sound of the ax cutting down the trees at the play's end is a nonverbal sign, communicating the destruction of the family's treasure and their way of life. But it also communicates the arrival of a *new* social order with new values and strengths. Verbal symbol and aural sign reinforce one another in communicating the play's meaning.

Examples of Theatre Language

To understand communication in the theatre, we must ask basic questions about theatre language: What do we hear? What do we see? What is taking shape before us? What growing image creates the life of the play? How does the special strength of the language help create the unique presentness of the theatre? When the various elements of theatre language are really

Anton Chekhov

Anton Pavlovich Chekhov (1860–1904) was born in southern Russia and studied medicine at Moscow University. During his student years he wrote short stories to earn money. He began his playwriting career in the 1880s with one-act farces, *The Marriage Proposal* and *The Bear*. *Ivanov* (1887) was his first full-length play to be produced.

Chekhov redefined stage realism during the years of his association with the Moscow Art Theatre (1898–1904). The meaning of his plays is not in direct, purposive action, but in the representation of a certain kind of rural Russian life, which he knew firsthand. Director Constantin Stanislavsky's style of interpreting the inner truth of Chekhov's characters and the mood of his plays resulted in one of the great theatrical collaborations.

During his last years, Chekhov lived in Yalta, where he had gone for his health, and made occasional trips to Moscow to participate in the productions. He died of tuberculosis in a German spa in 1904, soon after the production of *The Cherry Orchard*, and was buried in Moscow.

During his short life Chekhov wrote four masterpieces of modern stage realism: *The Sea Gull, Uncle Vanya, The Three Sisters, The Cherry Orchard*.

THE CHERRY ORCHARD

After some years abroad, the widowed Madame Ranevskaya returns to her Russian estate to find that it has been heavily mortgaged to pay her debts, and that it is to be auctioned. Generous and irresponsible, she seems incapable of recognizing her financial situation. A half-hearted attempt is made to collect money owed her by a neighboring landowner, but he is also in financial straits. Gaev, Madame Ranevskaya's brother, makes some suggestions, but his chief hope lies in an uncertain legacy from a relative, or a rich marriage for Anya, Madame Ranevskaya's young daughter. The only realistic proposal comes from Lopakhin, a merchant whose father was once a serf of the Ranevskaya family. He suggests cutting down the famous cherry orchard and dividing the land into plots for summer cottages. The family rejects the idea of destroying such beauty and tradition.

With no specific plan in mind for saving the estate, the family drifts aimlessly toward the day set for the auction. On the evening of the sale, Madame Ranevskaya gives a party she cannot afford. In the middle of the festivities, Lopakhin arrives; when questioned, he reveals that he has bought the estate and intends to carry out his plan for cutting down the orchard.

With the estate and orchard now sold, the family prepares to leave. Forgotten in the confusion is the old and dying Firs, the devoted family servant. As the sound of the ax rings from the orchard, he lies down to rest and is soon motionless in the empty house.

SOLILOQUY FROM HAMLET

The Shakespeare soliloquy is a stage convention for expressing a character's inner thoughts and feelings: As the actor speaks, we hear the way the character's mind works and understand those hidden thoughts that result in action. (See Figure 11.3.)

HAMLET: How all occasions do inform against me,
And spur my dull revenge! What is a man,
If his chief good and market of his time
Be but to sleep and feed? A beast, no more.
Sure, He that made us with such large discourse,
Looking before and after, gave us not
That capability and godlike reason
To fust in us unused. Now, whether it be
Bestial oblivion, or some craven scruple
Of thinking too precisely on the event,
A thought which, quartered, hath but one part wisdom
And ever three parts coward — I do not know
Why yet I live to say, "This thing's to do,"
Sith I have cause, and will, and strength, and means
To do't. Examples gross as earth exhort me.
Witness this army, of such mass and charge,
Led by a delicate and tender prince,
Whose spirit, with divine ambition puffed,
Makes mouths at the invisible event,
Exposing what is mortal and unsure
To all that fortune, death, and danger dare,
Even for an eggshell. Rightly to be great
Is not to stir without great argument,
But greatly to find a quarrel in a straw
When honor's at the stake. How stand I then,
That have a father killed, a mother stained,
Excitements of my reason and my blood,
And let all sleep, while to my shame I see
The imminent death of twenty thousand men
That for a fantasy and trick of fame
Go to their graves like beds, fight for a plot
Whereon the numbers cannot try the cause,
Which is not tomb enough and continent
To hide the slain? O, from this time forth,
My thoughts be bloody, or be nothing worth!
(4, iv)

working together, however, we do not ask these questions, for there is no time; we experience sensation, sounds, and presence, without particularly analyzing the experience. Let us consider several examples from familiar plays of theatre language's variety and immediacy.

FIGURE 11.3

The actor's language. Hamlet's costume in the final two acts is that of a man of action. He is no longer dressed in the "solemn black" of mourning, nor in the disheveled dress of his "antic disposition." In addition, the actor's speech, gestures, and movements convey the character's determination to rid Denmark of the corrupt king. Albert Finney plays Hamlet in the 1976 production at London's National Theatre.

Hamlet

The Shakespearean soliloquy is a means of taking the audience into the character's mind to see and hear its contents. In Hamlet's "How all occasions do inform against me," he begins with concern for his delayed revenge, then meditates on man's nature, and on the "thing" to be done. The precision of Hamlet's argument with himself reveals the brilliance of a mind that perceives the cause, proof, and means of revenge. The speech's length betrays the habit of mind that has delayed revenge against Claudius, filling time and space with words rather than actions. Measuring himself against his kinsman, the warrior-soldier Fortinbras, the man of action, Hamlet finds the example by which to act.

It is important that this speech is delivered as a soliloquy, for Hamlet is indeed alone in the charge from his father's ghost and in the eventual killing of Claudius.

The speech moves in thirty-five lines from inactivity to activity, concluding with: "O, from this time forth,/My thoughts be bloody, or be nothing worth!" Hamlet, the hitherto *invisible* man of action, takes shape before our eyes, ears, and minds, in sixty lines of blank verse.

Ghosts

The language of the nineteenth-century play was influenced by a theatre technology unknown in Shakespeare's day, and reflects a concern for reproducing speech appropriate to the characters' socioeconomic background

Ibsen's stage directions relate the characters' words to their physical gestures and to the stage lighting in the final scene from *Ghosts* (see Figure 11.4). His concern is to make visible the symbolic truth of the light (the sunrise illuminating the situation) and the darkness (Oswald's disease and society's repression). Ibsen's symbols are found both in dialogue and stage directions.

OSWALD: . . . And now let's live together as long as we can. Thank you, Mother.

(*He settles down in the armchair that* MRS. ALVING *had moved over to the sofa. The day is breaking; the lamp still burns on the table.*)

MRS. ALVING: Now do you feel all right?
OSWALD: Yes.
MRS. ALVING (*bending over him*): What a fearful nightmare this has been for you, Oswald — but it was all a dream. Too much excitement — it hasn't been good for you. But now you can have your rest, at home with your mother near, my own, my dearest boy. Anything you want you can have, just like when you were a little child. There now, the pain is over. You see how quickly it went. Oh, I knew it would — And look, Oswald, what a lovely day we'll have. Bright sunlight. Now you really can see your home.

(*She goes to the table and puts out the lamp. Sunrise. The glaciers and peaks in the background shine in the brilliant light of morning.*

With his back toward the distant view, OSWALD sits motionless in the armchair.*)

OSWALD (*abruptly*): Mother, give me the sun.
MRS. ALVING (*by the table, looks at him, startled*): What did you say?
OSWALD (*repeats in a dull monotone*): The sun. The sun.
MRS. ALVING (*moves over to him*): Oswald, what's the matter?

(OSWALD *appears to crumple inwardly in the chair; all his muscles loosen; the expression leaves his face; and his eyes stare blankly.*)

MRS. ALVING (*shaking with fear*): What is it? (*in a shriek*) Oswald! What's wrong! (*drops to her knees beside him and shakes him*) Oswald! Oswald! Look at me! Don't you know me?
OSWALD (*in the same monotone*): The sun — the sun.
MRS. ALVING (*springs to her feet in anguish, tears at her hair with both hands and screams*): I can't bear this! (*whispers as if paralyzed by fright*) I can't bear it! Never! (*suddenly*) Where did he put them? (*Her hand skims across his chest.*) Here! (*She shrinks back several steps and shrieks.*) No, no, no! — Yes! — No, no! (*She stands a few steps away from him, her fingers thrust into her hair, staring at him in speechless horror.*)
OSWALD (*sitting motionless, as before*): The sun — the sun.[4]

and psychological makeup. Ibsen introduces nonverbal signs and symbols in stage directions that are like descriptive passages in realistic novels.

The final scene of *Ghosts* begins with stage directions that indicate that Mrs. Alving puts out the table lamp as the sun rises. She is alone with her dying son, Oswald, who is talking about the sun. In Ibsen's play the *sun* (also a play on the word *son*) is a symbol for the *truth* about the secrets of the past.

Oswald is seated in a chair facing the audience, and we see the change that comes over him. As Oswald slumps into the immobile state of the catatonically ill, Mrs. Alving's truth is made visible. She has not eradicated the ghosts of the past, and she is faced with a terrible choice in the present:

FIGURE 11.4

In a final scene of Ghosts, *Oswald tells his mother about his mysterious disease, and she reveals to him its cause: the kind of corrupt life his father really led. The Stratford, Ontario, Shakespeare Festival Theatre production (1977) featured Margaret Tyzack and Nicholas Pennell.*

to give Oswald drugs that will kill him, or to permit him to live. Ibsen's language reflects Mrs. Alving's horror over the truth and her indecision. Using monosyllables, Ibsen indicates the choice Mrs. Alving will make. Five "no's," indicating that she can't give Oswald the drug, are placed against the one "yes." The repressiveness of nineteenth-century society that has dictated Mrs. Alving's principal life decisions becomes visible in her frantic inability to speak or to act.

Light, gesture, movement, physical relationships—in addition to the spoken word—help convey the play's meaning. The background lighting effect ("the sun rises") reinforces the truth of Mrs. Alving's tragic dilemma: The visual design is repeated in Oswald's words "the sun." Truth and light have come too late for them.

The Cherry Orchard

Chekhov ends *The Cherry Orchard* with language that also combines verbal and nonverbal effects: sounds with silence, words with noise, inactivity with activity.

Firs is the elderly valet left behind by the family in their hurried departure from the estate that has been sold at auction. His last speech is placed

FIGURE 11.5

At The Cherry Orchard*'s end, Firs, the old valet, lies down alone — the final symbol of the passing of a way of life. This visual image of the dying man is reinforced by the sound of a breaking string. Finally, the sounds of ax strokes suggest the arrival of a vital force taking over from the old. This scene was staged by director Andrei Serban in the 1977 New York Shakespeare Festival production at Lincoln Center, New York.*

between stage directions suggesting offstage sounds of departure, of a breaking string, and of the stroke of an ax. The *pauses* in Firs' speech indicate the ending of a life and also of a way of life. The fact that he is alone, locked in the house, forgotten and dying, tells us more vividly that "life has passed him by" than his saying it.

In Chekhov's plays, what people do — their gestures — is frequently more important than what they say. Like gesture, the abstract sound of the breaking string in the distance juxtaposed against the immediate sound of the ax is more important than the character's words. Even the order of the sound effects is important. The breaking string's mournful sound, symbolic of the release of tensions and the passing of a way of life, subsides into silence *before* the ax stroke, the sound of the aggressive new order, intrudes on the scene. At the end of *The Cherry Orchard*, the audience hears and sees a world in transition (see Figure 11.5).

In the modern theatre, stage directions have become important means by which playwrights communicate imaginative worlds to directors, actors, and designers. In the final scene of *The Cherry Orchard*, Chekhov describes the stage's appearance; Firs' costume, manner, and words; and the final powerful sounds.

(They go out. The stage is empty. We hear the doors being locked. The carriages leave. It becomes very quiet. There is only the muffled sound of an ax hitting a tree, a lonely and sad sound. Some steps. Firs appears at the door on the right. He is dressed as usual in a frock coat, a white vest, and slippers. He is sick.)

FIRS: *(Going to the door, turning the handle.)* It's locked. They're gone . . . *(He sits on the couch.)*

they've forgotten me. It doesn't matter . . . I'll rest here. I'm sure Leonid Andreyevich didn't put on his fur coat; he's gone out in his thin overcoat. *(He sighs anxiously.)* And I didn't watch him . . . ach, still like a child . . . *(He mutters some words which we cannot understand.)* so life has gone by now . . . and it seems I still haven't lived. *(He lies down on the couch.)* I'm going to lie down for a while. You have no more strength, nothing left in you . . . nothing . . . ah, go on, you nincompoop . . . good for nothing . . . *(He remains lying down, not moving. In the distance, as if from the sky, there is the sound of a snapped string, a melancholy sound which dies away little by little. Then silence, we hear only the sound of the axes against the trees, far away in the orchard.)*[5]

Brecht's "Epic" Language: *The Caucasian Chalk Circle*

Brecht includes music, songs, placards, film projections, and *gest* in his theatre language. Brecht's concept of gest or gestic language is a matter of the actors' overall attitude to what is going on around them and what they are asked to do on stage (see Figures 9.9 and 11.6). Brecht insisted that words follow the gest of the person speaking.

"Gest" is not supposed to mean gesticulation: it is not a matter of explanatory or emphatic movements of the hands, but of overall attitudes. A language is gestic when it is grounded in a gest and conveys particular attitudes adopted by the speaker towards other men. The sentence "pluck the eye that offends thee out" is less effective from the gestic point of view than "if thine eye offend thee, pluck it out." The latter starts by presenting the eye, and the first clause has the definite gest of making an assumption; the main clause then comes as a surprise, a piece of advice, and a relief.[6]

The characters' gestic language becomes visible in the test of the chalk circle. The materialistic attitudes of the lawyers and the governor's wife toward the child are contrasted with Grusha's humanitarian feelings. Grusha refuses to tug at the child, while the governor's wife pulls the child twice out of the circle. The wife's attitudes, words, and gestures betray the fact that her access to wealth and power depends on the return of the child to her. We see that she is selfish and "grasping."

Brecht used music and song as well as dialogue to express characters' thoughts and feelings. The narrator in *The Caucasian Chalk Circle* (scene vi) sings the girl's thoughts as a means of expressing, without becoming sentimental, Grusha's love for the child.

THE SINGER: Hear now what the angry woman thought and did not say:
(*Sings*)
If he walked in golden shoes
Cold his heart would be and stony.
Humble folk he would abuse
He wouldn't know me.
Oh, it's hard to be hard-hearted
All day long from morn to night.
To be mean and high and mighty
Is a hard and cruel plight.
Let him be afraid of hunger
Not of the hungry man's spite
Let him be afraid of darkness
But not fear the light.[7]

FIGURE 11.6

Brecht's gestic language. The circle drawn in white chalk on the stage signifies a test of true motherliness and rightful ownership based on mutual interests and well-being. The governor's wife (left) and Grusha pull at the child as Judge Azdak looks on in the 1965 pro-duction of The Caucasian Chalk Circle *at the Guth-rie Theater. Grusha (Zoe Caldwell) releases the child before harming him.*

Brecht's working notes call for musicians to be included on stage. A narrator interrupts the play's action to sing songs that pinpoint social atti-tudes and wrongs. A song is sung to reveal what Grusha *thinks* but does not say. As the narrator sings Grusha's thoughts, Brecht allows us to un-derstand, without sentiment, Grusha's selfless concern for the child.

Chekhov's Theatre Language in Modern Performance

The New York Shakespeare Festival Theatre opened a production of Chekhov's play *The Cherry Orchard* on February 17, 1977, at the Vivian Beaumont Theatre, Lincoln Center. It was directed by Andrei Serban and designed by Santo Loquasto. Influenced by Peter Brook, Serban builds a production from movement, myths, and sounds. For this reason his work is sometimes called "theatre of ritual." It involves the use of carefully posed sculptural groups, choreographic masses of people, and a specific acting style.

    Designer Loquasto's basically white setting and draped furniture create a sculptural effect as Irene Worth (as Madame Ranevskaya, center) rejoices over the cherry trees in full blossom.

In *The Three Sisters*, 1983, at the American Repertory Theatre, Cambridge, scenic designer Beni Montresor created a playing space with mirrored floor, massive red velvet curtains in the rear, and banks of footlights on either side of the floor. The Prozorov house becomes a stage within a stage where Chekhov's "poor players" strut and fret away their hours. Director Andrei Serban heightens the actors' energy to show people living to the hilt. Masha (Cheryl Giannini) twirls alone to a Chopin mazurka. All engage frantically in the dance, creating a striking visual image of people trying to forget, to avoid, the inevitability of their lives.

A scene from *The Cherry Orchard* staged by Peter Brook at the Brooklyn Academy of Music in 1981. Here, Natasha Parry (center) as Madame Ranevskaya sits with her companions on the large carpet that was the production's visual centerpiece.

Director Peter Stein at the Schaubühne am Lehniner Platz, West Berlin, 1984, staged the ending of *The Three Sisters* so that the empty house, the trunks and valises, the dilapidated fence, the encompassing trees with open space beyond make a visual statement about leavetaking. Vershinin (O. Sander), standing apart, takes his farewell of Olga (Edith Clever), Anfisa (John Hofer), the elderly nurse, and Irina (Corinna Kirchhoff). The total stage picture communicates parting, nostalgia, and change.

The body language of Chekhov's "three sisters," as directed by Liviu Ciulei, at the Guthrie Theatre, 1984, shows their physical and emotional isolation. The women — Joan MacIntosh as Masha, Frances McDormand as Irina, and Trish Hawkins as Olga — are frozen in a tableau against the darkness of the trees in the background and the emptiness of the foreground. Director Ciulei has captured in both his scenic design and staging, more than in Chekhov's words, the sisters' grief and aloneness in the play's final moments.

267

New Trends

French playwright and theatre theorist Antonin Artaud (1896–1948), one prophet of the new theatre, militated against traditional dialogue that furthers plot and reveals character. He favored inducing in audiences a shock reaction and a visceral response. He called for a "theatre of cruelty" to purge the audience's feelings of hatred, violence, and cruelty through use of nonverbal effects: sounds, lighting, unusual theatre spaces, violent movements. Artaud wanted to assault the audience's senses, to cleanse us morally and spiritually, for the improvement of humankind. Followers of Artaud, like Peter Brook, have taken theatre language in two directions, toward *violent images* and toward *physicalization*.

Violent Images in *Marat/Sade*

Peter Brook's 1965 production of *Marat/Sade* for the Royal Shakespeare Company played up the grimness of Peter Weiss' play. The opening scenes confront the audience with violent images and sounds of life in a nineteenth-century asylum that communicate viscerally more than intellectually. A quartet of inmates wearing colored sacks sings sardonic songs while the action described by the songs is mimed by other inmates. Some inmates wear shapeless white tunics and straitjackets to contrast with the formal nineteenth-century costumes of de Sade, the asylum director, and his family. The verbal debate between Jean-Paul Marat and the Marquis de Sade is repeatedly interrupted by the lunatics acting out Marat's story and their own passions. In the mass guillotining sequence, inmates make metallic rasping noises and pour buckets of paint — blood — down drains, while other inmates jump into a pit in the center of the stage so that their heads are piled above stage level, next to the guillotine.

Marat/Sade uses shock to make its point. Marat, the political idealist committed to violent social reform (played by a naked asylum inmate seated in a bathtub; see Figure 11.7), and the Marquis de Sade, the skeptic committed to anarchic individualism, debate the value of revolution during one of de Sade's theatrical productions. For de Sade, humanity, not the

FIGURE 11.7

Jean-Paul Marat, the social reformer (played by Ian Richardson in the Peter Brook production) debates the importance of violent revolution while an asylum inmate (Susan Williamson) attends to his skin disease.

political or economic system, is the root of all social evil. He argues, therefore, that revolution is futile and merely perpetuates violence. To make his point that the guillotine—the Revolution's tool—made dying wholesale and meaningless, de Sade describes the four-hour execution of Damiens, King Louis XV's would-be assassin. Damiens' death, for de Sade, is an example of significant individual suffering lost in the impersonal mass deaths of the guillotine.

Words are only one vehicle for the visceral impact of Weiss' language. The verbal images that describe Damiens' violent death are reinforced by the starkness of the white bathhouse where the performance of de Sade's play takes place. The onstage sexual and physical violence of the inmates — Charlotte Corday stabs Marat to death in his bathtub and the inmates revolt against their keepers—blends image and gesture, words and actions, into a total theatrical effect.

Peter Weiss' concrete verbal images of torture and death express de Sade's attitudes toward human corruption and unreason. The actor playing de Sade can also express, by luxuriating in the vowel sounds, how the witnesses to the execution luxuriated in the spectacle of Damiens' death. By doing so, the actor's word-sounds have a visceral effect on the audience.

DE SADE (*to Marat*):
Let me remind you of the execution of Damiens
after his unsuccessful attempt to assassinate
Louis the Fifteenth (now deceased)
Remember how Damiens died
How gentle the guillotine is
compared with his torture
It lasted four hours while the crowd goggled
and Casanova at an upper window
felt under the skirts of the ladies watching

    [*pointing in the direction of the tribunal
    where* COULMIER *sits*]

His chest arms thighs and calves were slit open
Molten lead was poured into each slit
boiling oil they poured over him burning tar
    wax sulphur
They burnt off his hands
tied ropes to his arms and legs
harnessed four horses to him and geed them up
They pulled at him for an hour but they'd never
    done it before
and he wouldn't come apart
until they sawed through his shoulders and hips

So he lost the first arm then the second
and he watched what they did to him and then
    turned to us
and shouted so everyone could understand
And when they tore off the first leg and then the
    second leg
he still lived though his voice was getting weak
and at the end he hung there a bloody torso
    with a nodding head
just groaning and staring at the crucifix
which the father confessor was holding up
    to him

    [*In the background a half-murmured litany
    is heard*.]

That
was a festival with which
today's festivals can't compete
Even our inquisition gives us no pleasure
nowadays
Although we've only just started
there's no passion in our post-revolutionary
    murders
Now they are all official
We condemn to death without emotion
and there's no singular personal death to be had
only an anonymous cheapened death
which we could dole out to entire nations
on a mathematical basis
until the time comes
for all life
to be extinguished[8]

The Open Theatre

In the late 1960s and early 1970s, language took on new characteristics in the American theatre. In many workshops and productions by groups such as the Living Theatre and the Open Theatre, ordinary stage dialogue, or the text, was replaced by two basic kinds of physical work: exercises in *sound-and-movement* and *character transformation*. The work of the Open Theatre, Joseph Chaikin's group, involved actors, directors, playwrights, and sometimes audiences to develop theatre pieces using physicalization to convey situation, relationships, character, sound, and action. The group

Joseph Chaikin

Joseph Chaikin (b. 1935), American actor and director, founded the Open Theatre in New York City in 1963 after working with the Living Theatre for three years. Among works that he directed or co-directed for the Open Theatre were *America Hurrah!*, *Viet Rock*, *The Serpent*, *Terminal*, *The Mutation Show*, and *Nightwalk*. In 1972 he published *The Presence of the Actor*, notes on his work with the Open Theatre.

From 1963 to 1973 the Open Theatre was a leading experimental company, engaging actors and playwrights in a group effort to explore questions about acting, audience, and performance. It was a "poor theatre," putting aside all such nonessentials as costume, makeup, scenery, and properties. The emphasis was on the actor, as well as contemporary political and social problems. After ten years the group disbanded, largely to avoid becoming an "institution."

Since then, Chaikin has directed *The Sea Gull* (1975), acted in *Woyzeck* (1976) and *Endgame* (1980), and has renewed interest in the "written theatre." He co-authored (with Sam Shepard) *Tongues* and *Savage/Love* (1978–79) and created *Texts* (1981) with Steve Kent, an adaptation of Beckett's *Texts For Nothing* and *How It Is*. *Imagining the Other* (1982), a political theatre piece developed in the Middle East, was staged in Israel.

celebrated the notion of the work-in-progress and formulated as their theatrical signature the actor in transformation from one role to another — before the audience's eyes.

Under Chaikin's leadership, the Open Theatre evolved a "physical" theatre language: exercises, sound, movement, silence, improvised situations, words, images, transformations. The group members' backgrounds, interests, training, and lifestyles were put to use in workshop performances. Writers participated in the workshops before writing anything down — their scripts were related to the group's improvisations, from which they selected the most effective work within a social or political context. The scripts were usually performed by the same actors who had been in the workshops. Jean-Claude van Itallie, Megan Terry, and María Irene Fornés wrote most consistently with the Open Theatre during those years. In a special 1977 issue of *The Drama Review* on playwriting, van Itallie talked about writing for the theatre as the expression of a new way of seeing. He said:

> A play is the expression of a new way of seeing, not only because you've decided to see things in a new way, but because you are seeing something clearly, being who you are right then. There's a discrepancy between your

point of view and the way that, say, the audience is accustomed to seeing. It's called "new" more by them than by you. You have to find the language with which to express the particular vision you have of ordinary reality. It may seem to you to be absolute common sense and obvious, but often the more obvious it seems to you, the more "new" it will seem to the world.[9]

Chaikin developed two performance techniques that later came to be known as "Open Theatre techniques": *sound-and-movement*, in which the actor developed physical movements and sounds to communicate emotions, and character *transformation*, in which the actor switched from one identity to another without establishing motivation or a realistic transition. "Image plays" were the results of these techniques. Each play presented an image or series of images coordinated by a central theme or idea. The literal meanings of spoken words were of relatively minor importance. Communication with the audience depended on the effectiveness of the actor's sound-and-movement patterns and the transformational roles. Chaikin's basic strategy was to *make things visible in action*. His questions, subjects, and ideas were not talked through but acted out by the group — physicalized.

In *Interview*, one of three short plays produced as *America Hurrah!* (1966; see Figure 11.8), Chaikin's group with playwright van Itallie re-created the mechanical behavior, isolation, and depersonalization of urban America. *Interview* begins and ends with automatic questions: What's your name? What job do you want? What experience have you had? How many years' experience? Age? Dependents? Social Security number?, and so on. A typical interview begins and ends the play. In the middle are short scenes revealing the sounds and rhythms of people's lives: a telephone switchboard operator, cocktail party loner, analyst's patient.

Interview's essential language, like that of most Open Theatre pieces, is:

- ▼ *Physicalization* — actors mime the action of electronic circuitry.

- ▼ *Basic scene ideas and images* — job interview, psychiatrist's couch.

- ▼ *Transformations* — the interviewer becomes a telephone operator who becomes a party loner.

FIGURE 11.8
Interview *was produced as part of* America Hurrah! *(Pocket Theatre, New York, 1966) on a bare stage with gray lighting. Wearing nondescript clothing, the actors worked in a depersonalized space with modules (a set of boxes) as furniture and props. The sparseness and colorlessness of the stage reinforce the playwright's statement about the quality of urban American life.*

- *Sounds* (by humans rather than a sound system) — actors make the sounds of ambulance sirens, subway noises, hum of telephone circuits.

- *Visual and aural images* — of social behavior in the America of the 1960s.

- *Masks* — to capture expressionless and anonymous lives.

- *Words and phrases* — brief sounds and movements repeated a number of times to label social types.

   Interview is an example of theatre language that makes a whole way of life visible through actors' physical and vocal techniques.

In *Interview*, playwright Jean-Claude van Itallie writes into the stage directions the various characters that the actors become (Third Interviewer, Telephone Operator, and so on). He also describes the sounds-and-movements that the actors must improvise to resemble telephone circuits and their sounds.

(The actress who played the Third Interviewer slips out of the subway as though it were her stop and sits on a box, stage right, as a Telephone Operator. The other actors form a telephone circuit by holding hands in two concentric circles around the boxes, stage left; they change the hissing sound of the subway into the whistling of telephone circuits.)

TELEPHONE OPERATOR: Just one moment I will connect you with Information.

(The Telephone Operator alternates her official voice with her ordinary voice; she uses the latter when she talks to her friend Roberta, another operator whom she reaches by flipping a switch. When she is talking to Roberta, the whistling of the telephone circuits changes into a different rhythm and the arms of the actors, which are forming the circuit, move into a different position.)

TELEPHONE OPERATOR: Just one moment and I will connect you with Information. Ow! Listen, Roberta, I said, I've got this terrible cramp. Hang up and dial again, please; we find nothing wrong with that number at all. You know what I ate, I said to her, you were there. Baked macaroni, Wednesday special, maple-nut fudge, I said. I'm sorry but the number you have reached is not — I can feel it gnawing at me at the bottom of my belly, I told her. Do you think it's serious, Roberta? Appendicitis? I asked. Thank you for giving us the area code but the number you have reached is not in this area. Roberta, I asked her, do you think I have cancer? One moment, please. I'm sorry the number you have reached — ow! Well, if it's lunch, Roberta, I said to her, you know what they can do with it tomorrow. Ow! One moment, please, I said. Ow, I said, Roberta, I said, it really hurts.

(The Telephone Operator falls off her seat in pain. The whistling of the telephone circuit becomes a siren. Three actors carry the Telephone Operator over to the boxes, stage left, which now serve as an operating table. Three actors imitate the Telephone Operator's breathing pattern while four actors behind her make stylized sounds and movements as surgeons and nurses in the midst of an operation. The Telephone Operator's breathing accelerates, then stops. After a moment the actors begin spreading over the stage and making the muted sounds of a cocktail party: music, laughter, talk. The actors find a position and remain there, playing various aspects of a party in slow motion and muted tones. They completely ignore the First Interviewer who, as a Girl At The Party, goes from person to person as if she were in a garden of living statues.)[10]

Language and the "New" Realism

By the 1970s, the experiments of the collectives, like the Open Theatre, had worked themselves into a dead end of one sort or another. Political consciousness was largely dissipated with the end of the Vietnam War; the "new" performance techniques had become stale and predictable, and

John Osborne

John Osborne (b. 1929 in London) is both playwright and film writer. Osborne was a little-known actor in repertory companies before he made his debut in 1956 as a playwright with *Look Back in Anger* (a film version appeared in 1958). The play established Osborne as the most important of the "angry young men." He quickly followed this play with *The Entertainer* (with Laurence Olivier), *Luther* (with Albert Finney), and *Inadmissible Evidence* (with Nicol Williamson), consolidating his reputation.

In 1958 Osborne became co-director of the Woodfall film company for which he wrote the screenplay of *Tom Jones* (1962), also starring Albert Finney. His later plays have been produced at the Royal Court and also at the National Theatre. His more recent ones include *A Patriot for Me* (1965), *West of Suez* (1971), and *Watch It Come Down* (1976). Osborne's *A Better Class of Person: An Autobiography 1929–1956* (1981) describes his childhood and early struggles in the theatre; it ends with the optioning of *Look Back in Anger* for the English Stage Company.

the games and transformations had been appropriated by the commercial theatre as *Hair* (1968) and *A Chorus Line* (1975) moved onto Broadway. Groups made decisions to break up (the Open Theatre) or collapsed completely (the Performance Group). Individuals, like Chaikin, chose to work as actors or directors with more structured theatres and texts. In the '70s, the written text with recognizable characters and plots was in again.

The importance of the written text was reasserted in 1956 in Britain by John Osborne in *Look Back in Anger*. What distinguished Osborne's play (and was to influence the work of an entire generation of British playwrights) was its social content and savage dialogue. But scenically, Osborne's play returned to old-fashioned realism: a one-room flat with a double bed, bookshelves, a chest of drawers, a gas stove, cupboard, ironing board, dining table and chairs, and two shabby armchairs.

Osborne's Language of Rage

Look Back in Anger deals with a postwar generation of young, disaffected working-class characters. Jimmy Porter represented a generation who became disillusioned, sullen, and full of rage when a "brave new world" failed to materialize. Osborne's dialogue is the "smart" language of post-World War II youth, detached in its rejection of politics, social movements, and the arts. Osborne's language does not represent ideas shared among people;

Jimmy Porter's opening diatribe in Osborne's *Look Back in Anger* took audiences by surprise in 1956. Jimmy's savage rage shocked and offended the average London theatregoer. *Look Back in Anger* was the first modern British play to express the feelings of a postwar generation. Osborne's characters turned their backs on the middle-class world, with its values of work, getting ahead, and suburban life. These city dwellers rage at a world they neither made nor asked to be brought into. In their defiantly shabby one-room flats they lash out at each other because "There aren't any good, brave causes left. . . ."

JIMMY PORTER: Nobody thinks, nobody cares. No beliefs, no convictions and no enthusiasm. Just another Sunday evening.

Cliff sits down again, in his pullover and shorts.

Perhaps there's a concert on. (*Picks up* Radio Times.) Ah. (*Nudges Cliff with his foot.*) Make some more tea.

Cliff grunts. He is reading again.

Oh, yes. There's a Vaughan Williams. Well, that's something, anyway. Something strong, something simple, something English. I suppose people like me aren't supposed to be very patriotic. Somebody said — what was it — we get our cooking from Paris (that's a laugh), our politics from Moscow, and our morals from Port Said. Something like that, anyway. Who was it? (*Pause.*) Well, you wouldn't know anyway. I hate to admit it, but I think I can understand how her Daddy must have felt when he came back from India, after all those years away. The old Edwardian brigade do make their brief little world look pretty tempting. All homemade cakes and croquet, bright ideas, bright uniforms. Always the same picture: high summer, the long days in the sun, slim volumes of verse, crisp linen, the smell of starch. What a romantic picture. Phoney too, of course. It must have rained sometimes. Still, even I regret it somehow, phoney or not. If you've no world of your own, it's rather pleasant to regret the passing of someone else's. I must be getting sentimental. But I must say it's pretty dreary living in the American Age — unless you're an American of course. Perhaps all our children will be Americans. That's a thought isn't it? . . ."

it consists mainly of Jimmy Porter's taunting, savage, and uncompromising stream-of-consciousness monologues on his wife's upper-class family and other subjects.

Osborne has been followed by such playwrights as Harold Pinter, Edward Bond, Howard Brenton, David Hare, and Caryl Churchill. These playwrights construct texts out of savage, taunting language; their characters, neglected by parents and society, have been transformed into inarticulate, violent people who claw, maim, kill, and survive. In Bond's most notorious play, *Saved* (1965), the characters are restless, aimless young people — products of their urban environment — resentful of their ineffectual and selfish parents (see Figure 11.9). Bond uses realistic lower-class speech to deal with the theme of the corruption of natural innocence by "upbringing and environment."

Author of *The Birthday Party, The Caretaker, The Homecoming,* and *Old Times,* Harold Pinter creates a brand of ambiguous realism by injecting

FIGURE 11.9

The notorious "stoning" scene in Edward Bond's Saved, *directed by William Gaskill, staged by the English Stage Company at the Royal Court Theatre, London, in 1965. The play was initially banned from the stage by the Lord Chamberlain for its language and for its depiction of the stoning of a baby in its pram. Clearly, Bond had found a frightful stage image to bring the atrocities — the bombing of Dresden, concentration camps, My Lai, Rumania's mass graves — perpetrated by civilized society closer to home.*

pauses and silences into fairly innocuous dialogue. These "word-gaps" are clues to the tensions and fears, doubts and uncertainties, that Pinter's characters experience. Words and even silences are used as weapons to protect themselves from the hostility and coerciveness of others. Of his use of ambiguous speech and situations, Pinter has said that we cannot understand other people; we cannot even understand ourselves; and the truth of any situation is almost always beyond our grasp. If this is true in life, why should it not be true in the theatre?[12]

Exactly ten years after *Look Back in Anger* opened in London, Sam Shepard wrote his first play. He is now part of a third postwar wave of American writers that includes David Mamet, Lanford Wilson, David Rabe, Marsha Norman, Ntozake Shange, August Wilson, and many others. All have tested the American character, family, and dreams, and found them wanting. Shepard's most recent plays — *Buried Child, True West, Fool for Love,* and *A Lie of the Mind* — take audiences into the inner workings of modern American family life, using bizarre verbal and nonverbal language in a carefully structured, carefully written text. Recognizable places and events are twisted and warped by sexually explicit language and acts of gratuitous violence. The lives of Shepard's characters are filled with incidents of murder, adultery, incest, and mutilation. In Shepard's Pulitzer

In Act I of Sam Shepard's *Buried Child*, Halie enters and discovers the corn (and husks) that her son Tilden has brought into the living room. Dodge, the husband and father, is a husk of his former self, emptied of his potency and usefulness by age, sickness, and guilt. He remains indoors, ill, isolated from the soil that holds his crime: child murder.

> *She stops abruptly and stares at the corn husks. She looks around the space as though just waking up. She turns and looks hard at* TILDEN *and* DODGE *who continue sitting calmly. She looks at the corn husks.*

HALIE: (*pointing to the husks*) What's this in my house! (*kicks husks*) What's all this!

TILDEN *stops husking and stares at her.*

HALIE: (*to* DODGE) And you encourage him!

DODGE *pulls blanket over him again.*

DODGE: You're going out in the rain?

HALIE: It's not raining.

TILDEN *starts husking again.*

DODGE: Not in Florida it's not.

HALIE: We're not in Florida!

DODGE: It's not raining at the race track.

HALIE: Have you been taking those pills? Those pills always make you talk crazy. Tilden, has he been taking those pills?

TILDEN: He hasn't took anything.

HALIE: (*to* DODGE) What've you been taking?

DODGE: It's not raining in California or Florida or the race track, only in Illinois. This is the only place it's raining. All over the rest of the world it's bright sunshine.

HALIE *goes to the night table next to the sofa and checks the bottle of pills.*

HALIE: Which one did you take? Tilden, you must've seen him take something.

TILDEN: He never took a thing.

HALIE: Then why's he talking crazy?

TILDEN: I've been here the whole time.

HALIE: Then you've both been taking something!

TILDEN: I've just been husking the corn.

HALIE: Where'd you get that corn anyway? Why is the house suddenly full of corn?

DODGE: Bumper crop!

HALIE: (*moving center*) We haven't had corn here for over thirty years.

TILDEN: The whole back lot's full of corn. Far as the eye can see.

DODGE: (*to* HALIE) Things keep happening while you're upstairs, ya know. The world doesn't stop just because you're upstairs. Corn keeps growing. Rain keeps raining.

HALIE: I'm not unaware of the world around me! Thank you very much. It so happens that I have an over-all view from the upstairs. The back yard's in plain view of my window. And there's no corn to speak of. Absolutely none!

DODGE: Tilden wouldn't lie. If he says there's corn, there's corn.

Prize winner *Buried Child* (1978), for example, carrots as phallic symbols are sliced up on stage with malicious energy, an amputee is robbed of his artificial leg, an old man's head is brutally shaved with an electric razor, and a baby's skeleton is brought on stage (see Figure 11.10).

Shepard's characters are all searching out their personal histories that might explain who they are and how they came to be that way. The central action of *Buried Child* is the grandson Vincent's quest for his roots and identity. Shepard is writing here within the mainstream of Western drama, from Sophocles' *Oedipus the King* to Edward Albee's *Who's Afraid of Virginia Woolf?* The grandson returns to his family, who live in a Midwestern

HALIE: What's the meaning of this corn Tilden!
TILDEN: It's a mystery to me. I was out in back there. And the rain was coming down. And I didn't feel like coming back inside. I didn't feel the cold so much. I didn't mind the wet. So I was just walking. I was muddy but I didn't mind the mud so much. And I looked up. And I saw this stand of corn. In fact I was standing in it. So, I was standing in it.
HALIE: There isn't any corn outside Tilden! There's no corn! Now, you must've either stolen this corn or you bought it.
DODGE: He doesn't have any money.
HALIE: (to TILDEN) So you stole it!
TILDEN: I didn't steal it. I don't want to get kicked out of Illinois. I was kicked out of New Mexico and I don't want to get kicked out of Illinois.
HALIE: You're going to get kicked out of this house, Tilden, if you don't tell me where you got that corn!

> TILDEN starts crying softly to himself but keeps husking corn. Pause.

DODGE: (to HALIE) Why'd you have to tell him that? Who cares where he got the corn? Why'd you have to go and tell him that?
HALIE: (to DODGE) It's your fault you know! You're the one that's behind all this! I suppose you thought it'd be funny! Some joke! Cover the house with corn husks. You better get this cleaned up before Bradley sees it.

DODGE: Bradley's not getting in the front door!
HALIE: (kicking husks, striding back and forth) Bradley's going to be very upset when he sees this. He doesn't like to see the house in disarray. He can't stand it when one thing is out of place. The slightest thing. You know how he gets.
DODGE: Bradley doesn't even live here!
HALIE: It's his home as much as ours. He was born in this house!
DODGE: He was born in a hog wallow.
HALIE: Don't you say that! Don't you ever say that!
DODGE: He was born in a goddamn hog wallow! That's where he was born and that's where he belongs! He doesn't belong in this house!
HALIE: (she stops) I don't know what's come over you, Dodge. I don't know what in the world's come over you. You've become an evil man. You used to be a good man.
DODGE: Six of one, a half a dozen of another.
HALIE: You sit here day and night, festering away! Decomposing! Smelling up the house with your putrid body! Hacking your head off til all hours of the morning! Thinking up mean, evil, stupid things to say about your own flesh and blood!
DODGE: He's not my flesh and blood! My flesh and blood's buried in the back yard!

> They freeze. Long pause. The men stare at her.[13]

farmhouse, to find out who he is. The past, once so promising, is filled with horror: one son killed in a gangland murder; a baby born of incest drowned; another son maimed in a chainsaw accident. Without the touchstones of normal family life and friendship, Shepard's characters live in a world that is indifferent to their betrayal, guilt, and violence. The family is locked together in mutual dependence, caring for the sick and looking after the physically and psychologically lame. But these are surface, automatic gestures. The characters do not really care about one another. Hostile and ineffectual, they assert themselves in the present with violence, for the past has too many hidden meanings.

FIGURE 11.10
In Buried Child, *New York, 1978, Bradley (Jay Sanders, right) is threatened with his own artificial leg by Vincent (Christopher McCann). Shelly (Mary McDonnell), Vincent's girlfriend, looks on.*

Summary

Language in the theatre is not merely the spoken word, although we tend to equate theatre language with words and words with the playwright's text, meaning, and message. But theatre is not a philosophical treatise or critical essay. It is a means of participating in a *universal way of seeing*.

In the theatre we are subjected to sounds, silences, images, and other people. All contribute to the overall illusion that life is taking place before us. These images may be familiar, strange, or fantastic. Oedipus' bleeding eyes, Oswald's likeness to his father, Marat's skin disease, and Bradley's artificial leg are *visible* images of certain kinds of experiences.

One critic says: "Theatre is the art of the self-evident, of what everybody knows — the place where *things mean what they sound and look like they mean*."[14] At the end of *The Cherry Orchard* Chekhov's meaning *is* the sound of the breaking string, for a way of life is dying even as noises from the new order are rapidly encroaching on the scene. In *The Three Sisters* the fading sounds of the briskly tuneful military band underscore the hopeless isolation of the sisters in their situation.

Chekhov, like most playwrights, shows us that theatre does not communicate images and aliveness through words alone. As Ionesco says, "Words are only one member of theatre's shock troops."[15] In the next chapter we will think about how to visualize all of theatre's "shock troops" in the mind's eye as we read a script.

Questions for Study

1. Study Figure 11.1. What aspects of theatre language communicate meaning to us?

2. What is a *sign*? Why is a sign important in the theatre?

3. What is the function of a *soliloquy*?

4. Read the section from *Ghosts* on page 260 and comment on Ibsen's use of lighting, movement, properties, and sentence structure. What are the characteristics of Ibsen's realistic language?

5. What nonverbal language does Chekhov use in the final stage direction of *The Cherry Orchard*?

6. What is an example of Brecht's *gestic* language?

7. What were two trends in language for the "new" theatre of the '60s?

8. How does Peter Weiss achieve a visceral impact with language in *Marat/Sade*?

9. Study the excerpt from *Interview* on page 274. How does the language of *Interview* communicate to us the mechanical quality of modern American life?

10. What do the following terms mean: *physicalization, sound-and-movement* exercises, *character transformation*?

11. What is the impact of the torrential monologue spoken by John Osborne's "angry young man" in *Look Back in Anger*?

12. How does Sam Shepard use verbal and nonverbal effects to reveal the degeneration of American character, values, and family life?

13. *Plays to Read*: John Osborne's *Look Back in Anger*, Sam Shepard's *Buried Child*, Jean-Claude van Itallie's *Interview*.

BARNARDO: Who's there?
FRANCISCO: Nay, answer me. Stand and
unfold yourself.
HAMLET, 1, i

As readers we must "see" the script being performed in our mind's eye and ear. It takes a special skill to bring characters, settings, words, and events to life as we read the printed page. With this practiced skill, we can read a script and hold an imprint of it — an afterimage — in our imaginations.

Chapter 12

Visualizing the Script

When Anton Chekhov was asked about the meaning of life, he replied, "It is the same as asking what is a carrot. A carrot is a carrot, and that's all that's known."[1] In life, unless the circumstances are extreme and arresting, we ordinarily do not ask ourselves what a certain event or accident *means*. We simply respond to and flow with our experiences. But when we see or read a play, we frequently do the reverse. We ask *what it means*, forgetting that theatre is theatre and not philosophy, literature, psychology, or history, although it may include some of each.

Like Chekhov's carrot, the theatre does not mean, but *is*. As we read the script of a play, although we are dealing with words on a printed page, we must go beyond asking what they mean. We must "see" them in our imagination taking place as a performance — as theatre. We must *hear* the words spoken by the actors, as well as the music and special sounds; *observe* the events' shape and dynamics; and *see* the visual elements of scenery, lighting, costume, and properties. Like the two guards at the beginning of *Hamlet*, we must as we read ask "Who's there?" as the play unfolds before us.

What follows is a discussion of six tools for seeing and hearing the script in our mind's eye as theatre.

A Model

How do we use our imagination to see and hear a script enacted on stage? It helps to think of the script as a blueprint composed of words, people, images, and objects of light, sound, and movement that set forth the performance's emotional, intellectual, and graphic values. These values can be divided into six components: imagined human activity, space, character, purpose (or concept), organization, and performance style.

- ▼ *Human Activity* Imaginative material (composed of human behavior) for actors to work with as individuals and in groups.

- ▼ *Space* Specifications as to the nature or configuration of the performance space or environment.

- ▼ *Character* Communication of patterns of behavior based on language, dress, gesture, attitudes, sound, and movement.

- ▼ *Purpose* The concept behind the action; the writer's intentions, strategies, and solutions.

- ▼ *Organization* The sequence or shape of incidents, including plot and structure, that makes the concept visible.

- ▼ *Performance Style* The visual, physical, and aural projection of the play's inner nature.[2]

Let us examine these six components as they appear in *The Trojan Women, Hamlet, Tartuffe, The Cherry Orchard, A Streetcar Named Desire,* and *Buried Child.*

Human Activity

A play is fabricated out of imagined activities engaging one or more human beings in some kind of conflict leading to crisis and change. The script's imaginative material, therefore, has a unity and completeness that life does not have. The material provides for physical and psychological behavior that the actor brings to life — makes *visible* — in words and actions while we watch. Hecuba's grieving, Tartuffe's plotting, and Blanche DuBois' disintegrating can be seen, heard, and felt. Each play's imaginative material is different.

FIGURE 12.1

Tartuffe, *directed at The Guthrie Theater, Minneapolis, in 1984 by Lucian Pintilie, the acclaimed Rumanian-born director. Harris Yulin (center) plays the "con man" Tartuffe in this contemporary restaging of Molière's classic comedy.*

The Trojan Women Euripides' *The Trojan Women* deals with the plight of war's often forgotten victims — women and children. What turned Euripides' dramatic imagination to the story of Troy was a similar occurrence during the Peloponnesian Wars between Athens and Sparta. In the winter of 416–415 B.C., Athens invited the neutral island city of Melos to join the Athenian Alliance. Melos refused and was besieged and captured. The Athenians put all adult males to death and enslaved the women and children.

In the play Euripides concentrates on what is left of the House of Troy, specifically the women and children. They are waiting to be divided up as slaves among their conquerors. The chief activity in Euripides' play is *waiting* — to learn of further deaths, separation, transportation, and ending.

Hamlet In Shakespeare's *Hamlet* the chief activities are the effects of the ghost's admonition, Claudius' villainy, Gertrude's fragile virtue, Ophelia's torn allegiances, and Laertes' naiveté. Out of this material, which has its source in the murder of a king, Shakespeare shapes a tale about the corrosive power of human evil and moral frailty to destroy lives and kingdoms.

Tartuffe Molière's romp of overweening greed and manipulation of money, property, and sexual favors plunges Orgon's family into chaos and ruin until the king's messenger arrives to save them from Tartuffe, the comic perpetrator in clerical garb (see Figure 12.1).

The Cherry Orchard In Chekhov's *The Cherry Orchard*, the life of the play occurs in and about the Ranevskaya estate. Chekhov's people react to their situations, expressing feelings of love, happiness, anxiety, frustration, and despair while they talk of beauty, the weather, work, money, property, cherry trees, relatives, Paris, ideals, the past and the future. All the while they talk, they fail to deal with the immediate problem in their lives: the scheduled auction of the estate to pay their debts. The chief activity in Chekhov's human comedy is the state of perpetual change that people knowingly or unknowingly experience while life goes on around them.

A Streetcar Named Desire   In Tennessee Williams' *A Streetcar Named Desire*, Blanche DuBois comes from Laurel, Mississippi, to Stanley Kowalski's home in New Orleans, where she clashes tragically with his personality and lifestyle.

Buried Child   The activity of Sam Shepard's *Buried Child* deals with the digging up of the family's terrible secrets (adultery, incest, and child murder). Once the secret crimes are revealed and the family's guilt exorcised, the grandson takes command of the family, and Shepard suggests there is hope for a future generation.

Space

How is space defined in the script? At the beginning of a playscript, the playwright builds in the mind's eye a three-dimensional space within which characters move about and interact. When we read, we need to ask ourselves certain questions: What does the space look like? What are the setting's configuration, color, details? How is the space filled by the characters? What are the visual clues about the manners, style, thoughts, and attitudes? It is important to visualize how the playwright uses the space, since this use sets the action and defines the characters' lives.

Opening speeches and stage directions give detailed information about how the playwright has imagined the stage space, including geography, time of day, weather, dress, mood, and general impressions of place.

Hamlet   At the beginning of *Hamlet* the two guards on the castle ramparts set the scene of betrayal, murder, and revenge. The guards are cold, nervous, cautious. They challenge one another to identify themselves during a routine changing of the castle guard at midnight. Their fear hints that something is "out of joint" in their world. Shakespeare's midnight scene stresses that the main events of the play are obscured in the darkness of moral confusion and evil deeds, and that these events will shortly be brought into question by the ghost's narrative.

There were no stage directions until after Shakespeare's time. All clues about movement, time, place, and behavior are in Shakespeare's verse, although frequently modern editors assist us in locating places and sounds. So we must read carefully what the characters say. In their actions and speech (especially in the great soliloquies), they define their environment, thoughts, and emotions.

The Cherry Orchard In scripts written toward the end of the nineteenth century, playwrights explicitly spelled out details of setting, lighting, costume, sounds, and properties, and of the characters' age, sex, coloring, class, and dress. These details were usually set down in descriptive stage directions at the beginning of each act. Both Ibsen and Chekhov were masters at visualizing in stage directions the stage environment as well as the time of day, weather, the characters and their activities.

Chekhov begins *The Cherry Orchard* with a description of the children's room in the Ranevskaya estate house where Lopakhin, the rich merchant, and Dunyasha, the young maid, have waited through the night for the family's arrival. The setting is highly specific in the stage directions.

> *The nursery, or children's room, now no longer in use. One of the doors leads to Anya's room. Daybreak, just before sunrise. It is already May. The cherry trees are in bloom but it is still cold; there is a frost on the blossoms. The windows are closed.*

The month of the year, time of morning, weather, condition of the room, and the cherry trees in bloom are all established in stage directions. In the opening dialogue we are told what the characters do (for example, Dunyasha blows out the candle she carries); what they wear (Lopakhin wears "a white vest and leather boots" as a sign of his wealth); what is heard (dogs barking offstage and the clerk Yepikhodov's new boots squeaking as he walks). Finally, we "hear" carriages driving up to the house, and the family dressed in traveling clothes with luggage, servants, dog, and neighbors fill the "empty stage" with life—with shouts of joy, greetings, anticipation, motion, and general confusion.

A Streetcar Named Desire The opening stage direction, a page in length, must be read carefully for clues about mood, style, environment, and attitudes. In this description, Williams evokes atmosphere with graphic details of place, time, light, and sound: New Orleans, Elysian Fields Avenue, a May twilight, blue sky, barroom piano music. Stanley and Mitch are described in age, dress, and movement: They are twenty-eight or thirty years old and wear blue denim work clothes.

SCENE ONE

The exterior of a two-story corner building on a street in New Orleans which is named Elysian Fields and runs between the L & N tracks and the river. The section is poor but, unlike corresponding sections in other American cities, it has a raffish charm. The houses are mostly white frame, weathered grey, with rickety outside stairs and galleries and quaintly ornamented gables. This building contains two flats, upstairs and down. Faded white stairs ascend to the entrances of both.

It is first dark of an evening early in May. The sky that shows around the dim white building is a peculiarly tender blue, almost a turquoise, which invests the scene with a kind of lyricism and gracefully attenuates the atmosphere of decay. You can almost feel the warm breath of the brown river beyond the river warehouses with their faint redolences of bananas and coffee. A corresponding air is evoked by the music of Negro entertainers at a barroom around the corner. In this part of New Orleans you are practically always just around the corner, or a few doors down the street, from a tinny piano being played with the infatuated fluency of brown fingers. This "Blue Piano" expresses the spirit of the life which goes on here.

Two women, one white and one colored, are taking the air on the steps of the building. The white woman is Eunice, who occupies the upstairs flat; the colored woman a neighbor, for New Orleans is a cosmopolitan city where there is a relatively warm and easy intermingling of races in the old part of town.

Tennessee Williams

Born Thomas Lanier Williams in Columbus, Mississippi, Tennessee Williams (1911 – 1983) was the son of a traveling salesman and an Episcopalian minister's daughter. The family moved to St. Louis in 1918. He was educated at Missouri University, Washington University in St. Louis, and later the University of Iowa, where he received his B.A. degree.

In 1939, *Story* magazine published his short story "A Field of Blue Children," the first work to appear under his nickname Tennessee, which was given to him because of his Southern accent. That same year he compiled four one-act plays under the title *American Blues*, and won a prize in the Group Theatre's American play contest. This aroused the interest of New York agent Audrey Wood, who asked to represent him.

The Glass Menagerie in 1944–45 marked Williams' first major success and established him as an important American playwright. It was followed by his major plays: *A Streetcar Named Desire* (1947), *The Rose Tattoo* (1951), *Cat on a Hot Tin Roof* (1955), *Sweet Bird of Youth* (1959), and *The Night of the Iguana* (1961). Although his later plays failed to please critics, he continued to write and be produced in New York and London until his death.

> *Above the music of the "Blue Piano" the voices of people on the street can be heard overlapping.*
>
> *[Two men come around the corner, Stanley Kowalski and Mitch. They are about twenty-eight or thirty years old, roughly dressed in blue denim work clothes. Stanley carries his bowling jacket and a red-stained package from a butcher's. They stop at the foot of the steps.]³*

Blanche, Stella's sister — dressed for a garden party in white suit, hat, gloves — comes unexpectedly into this setting. Williams describes her appearance:

> *She is about five years older than Stella. Her delicate beauty must avoid a strong light. There is something about her uncertain manner, as well as her white clothes, that suggest a moth.*

Jo Mielziner, scene designer for the 1947 Broadway production, visualized a single setting with several levels that showed all rooms of the apartment simultaneously (see Figure 12.2). The furniture and details of the set (the naked light bulb, for example) are clues to the Kowalski lifestyle that destroys Blanche's fragile truce with reality. She has nowhere to go — this is her last refuge — and when this environment becomes threatening, she retreats into a fantasy world. Yet the quality of the stage lighting and the open walls of Mielziner's setting suggest this very fantasy world.

FIGURE 12.2

Setting for A Streetcar
Named Desire *(1947).
Stanley Kowalski's friends
play poker while Blanche
DuBois is taken away to an
asylum. The foreground
shows the realistic details of
Jo Mielziner's setting: bed,
tables, and chairs. Stanley
comforts Stella on a stair-
way while Blanche is led
away by a doctor and nurse
in an upstage area that
seems far removed from the
poker game.*

Buried Child   Sam Shepard's *Buried Child* takes place in the living room
of Dodge and Halie's Midwestern home:

> *Day. Old wooden staircase down left with pale, frayed carpet laid down on the
> steps. The stairs lead off stage left up into the wings with no landing. Up right
> is an old, dark green sofa with the stuffing coming out in spots. Stage right of
> the sofa is an upright lamp with a faded yellow shade and a small night table
> with several small bottles of pills on it. Down right of the sofa, with the screen
> facing the sofa, is a large, old-fashioned brown T.V. A flickering blue light
> comes from the screen, but no image, no sound. In the dark, the light of the
> lamp and the T.V. slowly brighten in the black space. The space behind the
> sofa, upstage, is a large, screened-in porch with a board floor; a solid interior
> door to stage right of the sofa, leading into the room on stage; and another screen
> door up left, leading from the porch to the outside. Beyond that are the shapes of
> dark elm trees.*
>
> *Gradually the form of* DODGE *is made out, sitting on the couch, facing
> the T.V., the blue light flickering on his face. He wears a well-worn T-shirt,
> suspenders, khaki work pants and brown slippers. He's covered himself in an
> old brown blanket. He's very thin and sickly looking, in his late seventies. He
> just stares at the T.V. More light fills the stage softly. The sound of light rain.*
> DODGE *slowly tilts his head back and stares at the ceiling for a while, listening
> to the rain. He lowers his head again and stares at the T.V. He turns his head
> slowly to the left and stares at the cushion of the sofa next to the one he's sitting
> on. He pulls his left arm out from under the blanket, slides his hand under the
> cushion, and pulls out a bottle of whiskey. He looks down left toward the stair-
> case, listens, then uncaps the bottle, takes a long swig and caps it again. He*

FIGURE 12.3
Bradley (actor Jay Sanders) brutalizes Shelly (Mary McDonnell) in the New York production of Sam Shepard's Buried Child, *1978.*

puts the bottle back under the cushion and stares at the T.V. He starts to cough slowly and softly. The coughing gradually builds. He holds one hand to his mouth and tries to stifle it. The coughing gets louder, then suddenly stops when he hears the sound of his wife's voice coming from the top of the staircase.[4]

In this scene of forlorn emptiness and neglect, Dodge, the ailing father, continues to lie on the sofa — drinking occasionally — as, offstage, his wife addresses him for some 350 lines. Though Dodge shouts answers at Halie, hers is essentially a solo speech. As she talks about the weather and Dodge's health, we realize their relationship is as empty and frayed as the stark room, the tattered sofa, and the blank television screen.

Shepard, within the tradition of stage realism, has established a scene of illness and spiritual emptiness. Even before we meet the entire family, there are visual clues as to the decay of American values of family, religion, and relationships. (See Figure 12.3.)

Character

In drama, characters are defined by their physical characteristics, their socioeconomic status, their psychological makeup, and their moral or ethical choices. And characters are made visible through what the playwright says about them in stage directions (age, dress, demeanor, social status), what others say about them, and what they remark about themselves.

As readers we must use our imaginations to hear and see characters as the actors would represent them in performance: the words spoken, the stresses, nuances, and attitudes of the speakers; their costumes, movements and inactivity, silences, visual strengths, psychological makeup, and so on.

The Trojan Women   Since the Greek audience knew the story of the Trojan war, of Helen's abduction by Paris, of Hector's death in battle with the Greek hero Achilles, of the wooden horse and the fall of the city after a ten-year siege, Euripides could introduce his characters by simply *naming* them. He could then move along without explanation to the intensity of their tragic plight. The principal women are of royal birth, but Euripides depicts their common plight as recognizable people displaying ordinary emotions in a dire situation.

Hecuba, Troy's aging queen, has lost husband, sons, and — soon — grandson and daughters. However, her noble suffering is undercut by her desire for revenge against Helen, whose beauty and promiscuity are seen as the essential cause of their grief and enslavement. The Greek messenger Talthybius is presented as a compassionate but loyal soldier. He pities the women and children but performs his duty, even to removing Hector's young son for execution. Euripides' characters exhibit admirable as well as unattractive human qualities. For instance, Cassandra's clairvoyance is counterbalanced by her emotional instability, and Helen's culpability is offset by her startling argument that she has been innocent ("a bride of force"), wronged by the Trojans.

Because the play's events, specifically the consignment of the women to the Greek generals, are well known, Euripides concentrates on the psychology of war's victims. Despite the fact that the women are trapped and their destinies determined, they do more than react passively to their fates. They rage against the cruelties of the Greeks, especially against the murder of Hector's small son. They display fury, humiliation, grief, and nobility in the presence of colossal human waste and destruction (see Figure 12.4).

Hamlet   Character relationships in *Hamlet* are one thing on the surface and another underneath, but they are always clear to the audience. This

FIGURE 12.4

The Royal Shakespeare Company's 1979 production of The Greeks, directed by John Barton, was ten Greek plays performed over three evenings as The Wars, The Murders, and The Gods. The Trojan Women was the final play of Part One: The Wars. As we read the text we must imagine the abuse of the women by their captors. The photo captures plainly the rage and triumph of King Agamemnon over Cassandra, daughter of the defeated King Priam. John Shrapnel plays the Greek king Agamemnon with Celia Gregory as his captive, Cassandra, one of Hecuba's daughters, in Part Two: The Murders (from Aeschylus' Agamemnon).

is not true in many modern plays. Shakespeare has his characters tell us directly, in dialogue, **asides,** and soliloquies, what they are planning and feeling.

Plays such as *Hamlet, Othello,* and *Macbeth* illustrate tragic social, psychological, and political relationships. Most of the characters in *Hamlet* lack psychological subtlety and take their identities from broad stage types of the time. Some **stock characters** are king, tyrant, avenger, assassin, loyal friend, retainer. However, Gertrude, Ophelia, and of course Hamlet have interior lives that give them individuality. Hamlet is considered Shakespeare's most complex **protagonist,** but before we psychoanalyze any of Shakespeare's characters — and most especially Hamlet — we must remember that Shakespeare was writing for the public stage at the end of the sixteenth century. Shakespeare first gives his audience a **revenge play** with ghosts, murders, bizarre plots, suicides, graveyards, skulls, duels, and the avenger. (See Figure 12.5.)

In many ways Hamlet is typical of his time. Educated to rule his country, Hamlet possesses qualities of the ideal Renaissance gentleman: courage, generosity, learning, wit, courtly manners, sword skills, and a taste

FIGURE 12.5

The chamber scene in Hamlet *in which Hamlet taunts Gertrude and kills Polonius who is hidden behind the arras. Nan Martin as Gertrude with Robert Burr as Hamlet in the 1964 New York Shakespeare Festival production.*

for the arts. His melancholic attitude is not normal for him, and others say he was not always ineffectual in action. Only since his father's death and his mother's hasty marriage before the "funeral meats were cold" has he become apathetic and slow to act. Though in a state of grief, Hamlet is a man with a philosophic approach to life. He has been trained to analyze problems and to make decisions based on reason.

> And thus the native hue of resolution
> Is sicklied o'er with the pale cast of thought,
> And enterprises of great pitch and moment
> With this regard their currents turn awry
> And lose the name of action. . . .
> (3, i)

Nor would he neglect his duties, though he might be reluctant to correct the evils around him. However, he is also capable of understanding the implications of any potential action. Thus, he does not kill Claudius at prayer and risk sending the king's soul to heaven. In contrast, Laertes would have acted first and considered the consequences of his actions later.

Like the other characters in the play, Hamlet is a highly elaborate type: the philosophic mind who analyzes, reasons, and then acts. As he says, "I'll have grounds" before killing a king (who is also his uncle and stepfather).

The Cherry Orchard We ordinarily assume that words spoken by characters clarify relationships, define what is happening between characters, amplify emotions, and provide information. This is usually true. But Chekhov teaches us most forcefully that characters also use language, not to reveal their intentions, but to *conceal* them. In Chekhov's plays, meaning is frequently visible in the wide gap between *what is being said* and *what is being done*. The reader must listen beneath the surface of Chekhov's dialogue — and the dialogue of many modern plays — to hear and see the characters' unspoken feelings and needs.

How do we read Chekhov's silences and pauses and relate them to understanding character? First, we must know where the silences come in the script, gauge their length, and imagine their effect. Playwrights indicate silences in stage directions by writing a phrase like "after a pause" or "hesitating." But a more difficult kind of stage silence is that disguised by a rush of words, when characters fill the stage with talk in order to hide feelings. British playwright Harold Pinter (b. 1930) describes his theory of sound, silence, and words on stage:

> There are two silences. One when no word is spoken. The other when perhaps a torrent of language is being employed. This speech is speaking of a language locked beneath it. That is its continual reference. The speech we hear is an indication of that we don't hear. It is a necessary avoidance, a violent, sly, anguished or mocking smokescreen which keeps the other in its place. When true silence falls we are still left with echo but are nearer nakedness. One way of looking at speech is to say it is a constant stratagem to cover nakedness.[5]

Chekhov uses both pauses and torrents of language to get at the truth of human behavior. In the final act of *The Cherry Orchard* among the bustle of packing, leavetaking, and general farewells, Lopakhin, who has bought the estate, speaks volumes about his plans for the winter and the estate. In contrast, Madame Ranevskaya and her brother Gaev say farewell to a house, to one another, and to a way of life — forever. What is impressive about the scene is their need to make speeches, to fill the painful silences, to mask their anguish. Ellipses (the three or four periods that suggest the pauses in conversation) mark the places where the inner pain swells to the surface and stifles speech. This occurs three times in Madame Ranevskaya's farewell to her home.

MADAME RANEVSKAYA: In another ten minutes we'll have to get into the carriage. (*She looks around her.*) Goodbye, my dear house, my old ancestor . . . Winter will be over, and in the spring, you'll no longer exist . . . demolished. . . . (Act 4)

A Streetcar Named Desire   The relationships among Blanche, Stanley, Stella, and Mitch are based on the "law of the jungle": The weaker, in this case Blanche and Mitch, are physically and psychologically violated by Stanley, the stronger. Stanley's need to control his world destroys Mitch's happiness and Blanche's ability to cope with reality.

The character relationships are illustrated in a seesaw manner. We see Stanley, Stella, and Mitch as a compatible threesome, the sort who go bowling together. Blanche arrives on the scene with airs of sophistication and tries to alienate Stella's affections from Stanley. She engages Mitch's affections and he wants to marry her. Sensing his loss of affection and authority, Stanley retaliates physically and psychologically. He fights to preserve his home and family just as Blanche struggles to create a last refuge for herself. His explanation to Stella of why he has bought the one-way ticket back to Laurel for Blanche delineates the struggle:

> STANLEY: When we first met, me and you, you thought I was common. How right you was, baby. I was common as dirt. You showed me the snapshot of the place with the columns. I pulled you down off them columns and how you loved it, having them colored lights going! And wasn't we happy together, wasn't it all okay till she showed here? And wasn't we happy together? Wasn't it all okay? Till she showed here. Hoity-toity, describing me as an ape. . . .

Stanley finally destroys Blanche's relationship with Mitch by revealing her past sexual escapades; then he rapes her. At the play's end, Stanley has re-established control of his world, while Blanche has relinquished her tenuous hold on a world she could not cope with.

Williams' characters in *A Streetcar Named Desire* fall into two categories: survivors and nonsurvivors. The sensitive and the fragile fall before the coarse and brutal in Williams' violent world. (See Figure 12.6.)

Purpose

What is the purpose or concept behind the action? As readers, we must visualize what the characters do, where they do it, and with or against whom. We must also consider *why* characters do what they do, for a play

FIGURE 12.6

Blythe Danner as Blanche DuBois in the play's final scene with the Doctor and Nurse. Sigourney Weaver as Stella and Wendy Barrie as Eunice look on as the Doctor (George Morfogen) and nurse (Patricia Swanson) comfort Blanche before escorting her to the asylum in the 1986 production of A Streetcar Named Desire *at the Williamstown Theatre Festival, Massachusetts.*

represents persons in effective, complete, and meaningful action. In order to be complete and meaningful, dramatic action is shaped with some purpose in mind. It is not a random collection of unrelated events, although in plays like Chekhov's, action may *appear* to be random. The purpose of the action and the playwright's underlying concept are usually not entirely clear until the end of the play. However, there are five clues to it: title, climax, resolution, metaphor, and theme.

The Trojan Women: Title and Theme   Euripides names the play after the captives waiting to learn of their fates in exile. In this play that tells the story of Troy's destruction, Euripides' principal emphasis is on *theme* or his anti-war message: He stresses the irrationality of gods as well as of human beings and the cost of war in human lives. Euripides' attitude toward humanity's plight is summed up in Hecuba's lyric lament that ends the play:

> That mortal is a fool who, prospering,
> thinks his life has any strong foundation;
> since our fortune's course of action is the
> reeling way a madman takes, and no one
> person is ever happy all the time.[6]

A pacifist, Euripides was at pains to represent his nation's *hubris*, or overbearing pride, during the long wars with Sparta in the fifth century B.C. Speaking to contemporary politicians and generals in his audience, Euripides documents in Cassandra's rape and Astyanax's murder how very much the Greeks deserved their doom. The story of the Trojan women also commented indirectly on the genocide at Melos, the action of a barbaric (and degenerate) polity, and warned of disaster to come in the conduct of present and future wars.

A Streetcar Named Desire: Title and Climax Williams' play takes its title from an object and an emotion rather than a person. The "Desire" streetcar literally transports Blanche DuBois to the Kowalski tenement on Elysian Fields Avenue (in Greek mythology, the Elysian fields were the equivalent of heaven); at the same time, her personal desires for refuge, love, and sexual gratification have brought her to an emotional and mental dead end. The fact that the play climaxes with Blanche's rape underscores the purpose of the action: to demonstrate that, without refuge, the emotionally lame cannot survive a harsh and insensitive world.

Buried Child: Title, Metaphor, Theme The buried child of the play's title is both sign and symbol of the decay of the modern American family. The family in the play engaged for years in covering up the murder of a baby born to Halie and her son Tilden, later drowned by her husband Dodge and buried in the backyard. Shepard's Midwesterners of the 1970s are out of touch with the soil (which is in fact contaminated with incest and murder), once the quintessential symbol of America's work ethic and psychic vitality. American dreams of familial love, personal integrity, and success achieved by hard work have been replaced by realities of disease, betrayal, and death. The father is dying; the mother has deceived him many times over; and the sons are either dead or maimed. Ansel died in a gangland murder; Bradley was mutilated in a chainsaw accident; and Tilden is psychologically damaged. The return of the legitimate grandson seeking his heritage forces the family to face their betrayal and guilt. Their crimes are literally unearthed from the soil where they have been concealed for years.

As Dodge goes gently into death after the climactic revelation of his murder and burial of the unwanted child, the backyard (offstage) springs into growth with an abundance of vegetables (corn, carrots, potatoes, and peas), establishing the old agrarian rhythm of birth, death, and rebirth. At this point Shepard's themes, metaphors, and title become wholly clear: The American soil may be a sterile wasteland because of the degeneration of American character and values, but both are capable of renewal.

Organization

How are the incidents shaped and organized? To visualize a script, we must hear what the characters *say* to one another and see what they *do* under the pressure of developing events and relationships. We must also visualize the connections between plot and action, word and gesture. And, what is frequently more difficult while reading, we must see in the mind's eye the changing focus of attention on individuals within a group.

Let us look at three important scenes from *Tartuffe, A Streetcar Named Desire,* and *Buried Child*, considering the *organization* of these scenes and their *connection* to what has gone before and what is to come after.

Tartuffe: The Seduction Scene (Act IV, scene v)   Tartuffe's mask of religious piety conceals a monster of greed, lechery, and ingratitude. Stripping away Tartuffe's mask so that his benefactor Orgon can see the real Tartuffe and understand his own folly becomes the central action of the play. Orgon must learn that his affection for Tartuffe — to the extent of ignoring his wife's illness, disinheriting his son, betrothing his daughter to a man she detests, and entrusting a friend's secrets to a stranger — borders on unnaturalness of feeling and obstinate stupidity. Once the family's dilemma is clear, they — Cléante, Elmire, Valère, Mariane, Dorine — conspire to open Orgon's eyes. Elmire proposes herself as bait to lure Tartuffe into giving himself away.

The first four scenes of Act IV expose the hopelessness of convincing Orgon of Tartuffe's hypocrisy. In the first scene, Cléante tries to reason with Tartuffe to restore Orgon's estate (now signed over to him) to the rightful heir, Orgon's son Damis. In scene ii the family assembles to try to change Orgon's mind about marrying his daughter Mariane to Tartuffe. Mariane begs to be spared an abhorrent marriage (scene iii). Orgon refuses

and Elmire proposes a "test" of Tartuffe's virtue; Orgon agrees to the "challenge." Elmire hides her husband beneath a table (scene iv), explaining that she proposes to seduce Tartuffe and she will cease whenever her husband's "doubts are fully satisfied."

The seduction scene (scene v) — which usually takes place on the table beneath which Orgon is hiding — is an extreme act built upon all the family's failed arguments with Tartuffe and Orgon. (See Figure 12.7.) In one sense, it is a typical farce sex scene in which wife and lover are discovered by the husband. However, Molière's farce scene concerns the unmasking not of a too amorous lover but of a lecherous hypocrite, consuming all in his path with monstrous greed.

Emerging from beneath the table fully convinced of Tartuffe's treachery, Orgon concludes that the "man's a perfect monster"; but the family is not out of harm's way for Orgon has given his house, money, and property to Tartuffe. For the moment it seems as though the family will be destroyed by the evil intruder, but Molière introduces a **deus ex machina** (a person, or fact, outside the story who steps in to resolve a hopelessly deadlocked situation). In this case, the unexpected force is King Louis XIV's officer who arrests Tartuffe for other "vicious crimes" committed under another name, thus proving that sometimes an all-powerful hand must intercede to save the innocent from evil powers (see Figure 12.8). Molière's simple truth is that discovery (scene v) of one's errors and sincere remorse do not necessarily extract one from the consequences of folly and stupidity.

A Streetcar Named Desire: Blanche's Birthday Party This scene (see Figure 12.9) illustrating the beginning of Blanche's retreat from reality

FIGURE 12.8 (above)

Tartuffe. *Director Lucian Pintilie's staging of Molière's Tartuffe at the Guthrie Theater, Minneapolis, in 1984. This scene depicts Tartuffe's associates surrounded by the "disorder" they have created in the life of Orgon's family. Scenery by Radu Boruzescu, costumes by Miruna Boruzescu, and lighting by Beverly Emmons.*

FIGURE 12.9

The birthday party. Marlon Brando as Stanley (left) prepares to throw his cup and plate on the floor during Blanche's birthday party in A Streetcar Named Desire. *Jessica Tandy as Blanche (center) and Kim Hunter as Stella (right) are seated at the table.*

begins with Stanley, Blanche, and Stella seated around a table set for four. A birthday cake and flowers are on the table. Stanley is sullen, Stella is embarrassed and sad, and Blanche is putting up a brave front with an artificial smile.

Blanche assesses the situation: Her "beau," Mitch, has stood her up. She tells a lame joke to fill the awkward silence, Stella corrects Stanley's table manners, and he throws his plate on the floor. Blanche wants to know what happened while she was taking a bath, but Stella avoids telling her that Stanley has found out about her past and told Mitch, and that this is the reason Mitch is not coming to the party. Stanley gives Blanche a birthday present: a bus ticket back to Laurel. Blanche runs into the bathroom to be sick. Stella and Stanley argue about his treatment of Blanche and he accuses Blanche of changing their lives. The scene ends with Stella quietly asking to be taken to the hospital to have their baby.

Williams shapes scenes vii–ix to illustrate that hostile forces have turned on Blanche. In vii, Stanley tells Stella the facts about Blanche's past and sets the stage for his ultimatum: She must leave. Scene ix is a confrontation between Mitch and Blanche in which she realizes he is not to be that "cleft in the rock of the world" she needs.

In these three scenes, Blanche is the focus of the conflict among the characters. Williams develops the relationships to the crisis point at which the bus ticket signals to Blanche that she has no place of refuge. What follows is rape — Stanley's ultimate violation of her — and psychosis. Williams' concept is clear: Certain fragile souls must have protection — otherwise they are destroyed by the world's brute forces.

Buried Child: Ceremony of the Corn Husks Like many contemporary playwrights, Shepard is master of the unexpected event and stage metaphor. Tilden, the son who is a former all-American fullback, a jailbird, and of marginal intelligence, enters in Act 1 carrying an enormous armful of fresh-picked corn and drops the bundle in the middle of the living room floor. He methodically shucks the corn, dropping the clean ears into a bucket and the husks around him on the floor, as his parents, Dodge and Halie, shout at one another. Halie complains about the litter in the room and accuses Tilden of stealing the corn from the neighbors.

After the corn is shucked and the house quiet, for Halie has left for her "lunch" with the preacher and Dodge has fallen asleep on the sofa, Tilden begins a remarkable ceremony of gathering the husks off the floor and gently spreading them over his father's sleeping body. He repeats this ceremony until the floor is clean of corn husks and Dodge is completely covered by them. The symbolism implies that Dodge is a husk of his former self. He no longer farms the land, but rather remains indoors, away from the soil that holds his crime. The corn itself is a symbol of life — of sustenance, sexuality, and procreation. Only Tilden at this point can see the "fantastic field" behind the house where he has gotten the corn. Symbolically, he has access to the field because he knows the truth. According to critic Richard Gilman, the field is a metaphor for fecundity and at the same time a hope for the future against bitter hidden truths.[7]

Tilden's gentle ceremony speaks more than a thousand words about Dodge's disease, the family's moral disorder, and the hope for the future in the next generation. It stands in contrast to Bradley's malicious shaving of Dodge's head while he still sleeps. Both the gentle and violent gestures point up the play's moral ambivalence. With Dodge's confession and death in Act 2, the family's guilt will be exorcised and the mysterious field made visible to all.

Performance Style

As readers, how do we think about a play's style of **performance**? *Style* is one of the most difficult words in our language to define. Fashion magazines, like *Harper's Bazaar* and *Gentlemen's Quarterly*, define style as the look of the season's high fashion. It is displayed in their pages in the fashion model's hairstyle, makeup, clothes, accessories, posture. In theatre, the word *style* has a different and more complex meaning. In general, *theatrical style is the physical projection of a play's inner nature.* In other words, style and the play's *physical reality* are the same. The reader must always think aurally, visually, and three dimensionally about the play's physical look.

The two principal performance styles in today's theatre are *realism* and *theatricalism.* We need to know what these terms mean, and how to detect these two general styles in the reading of a play.

The most influential book on theatrical style is Michel Saint-Denis' *Theatre: The Rediscovery of Style* (1960). He defines style as "the perceptible form that is taken by reality in revealing to us its true and inner character."[8] What do we look for to visualize this outer reality? What basic questions get at a play's style?

First, we must look for outer or visible characteristics. What are the characters' nationalities and ethnic characteristics? Are they Russian, British, American? Are they Afro-American, Asian-American, East Indian, Mexican-American, Italian-American? What manner and everyday habits do these characters exhibit? What are their ways of speaking, sitting, walking, dressing, gesturing, smiling, eating, and drinking? How are their cultural rhythms expressed?

We must also ask where and when the play takes place. Is it a house, or street, or castle, or nonspecific locale? What does the setting look like? Is it a room, or arranged platforms? What is the historical period? Or has the writer chosen to mix elements from various periods? And we must ask about the psychological, emotional, and social reality of the characters. How do they speak and behave? Do they speak in verse or ordinary prose? Is their conversation formal or informal? Are their gestures and movements those that we observe around us, or grander? All of these questions about style get at the play's inner nature from the outside — from the setting, costumes, lighting, sounds, speech, and movements.

Realism

Realism is a production style whose intention is to represent life in such a way that the audience accepts what is seen as a picture of *everyday* reality. One major movement of the nineteenth- and twentieth-century European and American theatres has been to re-create everyday life on stage. American critic Eric Bentley defines realism as "the candid presentation of the natural world."[9] It is exact, detailed, and recognizable, with an "everyday" quality about it. The actors, dressed as real people, are put in the middle of real furniture, properties, doors, ceilings, and windows. The box set, the basic environment for the realistic play, uses three walls and a ceiling — the illusion is created that a "fourth wall," between stage and audience, has been removed. The box set was in common use in European theatres around 1875.

The Cherry Orchard

In the 1904 production at the Moscow Art Theatre, director Constantin Stanislavsky set a standard for stage realism. He worked to re-create the play's **mise-en-scène**, or total stage picture. He paid particular attention to stage sounds (birds singing, dogs barking) to create a sense of the play's living reality. Details of costume, setting, locale, furniture, properties, speech, and movement were scrutinized to make certain they were like the life they imitated: rural Russia around 1904. Ordinary objects and activities of everyday existence were brought onstage: samovar, piano, harmonica, stove, lamp, tobacco, singing, drink, twilight, window frost. Stanislavsky's actors turned their backs to the audience, as if it did not exist, and moved with familiarity within their stage environment. There was no star, but a perfect **ensemble**. The foreground and background were one, and properties, costumes, doors, lamps, window curtains, and lights, no less than the actors, performed their parts.

A Streetcar Named Desire

The 1947 production directed by Elia Kazan and designed by Jo Mielziner, shows us a "selected realism"—a detailed stage environment that also evokes a mood of detachment and fantasy. The blues piano, played in the distance, for instance, is appropriate to the play's setting—New Orleans. The blues is also an expression of loneliness, rejection, and a longing for love. The piano music is a real part of New Orleans' back streets and also a way of calling attention to Blanche's drift into a fantasy world.

The performance style is one of contrasting effects. Upstage, there are mood music, soft lighting, and blurred shapes. Downstage, there are realistic details: table, chairs, bed, light bulb, stairwell, flowers, birthday cake, poker game. The scenic style sets forth both the harsh facts of Stanley's world and the dreamlike quality of Blanche's existence (see Figure 12.2).

The director's notebook Elia Kazan kept before and during the Broadway rehearsals shows that he concentrated from the beginning on the play's style. For Kazan, *Streetcar* is about a confused bit of light and culture being snuffed out by violence and vulgarity. Kazan wanted to contrast Stanley's brutality with Blanche's fragile memories and emotions visually, and the set designer Jo Mielziner selected realistic details to do so. Even though the play's outer world is physically and socially realistic, it also calls for moods and sounds that are not objectively present in the environment; for example, polka music (the "Varsouviana") plays each time Blanche remembers the past. It acts as a signal to the audience that Blanche is drifting into her fantasy world where she is loved, respected, cared for, and treated as an elegant lady.

New British Writing

Following the successes in London of John Osborne's *Look Back in Anger* and *The Entertainer* a year later, the language, subjects, passions, and characters of the British working class gained a secure foothold on the modern British stage. Those writers for whom Osborne's play opened up stages and audiences include Arnold Wesker, Shelagh Delaney, Ann Jellicoe, Edward Bond, David Storey, Harold Pinter, David Hare, Howard Brenton, Caryl Churchill, and many more. New actors and directors emerged to bring the new plays to life in the new realistic performance style. Alan Bates, Glenda Jackson, Joan Plowright, Albert Finney, Vivian Merchant, and Colin Blakely found themselves in plays about England's postwar working class. A new generation of directors, including Peter Hall, Joan Littlewood, Tony Richardson, Lindsay Anderson, William Gaskill, and Howard Davies, came forth.

The plays of the new British realism were set in solidly recognizable working-class milieus, peopled by characters who were largely products of an urban, industrial society. Edward Bond's characters, especially in *Saved* (1965), are resentful young people, violent and inarticulate. Bond uses realistic lower-class speech to deal with the theme of the corruption of natural innocence by "upbringing and environment." David Storey writes about rough-hewn tradesmen engaged in the activities of their various jobs or the games they play after work. *The Contractor* (1969) is an example of his method of constructing a play around a central activity in an ordinary laborer's day, such as putting up a tent for the wedding of the boss's daughter to an upper-middle-class doctor (see Figure 12.10). Class barriers and routine-filled lives are Storey's central concerns.

Stage realism has dominated the mainstream of the serious British theatre since the Royal Court Theatre produced *Look Back in Anger* in 1956.

FIGURE 12.10

The Contractor *by David Storey, at the Royal Court Theatre, London, 1969, directed by Lindsay Anderson. Actors as workmen raise the wedding tent on stage as part of the action.*

Osborne expressed the speech, resentments, and shabby lifestyle of an entire generation. Moreover, he represented a new breed of playwright, out of touch with the drawing-room comedies of Noel Coward and Christopher Frye in the commercial **West End** theatre. Alienated themselves from middle-class values, these newcomers felt that plays about the working class with recognizable characters, speech, subjects, and environments would find an audience. Critic Kenneth Tynan recognized what was shortly to be called the "new wave" of modern British writing when he wrote his prophetic review of Osborne's play in the *Observer*:

> I agree that *Look Back in Anger* is likely to remain a minority taste. What matters, however, is the size of the minority. I estimate it at roughly 6,733,000, which is the number of people in this country between the ages of twenty and thirty . . . I doubt if I could love anyone who did not wish to see *Look Back in Anger*. It is the best young play of its decade.[10]

Since the forties, American playwriting and production styles have likewise continued a strong current of realism and social protest, from the plays of Clifford Odets and Arthur Miller to the recent work of David Mamet, David Rabe, Marsha Norman, August Wilson, Lanford Wilson, and Sam Shepard.

Realism and Theatricalism

Realism and theatricalism are two broad categories of performance styles seen in today's theatre. In realistic style, all stage elements, including the actor's performance, simulate details of everyday life appropriate to the play's characters and environment. Realism has predominated in our time, but some theatre artists, feeling constrained by the limitations of stage realism, have sought other modes of expression. They have turned increasingly to purely theatrical devices — open stages, minimal scenic pieces and properties, ritual with highly stylized sounds and movement, and actor–audience participation.

REALISM

Chekhov's plays have long been considered major works of modern stage realism. Revolting against artificiality in the nineteenth-century theatre, he asked the audience to believe that they were seeing someone else's everyday life. The play's settings, costumes, dialogue, and general milieu were essential to his total purpose. Actor-director Constantin Stanislavsky created a performance style at the Moscow Art Theatre compatible with Chekhov's concepts of stage realism. The actor was placed *in* the setting, not against a painted drop as background. A "realistic" acting style developed to complement the mise-en-scène, and acting became an ensemble art.

THEATRICALISM

Director Andrei Serban collaborated with designers Santo Loquasto and Jennifer Tipton to stage in a theatrical style a play long thought to be the hallmark of stage realism. The 1977 production of *The Cherry Orchard* at the Vivian Beaumont Theatre in New York excited audiences with its boldness and innovation. Dispensing with a traditional room with walls, director and designer opened up the stage to suggest a central room flowing into and receding from the orchard. Loquasto designed a vast white carpet, the suggestion of white walls at the side, and a large cyclorama across the back of the stage. Furniture and actors became sculptured groups in silhouette against the whiteness. Using the metaphor of the death of a house, Serban's production aimed to *ritualize* Chekhov's play to comment on the death of a civilization.

In this photo from the 1904 Moscow Art Theatre production of *The Cherry Orchard*, directed by Constantin Stanislavsky, the attention to realistic detail conveys visually the minutiae of daily life on the estate. The realistic details of a family leaving a house that has been sold include packing crates containing the family's belongings; furniture, carpets, and curtains removed; and luggage stacked to one side. In the right of the photo, Lopakhin prepares a farewell toast. The wall treatment replicates leaves and tree trunks of the cherry orchard so everpresent in the life and minds of Chekhov's characters.

The Cherry Orchard, directed by Andrei Serban in 1977. Actors and furniture half-hidden by dustcovers are sculpted against the vast stage space and the whiteness of the carpet and trees. Irene Worth (center) as Madame Ranevskaya is being comforted by Priscilla Smith as Varya upon their return to the old family estate.

Meticulous attention to realistic details of design and performance is evident in this photo of the 1978 National Theatre production of Chekhov's *Cherry Orchard* in London, directed by Peter Hall. Dorothy Tutin (center) as Madame Ranevskaya with (left to right) Ben Kingsley (Trofimov), Robert Stephens (Gaev), and Susan Fleetwood (Varya).

Director Peter Brook took Shakespeare's *Midsummer Night's Dream* (1970) out of Elizabethan costumes, painted scenic backdrops, and green forests. Brook's actors performed while balancing on trapezes, juggling plates, hurling streamers, or stumbling about on stilts.

An early scene from *The Cherry Orchard* staged by Peter Brook in Paris in 1981. Madame Ranevskaya (Natasha Parry) experiences the joy of returning to her old home and friends. The furniture is still draped with dustcovers but the large white carpet was the visual centerpiece of Brook's openly theatrical production.

Liviu Ciulei's concept for Shakespeare's *The Tempest* (Guthrie Theater, 1981) placed Prospero's enchanted island on a stage surrounded by a trough of blood, in which floated debris reminiscent of Western civilization. In this photo the horse's head beside Prospero (Ken Ruta) and the clock without hands center stage are only two of the symbolic props that littered the borders of the playing area.

Theatricalism

Theatricalism refers to a nonrealistic mode of performance. In its broadest sense, it represents a revolt against realism by insisting that the stage be used in an openly nonrepresentational way. Under the auspices of such modern directors as Vsevelod Meyerhold, Max Reinhardt, Bertolt Brecht, Peter Brook, Liviu Ciulei, John Dexter, Andrei Serban, and Peter Sellars, theatricalism has come to be associated with:

- large, spectacular productions
- new interpretations of classics or familiar plays
- emphasis on pageantry and sensory effects
- de-emphasis on the script's verbal qualities
- unusual interpretations of scripts, rather than predictable ones
- the stage used as a stage rather than transformed into such realistic environments as living rooms, porches, or kitchens[11]

The success in this country of Peter Brook's *A Midsummer Night's Dream* (1970) and *The Mahabharata* (1987), John Dexter's *Equus* (1973), and Andrei Serban's *The Cherry Orchard* (1977) has fueled a growing interest in theatricalism, especially among the professional regional theatres.

The Trojan Women

In the early '70s, director Andrei Serban developed a starkly theatrical style to project Greek tragedy's inner reality to modern American audiences. Working with composer Elizabeth Swados on three plays by Euripides (*Medea, Electra,* and *The Trojan Women*), he produced selections from the texts in repertory on successive nights at La Mama Experimental Theatre Club in New York in 1974. The ancient material was sung, chanted, spoken, shouted, screamed, whispered, and even gasped in ancient languages.

▼▼▼

Andrei Serban

Andrei Serban (b. 1943), Rumanian-born director, came to the United States in 1969 at the invitation of Ellen Stewart to work at her La Mama Experimental Theatre Club on a Ford Foundation grant. After participating in Peter Brook's International Research Institute in Paris and Shiraz, Iran, he returned to New York to direct La Mama ETC productions of *Medea, Electra,* and *The Trojan Women* (see Figure 12.11).

During 1975 he directed Bertolt Brecht's *Good Person of Setzuan* at the Berlin International Festival; and in 1976 Shakespeare's *As You Like It* for summer festivals in France. In 1977, he directed Chekhov's *Cherry Orchard* and Aeschylus' *Agamemnon* at Lincoln Center and Chekhov's *Sea Gull* at the Public Theater, New York. Periodically returning to La Mama (where he staged Chekhov's *Uncle Vanya* in 1983), he divides his time between regional theatres in this country and abroad. He directed *The Three Sisters* (1983), *The Serpent Woman* (1988), and *The Miser* (1989) at the American Repertory Theatre, Boston; and Molière's *Imaginary Invalid* at the Guthrie Theater, Minneapolis, in 1984.

The meanings of the texts were communicated not through words but through sounds, actions, emotions, and music. In *The Trojan Women,* the audience was treated as participants and bystanders who watched Troy's women and children being driven from their ruined towers to tumbrils on the beachhead, there to be murdered, raped, or claimed as prizes. Hector's wife and son were exhibited in cages. Andromache was illuminated in a frozen farewell to her child before plunging to her death by leaping from a balcony into the center of the crowd. On a cart in the middle of the theatre's large rectangular space, Helen of Troy was stripped of her clothes, her hair cut; she was dirtied, mocked, and put to death with an ax blade.

Serban used a *universal language* — the sounds of music and the human voice in pain and anger — to enact Euripides' story. By restaging the ancient material in this way, it awakened the audience's collective memories and emotions in recognition of the pain and suffering common to all victims of war.

Whether we are reading *A Streetcar Named Desire* or *The Trojan Women,* a play's performance style is inherent in the text. As we read a play, we must ask if it should be staged with photographic realism or with flamboyant theatricality. When the experience that the play deals with is larger and grander than our living rooms, coffee cups, and card games, its performance style must be approached theatrically to suggest this larger-than-life quality of the characters and events. Greek and Elizabethan texts lend

FIGURE 12.11
Director Andrei Serban's theatrical style is evident in his treatment of the Greek chorus in Euripides' Medea, *produced at La Mama Experimental Theatre Club (New York, 1974).*

themselves to the theatrical, whereas our modern psychological and sociological plays adapt better to realistic staging. However, as shown by the photo essay, many directors in the last decade have taken to staging the father of modern stage realism, Anton Chekhov, in extraordinary theatricalist ways.

Summary

A play's meaning emerges not just from the words of the text, but from all the relationships that develop among all the elements of performance. Therefore, it is important to imagine the performance in our mind's eye as we read the play. Here is a play reader's checklist to assist with translating the written text into the theatre experience:

1. Imagine the playwright's material three dimensionally.

2. Visualize the set, atmosphere, costumes, sounds, decor, and space, and how the actors fill the space individually and in groups.

3. Read all opening speeches and stage directions carefully for details of time, place, weather, sounds, and mood.

4. Ask basic questions about what's happening: Who's there? Where and why? What are they doing?

5. Observe the relationships that develop or unfold between characters and among the groups.

6. Think carefully about what the characters say to one another, as well as what they don't say. Give particular attention to the pauses and silences, as well as to the word torrents occurring in the text.

7. Look at the visible relationships and search out the invisible and unspoken. Give attention again to pauses, silences, and sounds for related meanings.

8. Observe how the incidents are related to those that come before and after in the chain of events. Ask why the playwright has organized the incidents and events in the way that he or she has done.

9. Listen in the mind's ear to the play's story as it unfolds; visualize in the mind's eye the action's shape as it develops.

10. Imagine the production style that the script lends itself to, and think in terms of the look of the play in performance. Consider such things as historical period, environment, movement, scenery, costumes, properties, sounds, music, and lighting.

Questions for Study

1. Select one of the representative plays and discuss the playwright's use of *imaginative material*.

2. What does Anton Chekhov mean when he talks about life and a carrot?

3. What are six tools for seeing and hearing the script as theatre?

4. Discuss the six tools in relation to one of the following plays: *The Trojan Women, Hamlet, Tartuffe, The Cherry Orchard, A Streetcar Named Desire,* or *Buried Child.*

5. How do various playwrights indicate the use of *space* in a script?

6. How does Shakespeare usually organize opening speeches in his plays? Discuss specifically *Hamlet.*

7. What details do Ibsen or Chekhov provide in opening stage directions?

8. How do the realistic playwrights' stage directions or opening speeches differ from, for example, those of Shakespeare?

9. How do we discover the *concept* or *purpose* behind a play's action? Sometimes this is called the playwright's *intention.*

10. Discuss what you consider to be the most "actable" dramatic characters that we have studied in this chapter. Be specific about your reasons.

11. How are *pauses* and *silences* used for effect in the theatre? Comment specifically on the plays of Chekhov.

12. What does Harold Pinter mean by a "torrent of language"? Find examples of the technique in *The Cherry Orchard.*

13. Select one of the representative plays and discuss the five clues to the purpose or concept behind the play's action: title, climax, resolution, metaphor, and theme.

14. How do playwrights shape and organize *incidents* or *events*? Discuss specifically *Tartuffe, A Streetcar Named Desire,* or *Buried Child.*

15. Why is the seduction scene so important in *Tartuffe*?

16. Discuss Shepard's use of vegetables as stage metaphors in *Buried Child.*

17. Why is *style* difficult to define? Discuss its different uses in the world of fashion, literature, and theatre.

18. What are some basic questions to ask about a play's style?

19. Define *realism* as a performance style in the theatre.

20. Discuss *Ghosts, The Cherry Orchard,* and *Buried Child* as plays of stage realism.

21. What is a *box set*? When was it first in common use in European theatres?

22. Define *theatricalism* as a performance style.

23. Describe *six* features of performance style associated with theatricalism. How does Andrei Serban's 1974 production of *The Trojan Women* reflect these particular features of theatricalism as a performance style?

24. How is the reader's checklist on page 315 helpful in imagining *A Streetcar Named Desire* as a play in performance?

25. Apply what you have learned about visualizing a script to one of the following scenes: The staging of the play-within-the-play in *Hamlet* (Act 3, scene ii); the king's messenger's entrance at the climax and resolution of *Tartuffe* (Act 5, scene iii); the rape scene in *A Streetcar Named Desire* (scene x); the carrot-chopping scene in *Buried Child* (Act 2).

26. *Suggested Reading*: Elia Kazan's "Notebook for *A Streetcar Named Desire*" in *Directors on Directing: A Source Book of the Modern Theatre*, edited by Toby Cole and Helen K. Chinoy (Indianapolis: Bobbs-Merrill, 1976); *Peter Brook: A Theatrical Casebook*, compiled by David Williams (New York: Methuen, 1988).

VLADIMIR: **Moron!**
ESTRAGON: **Vermin!**
VLADIMIR: **Abortion!**
ESTRAGON: **Morpion!**
VLADIMIR: **Sewer-rat!**
ESTRAGON: **Curate!**
VLADIMIR: **Cretin!**
ESTRAGON: **(with finality) Crritic!**
SAMUEL BECKETT, *WAITING FOR GODOT*

Theatre critics add new dimensions to our awareness of the art. Critics acquaint readers and audiences with both good and bad productions; they hope, at best, to connect the good work with audiences and to preserve it for future generations.

Chapter 13

Viewpoints

Theatre criticism gives us a public view or assessment of what we see in the theatre. There are two distinct kinds of **criticism**: *Drama criticism* comments on the written text from a literary and cultural-historical perspective; *theatre criticism* deals with a play's performance, focusing on all elements of production, including the text in performance.

Present-day theatre criticism reflects the fact that we live in a consumer-oriented society. The business of journalistic theatre reviewers at newspapers and magazines such as the *New York Times, Los Angeles Times,* the *Washington Post,* the *New Yorker, New York Magazine,* and *The Village Voice* is to appraise theatrical performances found on Broadway, Off-Broadway, and in our regional theatres. But theatre criticism is more than appraisal. It is also an economic force (although many critics often deny this fact). In the commercial theatre, criticism often determines whether a play will continue or close after opening night. Given that critics for the *New York Times* and other metropolitan newspapers and television stations have the power to close a Broadway play or keep it running for months, we would do well to consider how critics' views affect the quality of our theatres and what we are seeing. It is also interesting to reflect on our own roles as critics in which we are cast by simply attending a show.

Seeing Theatre

Audiences as Critics

After the curtain comes down, we often go with friends to our favorite restaurant or hangout to

talk about the good and bad points of the production we have just seen. It's hard to put out of our minds a powerful performance of a play, whether we've just experienced Blanche DuBois' dependence on the kindness of strangers or the Orgon family's triumphant return to their house after their ordeal with Tartuffe. As we leave the theatre, we carry with us the emotional residue of the bleak pathos of Blanche's future or pleasure in Orgon's escape. A well-performed and meaningful play remains in our minds and in our emotions.

All audiences are critics by virtue of seeing a play in performance (see Figure 13.1). We may like the play and not the performance; or like the performance and not the play; or like neither or both. We may even praise certain strong scenes or single out powerful performances by certain actors. It is generally agreed that audiences bring at least *four viewpoints* to the theatre: We relate to a play's human significance, its social significance, its artistic qualities, and its entertainment value, but not necessarily in any particular order.

Human Significance As we have discussed throughout this book, the playwright and other theatre artists connect us with a common humanity between the stage action and where we are seated in the auditorium, or "the seeing place." Great plays, such as the model plays cited in this book, confront us with life's verities, conveying the hope, courage, despair, compassion, violence, love, hate, exploitation, and generosity experienced by all humankind. They show us ways of fulfilling ourselves in relationships and even with material things; they also show us the possibility of losing our families and property through accidents or catastrophes of war and tyranny. The best plays explore what it means to be human beings in *special* circumstances. These circumstances can be bizarre, like the witches' fortuitous appearance before Macbeth, or recognizable, like an unwanted relative appearing at a New Orleans tenement building. Theatre is an extraordinary medium that links us as audiences with actors as characters. They become reflections of ourselves, or what potentially could be ourselves. Theatre's best achievements lead us to discoveries and reflections about our own personalities, circumstances, desires, and anxieties.

Social Significance   Of all the arts, theatre has a built-in relation to society because by definition an audience is *an assembled group of spectators*. We become part of a *community* as we watch theatre. Communities vote, express themselves at town council meetings, and respond to local, national, and international events.

Since the days of the classical Greek theatre, the playing space has served as an arena wherein to discuss social and political issues, popular and unpopular. Euripides and the Greek comic playwright Aristophanes were often scorned because of their unpopular pacifist beliefs in a time of great nationalistic fervor. The modern theatre likewise deals with controversial issues. The theatre section of any Sunday edition of the *New York Times* lists plays that deal with almost every imaginable social issue: gay rights, drugs, civil rights, AIDS, abortion, racism, sports scandals, real estate fraud, family strife, sexual discrimination, financial hardship, marriage, show business, incest, feminism, nuclear war, terminal disease, mental illness, capital punishment, political chicanery, and so on. But the best plays and performances present social issues only as fuel for thought, not as propaganda.

Playwrights, along with their artistic associates, focus our attention, compassion, and outrage on social injustices and political corruption. *Tartuffe* celebrates triumph over injustice and *Macbeth* deplores subversion by evil forces and personal ambition. The playwright stimulates social awareness and puts us, as audiences, in touch with our own thoughts and feelings about issues — both as individuals and as groups. The aim of great playwrights is *to give us new perspectives*, to expand our consciousness, on old and new social issues.

Aesthetic Significance Each of us has aesthetic standards. We know what we like and what we don't like. We have seen a lot of television and many movies. As we attend more and more plays, we quickly come to spot honesty in acting, writing, and directing. We see the gimmicks for what they are. We sense the miscasting and the awkward moments. We have no checklist of what makes one performance more effective, provocative, or moving than another, but there are a number of questions we can ask ourselves about any play or performance. Does the play, as performed, excite or surprise us? Does it barely meet our expectations, or worse? Does it stimulate us to think? Are the actors convincing? Or are they more than just convincing, are they mesmerizing? Does the performance seem wooden or lively? Does what we are seeing seem in any way original, or does it seem a carbon copy of something else? Is it complete and logically sound? Are we caught up in the characters' lives, or are we simply waiting for the play to end?

As we see more theatre, we develop a more sophisticated awareness of sights, words, characters, action, actors, sounds, and colors. We appreciate balance and harmony — beginnings, middles, and ends. We also appreciate stage performances that exceed our expectations — that reveal issues and viewpoints that we did not know existed, and in theatrical ways we did not anticipate.

Entertainment Great theatre is always diverting in one or more ways. Even tragedy delights us in an unusual way. Aristotle called the way *catharsis*, or the cleansing of the emotions of pity and fear. In addition, tragedy has its share of just plain thrills. *Hamlet* and *Macbeth* offer ghosts, witches, murders, and duels, but they also please us at a deeper level. By witnessing the trials and insights of the tragic heroes, we are liberated from despair over the senselessness of human deeds.

Comedy and farce openly entertain us with romance, reason, pratfalls, gags, misunderstandings, wit, and nonsense while assuring us that wishes can be fulfilled (and even if *our* wishes cannot, farce assures us that it's safe at least to *wish for* the unheard of or for the socially unacceptable). Comedy and farce persuade us that society is really not so bad after all. In effect, they affirm that society will survive humanity's bungling.

In short, theatre is a dependable source of pleasure, laughter, tears, and companionship in an uncertain world. It is a place where we meet people and join with them in a collective experience: We laugh together and we cry together. Theatre entertains by involving us with others both on the stage and around us in the auditorium.

The Professional Critic

The Critic's Role

Unlike theatre itself, which always takes place in the present, the writing of criticism takes place after the fact. After the curtain comes down on the opening-night performance, critics begin their formal work — writing the review or preparing their sound bites for television journalism. The critic's education, background, experience in the theatre, and critical skills make it possible for him or her to produce instant reviews for radio and television or to write within an hour five paragraphs on the play for the late-night newspaper deadline. Those critics writing for Sunday editions or for weekly or monthly magazines have more leisure and usually write longer reviews. However, in all instances the professional critic has deadlines and a specific number of words allowed for the review. Critic Stanley Kauffmann of the *New Republic* calls the theatre critic "a kind of para-reality to the theater's reality. . . ."

> . . . His [the critic's] criticism is a body of work obviously related to but still distinct from what the theater does; possibly influential, possibly not, but no more closely connected than is political science to the current elections. The critic learns that, on the one hand, there is the theater, with good and bad productions, and, on the other hand, there is criticism, which ought to be good about both good and bad productions. Life is the playwright's subject, and he ought to be good about its good and bad people; the theater is the critic's subject, and he ought to be good about its good and bad plays.[1]

Theatre, according to Kauffmann, is a subject that critics often approach with an attitude of open hostility. And the hostility is frequently requited by artists, producers, and managers. They often resent the critic's power

FIGURE 13.2

Artist Jasper Johns demonstrated his sense of irony in "The Critic Sees" in 1961 (sculpmetal on plaster with glass).

to sit in public judgment on the production. (See Figure 13.2.) The resentment is not so much against the individual critic, or the review, but against the very practice of theatre criticism. Shakespeare has Berowne in *Love's Labour's Lost* speak of "A critic; nay, a night-watch constable." Chekhov, according to one report, referred to critics as "horse-flies . . . buzzing about anything." And Max Beerbohm acknowledged in "The Critic as Pariah" (1903): "We are not liked, we critics."

Critics actually perform many services for the theatregoing public, its artists, and producers. They recognize and preserve the work of good artists for future generations. Plays that receive favorable critical attention are usually published. Critics are also publicists of the good and the bad, helping the public decide what productions to see. Critics mediate between artist and audience, as Kenneth Tynan did with his 1956 review of *Look Back in Anger* (see pages 336–337). They also serve as historians of sorts. Analyses of the professional theatre by Brooks Atkinson, Robert Brustein, Kenneth Tynan, Benedict Nightingale, Martha Croyden, Mel Gussow, and many others provide historical accounts of theatre seasons, special theatre events, and performances. Critics discover new playwrights and call attention to electrifying performances.

The most brutal (and dishonest) argument levied against theatre critics is that they are no more than failed creative artists. This is also said of literary, art, music, and architecture critics. Sometimes first-rate criticism is written by second-rate artists. Often the reverse is true. George Bernard Shaw (1856–1950) excelled in both. Criticism is a true talent, combining artistic sensibilities, writing ability, performance insights, and knowledge of theatre past and present. It requires a special creative flair. Kauffmann

George Jean Nathan

George Jean Nathan (1882–1958) was for many years a leading American theatre critic, writing largely for New York City newspapers. He fought for a drama of ideas in America, and championed plays by Henrik Ibsen, George Bernard Shaw, and August Strindberg. He discovered the great American playwright Eugene O'Neill, and published his early work in *The Smart Set*, a magazine he edited with H. L. Mencken. Nathan's more than thirty books on theatre include the volumes on the New York season that he produced annually for many years.

defines *creation* . . . "as the imaginative rendering of experience in such a way that it can be essentially re-experienced by others." This is why the critic writes and why the reader (although he or she may not often go to the theatre) reads. The critic re-creates the experience of theatre in another medium for the reader. And the critic holds a mirror up to theatre's nature, serving in the long run even those who most resent the role of the critic in the theatre.

The Critic's Questions

Theatre criticism evaluates, describes, or analyzes a performance's merits and a production's effectiveness. Since the time of the great German playwright and critic Johann Wolfgang von Goethe (1749–1832), the theatre critic traditionally has asked three basic questions of the work:

- What is the playwright trying to do?
- How well has he or she done it?
- Is it worth doing?

The first question concedes the playwright's creative freedom to express ideas and events within the theatre. The second question assumes that the critic is familiar with the playwright, as well as with the forms and techniques of the playwright's time. The third question demands a sense of production values and a general knowledge of theatre. These questions show up in varying degrees of emphasis in the review.

If critics work with these essential questions (and each one usually generates more questions about the performance), they first consider the

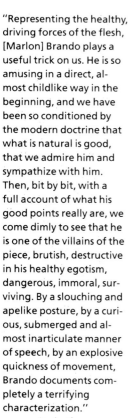

"Representing the healthy, driving forces of the flesh, [Marlon] Brando plays a useful trick on us. He is so amusing in a direct, almost childlike way in the beginning, and we have been so conditioned by the modern doctrine that what is natural is good, that we admire him and sympathize with him. Then, bit by bit, with a full account of what his good points really are, we come dimly to see that he is one of the villains of the piece, brutish, destructive in his healthy egotism, dangerous, immoral, surviving. By a slouching and apelike posture, by a curious, submerged and almost inarticulate manner of speech, by an explosive quickness of movement, Brando documents completely a terrifying characterization."

Irwin Shaw
The New Republic
22 December 1947

326

"What also makes Mr. Galati's production so impressive is its ability to give the everyday a poetic suggestiveness. Almost the best moment is the loading-up of the Joad family's jalopy with bed-linen, buckets, boxes of clothes and kitchen utensils; hardly a word is spoken, but you sense both the pathos and the quirky optimism that lies behind the migration."

Michael Billington
Guardian
24 June 1989

". . . *Look Back in Anger* was a sensation in England because Mr. Osborne has put into words an almost inarticulate point of view about the condition of British society today. . . . Although Jimmy Porter is, as one of the other characters phrases it, "angry and helpless," Mr. Osborne is not helpless. He has a savage vocabulary on the tip of his tongue."

Brooks Atkinson
The New York Times
13 October 1957

Harold Clurman

Harold Clurman (1901–1980) was an American director, author, and critic. Founding member and managing director of the Group Theatre (1931–41), he directed the early plays of Clifford Odets and many distinguished Broadway plays by Eugene O'Neill, Lillian Hellman, Arthur Miller, and Tennessee Williams. Clurman was for over fifteen years theatre critic for *The Nation*. He told the story of the Group Theatre in *The Fervent Years* (1945) and wrote an autobiography, *All People Are Famous* (1974). He published collections of his theatre essays and reviews in *Lies Like Truth* (1958) and *The Naked Image* (1966). The Harold Clurman Theater on 42nd Street in New York is named for him.

imaginative material, the concept, and the themes. Second, they judge how well the performance accomplishes the playwright's intentions. Plot, character, setting, lighting, sound, acting, and directing may be considered, depending on their relative contribution to the effectiveness of the production. Third, the response to the question "Was it worth doing?" is the most sensitive and influential aspect of the review, for critical standards are on the line as well as the fate of the production. Brooks Atkinson and Kenneth Tynan had the innate good judgment to know that Tennessee Williams and John Osborne had said something significant about human vulnerability and anger. Their reviews of *A Streetcar Named Desire* and *Look Back in Anger* are included here to demonstrate the critical standards and evaluations that get at the heart and substance of great plays and performances.

Whatever the order of the critic's essential questions about the performance, theatre criticism *describes, evaluates,* and *assesses* to one degree or another depending on the critic's tastes, talents, and preferences. Where the critic places his or her emphasis also depends on the production itself. Is it an old play dressed out in fresh designs and interpretations, as was Peter Brook's *A Midsummer Night's Dream*? Unless the critic *describes* that new look, the reader won't understand the critic's estimation of the production. Kenneth Tynan felt that *Look Back in Anger* required an *evaluation* of the truthfulness of Osborne's portrait of postwar youth, not a description of the scenery, costumes, and lighting.

Performance Notes

American Theatre, Theater, and the *Performing Arts Journal* have in recent years published relatively brief critical descriptions of distinguished productions in the noncommercial theatre both in the United States and in

FIGURE 13.3

A recent revival of Ionesco's The Chairs *with Roberts Blossom and Tresa Hughes, directed by Andrei Belgrader for the American Repertory Theatre, 1989–1990 season. As the stage gradually fills with chairs, Ionesco makes a powerful visual statement about the emptiness and fantasies that fill our lives.*

Europe. These performance notes provide, first, a record of a production, stressing its experimental qualities in acting, directing, and design, along with the fresh interpretation that emerged from nontraditional staging. The notes, usually about six paragraphs in length, are accompanied by photographs to give a sense of the performance style.

Performance notes offer an impression of trends in the avant-garde theatre, as well as some familiarity with directors (many of whom we have already mentioned) whose tastes and directorial styles are gradually finding their way into the commercial theatre. A glance at a collection of performance notes for recent theatrical seasons turns up such directors as Andrei Serban, Lee Breuer, Peter Brook, Ariane Mnouchkine, Martha Clarke, Robert Wilson, Andrei Belgrader, Jonathan Miller, and JoAnne Akalaitis. (See Figure 13.3.)

It takes years of seeing theatre to develop critical standards. But the best professional critics remain flexible even in their immense knowledge of theatre. George Jean Nathan, writing in the 1920s and '30s, got at the heart of the matter: ". . . Criticism, at its best, is the adventure of an intelligence among emotions."[2] After all is said and done, theatre criticism is the encounter of one person's sensibility with the theatrical event. Thus it is important that the critic tell us about the performance, humankind, society, and perhaps even the universe in the course of evaluating the theatre event. Harold Clurman once said that whether the critic is good or bad doesn't depend on his opinions, but on the reasons he can offer for those opinions.[3]

Writing the Theatre Review

Although there is no general agreement on criteria for judging a performance, the first step in writing theatre criticism is the ability *to see*. If we can describe what we see in the theatre, then we can begin to arrive at critical judgments. The play or production or both determines the approach — the structure of the review and the critical priorities. If the staging justifies a detailed account of what we observe, then the review incorporates a great deal of description. However, what we see in the theatre must connect with the play's meaning. For this reason, *all theatre criticism involves both description and evaluation*.

Since theatre is something perceived by the audience, writing about performance should be based on sensory impressions. As audiences, we are exposed to many significant details, sounds, and images, and only from them do we derive concepts or abstract meanings. Because we build critical concepts on the foundation of our perceptions, we can begin the process of seeing theatre critically by learning to describe our perceptions. A model for a theatre review written according to this method might take the following form (Figure 13.4):

Heading or logo
Substance or meaning of play
Setting or environment
Acting (actor and character)
Language   *Select and*
Stage business   *prioritize*
Directing   *these*
Costumes   *elements*
Lighting and sound effects
Other significant human details

In writing any commentary it is necessary, first, to identify the performance to be discussed. Kenneth Tynan identifies both play and playwright in the first paragraph of his review of *Look Back in Anger*. Frank Rich of the *New York Times* identifies actress, play, and playwright in the two short opening paragraphs of his review of *Rockaby*.

Frank Rich

Frank Rich, *New York Times* theatre critic since 1980, reviews Broadway almost entirely. Rich is a theatre critic whose influence determines the fates of multimillion dollar investments in one of the major theatre capitals of the world — New York City. His obligation is not to producers, playwrights, or actors but to a balanced and astute assessment of their work.

A STREETCAR NAMED DE-SIRE, a play in three acts by Tennessee Williams. Staged by Elia Kazan; scenery and lighting by Jo Mielziner; costumes by Lucinda Ballard; produced by Irene M. Selznick. At the Barrymore Theatre.

Negro Woman	Gee Gee James
Eunice Hubbell	Peg Hillias
Stanley Kowalski	Marlon Brando
Harold Mitchell (Mitch)	Karl Malden
Stella Kowalski	Kim Hunter
Steve Hubbell	Rudy Bond
Blanche DuBois	Jessica Tandy
Pablo Gonzales	Nick Dennis
A Young Collector	Vito Christi
Mexican Woman	Edna Thomas
A Strange Woman	Ann Dere
A Strange Man	Richard Garrick

FIGURE 13.4

A logo is a standardized format for listing the play's title, author, artists, producer, theatre, and cast list in a box separate from the review. This New York Times *logo for* A Streetcar Named Desire *was published in the December 4, 1947, edition. (Copyright © 1947 by* The New York Times *Company. Reprinted by permission.)*

Next, commentary on the play's substance or meaning informs the reader about the playwright's particular perspective on human affairs. Third, the performance involves what J. L. Styan calls "an environment of significant stimuli": sights, sounds, color, light, movement, space.[4] These stimuli can be described by answering questions related to setting, costumes, sound, lighting, acting, and stage business. Is the stage environment open or closed, symbolic or realistic? What are the effects of the stage

STAGE: BILLIE WHITELAW IN THREE BECKETT WORKS

By Frank Rich

It's possible that you haven't really lived until you've watched Billie Whitelaw die.

The death occurs in "Rockaby," the last of three brief Beckett pieces that have brought the English actress to the newly named Samuel Beckett Theater. In "Rockaby," she plays a woman in a rocking chair, rocking herself to the grave. The assignment looks simple. The only word Miss Whitelaw speaks on-stage is "more," repeated four times. The "more"'s are separated by a litany of other words — the tortured final thrashings of a consciousness, as recorded by the actress on tape. Then there is no more.

At that point, Miss Whitelaw stops rocking. The lone light that picks her face out of the blackness starts to dim, and, in the longest of Beckett pauses, we watch the light within the face's hollow eyes and chalky cheeks dim, too. During the long silence, the actress doesn't so much as twitch an eyelash — and yet, by the time the darkness is total, we're left with an image different from the one we'd seen a half minute earlier. Somehow Miss Whitelaw has banished life from her expression: what re-

mains is a death mask, so devoid of blood it could be a faded, crumbling photograph. And somehow, even as the face disintegrates, we realize that it has curled into a faint baby's smile. We're left not only with the horror of death, but with the peace.

And there you have it. With no words, no movement and no scenery, the world's greatest playwright and one of his greatest living interpreters have created a drama as moving as any on a New York stage. Indeed, one might almost say that the entire Beckett canon is compressed into this short coda to a 15-minute play. In the long pause, we feel the weight of the solitary, agonizing, seemingly endless night of living. In Miss Whitelaw's descent to extinction, we see the only escape there can be — and we feel the relief. Death becomes what it must be in a Beckett play: a happy ending.

Like the other works of this evening, "Rockaby" is late Beckett. . . . The author's dramatization of stasis has been distilled to its most austere, pitch-black quintessence; the writing is so minimalist that even the scant, incantatory language has been

drained of color, vocabulary and at times even of feeling. Yet if "Rockaby" (1980) and its predecessor on the bill, "Footfalls" (1976), make unusual demands on the audience, they are riveting theater. Or so they are as performed by Miss Whitelaw, for whom Mr. Beckett wrote them, and as impeccably directed by Alan Schneider. . . .

In "Rockaby," the actress continues to create variations within a tiny palette. Each of the four "more"'s becomes more fearful; the speaker's "famished eyes" more and more dominate her face. Though the recorded speeches that follow the request for "more" tend to sound alike, subtle differences in both the writing and the performance gradually unfold the desolate tale of a woman's terrifying search for "another creature like herself" — for "one other living soul." An echoed phrase — "time she stopped" — serves as a refrain in each speech until we at last reach the "close of a long day." Then Mr. Beckett and Miss Whitelaw make time stop, and it's a sensation that no theatergoer will soon forget.

FIGURE 13.5

The New York Times *review of Samuel Beckett's* Rockaby, *published February 17, 1984.*[5]

shape on the actor's speech, gesture, and movement? Is the lighting symbolic or suggestive of realistic light sources? What details of color, period, taste, and socioeconomic status are established by the costumes? What use is made of music and sound or light effects? What details separate the actor-at-work from his or her character-in-situation? What do the characters do in the play's action? What stage properties do the actors use and how are they significant? Finally, what visual and aural *images* of human experience and society develop during the performance? How effective are they?

In his review of *Rockaby* (see Figure 13.5), Frank Rich describes the actress seated in the single piece of furniture (the rocking chair), and the recorded sounds of her voice in contrast to the single word that she speaks ("more"). The stark stage environment, the lighting (or the absence thereof), the rocking movements of the woman in the chair, and the death mask-like makeup Billie Whitelaw wears precede any concern for the "meaning" of it all. The critical properties are clear. The look and minimal speech of the performance project an *image* of the playwright's meaning: ". . . the tortured final thrashings of a consciousness" before her extinction in death, or, as Beckett writes, before "the close of a long day."

Two Critics at Work

Brooks Atkinson (1894–1984) and Kenneth Tynan (1927–1980) wrote significant first-night reviews of two plays that made stage history: *A Streetcar Named Desire* and *Look Back in Anger*. Atkinson reviewed a play enthusiastically embraced by critics and audiences; Tynan, in contrast, found himself a lone voice supporting a play most critics had vilified. Let us examine the choices made by each of these critics as they organized the elements of their reviews. In them, both highly influential critics said to their readers, I have just seen a masterpiece, and so should you.

Atkinson on *Streetcar*

The opening-night reviewers for three of the New York newspapers — the *Post*, the *Daily News*, and the *Herald Tribune* — were unanimously ecstatic, calling Williams' new play "brilliant," "powerful," and "a smash hit." They compared him to Eugene O'Neill, Clifford Odets, and William

STREETCAR TRAGEDY: MR. WILLIAMS' REPORT ON LIFE IN NEW ORLEANS

By Brooks Atkinson

By common consent, the finest new play on the boards just now is Tennessee Williams' "A Streetcar Named Desire." As a tribute to the good taste of the community, it is also a smash hit. This combination of fine quality and commercial success is an interesting phenomenon. For if the literal facts of the story could be considered apart from Mr. Williams' imaginative style of writing, "Streetcar" might be clattering through an empty theatre. It is not a popular play, designed to attract and entertain the public. It cannot be dropped into any of the theatre's familiar categories. It has no plot, at least in the familiar usage of that word. It is almost unbearably tragic.

After attending a play of painful character, theatregoers frequently ask in self-defense: "What's the good of harrowing people like that?" No one can answer that sort of question. The usual motives for self-expression do not obtain in this instance. There is no purpose in "Streetcar." It solves no problems; it arrives at no general moral conclusions. It is the rueful character portrait of one person, Blanche DuBois of Mississippi and New Orleans. Since she is created on the stage as a distinct individual, experiences identical with hers can never be repeated. She and the play that is woven about her are unique. For Mr. Williams is not writing of representative men and women; he is not a social author absorbed in the great issues of his time, and, unlike timely plays, "Streetcar" does not acquire stature or excitement from the world outside the theatre.

Character Portrait

These negative comments are introduced to establish some perspective by which "Streetcar" may be appreciated as a work of art. As a matter of fact, people do appreciate it thoroughly. They come away from it profoundly moved and also in some curious way elated. For they have been sitting all evening in the presence of truth, and that is a rare and wonderful experience. Out of nothing more esoteric than interest in human beings, Mr. Williams has looked steadily and wholly into the private agony of one lost person. He supplies dramatic conflict by introducing Blanche to an alien environment that brutally wears on her nerves. But he takes no sides in the conflict. He knows how right all the characters are — how right she is in trying to protect herself against the disaster that is overtaking her, and how right the other characters are in protecting their independence, for her terrible needs cannot be fulfilled.

There is no solution except the painful one Mr. Williams provides in his last scene.

For Blanche is not just a withered remnant of Southern gentility. She is in flight from a world she could not control and which has done frightful things to her. She has stood by during the long siege of deaths in the family, each death having robbed her of strength and plunged her further into loneliness. Her marriage to an attractive boy who looked to her for spiritual security was doomed from the start; and even if she had been a super woman she could not have saved it.

By the time we see her in the play she is hysterical from a long and shattering ordeal. In the wildness of her dilemma she clings desperately to illusions of refinement — pretty clothes that soothe her ego, perfumes and ostentatious jewelry, artifices of manners, forms and symbols of respectability. Since she does not believe in herself, she tries to create a false world in which she can hide. But she is living with normal people who find her out and condemn her by normal standards. There is no hope for Blanche. Even if her wildest dreams came true, even if the rich man who has become her obsession did rescue her, she would still be lost. She will always have to flee reality.

Poetic Awareness

Although Mr. Williams does not write verse nor escape into mysticism or grandeur, he is a poet. There is no fancy writing in "Streetcar." He is a poet because he is aware of people and of life. His perceptions are quick. Out of a few characters he can evoke the sense of life as a wide, endlessly flowing pattern of human needs and aspirations. Although "Streetcar" is specific about its characters and episodes, it is not self-contained. The scenes of present time, set in a New Orleans tenement, have roots in the past, and you know that Mr. Williams' characters are going on for years into some mysterious future that will always be haunted by the wounding things we see on stage. For he is merely recording a few lacerating weeks torn out of time. He is an incomparably beautiful writer, not because the words are lustrous, but because the dialogue is revealing and sets up overtones. Although he has confined truth to one small and fortuitous example, it seems to have the full dimension of life on the stage. It almost seems not to have been written but to be happening.

"Streetcar" deserves the devotion of the theatre's most skillful craftsmen; and, not entirely by accident, it has acquired them. Elia Kazan, who brilliantly di-rected "All My Sons" last season, is versatile enough to direct "Streetcar" brilliantly also. He has woven the tenderness and the brutality into a single strand of spontaneous motion. Confronted with the task of relating the vivid reality of "Streetcar" to its background in the city and to its awareness of life in general, Jo Mielziner has designed a memorable, poetic setting with a deep range of tones.

Excellent Performances

The acting cannot be praised too highly. Marlon Brando's braggart, sullen, caustic brother-in-law, Karl Malden's dull-witted, commonplace suitor, Kim Hunter's affectionate, level-headed sister are vivid character portraits done with freshness and definition. As Blanche DuBois, Jessica Tandy has one of the longest and most exacting parts on record. She plays it with an insight as vibrant and pitiless as Mr. Williams' writing, for she catches on the wing the terror, the bogus refinement, the intellectual alertness and the madness that can hardly be distinguished from logic and fastidiousness. Miss Tandy acts a magnificent part magnificently.

It is no reflection on the director and the actors to observe that Mr. Williams has put into his script everything vital we see on the stage. A workman as well as an artist, he has not only imagined the whole drama but set it down on paper where it can be read. The script is a remarkably finished job: it describes the characters at full length, it foresees the performance, the impact of the various people on each other, the contrasts in tone and their temperaments and motives.

In comparison with "The Glass Menagerie," "Streetcar" is a more coherent and lucid drama without loose ends, and the mood is more firmly established. "Summer and Smoke," which has not yet been produced in New York, has wider range and divides the main interest between two principal characters. If it is staged and acted as brilliantly as the performance of "Streetcar," it ought to supply the third item in a notable trilogy. For there is considerable uniformity in the choice of characters and in the attitude toward life. That uniformity may limit the range of Mr. Williams' career as a playwright; so far, he has succeeded best with people who are much alike in spirit. In the meantime he has brought into the theatre the gifts of a poetic writer and a play that is conspicuously less mortal than most.

FIGURE 13.6

A Streetcar Named Desire *was reviewed for the* New York Times *by Brooks Atkinson as a Sunday edition feature article on December 14, 1947. Williams' play opened at* The Barrymore Theatre *on December 3, 1947.* [6]

LOOK BACK IN ANGER AT THE ROYAL COURT

By Kenneth Tynan

"They are scum" was Mr. Maugham's famous verdict on the class of State-aided university students to which Kingsley Amis' Lucky Jim belongs; and since Mr. Maugham seldom says anything controversial or uncertain of wide acceptance, his opinion must clearly be that of many. Those who share it had better stay away from John Osborne's *Look Back in Anger*, which is all scum and a mile wide.

Its hero, a provincial graduate who runs a sweet-stall, has already been summed up in print as "a young pup," and it is not hard to see why. What with his flair for introspection, his gift for ribald parody, his excoriating candour, his contempt for "phoneyness," his weakness for soliloquy, and his desperate conviction that the time is out of joint,

Jimmy Porter is the completest young pup in our literature since Hamlet, Prince of Denmark. His wife, whose Anglo-Indian parents resent him, is persuaded by an actress friend to leave him; Jimmy's prompt response is to go to bed with the actress. Mr. Osborne's picture of a certain kind of modern marriage is hilariously accurate: he shows us two attractive young animals engaged in competitive martyrdom, each with its teeth sunk deep in the other's neck, and each reluctant to break the clinch for fear of bleeding to death.

The fact that he writes with charity has led many critics into the trap of supposing that Mr. Osborne's sympathies are wholly with Jimmy. Nothing could be more false. Jimmy is simply and abundantly alive; that rarest of

dramatic phenomena, the act of original creation, has taken place; and those who carp were better silent. Is Jimmy's anger justified? Why doesn't he *do* something? These questions might be relevant if the character had failed to come to life; in the presence of such evident and blazing vitality, I marvel at the pedantry that could ask him. Why don't Chekhov's people *do* something? Is the sun justified in scorching us? There will be time enough to debate Mr. Osborne's moral position when he has written a few more plays. In the present one he certainly goes off the deep end, but I cannot regard this as a vice in a theatre that seldom ventures more than a toe into the water.

Look Back in Anger presents post-war youth as it really is,

Saroyan. But the *New York Times'* Brooks Atkinson, then dean of New York reviewers, best put the play in perspective (see Figure 13.6).

In an unusual approach, Atkinson wrote two reviews of *Streetcar*. The first appeared after opening night. The second, and now very famous, review appeared ten days later, on Sunday, December 14, 1947. In both reviews Atkinson recognized that Williams' play did not address the great social issues of the times, that it solved no problems and arrived at no general moral conclusions. Nor did it deal with "representative" men and women. But, as Atkinson wrote, it was a work of art. Its audiences sat in the "presence of truth."

Atkinson's review is organized so that he deals first with the play's truthfulness about the human beings portrayed. He then deals with Williams' "poetic language," directing and scenic details, the fine performances of the actors, and, finally, with Williams' career as the author of two Broadway successes in two years: *The Glass Menagerie* and *A Streetcar Named Desire*.

with special emphasis on the non-U intelligentsia who live in bed-sitters and divide the Sunday papers into two groups, "posh" and "wet." To have done this at all would be a signal achievement; to have done it in a first play is a minor miracle. All the qualities are there, qualities one had despaired of ever seeing on the stage — the drift towards anarchy, the instinctive leftishness, the automatic rejection of "official" attitudes, the surrealist sense of humour (Jimmy describes a pansy friend as "a female Emily Brontë"), the casual promiscuity, the sense of lacking a crusade worth fighting for, and, underlying all these, the determination that no one who dies shall go unmourned.

One cannot imagine Jimmy Porter listening with a straight face to speeches about our inalienable right to flog Cypriot schoolboys. You could never mobilise him and his kind into a lynching mob, since the art he lives for, jazz, was invented by Negroes; and if you gave him a razor, he would do nothing with it but shave. The Porters of our time deplore the tyranny of "good taste" and refuse to accept "emotional" as a term of abuse; they are classless, and they are also leaderless. Mr. Osborne is their first spokesman in the London theatre. He has been lucky in his sponsors (the English Stage Company), his director (Tony Richardson), and his interpreters: Mary Ure, Helena Hughes, and Alan Bates give fresh and unforced performances, and in the taxing central role Kenneth Haigh never puts a foot wrong.

That the play needs changes I do not deny: it is twenty minutes too long, and not even Mr. Haigh's bravura could blind me to the painful whimsey of the final reconciliation scene. I agree that *Look Back in Anger* is likely to remain a minority taste. What matters, however, is the size of the minority. I estimate it at roughly 6,733,000, which is the number of people in this country between the ages of twenty and thirty. And this figure will doubtless be swelled by refugees from other age-groups who are curious to know precisely what the contemporary young pup is thinking and feeling. I doubt if I could love anyone who did not wish to see *Look Back in Anger*. It is the best young play of its decade.

FIGURE 13.7

Kenneth Tynan reviewed Look Back in Anger *for the* Observer, London. *Osborne's play opened at the Royal Court Theatre on May 8, 1956, and was produced by the English Stage Company.*[7]

Tynan on *Anger*

After John Osborne's *Look Back in Anger* by the English Stage Company opened in London on May 8, 1956, critic Kenneth Tynan found himself in the minority, defending a play that many considered offensive and dismissed as self-indulgent drivel. Again, Tynan focused on the play's central character and Jimmy Porter's "desperate conviction that the time is out of joint. . . ." Praising the character as an act of original creation on Osborne's part — a truthful portrait of postwar youth — he wrote, "Mr. Osborne is their first spokesman in the London theatre. . . ." Tynan emphasized the human, social, and political significance of Osborne's young people as characters never before seen on the British stage (see Figure 13.7).

Summary

As we gain experience seeing theatre and describing our perceptions from a critical viewpoint, we learn that in some performances, elements such as costumes or lighting may be more important than in others. We become able to arrange priorities, to describe those details that enhance the performance, and omit those that contribute little to it. We develop criteria based on sensory stimuli for judging the performance's effectiveness.

Meaning does not *precede* the performance. A performance's meaning is the sum total of the audience's perceptions. Our experience of the relationship among visual and aural stimuli during a performance leads us to conclusions about the meaning of *Hamlet* or *Rockaby*, for example. To become skilled theatre critics is to hone our perceptions of the when, where, and how of the event taking place before us.

The professional theatre critic confronts the work in performance as the end product of the theatre's creative process. At best, the theatre critic enhances our understanding of the play as performance by enabling us to perceive the theatrical experience from a perspective other than our own or that of our friends.

Theatre criticism — carefully weighed by the reader — adds a new dimension to our discovery of theatre.

Questions for Study

1. What are the essential differences between *drama criticism* and *theatre criticism*?

2. In what way can theatre criticism be an *economic* force?

3. In what ways do general audiences become critics of the performances they see?

4. Name four main viewpoints that audiences bring to the theatre. Can you think of others?

5. Discuss these four viewpoints in relation to one or more of the model plays we have talked about.

6. Comment on the strengths and weaknesses of the most recent production you have seen.

7. How does theatre entertain us?

8. What is the job of the professional theatre critic?

9. What were Brooks Atkinson's special insights into *A Streetcar Named Desire*?

10. What were Kenneth Tynan's arguments in favor of an unusual and potentially unpopular play like *Look Back in Anger*?

11. What information is contained in the *logo* for theatre reviews printed in the *New York Times*?

12. Bring the theatre section of the Sunday edition of the *New York Times* to class and discuss the different issues that playwrights are presenting to audiences today.

13. Select a production that you have seen recently and discuss the basic questions dating from Goethe's time: *What is the playwright trying to do? How well has he or she done it? Is it worth doing?* How well do these questions help you get at the merits of a play in performance?

14. Around what priorities did Frank Rich organize his review of *Rockaby*? See page 332.

15. Attend one or more plays on your campus or in your community during the semester. Write one or more *reviews* of these performances keeping in mind the model on page 330.

16. *Suggested Reading*: Bring reviews to class from various local and national newspapers and magazines. Comment on the content and structure of the review, as well as the critic's viewpoint. Read Diana Rigg's collection of the world's most unfavorable theatre reviews, *No Turn Unstoned* (London: H. Hamilton, 1983); in paperback from Doubleday.

Glossary

Actors' Equity Association The professional union for actors, stage managers, dancers, and singers. The union controls contracts on Broadway and in the professional regional theatres. It classifies theatres, sets a minimum wage scale, and prescribes the percentage of actors and stage managers who must be members of Equity for any show within a given professional theatre. The union also prescribes conditions for auditions, working conditions, and sets down rules for becoming an "Equity" actor.

Aesthetic distance A theatre term implying a detachment between the work of art and the receptor. In order to experience a play as a work of art and not as life, there must be some sort of "psychical distance" between the viewer and the theatre event itself. If we become too involved in a play for personal reasons (perhaps its subject matter is too painful for us based on a recent experience, like rape), then we may not be able to view the play as art but only as a real life experience.

Aesthetic distance does not mean that we are totally detached or unmoved by a play or a production; rather, it means we are aware of ourselves as receptors and can experience with a new interest the work of art as something that is like life, but is not life. Our thoughts and feelings evoked by a play are not the same as those evoked by a roughly similar situation in real life. There exists emotional and intellectual distance between us and the art work.

Agon A Greek word meaning contest or debate between opposing characters and viewpoints in Greek tragedy and comedy. The fierce debate between Oedipus and Teiresias in *Oedipus the King* is called an *agon*.

Alienation effect (Verfremdungseffekt) Bertolt Brecht called his theory and technique of distancing or alienating audiences from emotional involvement with characters and situations an "alienation effect."

Brecht wanted a thinking audience rather than an emotionally involved audience. To break down emotional involvement Brecht used white light, placards, loudspeakers, projections, loosely connected scenes, songs, and music to make things on stage appear unfamiliar, even strange, so audiences would observe and think about what they were seeing. Brecht's staging devices were employed to break with traditional stage illusion; that is, we are peering into others' lives and feeling what they feel.

Allegory A narrative in which abstractions, such as virtue, charity, hope, are made concrete for the purpose of communicating a moral. In a drama, like *Everyman* (written around 1500), characters are personified abstractions, a device typical of a morality play for teaching lessons to audiences. In *Everyman*, the most famous dramatic allegory of its time, we find Good Deeds, Beauty, Five Wits, Death, and more, represented on stage by actors.

Anagnorisis, Recognition Aristotle introduced *recognition* in the *Poetics* as a simple recognition of persons by such tokens as footprints, clothes, birthmarks, and so on. The term has since taken on a larger meaning to include the tragic hero's self-understanding. All of Shakespeare's heroes have great moments of recognition wherein they realize who they are, what they have done, and what their deeds mean for others as well.

Antagonist The character in a play who commonly opposes the chief figure or *protagonist*. The *agon* in Greek tragedy is usually centered on the debate between protagonist and antagonist; for example, in *Oedipus the King* the great antagonists to Oedipus in various debates are Teiresias, Creon, Jocasta, and the Shepherd.

Arena stage See **Stages**

Aside A short statement made by a character directly to the audience to express aloud a personal attitude or to comment upon another character or event. The convention of the aside is that it cannot be overheard by another character. The aside is one of drama's many unrealistic devices, such as the soliloquy, that audiences readily accept.

Black box See **Stages**

Box set An interior setting, such as a living room or a dining room, using flats to form the back and side walls and often the ceiling of the room. The Moscow Art Theatre settings for Chekhov's *The Three Sisters* and *The Cherry Orchard* have box settings.

Broadway Broadway is one of the longest streets in Manhattan, extending diagonally the length of the island. However, for theatregoers, "Broadway" is the thirty to forty theatres clustered between 44th Street and 52nd Street two or more blocks to the west and east of the thoroughfare. Most Broadway playhouses were built at the turn of the century, tending to have small foyers, proscenium stages, outmoded equipment, and drafty dressing rooms. Called the "Great White Way" for its glitter, Broadway remains the area where the most important commercial theatre in the world is produced. When it has a dud of a season, it is then referred to as "the fabulous invalid."

Catharsis Aristotle considered *catharsis* the release of twin emotions of pity and fear in the audience as it experienced tragedy. Catharsis is thought of as psychologically purgative, for it produces in an audience a purgation (or purification) of the emotions of pity and fear. Thus, an audience comes away from tragedy having felt and even modified these emotions. Catharsis, it has been argued, produces a psychologically useful role for tragedy in society.

Character Drama's characters are sometimes divided into two types: *flat* and *round*. Flat characters represent a single trait (for example, a lecherous

villain or faithful wife) and are highly predictable. Round characters are more complex, seen as it were from many sides. Like Hamlet, Mrs. Alving, and Troy Maxson, their motives, insights, and behavior, though sometimes unexpected, are credible and provocative. See **Stock character**.

Climax A decisive turning point in the plot where tension is highest. The burning of the orphanage in *Ghosts* is a good example of climax.

Comic relief Humorous episodes in tragedy that briefly lighten the tension and tragic effect. Scenes of comic relief often deepen rather than alleviate the tragic effect. One such scene of comic relief is the gravedigger's scene in *Hamlet*, which, despite its jocularity, calls attention to the common end of all humanity — death and the grave.

Commedia dell' Arte Professional, improvisational companies of actors, including women, that flourished in Italy in the sixteenth century. The average size *commedia* company was ten to twelve members, divided usually into stock characters of two sets of lovers, two old men, and several *zanni* (the array of comic servants, braggarts, buffoons, tricksters, and dupes). Each character had an unvarying name, like Pantalone, costume, mask, and personality. The actors worked from a basic story outline (posted backstage), improvising dialogue, action, and stage business (called *lazzi*) from that outline. They performed on improvised platform stages; the best companies performed in the halls and palace theatres of dukes and kings. Since the *Commedia dell' Arte* was improvised theatre, even though we have some 700 or more *scenarios*, or plot outlines performed by the companies, we are left with only the bare bones of a theatre tradition: its characters, events, disguises, *lazzi*, and illustrations of costumes and masks.

Convention An understanding established through custom or usage in the theatre that certain devices will be accepted or assigned specific meaning or significance on an arbitrary basis, that is, without requiring that they be natural or real. In a soliloquy the actor stands alone on the stage speaking to himself or herself so that the audience can "overhear" private thoughts. Since this behavior is accepted as a convention we do not think it odd or unnatural when it occurs.

Criticism Criticism is the understanding and assessing of the play either as a literary text or as a play in performance. These types of criticism are called respectively drama and theatre criticism. Drama (or interpretive) criticism is usually associated with scholarly articles, books on theatre, and classroom teaching. The critic is concerned with the what and how of the play — with historical background, themes, genre, character, plot, and action. Theatre criticism is found in newspapers, magazines, and journals; it deals with the productions of new and revived plays as performances, not literary texts. Such specialized theatre journals as *The Drama Review, Theater, American Theatre,* and *The Performing Arts Journal* publish articles mainly on contemporary theatre performance and avant-garde movements in the United States, Europe, and Latin America.

Deus ex machina ("a god out of the machine") In Greek plays, a cranelike device (the *mechane*) was used to raise or lower "gods" into the playing space. It came to be used by playwrights, like Euripides, to solve a problem in a story, usually the ending. Hence, the term has come to mean in drama and literature any unexpected or improbable device used to unknot a plot and thus conclude the work. The king's officer who arrests Tartuffe and rewards Orgon in Molière's comedy is one such example.

Dionysus Greek god of wine, fertility, the phallus, and irrational impulses. It is commonly held that Greek tragedy evolved from choral celebrations (dithyrambic odes) in Dionysus' honor. The Greater Dionysia (or City Dionysia) in Athens was a festival held each year in the god's honor; popular dramatic contests — with Aeschylus, Sophocles, and Euripides competing — were held in the Theatre of Dionysus.

Double plot, subplot, simultaneous plots Drama's *plot* is the arrangement of incidents or sequences in the story, that is, the order of events. Aristotle not only called plot the "soul of tragedy" but "the whole structure of the incidents." He considered it more important than character or the personalities of the story's individuals. We discussed the elements of plot (exposition, point of attack, complication, crisis, climax, reversal, resolution) in Chapter 10 and the appeal of double plots to Renaissance writers.

The double or simultaneous plot (sometimes called a subplot or underplot) develops two plots, usually with some sort of connection between them. In the order of things, one will be more important than the other. The secondary plot (the story of Polonius' family in *Hamlet* or the Gloucester plot in *King Lear*) is a variation on the main plot. In *Hamlet,* the main plot and the subplot deal with two families whose children suffer parental loss, grief, and untimely deaths. In repeating themes, problems, and events, the double plot demonstrates the world's complexity by engaging a large number of people, events, and locales.

Dramaturg The dramaturg's profession, which was created in eighteenth-century Germany, has only recently been instituted in American regional theatres. Most often called a *literary manager* in this country, the dramaturg is a critic in residence who performs a variety of tasks before a play opens. He or she selects and prepares playtexts for performance; advises directors and actors on questions of the play's history and interpretation; and educates audiences by preparing lectures, program notes, and essays. To accomplish all of this, the dramaturg serves as script reader for new scripts, theatre historian, translator, play adaptor, editor, director's assistant, and critic of the work in progress. The commitment to producing new plays by our regional theatres has given rise to the dramaturg's employment by a number of not-for-profit regional theatres, including the Yale Repertory Theatre in New Haven, the Guthrie Theater in Minneapolis, the Mark Taper Forum in Los Angeles, and the American Repertory Theatre in Cambridge.

Ensemble acting or performance Acting that stresses the total artistic unity of the performance rather than the individual performance of a specific (or "star") actor. The photos of Stanislavsky's productions of *The Three Sisters* and *The Cherry Orchard* show the unity of acting style for which the Moscow Art Theatre became renown.

Epilogue Usually a concluding address following the play's ending. Many epilogues were written to encourage applause or to feature one final time a popular actor.

Hamartia (hybris; hubris) A Greek word variously translated as "tragic flaw," or "tragic error." Though Aristotle used *hamartia* to refer to those personality traits that lead heroes to make fatal mistakes, the idea of tragic flaw became simplified over the centuries to mean a single vice, frailty, or even a virtue (for example, pride, ambition, arrogance, overconfidence) that brings about the tragic hero's downfall. When applied to Sophocles' and to Shakespeare's great heroes, *hamartia* becomes a very complex concept related to human choice and action.

Hand properties See **Properties**

Irony Dramatic irony (Sophoclean irony or tragic irony) refers to a condition of affairs that is the tragic reverse of what the participants think will happen but what the audience knows at the outset. Thus, it is ironic that Oedipus accuses the blind prophet Teiresias of corruption and lack of understanding. By the play's end, Oedipus learns (as the audience has known from the beginning) that he himself is corrupt, that he has been mentally blind (ignorant), and the prophet has had superior sight (knowledge).

Dramatic irony also occurs when a speech or action is more fully understood by the audience than by the characters. Found in both tragedy and comedy, this sort of irony is usually based on misunderstanding or partial knowledge. It is ironic, for example, that Tartuffe thinks the king's officer has come to arrest Orgon when, in fact, he has come to arrest Tartuffe.

Mise-en-scène The arrangement of all the elements in the stage picture either at a given moment or dynamically throughout the performance. Modern directors give careful attention to the mise-en-scène, or total stage picture, integrating all elements of design, lighting, acting, and so forth. The mise-en-scène established by director Andrei Serban and designer Santo Loquasto for the 1977 New York production of *The Cherry Orchard* reflects the director's emphasis on the cherry trees and the dying civilization (see Photo Essay, Chapter 11).

Monologue Usually a long speech delivered by one character that may be heard but not interrupted by others. Or, it may refer to a performance by a single actor, which is called today a "solo performance." The term *monologue* has been applied to the soliloquy, the aside, and to "direct address" where a character steps out of the world of the play and speaks directly to the audience, like the narrator in Bertolt Brecht's *The Caucasian Chalk Circle*.

Off-Broadway A term that came into theatrical usage in the 1950s; defined by the Actors' Equity Association minimum basic contract as theatres located in the Borough of Manhattan outside the area bounded by Fifth and Ninth avenues, from 34th to 56th street, and by Fifth Avenue to the Hudson River from 56th to 72nd street. In addition to being outside that area, an Off-Broadway theatre has no more than 299 seats.

Off-Broadway playhouses developed in the '50s as alternatives to Broadway's commercialism. Today, the term refers to professional (Equity) theatres operating on significantly reduced budgets in comparison to Broadway, but under a financial structure prescribed by the Actors' Equity Association. Sam Shepard's plays are performed Off-Broadway, and some Broadway plays, like Marsha Norman's 'Night, Mother, are reopened Off-Broadway once they have closed on Broadway. This latter practice, of course, depends on the popularity of the play.

Off-Off-Broadway A term that came into theatrical usage in the 1960s, referring to experimental theatres (and spaces) located between West Houston Street ("Soho"), Greenwich Village, and the Bowery. These theatres are lofts, garages, warehouses, studios, churches, and coffee houses where noncommercial and experimental workshops and performances take place. As Broadway's commercialism and Actors' Equity encroached on the Off-Broadway theatres, adventuresome producers and artists moved elsewhere, looking for solutions to high production costs and union demands. The work of the Open Theatre, the Living Theatre, the Performance Group, the Wooster Group, and La Mama Experimental Theatre Club is in this category.

Open stage See **Stages**

Performance A word used, especially in modern theatre criticism, to describe the whole theatrical event. In environmental theatre the performance begins as the *first* spectator enters the performing space and ends when the *last* spectator leaves.

Producer In the American theatre the person who puts together the financing and management, publicity and artistic teams to "produce" a show, usually commercial. The producer is ordinarily not involved directly in the artistic direction of the production. The producer hires (and even fires) the artistic personnel and in this way may put a kind of stamp on the overall artistic effect. Producers who have significantly affected the Broadway theatre for some years are: Roger L. Stevens, David Merrick, Bernard Jacobs (of the Shubert organization), Alexander H. Cohen, James M. Nederlander, Morton Gottlieb, Emanuel Azenberg, and Elizabeth I. McCann.

Properties These fall into two categories: *set* and *hand* properties.

Set properties are those items of furniture or set pieces that the actor uses; they are placed on stage for design reasons, to accommodate the actor's movement, and to place the actors in the right degree of emphasis with relationship to them. The size and structure of properties, especially furniture, determine the sort of movement the actor can make around them and the use of costume.

Hand properties, such as fans, pistols, swords, or telephones, are required for personal use by the actor. Sometimes the distinction between the set and hand prop is unclear, but design is the main function of the set prop; the hand prop first satisfies the needs of the actor using it even though its "look" is important to the designer. The table lamp that Mrs. Alving turns out in the final act of *Ghosts* is a hand prop, one with symbolic significance. As a set prop, the tree in *Waiting for Godot* is part of the scenic design. Properties are the initial responsibility of the designer. There is a property head and crew responsible for acquiring or making props, supplying rehearsal props, handing out and storing props during the production, and repairing and returning props to storage at the production's close.

Proscenium theatre   See **Stages**

Protagonist   The major character in a play. The Greek word literally means "first" (*protos*), that is, the first contender or chief actor in the performance. For example, Oedipus, Hecuba, Hamlet, Macbeth, and Othello are all protagonists. The Greeks labeled the second role the *deuteragonist*, and the third the *tritagonist*. The character in conflict with the protagonist is the *antagonist*.

Regional or resident theatres   The terms *regional* and *resident* have been used interchangeably for the past twenty years to describe professional (Equity) not-for-profit theatres located outside New York City. Today, there are over sixty theatres (members of the League of Resident Theatres) in fifty-one cities with operating budgets ranging from $200,000 to more than $9 million. They produce over 600 productions yearly to audiences of more than 12,000,000. Most perform seasons from five to eleven months, generally to subscription audiences. Established in the '50s and '60s, these theatres from Seattle to Boston have been heralded as alternatives to the commercialism of Broadway and to the theatre's centralization in New York. In a society as diverse and as farflung as that of the United States, these theatres make up a matrix that many call our *national theatre*. Among the most prestigious of the regional theatres are: the Guthrie Theater (Minneapolis), American Repertory Theatre (Cambridge), the Arena Stage (Washington, D.C.), the Yale Repertory Theatre (New Haven), the Mark Taper Forum (Los Angeles), the New York Shakespeare Festival Theatre (New

York), the Milwaukee Repertory Theatre (Wisconsin), the Goodman Theatre (Chicago), and Actors Theatre of Louisville.

Revenge play   The development of revenge plays was influenced in the Renaissance by the work of the Roman author Seneca (4 B.C.–65 A.D.). Seneca's ten extant Roman tragedies, probably written not for the stage but for private readings, were filled with deranged heroes, ghosts, deeds of vengeance and horror, stoical speeches, messengers reporting offstage horrors, and pithy moralisms (called *sententiae*).

The Elizabethans read the Roman writers in their classrooms and transposed revenge conventions to the public stage. *Hamlet* has its ghost; its variety of deaths by sword, poison, trickery; and its revengers (Hamlet, Laertes, Fortinbras). In *King Lear*, Gloucester is blinded on stage and *Titus Andronicus* is a virtual feast of atrocities. The revenge play had its own excitement in its many variations on patterns and conventions (like today's horror films) but some, like *Hamlet*, achieved greatness in the writing, characters, originality, and universal insights.

Reversal (peripeteia; peripety)   A plot reversal occurs when an action produces the opposite effect of what was intended or expected. Reversals occur in both tragedy and comedy. A complex play may have several reversals before its ending. The reversal that occurs when Tartuffe's true nature is revealed to Orgon in the seduction scene is not at all what the characters anticipate. In fact, this reversal "reverses" their situation in the sense that it only makes it worse. The king's officer brings about the final reversal by restoring Orgon's family to good fortune and by punishing Tartuffe.

Satyr play The fourth play in the series of fifth-century classical Greek tragedies functioned as an afterpiece to the tragic trilogy. The satyr play burlesqued the serious themes or the major characters of the three earlier plays (the trilogy) by showing persons in ludicrous situations. The piece had a chorus of lewd satyrs (creatures half-man, the other half either horse or goat). Euripides' *The Cyclops* is the only complete satyr play in existence. It travesties the legend of Odysseus' encounter with Polyphemus.

Scenographer A designer with artistic control over all design elements, including set, lighting, and costume. The recent development of theatre technology, particularly the use of film projections and moving scenery, has called for unified production with one person integrating the various design elements. Although the scenographer works closely with the director, he or she is responsible for the totality of theatrical expression in time and space. Artistic unity is the goal. The idea that one person must have total control over design is derived from the theatrical concepts of the early twentieth-century theorists Adolphe Appia and Edward Gordon Craig.

   One of the world's most famous scenographers today is Josef Svoboda (b. 1920), the leading designer of the Prague National Theatre in Czechoslovakia. He became known in America through the Czech Pavilion at the 1967 Montreal Exposition, where he orchestrated films and stills, cascading images over surfaces and spectators. The result was a visually kinetic assault on the spectators. Svoboda's stage designs feature moving blocks, projections, and mirrors. The basis of his theory is that all scenic elements must appear and disappear, shift and flow, to complement the play's development.

Set properties See **Properties**

Soliloquy A speech delivered by an actor alone on stage, which, by stage convention, is understood by the audience to be the character's internal thoughts, not part of an exchange with another character or even with the audience.

Spine In the Stanislavsky method, a character's dominant desire or motivation, which underlies his or her action in the play. For a director, the spine is the throughline of a character's action that propels the play forward toward its conclusion. Director Elia Kazan conceived of the spine of Tennessee Williams' character Blanche DuBois in *A Streetcar Named Desire* as the search for refuge from a brutal and hostile world.

Stage business An actor's "business" in a role can be anything from the reading of a newspaper to smoking a cigarette to drinking a cup of coffee while he or she performs the text. Stage business is the actor's "busyness," activities devised by the actor (sometimes at the director's suggestion) to create a sense of character apart from the dialogue.

Stages — proscenium, arena, thrust or open, and black box Throughout theatre history, there have been five types of theatre buildings and basic arrangements of audience seating: (1) the proscenium or picture-frame stage, (2) the arena stage, or theatre in the round, (3) the thrust or open stage, (4) the black box, and (5) created or found space of the kind discussed as environmental theater in Chapter 3.

   The proscenium or picture-frame stage is most familiar to us. Almost all college campuses have proscenium theatres, and our Broadway theatres have proscenium stages. The word *proscenium* comes from the wall with a large center opening that separates the audience from the raised stage. In the past the opening was called an "arch" (the proscenium arch), but it is actually a rectangle. The audience faces in one direction before this opening, appearing to look through a picture frame into the locale on the other side. The auditorium floor slants downward from the back of the building to provide greater visibility for the audience; usually there is a balcony above the auditorium floor protruding about halfway over the main floor. Frequently there is a curtain just behind the proscenium opening that discloses or hides the event on the other side. The idea that a stage is a room with its fourth wall removed comes from this type of stage; the proscenium opening is thought of as an "invisible wall."

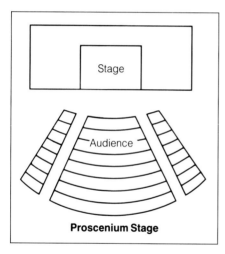

Proscenium Stage

The *arena* stage (also called a theatre in the round) breaks away from the formality of the proscenium theatre. It places the stage at the center of a square or circle with seats for the spectators around the circle or on the four sides. This stage offers more intimacy between actor and audience since the playing space usually has no barriers separating them. In addition, productions can usually be produced on low budgets since they require only minimal set pieces and furniture to indicate scene and place. Margo Jones (1913–

1955) pioneered arena theatre design and performance in America, establishing Theatre 47 in Dallas, Texas, in 1947. Today, the Arena Stage in Washington, D.C., founded by Zelda Fichandler and Edward Mangum, is one of the most famous.

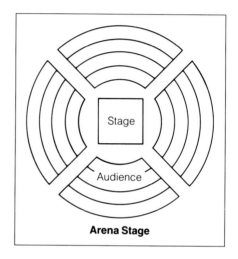

Arena Stage

The *thrust* or *open* stage, which combines features of the proscenium theatre and the arena stage, usually has three-quarter seating for the audience. The basic arrangement has the audience sitting on three sides or in a semicircle around a low platform stage. At the back of the stage is some form of proscenium opening providing for entrances and exits as well as scene changes. The thrust stage combines the best features of the other two stages discussed here: the sense of intimacy for the audience, and a stage setting against a single background that allows for scenic design and visual elements. After World War II a number of important thrust stages were built in the United States and Canada, including the Guthrie Theater in Minneapolis and the Shakespeare Festival Theatre at Stratford, Ontario.

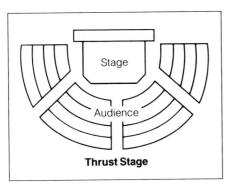

Thrust Stage

The *black box* is a type of minimal performance space developed in the '60s for experimental work and/or new plays. Essentially a large rectangular room (painted a flat black to avoid glare from the overhead lighting instruments), the black-box theatre is usually equipped with a complex overhead lighting grid with instruments and movable seating (approximately 90 to 200 seats). The movable seating permits experimentation with the shape and size of the performance space. The Cottesloe Theatre at the National Theatre, London, is a black-box theatre with two galleries surrounding three sides of the rectangular space. Designed along the lines of an Elizabethan inn-

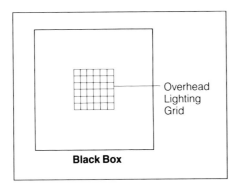

Black Box

yard, the galleries are permanent but the risers of seats positioned along the floor are movable. (See page 6.)

Stock character   The stock character is not only a "flat" character but a generic type found throughout drama: jealous husband, clever servant, braggart soldier, hypocrite, pedant, cuckold, miser. Though most common to comedy (Molière has a number of stock characters in *Tartuffe* ranging from hypocrite to clever servant), stock characters are also found in serious plays. In tragedy we find the avenger, the usurper, the tyrant, and so on.

Thrust stage   See **Stages**

Tiring-house   The backstage space in the Elizabethan public theatre. We know little about this area behind the stage wall used for preparing and maintaining productions. Some reconstructions suggest the space was used for dressing rooms, and for storing costumes, furniture, properties, and other equipment.

United Scenic Artists   The union composed of scenic designers, art directors for television and movies, scenic artists, costume designers, lighting designers, mural artists, as well as members in diorama and display. In order to accept jobs with some theatre organizations, designers must join the United Scenic Artists Union. There are two U.S.A. locals, No. 829 in New York City and No. 350 in Chicago. Both are affiliated with the International Brotherhood of Painters and Allied Trades of the AFL-CIO. There is a parallel union on the West Coast, local 816, the Scenic and Title Artists union, affiliated with the International Alliance of Theatrical Stage Employees (I.A.T.S.E.), the "stagehands" union.

To qualify for membership in the United Scenic Artists Union, an interview and samples of the designer's work are required. Those who become applicants are given rigid examinations in one or more categories chosen by the candidate (scenic designer, costume designer, lighting designer, and scenic artist). Sooner or later, membership in the union becomes an important professional step for the designer.

Unity A critical term implying a coherence in which the parts of a piece work together to contribute to the whole. *Unity* suggests completeness or a recognizable pattern that ties together beginning, middle, and ending. Aristotle thought a tragedy should have a unified action, meaning a completeness without loose ends or the *deus ex machina* abruptly resolving the play.

Italian critics of the late sixteenth century codified Aristotle's comments in *The Poetics* on unity of action and themselves established "three unities" of time, place, and action. These unities have often mistakenly been passed down to generations as Aristotle's prescription. The unities so revered by sixteenth-century Italian critics and by seventeenth-century French neoclassical writers were: (1) the action of a play must not cover more than twenty-four hours; (2) it must occur in a single place or room; and (3) it must be entirely tragic or entirely comic with no mixture of plots or characters from either kind of writing. What is interesting is that most Greek tragedies in some way violate these unities.

Well-made play (pièce bien faite) A commercially successful pattern of play construction. Its techniques were perfected by the nineteenth-century French playwright Eugène Scribe (1791–1861) and his followers.

The well-made play uses eight technical playwriting elements: (1) a plot based on a secret known to the audience but withheld from certain characters until it is revealed at the climax to unmask a fraudulent character and restore the suffering hero, with whom the audience sympathizes, to good fortune; (2) a pattern of increasingly intense action and suspense prepared by exposition, contrived entrances and exits, and devices like unexpected letters; (3) a series of gains and losses in the hero's fortunes, caused by a conflict with a hostile opponent or force; (4) a major crisis in the hero's bad fortune; (5) a revelation scene brought about by the disclosure of a secret that brings a turnabout in the hero's bad fortune and defeats the opponent; (6) a central misunderstanding made obvious to the audience but withheld from the characters; (7) a logical, credible resolution or tying-up of events with appropriate dispensations to good and bad characters; and (8) an overall pattern of action repeated in each act, and act climaxes that increase tension over the play's three or four acts.

The features were not new in Scribe's day, but represented the technical methods of most great writers of comedy and even serious drama. Scribe and his followers turned the techniques into a formula for commercially entertaining plays as well as serious plays dealing with social and psychological subjects. In plays by Henrik Ibsen, George Bernard Shaw, and Oscar Wilde we can see the well-made play machinery underpinning the action.

West End, London The theatre district in central London equivalent to our Broadway where commercial plays are produced. *Cats* and *The Phantom of the Opera* were first produced in the West End rather than in one of the government-subsidized theatres.

Suggested Projects for Students of Theatre

CHAPTER 1

1. Write a short essay contrasting and comparing your experience of a theatre performance with a film of your choice.

2. Attend a dance performance or an opera. What are the similarities and differences between theatre and these art forms?

CHAPTER 2

1. Describe in detail a contemporary theatre with which you are familiar. Discuss the location and function of the foyers, stage, and working areas.

2. Interview the technical director, designers, directors, and actors who work in this theatre. What are its successful features from their viewpoint? What are its difficulties? What is the audience's attitude toward the auditorium?

3. Discuss with the theatre's managing director, marketing, audience development, and box office personnel the kinds of jobs they do for this theatre. What are their priorities? How are they similar? Different?

CHAPTER 3

1. Seek out a "nontraditional" theatre group in your area. Interview members of the group and describe their goals, working environment or space, and the type of performance work they engage in.

2. Write a short research paper on the history of one of the following internationally known groups:
   - The Wooster Group, New York City
   - The Bread and Puppet Theatre, Vermont
   - Théâtre du Soleil, Paris
   - The San Francisco Mime Troupe
   - Mabou Mines, New York City
   - El Teatro Campesino, San Juan Bautista, California

CHAPTER 4

1. Interview a playwright and write a short essay on his or her working methods.

2. Talk with various writers about the sources of their inspiration and creative material. Make a list to share with the class.

3. Discover how a playwright goes about getting an agent.

4. What is the process for getting a playscript published?

CHAPTER 5

1. Interview a working director and write a short essay on how she or he approaches a text. What are the first steps?

2. Draw a ground plan for one of the model plays in this book.

3. Interview a stage manager. Draw up a checklist of his or her duties.

4. Make a list of what a stage manager's promptbook includes.

5. What are the audition and casting rules for your campus theatre?

CHAPTER 6

1. Interview an actor and describe his or her preparations for a role.

2. Read a biography (or autobiography) of a major professional actor. A few books are suggested in the bibliography of this text. Be prepared to discuss the difficulties of the profession, as well as the particular problems encountered by the actor whom you have studied.

3. Using Constantin Stanislavsky's methods, write out your imagined history of one of the following characters:
   - Ophelia (*Hamlet*)
   - Mrs. Alving (*Ghosts*)
   - Lopakhin (*The Cherry Orchard*)
   - Tartuffe
   - Varya (*The Cherry Orchard*)
   - Vincent (*Buried Child*)
   - Troy Maxson (*Fences*)
   - Mitch (*A Streetcar Named Desire*)
   - Grusha (*The Caucasian Chalk Circle*)

4. Attend a dress rehearsal of one of your campus productions, recording in a notebook all that takes place there. Review in the text the purpose of the dress rehearsal.

CHAPTER 7

1. Interview a working designer — scenery, costume, lighting, or sound — and describe his or her work on a particular production. What problems did the designer encounter? What solutions were tried and decided on for the production?

2. Research Bertolt Brecht's staging of *The Caucasian Chalk Circle* for the Berliner Ensemble in 1954. Discuss, in particular, his use of the half white curtain across the front of the stage, the scenic designs, and his use of the revolving stage.

3. Select one of the following characters and design a costume for that character to wear in a particular scene. Include swatches of material on the design to illustrate your sense of color and material textures:
   - Ophelia (*Hamlet*)
   - Elmire (*Tartuffe*)
   - Grusha (*The Caucasian Chalk Circle*)
   - The Fireman (*Bald Soprano*)
   - Stanley Kowalski (*A Streetcar Named Desire*)
   - Halie (Act 1; *Buried Child*)
   - Charlotta (*The Cherry Orchard*)
   - Lucky (*Waiting for Godot*)
   - Rose (*Fences*)
   - Mrs. Alving (*Ghosts*)

4. Describe particular makeup problems (and solutions) for a performance or a film that you have seen.

5. Make a list of stage properties that are needed for one of the following plays: *Buried Child, Ghosts, A Streetcar Named Desire, Waiting for Godot, Fences.*

6. Interview the technical director of your campus theatre and make a list of the lighting and sound equipment that is in current use. What new items of stage technology are needed by the theatre at this time?

CHAPTER 8

1. Report to the class on the latest trends listed in *Variety* regarding:
   - Broadway openings and closings
   - Broadway grosses for musicals and nonmusicals
   - national touring companies
   - events on the regional theatre scene

2. If possible, talk with several *producers* from the commercial, nonprofit, and educational theatre. What are the similarities and differences in their jobs and attitudes?

3. Develop a flow chart of the theatre organization best known to you including artistic and administrative staff.

4. Write a short essay on how the producer's job differs in the professional and educational setting.

5. Bring a copy of the *Actors' Equity Association Rules Handbook* to class. Discuss the scope of the union's concerns for working actors and stage managers.

CHAPTER 9

1. Make a diagram, like the one found on page 189, outlining the differences between *comedy* and the *theatre of the absurd*.

2. Make two diagrams showing the differences between tragedy and melodrama, and comedy and farce.

3. For a semester-long project, select a short story or a novel for the class as a group to adapt as a stage play. Keep a journal describing the methods, readings, and progress of the adaptation. Conclude the project with a staged reading of the adaptation by the class.

CHAPTER 10

1. Diagram the plot for one of the following plays: *Tartuffe, A Streetcar Named Desire, Fences, Buried Child*. Include in this diagram points of exposition, complication, climax, and resolution.

2. Write one-paragraph statements on the structure and content of:
   - exposition in *Tartuffe*
   - point of attack in *Ghosts*
   - complications in *A Streetcar Named Desire*
   - crisis and climax in *Fences*
   - resolution in *Buried Child*

3. After some research, describe Mabou Mines as a "theatre collective."

4. Describe Billie Whitelaw's preparation for her role in Samuel Beckett's *Rockaby*. (See videotape cited on page 359.)

CHAPTER 11

1. Using a tape recorder, record some "everyday" language that takes place at the family breakfast or dinner table, at restaurants with friends, or over coffee breaks between classes. Why is this language (or dialogue) essentially *undramatic*, or unstageworthy? Play back some of your best examples for the class.

2. Write a detailed analysis of one of Hamlet's or Macbeth's soliloquies. What makes Shakespeare's language stageworthy or dramatic?

3. Make a list of the nonverbal language in Ibsen's *Ghosts* or in Chekhov's *The Cherry Orchard*. In what way does the nonverbal language complement the "verbal" dialogue? Give other examples of how nonverbal language conveys meaning on stage.

4. Read the relevant chapter in *Notes and Counter-Notes* by Eugene Ionesco and describe the history of how he came to write *The Bald Soprano*.

CHAPTER 12

1. Design either on paper or as a three-dimensional model a box setting for *Ghosts, The Cherry Orchard* or *The Bald Soprano*.

2. Attend a play and describe the performance style of the production. Was the overriding style *realism* or *theatricalism*? Be specific in your answer.

3. Apply the model on page 284 to *Fences*. Describe in detail the six elements as they appear in August Wilson's play.

CHAPTER 13

1. Study the performance notes in *The Performing Arts Journal*. Select one production on your campus or in the community during the semester and write a performance note based on the model used in *PAJ*.

2. Bring a sample review from one of your local newspapers to class. Analyze the critic's writing style, approach to priorities in the production, and conclusions about the play in performance. With what points do you agree or disagree?

3. Write several theatre reviews during the semester using the method set forth in page 330.

Appendix B

Related Films and Videocassettes

CHAPTER 1

Oedipus Rex, by Sophocles. Directed for the Guthrie Theater in Minneapolis and filmed by Tyrone Guthrie. (90 min., video, 1956.) Facets Multimedia, distributors.

Hamlet. With Laurence Olivier. (153 min., black & white video, 1948.) Rank Productions, Learning Corporation of America, Twyman, distributors.

Macbeth. With Orson Welles. (89 min., black & white, 1948.) Republic Films, producers; Mac-Millan, Twyman, Ivy Films, distributors. (16mm; also available on VHS video.)

A Streetcar Named Desire. With Vivien Leigh and Marlon Brando. (122 min., black & white video, 1951.) United Artists, distributors.

CHAPTER 2

The Noh Drama: Hagoromo. (43 min., color, 1968.) Kajima, producers; UNIJAP, distributors.

Bunraku Puppet Theater. (35 min., black & white, 1968.) NBCEE, producers; Films, Inc., distributors.

Kabuki: Classic Theater of Japan. (30 min., color.) MTP, producers; Modern Talking Picture Service, distributors.

CHAPTER 3

Grotowski's *Akropolis*. (60 min., black & white video, VHS.) Arthur Cantor Film Collection, distributors.

Schechner's *Dionysus in 69*. (90 min., black & white, 1970.) Sigma III, distributors.

Mnouchkine's *1789*. (35 mm, color, 1974.) M. Mnouchkine Films Ariane, 44 Champs-Elysees, 75008 Paris, distributor.

The Brig, by Kenneth Brown, and performed by the Living Theatre. Directed by Jonas Mekas. (65 min., video, 1964.) Facets Multimedia, distributor.

The Connection, by Jack Gelber, and performed by the Living Theatre. Directed by Shirley Clarke. (105 min., video, 1961.) Facets Multimedia, distributor.

The Mahabharata, a film by Peter Brook. (16 mm and video, 1990.) MK2 Productions USA, distributors.

CHAPTER 4

"NPR Beckett Festival of Radio Plays (1989.)" A series of 5 cassettes, including Samuel Beckett's plays: *All That Fall* (2 cassettes), *Embers* (1 cassette), *Words and Music* (1 cassette), *Cascando* (1 cassette), *Rough for Radio 2* (1 cassette.) NPR Cassette Department N, Washington, D.C., distributors.

David Mamet, an interview with the playwright. (55 min., video.) Facets Multimedia, distributor.

'Night, Mother, by Marsha Norman, with Sissy Spacek and Anne Bancroft. Directed by Tom Moore. (96 mins., video, 1986.) Facets Multimedia, distributor.

True West, by Sam Shepard. Directed by Gary Sinise and performed by members of the Steppenwolf Theater Company, Chicago, for PBS, and starring John Malkovich and Gary Sinise as the brothers. (110 min., video, 1983.) Facets Multimedia, distributors.

A Raisin in the Sun, by Lorraine Hansberry. The film features Sidney Poitier and Ruby Dee. (128 min., video, 1971.) Facets Multimedia, distributors.

CHAPTER 5

Samuel Beckett's *Rockaby*. Alan Schneider directs Billie Whitelaw in the premiere performance of Beckett's play. The film documents the preparations and rehearsals of the director with the star, through the complete recording of the play at the Beckett Festival in Buffalo, New York. (60 min., color.) Pennebaker Associates, Inc., distributors. (Also available on 16mm and video.)

Stations: Robert Wilson. An original work for video by Robert Wilson. (60 min., video, 1985.) Facets Multimedia, distributors.

A Streetcar Named Desire, by Tennessee Williams. Film directed by Elia Kazan and starring Vivien Leigh as Blanche DuBois and Marlon Brando as Stanley Kowalski with Karl Malden and Kim Hunter. (122 min., black & white video, 1951.) Facets Multimedia, distributors.

Beckett Directs Beckett (*Waiting for Godot, Krapp's Last Tape*, and *Endgame*), performed by the San Quentin Drama Workshop with mise-en-scène derived from Samuel Beckett's production scripts. (Visual Press, video, 1990.) Smithsonian Institution, distributor.

CHAPTER 6

Speaking Shakespearean Verse. With members of the Royal Shakespeare Company, including actors Ian McKellen, Alan Howard and directors Trevor Nunn, John Barton, Terry Hands. (50 min., color.) Films for the Humanities, distributor. (Video only.)

Preparing to Perform Shakespeare. With members of the Royal Shakespeare Company, including Ian McKellen, Alan Howard and directors John Barton and Trevor Nunn. (50 min., color.) Films for the Humanities, distributor. (Video only.)

Approaches to Hamlet. With John Barrymore, Laurence Olivier, John Gielgud, and Nicol Williamson. (45 min., color.) Films for the Humanities, distributor. (16 mm, video.)

"What's the Score?": Text Analysis for the Actor. With Arthur Wagner. (85 min., color, video VHS.) Theatre Arts Video Library, distributor.

Death of a Salesman, by Arthur Miller. A CBS television video with Dustin Hoffman as Willy Loman and Kate Reid, John Malkovich and Stephen Lane. (135 min., video, 1986.) Facets Multimedia, distributor.

Our Town, by Thornton Wilder. Film stars William Holden, Martha Scott, and Frank Craven, recreating their original Broadway roles. (89 min., video, 1940.) Facets Multimedia, distributors.

CHAPTER 7

The Three Sisters. Directed by Laurence Olivier, with settings by Josef Svoboda and costumes by Beatrice Dawson, from the National Theatre production (London) with Alan Bates, Joan Plowright, Derek Jacobi, Laurence Olivier. (AFT 1973, 165 min., 16mm, color.) The American Film Institute, distributor.

Fundamentals of Scenic Painting. With Ron Ransom, Jr. (81 min., color, video VHS.) Theatre Arts Video Library, distributor.

CHAPTER 8

Presenting Performance. (Slide/tape by Thomas Wolf.) Deals with all aspects of performance administration, financial management, promotion, hiring, fundraising. (Carousel; 30 min. slide-and-sound.) ACA Books, 570 7th Ave., New York 10018, distributor.

CHAPTER 9

King Lear. With Laurence Olivier, Dorothy Tutin, Diana Rigg, Leo McKern, John Hurt. (2 hours, 38 min., color.) Films for the Humanities, distributor. (Video only.)

The Comedy of Manners/Molière: The Misanthrope. With Edward Petherbridge. (52 min., color.) Films for the Humanities, distributor. (Video only.)

The Life and Adventures of Nicholas Nickleby. With Roger Rees and the Royal Shakespeare Company. Directed by Trevor Nunn. (7 hours, 59 min., color.) Films for the Humanities, distributor. (Video only.)

The Grapes of Wrath, adapted from John Steinbeck's novel by director John Ford, with Henry Fonda as Tom Joad and John Carradine as Casy. (129 min., video, 1946.) Facets Multimedia, distributor.

CHAPTER 10

Swimming to Cambodia, by Spalding Gray. Spalding Gray is filmed in his one-man performance. (85 min., video, 1986.) Facets Multimedia, distributors.

The Trojan Women, by Euripides. Filmed in Greece by director Michael Cacoyannis with Katherine Hepburn, Genevieve Bujold, Vanessa Redgrave. English dialogue. (105 min., video, 1971.) Facets Multimedia, distributors.

CHAPTER 11

Marat/Sade. Directed by Peter Brook with the Royal Shakespeare Company. (116 min., color, 16mm, 1966.) United Artists, distributors.

Look Back in Anger, starring Richard Burton. (99 min., black & white, 1959.) ABP Woodfall Productions, distributor.

The Serpent: An Open Theatre Production. (115 min., MGM, 16mm, color, 1973.) VCI (Video Communications, Inc.), distributor. (80 min., black & white, video VHS, 1970.) Arthur Canton Film Collection, distributor.

Macbeth. Roman Polanski's 1972 adaptation with Jon Finch and Francesca Annis. (120 min., 16mm, color.) Swank Motion Pictures, distributor.

The Three Sisters. With Alan Bates, Joan Plowright, Laurence Olivier. The National Theatre (London) production, directed by Laurence Olivier and designed by Josef Svoboda. (AFT, 1973, 165 min., 16 mm, color.) The American Film Institute, distributor.

Molière. The Royal Shakespeare Company (England) presents a version of Mikhail Bulgakov's comedy based on the life of the French playwright. With Anthony Sher as Molière and directed by Bill Alexander. (112 min., video, 1984.) Facets Multimedia, distributors.

Suggested Readings

CHAPTER 1

Blau, Herbert. *The Audience*. Baltimore, Md.: Johns Hopkins University Press, 1990.

Brook, Peter. *The Empty Space*. New York: Macmillan, 1978.

Cole, David. *The Theatrical Event: A Mythos, A Vocabulary, A Perspective*. Middletown, Conn.: Wesleyan University Press, 1975.

Kott, Jan. *The Theatre of Essence*. Evanston, Ill.: Northwestern University Press, 1984.

Schechner, Richard. *The End of Humanism: Writings on Performance*. New York: Performing Arts Journal Publications, 1982.

CHAPTER 2

Bowers, Faubion. *Japanese Theatre*. New York: Hill and Wang, 1952.

Brockett, Oscar G. *History of the Theatre*. 4th ed. Boston: Allyn and Bacon, 1982.

Hodges, C. Walter. *The Globe Restored*. 2nd ed. London: Oxford University Press, 1968.

Kirby, E. T. *Ur-Drama: The Origins of Theatre*. New York: New York University Press, 1975.

Lommel, Andreas. *Shamanism: The Beginnings of Art*. New York: McGraw-Hill Book Company, 1967.

Mullin, Donald C. *The Development of the Playhouse: A Survey of Theatre Architecture from the Renaissance to the Present*. Berkeley: University of California Press, 1970.

Southern, Richard. *The Seven Ages of the Theatre*. New York: Hill and Wang, 1961.

Turner, Victor. *From Ritual to Theatre: The Human Seriousness of Play*. New York: Performing Arts Journal Publications, 1982.

CHAPTER 3

Carriere, Jean-Claude. *The Mahabharata*. Trans. Peter Brook. New York: Harper & Row, 1987.

Grotowski, Jerzy. *Towards a Poor Theatre*. New York: Clarion Books, 1968.

Malina, Judith. *The Diaries of Judith Malina 1947–1957*. New York: Grove Press, 1984.

McNamara, Brooks, Jerry Rojo, and Richard Schechner. *Theatres, Spaces, Environments: Eighteen Projects*. New York: Drama Book Specialists, 1975.

Roose-Evans, James. *Experimental Theatre from Stanislavsky to Peter Brook*. London: Routledge & Kegan Paul, 1984.

Schechner, Richard. *Environmental Theatre*, New York: Hawthorn Books, 1973.

Schevill, James. *Breakout! In Search of New Theatrical Environments*. Chicago: University of Chicago Press, 1972.

CHAPTER 4

Brater, Enoch, ed. *Feminine Focus: The New Women Playwrights*. New York: Oxford University Press, 1989.

Conversations with Lillian Hellman. Ed. Jackson R. Bryer. Jackson: University Press of Mississippi, 1986.

Conversations with Tennessee Williams. Ed. Albert J. Devlin. Jackson: University Press of Mississippi, 1986.

Dramatists Sourcebook 1989–90. Eds. Angela Mitchell and Gillian Richards. New York: Theatre Communications Group, 1989.

Interviews with Contemporary Playwrights. Eds. Kathleen Betsko and Rachel Koenig. New York: Beech Tree Books, 1987.

Macgowan, Kenneth. *Primer of Playwriting.* New York: Random House, 1951.

Mamet, David. *Writing in Restaurants.* New York: Viking Penguin, Inc., 1986.

Miller, Arthur. *Timebends: A Life.* New York: Grove Press, 1987.

"Playwrights and Playwriting Issue." *Drama Review* 21, No. 4 (December 1977).

Playwrights on Playwriting: The Meaning and Making of Modern Drama from Ibsen to Ionesco. Ed. Toby Cole. New York: Hill and Wang, 1961.

Savran, David, ed. *In Their Own Words. Contemporary American Playwrights: Interviews.* New York: Theatre Communications Group, 1988.

"The 'Woman' Playwright Issue." *Performing Arts Journal 21,* 7, No. 3 (1983): 87–102.

Women in American Theatre. 2nd ed. Eds. Helen Krich Chinoy and Linda Walsh Jenkins. New York: Theatre Communications Group, 1987.

CHAPTER 5

Bartow, Arthur. *The Director's Voice: Interviews.* New York: Theatre Communications Group, 1989.

Brook, Peter. *The Shifting Point: Theatre, Film, Opera 1946–1987.* New York: Harper & Row, 1987.

Chekhov, Michael. *To the Director and Playwright.* Comp. Charles Leonard. New York: Limelight Editions, 1984.

Clurman, Harold. *On Directing.* New York: Macmillan, 1972.

Cole, Toby, and Helen Krich Chinoy, eds. *Directors on Directing.* Rev. ed. New York: Macmillan, 1976.

Guthrie, Tyrone. *A Life in the Theatre.* London: Harrap Ltd., 1987.

Hall, Peter. *Peter Hall's Diaries: The Story of a Dramatic Battle.* Ed. John Goodwin. London: Hamish Hamilton, 1983.

Kazan, Elia. *A Life.* New York: Alfred A. Knopf, 1988.

Miller, Jonathan. *Subsequent Performances.* New York: Viking Penguin, Inc., 1986.

Schneider, Alan. *Entrances: An American Director's Journey.* New York: Viking Penguin, Inc., 1986.

Shyer, Laurence. *Robert Wilson and His Collaborators.* New York: Theatre Communications Group, 1989.

Willett, John, ed. and trans. *Brecht on Theatre: The Development of an Aesthetic.* New York: New Directions, 1964.

CHAPTER 6

Adler, Stella. *The Technique of Acting.* New York: Bantam, 1990.

Berry, Cicely. *The Actor and His Text.* London: Harrap Ltd., 1987.

———. *Voice and the Actor.* New York: Macmillan, 1974.

Boleslavsky, Richard. *Acting: The First Six Lessons.* New York: Theatre Arts Books, 1933.

Carnovsky, Morris, with Peter Sander. *The Actor's Eye.* New York: Performing Arts Journal Publications, 1984.

Chaikin, Joseph. *The Presence of the Actor: Notes on the Open Theatre, Disguises, Acting and Repression.* New York: Atheneum, 1972.

Cohen, Robert. *Acting Professionally: Raw Facts About Careers in Acting.* 4th ed. New York: Harper & Row, 1990.

Cole, Toby, and Helen Krich Chinoy, eds. *Actors on Acting: The Theories, Techniques, and Practices of Great Actors of All Times as Told in Their Own Words.* Rev. ed. New York: Crown Publishers, 1980.

Diderot, Denis. "The Paradox of Acting," in William Archer, *Masks or Faces?* New York: Hill and Wang, 1957.

Hagen, Uta. *Sources: A Memoir.* New York: Performing Arts Journal Publications, 1984.

————— with Haskel Frankel. *Respect for Acting.* New York: Macmillan, 1973.

Hirsch, Foster. *A Method to Their Madness: The History of the Actors Studio.* New York: W. W. Norton, 1984.

King, Nancy. *Theatre Movement: The Actor and His Space.* New York: Drama Book Specialists Publications, 1971.

Lewis, Robert. *Advice to the Players.* New York: Theatre Communications Group, 1989.

—————. *Slings and Arrows: Theater in My Life.* New York: Scarborough House, 1986.

Linklater, Kristin. *Freeing the Natural Voice.* New York: Drama Book Specialists Publications, 1976.

Marowitz, Charles. *The Act of Being: Toward a New Theory of Acting.* New York: Taplinger, 1978.

Mekler, Eva. *Masters of the Stage: Twenty-Seven British Acting Teachers Talk about Their Craft,* New York: Grove Press, 1989.

Olivier, Laurence. *On Acting.* New York: Simon & Schuster, 1986.

Redfield, William. *Letters from an Actor.* New York: Limelight Editions, 1984.

Rubin, Lucile S., ed. *Movement for the Actor.* New York: Drama Book Specialists Publications, 1980.

Saint-Denis, Michel. *Training for the Theatre: Premises and Promises.* Ed. Suria Saint-Denis. New York: Theatre Arts Books, 1982.

Skinner, Edith. *Speak with Distinction.* 2nd ed. Eds. Timothy Monich and Lilene Mansell. New York: Applause Theatre Book Publishers, 1989.

Stanislavsky, Constantin. *An Actor Prepares.* Trans. Elizabeth Reynolds Hapgood. New York: Theatre Arts Books, 1948.

—————. *Building a Character.* Trans. Elizabeth Reynolds Hapgood. New York: Theatre Arts Books, 1977.

—————. *Creating a Role.* Trans. Elizabeth Reynolds Hapgood. New York: Theatre Arts Books, 1961.

—————. *My Life in Art.* Trans. J. J. Robbins. New York: Theatre Arts Books, 1952.

Strasberg, Lee. *A Dream of Passion: The Development of the Method.* Ed. Evangelina Morphos. Boston: Little, Brown, 1987.

Suzuki, Tadashi. *The Way of Acting: The Theatre Writings of Tadashi Suzuki.* Trans. J. Thomas Rimer. New York: Theatre Communications Group, 1986.

CHAPTER 7

Anderson, Barbara, and Cletus Anderson. *Costume Design.* New York: Holt, Rinehart and Winston, 1984.

Aronson, Arnold. *American Set Design.* New York: Theatre Communications Group, 1985.

Bay, Howard. *Stage Design.* New York: DBS Publications, 1974.

Bellman, Willard F. *Scenography and Stage Technology: An Introduction.* New York: Thomas Y. Crowell, 1977.

Burdick, Elizabeth B., and others, eds. *Contemporary Stage Design U.S.A.* Middletown, Conn.: Wesleyan University Press, 1975.

Burris-Meyer, Harold, and Edward C. Cole. *Scenery for the Theatre.* 2nd ed. Boston: Little, Brown, 1972.

Collison, David. *Stage Sound.* 2nd rev. ed. New York: DBS Publications, 1982.

Corey, Irene. *The Mask of Reality: An Approach to Design for Theatre.* New Orleans: Anchorage Press, 1968.

Corson, Richard. *Stage Makeup.* 7th ed. Englewood Cliffs, N.J.: Prentice-Hall, 1986.

Ingham, Rosemary, and Liz Covey. *The Costume Designer's Handbook: A Complete Guide for Amateur and Professional Costume Designers.* Englewood Cliffs, N.J.: Prentice-Hall, 1983.

Izenour, George C. *Theatre Design.* New York: McGraw-Hill, 1977.

James, Thurston. *The Theater Props Handbook: A Comprehensive Guide to Theater Properties, Materials and Construction.* Crozet, Va.: Betterway Publications, 1989.

Jones, Robert Edmond. *The Dramatic Imagination: Reflections and Speculations on the Art of the Theatre.* New York: Methuen, 1987.

Leacroft, Richard, and Helen Leacroft. *Theatre and Playhouse: An Illustrated Development of Theatre Building from Ancient Greece to the Present Day.* New York: Methuen, 1984.

Palmer, Richard H. *The Lighting Art: The Aesthetics of Stage Lighting Design.* Englewood Cliffs, N.J.: Prentice-Hall, 1985.

Parker, Oren, and Harvey K. Smith. *Scene Design and Stage Lighting.* 5th ed. New York: Holt, Rinehart, and Winston, 1985.

Pecktal, Lynn. *Designing and Painting for the Theatre.* New York: Holt, Rinehart and Winston, 1975.

Rich, Frank, with Lisa Aronson. *The Theatre Art of Boris Aronson.* New York: Alfred A. Knopf, 1987.

Rosenthal, Jean, and Lael Wertenbaker. *The Magic of Light.* New York: Theatre Arts Books, 1972.

Russell, Douglas A. *Costume History and Style.* Englewood Cliffs, N.J.: Prentice-Hall, 1983.

———. *Stage Costume Design: Theory, Technique and Style.* 2nd ed. Englewood Cliffs, N.J.: Prentice-Hall, 1985.

Simonson, Lee. *The Stage Is Set.* New York: Theatre Arts Books, 1962.

CHAPTER 8

Botto, Louis. *At This Theatre: Playbill Magazine's Informal History of Broadway Theatres.* New York: Dodd, Mead, 1984.

Crawford, Cheryl. *One Naked Individual: My Fifty Years in the Theatre.* Indianapolis: Bobbs-Merrill, 1977.

David, Christopher. *The Producers.* New York: Harper & Row, 1972.

Farber, Donald C. *From Option to Opening: A Guide to Producing Plays Off-Broadway.* Rev. ed. New York: Limelight Editions, 1989.

———. *Producing Theatre: A Comprehensive Legal and Business Guide.* New York: Drama Book Specialists, 1981.

Goldman, William. *The Season: A Candid Look at Broadway.* Rev. ed. New York: Limelight Editions, 1984.

Hay, Peter. *Broadway Anecdotes.* New York: Oxford University Press, 1989.

Jacobs, Susan. *On Stage: The Making of a Broadway Play.* New York: Alfred A. Knopf, 1972.

Langley, Stephen, ed. *Producers on Producing*. New York: Drama Book Specialists, 1976.

————. *Theatre Management in America, Principles and Practices: Producing for Commercial, Stock, Resident, College and Community Theatre*. New York: Drama Book Publishers, 1980.

Newman, Danny. *Subscribe Now!* New York: Theatre Communications Group, 1977.

Reiss, Alvin. *The Arts Management Handbook*. Rev. ed. New York: Law-Arts Publishers, 1973.

Shagan, Rena. *The Road Show: A Handbook for Successful Booking and Touring in the Performing Arts*. New York: ACA Books, 1984.

Theatre Profiles 9: The Illustrated Guide to America's Nonprofit Professional Theatres. New York: Theatre Communications Group, 1990.

Goldman, Michael. *The Actor's Freedom: Toward a Theory Of Drama*. New York: Viking, 1975.

Heilman, Robert B. *Tragedy and Melodrama: Versions of Experience*. Seattle: University of Washington Press, 1968.

Langer, Susanne K. *Feeling and Form: A Theory of Art*. New York: Charles Scribner's Sons, 1953.

Marranca, Bonnie. *Theatre of Images*. New York: Drama Book Specialists, 1977.

Nichol, Allardyce. *The Theory of Drama*. New York: Thomas Y. Crowell, 1931.

Schechner, Richard. *Public Domain: Essays on the Theatre*. Indianapolis: Bobbs-Merrill, 1969.

Smith, James L. *Melodrama*. London: Methuen, 1973.

Willett, John. *The Theatre of Bertolt Brecht: A Study of Eight Aspects*. New York: New Directions, 1959.

CHAPTERS 9 and 10

Beckerman, Bernard. *Dynamics of Drama: Theory and Method of Analysis*. New York: Alfred A. Knopf, 1970.

Bentley, Eric. *The Life of the Drama*. New York: Atheneum, 1964.

Bermel, Albert. *Farce: A History from Aristophanes to Woody Allen*. New York: Simon & Schuster, 1982.

Corrigan, Robert W., ed. *Comedy: Meaning and Form*. Rev. ed. New York: Harper & Row, 1980.

————, ed. *Tragedy: Vision and Form*. Rev. ed. New York: Harper & Row, 1980.

Esslin, Martin. *An Anatomy of Drama*. New York: Hill and Wang, 1977.

————. *The Theatre of the Absurd*. 3rd ed. New York: Penguin, 1983.

Fergusson, Francis. *The Idea of a Theater: A Study of Ten Plays. The Art of Drama in Changing Perspective*. New Jersey: Princeton University Press, 1987.

CHAPTER 11

Blau, Herbert. *Blooded Thought: Occasions of Theatre*. New York: Performing Arts Journal Publications, 1982.

————. *Take Up the Bodies: Theater at the Vanishing Point*. Urbana: University of Illinois Press, 1982.

Cole, David. *The Theatrical Event: A Mythos, A Vocabulary, A Perspective*. Middletown, Conn.: Wesleyan University Press, 1975.

Ionesco, Eugene. *Notes and Counter-Notes: Writings on the Theatre*. Trans. Donald Watson. New York: Grove Press, 1964.

McLuhan, Marshall. *Understanding Media: The Extensions of Man*. New York: McGraw-Hill, 1964.

Pavis, Patrice. *Languages of the Stage: Essays in the Semiology of Theatre*. New York: Performing Arts Journal Publications, 1982.

Styan, J. L. *Drama, Stage and Audience*. London: Cambridge University Press, 1975.

CHAPTER 12

Bentley, Eric. *The Playwright as Thinker: A Study of Drama in Modern Times*. New York: Harcourt, Brace, Jovanovich, 1987.

Brook, Peter. *Peter Brook: A Theatrical Casebook*. Comp. David Williams. New York: Methuen, 1988.

Esslin, Martin. *The Field of Drama: How the Signs of Drama Create Meaning on Stage & Screen*. New York: Methuen, 1987.

Saint-Denis, Michel. *Theatre: The Rediscovery of Style*. New York: Theatre Arts Books, 1960.

Styan, J. L. *The Dramatic Experience: A Guide to Reading Plays*. London: Cambridge University Press, 1965.

————. *Modern Drama in Theory and Practice*. 3 vols. London: Cambridge University Press, 1983.

Szondi, Peter. *Theory of the Modern Drama*. Ed. Michael Hays. Minneapolis: University of Minnesota Press, 1987.

"Theatricalism Issue." *The Drama Review*, 21, No. 2 (June 1977).

CHAPTER 13

Atkinson, Brooks. *Broadway*. New York: Macmillan, 1970.

Brustein, Robert. *Who Needs Theatre?* Ed. Gray Fishetjon. New York: Atlantic Monthly Press, 1987.

"Criticism Issue." *Drama Review*, 18, No. 3 (September 1974).

Clurman, Harold. *Lies Like Truth: Theatre Reviews and Essays*. New York: Macmillan, 1958.

————. *The Naked Image: Observations on the Modern Theatre*. New York: Macmillan, 1966.

Kauffmann, Stanley. *Persons of the Drama: Theater Criticism and Comment*. New York: Harper & Row, 1976.

————. *Theatre Criticisms*. New York: Performing Arts Journal Publications, 1984.

Nathan, George Jean. *The Critic and the Drama*. New York: Alfred A. Knopf, 1922.

Rogoff, Gordon. *Theatre Is Not Safe*. Evanston, Ill.: Northwestern University Press, 1987.

Sontag, Susan. *Against Interpretation and Other Essays*. New York: Doubleday, 1966.

Tynan, Kenneth. *Curtains: Selections from the Drama Criticism and Related Writings*. New York: Atheneum, 1971.

Notes

CHAPTER 1

1. Peter Brook, *The Empty Space* (New York: Atheneum, 1968): 3. Copyright © 1968 by Peter Brook. Reprinted with permission of Atheneum Publishers, New York, and Granada Publishing Ltd., England.
2. Samuel Beckett, *Waiting for Godot* (New York: Grove, 1954): 36, 61. Copyright © 1954 by Grove Press, Inc. Renewed 1982 by Samuel Beckett. Reprinted by permission of Grove Press, Inc.
3. Martin Esslin, *The Theatre of the Absurd*, 3rd ed. (New York: Pelican Books, 1980): 19–21.

CHAPTER 2

1. Mircea Eliade, *The Sacred and the Profane: The Nature of Religion*, trans. Willard R. Trask (New York: Harcourt, 1959): 24. Copyright © 1957 by Rowohlt Taschenbuch Verlag GmbH, trans. © 1959 and renewed 1987 by Harcourt Brace Jovanovich. Reprinted by permission of Harcourt Brace Jovanovich, Inc.

CHAPTER 3

1. Jerzy Grotowski, *Towards a Poor Theatre* (New York: Clarion Press, 1968): 19–20. Reprinted by permission of H. M. Berg, Odin Teatret, Denmark.
2. Grotowski: 19–20. Reprinted by permission.
3. Grotowski: 75. Reprinted by permission.

4. Richard Schechner, *Environmental Theater* (New York: Hawthorn, 1973): 25. Copyright © 1973 by Richard Schechner. All rights reserved. Reprinted by permission of Hawthorn Books, Inc.
5. Mel Gussow, "The Living Theater Returns to Its Birthplace," *New York Times* (Jan. 15, 1984): II, 6.

CHAPTER 4

1. Tennessee Williams, Afterword to *Camino Real* (New York: New Directions, 1953): xii. Copyright © 1948, 1953 by Tennessee Williams. Reprinted by permission of New Directions Publishing Corporation.
2. Amy Lippman, "Rhythm & Truths: An Interview with Sam Shepard," *American Theatre*, 1, No. 1 (April 1984): 9. Reprinted by permission of the Theatre Communications Group Inc.
3. Lippman: 12. Reprinted by permission of the Theatre Communications Group Inc.
4. John Lion, "Rock 'n' Roll Jesus with Cowboy Mouth," *American Theatre*, 1, No. 1 (April 1984): 8. Reprinted by permission of the Theatre Communications Group Inc.
5. R. C. Lewis, "A Playwright Named Tennessee," *The New York Times Magazine* (7 December 1947): 19. Copyright © 1947 by The New York Company. Reprinted by permission.
6. August Wilson, *Fences* (New York: NAL Penguin, 1986): 69.
7. Lorraine Hansberry. *To Be Young, Gifted and Black*, adapted by Robert Nemiroff (Englewood Cliffs, N.J.: Prentice-Hall, 1969): 133–134. Copyright © 1969 by Prentice-Hall, Inc. Reprinted by permission.
8. Lillian Hellman, *Pentimento: A Book of Portraits* (Boston: Little, Brown & Company, 1973): 151–152.

9. María Irene Fornés, "The 'Woman' Playwright Issue," *Performing Arts Journal*, 7, No. 3 (1983): 91. Reprinted by permission.
10. Carol Lawson, "Caryl Churchill Wins Blackburn Drama Prize," *The New York Times* (25 February 1984), I, 16:5. Copyright © 1984 by The New York Times Company. Reprinted by permission.
11. Mel Gussow, "Women Playwrights: New Voices in the Theater," *The New York Times Magazine* (1 May 1983): 6, 26. Copyright © 1983 by The New York Times Company. Reprinted by permission.

CHAPTER 5

1. Alan Schneider, "Things to Come: Crystal-Gazing at the Near and Distant Future of a Durable Art," *American Theatre*, 1, No. 1 (April 1984): 17. Reprinted by permission of the Theatre Communications Group Inc.
2. Elia Kazan, "Notebook for *A Streetcar Named Desire*" in *Directing The Play: A Source Book of Stagecraft*, eds. Toby Cole and Helen Krich Chinoy (Indianapolis: The Bobbs-Merrill Company, 1953): 296.
3. Hubert Witt, ed., *Brecht: As They Knew Him* (New York: International Publishers, 1974): 126. Reprinted by permission.
4. Arthur Bartow, "'Images from the Id': An Interview," *American Theatre*, 5, No. 3 (June 1988): 56–57. Courtesy of the Theatre Communications Group Inc.
5. Bartow: 17.
6. Robert Wilson and David Byrne, *The Forest* (West Berlin: Theater der Freien Volksbühne, 1988): 29–32.
7. Wilson and Byrne: 36.

CHAPTER 6

1. Laurence Olivier, *On Acting* (New York: Simon & Schuster, 1986): 192. Reprinted by permission.
2. Hal Burton, ed., *Great Acting* (London: British Broadcasting Corp., 1967): 71–72. Reprinted by permission of International Creative Management, Ltd.
3. Richard Eder, "The World According to Brook," *American Theatre*, 1, No. 2 (May 1984): 38. Reprinted by permission of the Theatre Communications Group Inc.
4. Toby Cole and Helen K. Chinoy, eds., *Actors on Acting: The Theories, Techniques, and Practices of the Great Actors of All Times as Told in Their Own Words* (New York: Crown, 1959): 132. Reprinted by permission.
5. Lewis Funke and John E. Booth, eds., *Actors Talk About Acting* (New York: Random House, 1961): 14. Reprinted by permission.
6. Robert Hethmon, *Strasberg at the Actors Studio* (New York: Viking Press, 1965): 78.
7. Constantin Stanislavsky, *An Actor's Handbook*, ed. and trans. Elizabeth Reynolds Hapgood (New York: Theatre Arts, 1963): 100.
8. Uta Hagen with Haskel Frankel, *Respect for Acting* (New York: Macmillan, 1973): 37–38. Reprinted by permission.
9. Cicely Berry, *The Actor and The Voice* (New York: Macmillan, 1973): 121.
10. Lionel Gracey-Whitman, "Return by Popular Demand," *Plays and Players*, No. 367 (April 1984): 21–25. Reprinted by permission.

CHAPTER 7

1. Lynn Pecktal, "A Conversation with Ming Cho Lee," in *Designing and Painting for the Theatre* (New York: Holt, Rinehart, & Winston, 1975): 242. Reprinted by permission.
2. Pecktal: 51. Reprinted by permission.
3. Jarka Burian, *The Scenography of Josef Svoboda* (Middletown, Conn.: Wesleyan University Press, 1971): 31. Copyright © 1971 by Jarka Burian. From a speech by Josef Svoboda, the text of which was printed in *Zprávy Divadelního Ústavu*, no. 8 (1967): 28–29. Reprinted by permission of Wesleyan University Press.
4. Patricia Zipprodt, "Designing Costumes," in *Contemporary Stage Design U.S.A.* (Middletown, Conn.: Wesleyan University Press, 1974): 29.
5. John Gruen, "She Is One of Broadway's Most Designing Women," *The New York Times* (8 April 1984): II, 5, 14. Copyright © 1984 by The New York Times Company. Reprinted by permission.

CHAPTER 8

1. Cheryl Crawford, *One Naked Individual: My Fifty Years in the Theatre.* (Indianapolis: Bobbs-Merrill, 1977): 4.
2. Alexander H. Cohen, "Broadway Theatre," in *Producers on Producing*, ed. Stephen Langley (New York: Drama Book Specialists, 1976): 15.
3. Audrey Wood with Max Wilk, *Represented by Audrey Wood* (Garden City, N.Y.: Doubleday and Company, 1981): 7.
4. *Producers on Producing*: 78.

CHAPTER 9

1. Peter Brook, *The Empty Space* (New York: Atheneum, 1968): 15.

2. Lane Cooper, *Aristotle on the Art of Poetry* (Ithaca, N.Y.: Cornell University Press, 1947): 17.
3. "Lillian Hellman, Playwright, Author and Rebel, Dies at 79," *The New York Times* (1 July 1984): 20.
4. Eric Bentley, "The Psychology of Farce," in *Let's Get A Divorce! and Other Plays* (New York: Hill and Wang, 1958): vii–xx.
5. Danielle Sallenave, "Entretien avec Antoine Vitez: Faire théâtre de tout," *Digraphe* (April 1976): 117.
6. John Willett, trans. *Brecht on Theatre: The Development of an Aesthetic* (New York: Hill and Wang, 1964): 37. Copyright © 1957, 1963, and 1964 by Suhrkamp Verlag, Frankfurt Am Main. This translation and notes © 1964 by John Willett. Reprinted with permission of Hill and Wang, a division of Farrar, Straus & Giroux, Inc. and A.B. P. Ltd.
7. Willett: 121. Reprinted by permission.
8. Albert Camus, *The Myth of Sisyphus and Other Essays* (New York: Alfred A. Knopf, 1955): 5. Reprinted by permission.
9. Eugene Ionesco, *Notes and Counter-Notes: Writings on the Theatre*, translated by Donald Watson (New York: Grove Press, 1964): 257. Copyright © 1964 by Grove Press, Inc. Reprinted with permission.
10. Eugene Ionesco, *The Bald Soprano*, translated by Donald Watson (New York: Grove Press, 1958): 11–13. Copyright © 1958 by Grove Press, Inc. Reprinted with permission.

CHAPTER 10

1. David Mamet, *Writing in Restaurants* (New York: Viking Penguin, 1986): 8.
2. Laurence Olivier, *On Acting* (London: George Weidenfeld & Nicolson Limited, 1986): 192. Reprinted by permission of the publisher.

3. Francis Fergusson, *The Idea of a Theatre* (Princeton: University Press, 1949): 36.

4. For my understanding of climactic and episodic drama I am indebted to material from Bernard Beckerman, *Dynamics of Drama: Theory and Method of Analysis* (New York: Alfred A. Knopf, 1970).

5. Spalding Gray, "About *Three Places in Rhode Island*," *Drama Review*, 23, No. 1 (March 1979): 31–42.

6. Samuel Beckett, *Rockaby* (New York: Grove Press, 1980). Reprinted by permission of Grove Press.

7. Robert Wilson, *The Civil WarS*, edited by Jan Graham Geidt (Cambridge, Mass.: American Repertory Theatre, 1985): 16. Reprinted by permission.

CHAPTER 11

1. Eugene Ionesco, *Notes and Counter-Notes: Writings on the Theatre*, translated by Donald Watson (New York: Grove Press, 1964).

2. Peter Brook, *The Empty Space* (New York: Atheneum, 1968): 12.

3. George Steiner, *The Death of Tragedy*. Copyright © 1963, renewed 1989 by George Steiner. Reprinted by permission of the author's agent, George Borchardt, Inc.

4. *Henrik Ibsen: The Complete Major Prose Plays*, translated by Rolf Fjelde. Copyright © 1965, 1970, 1978 by Rolf Fjelde. Reprinted with permission of The New American Library, Inc.

5. Anton Chekhov, *The Cherry Orchard*, revised version in English by Jean-Claude van Itallie (New York: Dramatists Play Service, Inc., 1979): 57–58. Jean-Claude van Itallie, 1977, 1979. © 1979 by Jean-Claude van Itallie (Revised). © 1977 by Jean-Claude van Itallie. This excerpt is reprinted by permission of the author and Drama-

tists Play Service, Inc. No stock or amateur performance of the play may be given without obtaining in advance the written permission of the publisher and paying the requisite fee.

6. Bertolt Brecht, "On Gestic Music" in *Brecht on Theatre: The Development of an Aesthetic*, translated by John Willett (New York: Hill and Wang, 1964): 104. Reprinted by permission.

7. Bertolt Brecht, *The Caucasian Chalk Circle*, translated by Ralph Manheim, in *Collected Plays*, Volume 7, edited by Ralph Manheim and John Willett (New York: Random House, Inc., 1975). Reprinted with permission of Random House, Inc.

8. Peter Weiss, *The Persecution and Assassination of Jean-Paul Marat as Performed by the Inmates of the Asylum of Charenton Under the Direction of the Marquis de Sade*; English translation copyright © 1965 by John Calder Ltd.; originally published in German under the title *Die Verfolgung und Ermordung Jean Paul Marats Dargestellt Durch die Schauspielgruppe des Hospizes zu Charenton unter Anleitung des Herrn de Sade*; copyright © 1964 by Suhrkamp Verlag, Frankfurt Am Main. Reprinted with permission of Atheneum Publishers and Calder and Boyars Ltd.

9. Jean-Claude van Itallie, "A Reinvention of Form," *Drama Review* (Playwrights and Playwriting Issue), 21, No. 4 (December 1977): 66–74. Reprinted with permission.

10. Jean-Claude van Itallie, *America Hurrah!* Copyright © 1966 by Jean-Claude van Itallie as unpublished plays. Copyright © 1966, 1967 by Jean-Claude van Itallie. Reprinted with permission of Grove Press, Inc.

11. John Osborne, *Look Back in Anger*. Copyright © 1957 by John Osborne. Reprinted with permission of S. G. Phillips, Inc. and Faber and Faber Publishers.

12. John Russell Taylor, *The Angry Theatre: New British Drama* (New York: Hill and Wang, 1962): 356.
13. Sam Shepard, *Buried Child* (Urizen Books, 1979). Included in *Seven Plays* by Sam Shepard. Copyright © 1979 by Sam Shepard. Reprinted by permission of Bantam Books. All rights reserved.
14. David Cole, *The Theatrical Event: A Mythos, A Vocabulary, A Perspective* (Middletown, Conn.: Wesleyan University Press, 1975): 141. Reprinted with permission.
15. Eugene Ionesco, *Notes and Counter-Notes: Writings on the Theatre*, translated by Donald Watson (New York: Grove Press, 1964): 23.

CHAPTER 12

1. Anton Chekhov, *Letters of Anton Chekhov*, edited by Avrahm Yarmolinski (New York: Viking Press, 1973): 169. Reprinted with permission.
2. For the discussion of the script-as-model I am indebted to material from David Cole, "The Visual Script: Theory and Technique," *Drama Review*, 20, No. 4 (December 1976): 27–50.
3. Tennessee Williams, *A Streetcar Named Desire*. Copyright 1947 by Tennessee Williams. Quotations in this chapter are reprinted by permission of New Directions Publishing Corporation.
4. Sam Shepard, *Buried Child* (New York: Urizen, 1979).
5. Harold Pinter, "Writing for the Theatre," in *Modern British Drama*, edited by Henry Popkin (New York: Grove Press, 1969): 574–580. Reprinted with permission.
6. Euripides, *The Trojan Women*, in *The Complete Greek Tragedies*, edited by Richard Lattimore (Chicago: The University of Chicago, 1959). Quotations in this chapter are reprinted by permission of The University of Chicago Press.

7. Richard Gilman, "Introduction," in *Sam Shepard: Seven Plays* (New York: Bantam, 1981): xxiv–xxv.
8. Michel Saint-Denis, *Theatre: The Rediscovery of Style* (New York: Theatre Arts Books, 1960): 62.
9. Eric Bentley, *The Playwright As Thinker: A Study of Drama in Modern Times* (New York: Harcourt, Brace, 1946): 4.
10. Terry W. Browne, *Playwrights' Theatre: The British Stage Company at the Royal Court Theatre* (London: Pitman, 1975): 10.
11. "The Theatricalism Issue," *The Drama Review*, 21, No. 2 (June 1977).

CHAPTER 13

1. Stanley Kauffmann, *Persons of the Drama: Theater Criticism and Comment* (New York: Harper & Row, 1976): 369–380.
2. George Jean Nathan. *The Critic and the Drama* (New York: Alfred A. Knopf, 1922): 133.
3. Eric Bentley and Julius Novick, "On Criticism," *Yale/Theatre*, 4, No. 2 (Spring 1973): 23–36.
4. J. L. Styan, *Drama, Stage and Audience* (London: Cambridge University Press, 1975): 33.
5. Frank Rich, "Stage: Billie Whitelaw In Three Beckett Works," *New York Times* (17 February 1984): III, 3. Copyright © 1984 by The New York Times Company. Reprinted by permission.
6. Brooks Atkinson, "'Streetcar' Tragedy, Mr. Williams' Report on Life in New Orleans," *New York Times* (14 December 1947): II, 3. Copyright © 1947 by The New York Times Company. Reprinted by permission.
7. Kenneth Tynan, "*Look Back in Anger*, by John Osborne, at the Royal Court," in *Curtains: Selections from the Drama Criticism and Related Writings* (New York: Atheneum, 1971): 130–132.

Index

Aside, 293, 342, 344
Assistant director, 100
As You Like It (Shakespeare), 18, 313
  text of, 18
Atkinson, Brooks (critic), 12, 25, 113, 324, 327,
    328, 333
  on Jessica Tandy in *Streetcar*, 113
  review of *A Streetcar Named Desire*, 333–335, 336
Audience, 9–12, 14, 20–24
  actor-audience relationship, 10–12
  expectations of, 20–24
  feedback, 14
Auditions, 96
Auditorium (Greek), 30
Avignon Festival (France), 68, 70

Baal (Brecht), 205
B. Beaver Animation, The (Breuer), 243
Bacchae, The (Euripides), 64, 67
Bald Soprano, The (Ionesco), 209, 210–211, 222, 224,
    225
  as absurdist play, 209
  diagram of, 225
  situation in, 224
  as tragedy of language, 209
  text from, 210–211
Ballard, Lucinda (designer), 146, 147, 331
Barrault, Jean-Louis (actor), 112
Barrymore, Ethel (actor), 112
Barrymore, John (actor), 112
Barton, John (director), 227, 293
Bates, Alan (actor), 306, 327
Battle of Angels (Williams), 83
Beck, Julian (actor-director), 64, 66
  on theatre, 66
Beckett, Samuel (playwright), 4, 17, 18, 19, 21, 89,
    97, 109, 112, 114, 115, 193, 194, 195, 208, 235,
    236–239, 240–241, 243, 250, 318, 332, 333
  as absurdist writer, 208

biography of, 194
  See also Rockaby; Waiting for Godot.
Bel Geddes, Norman (designer), 137
Belgrader, Andrei (director), 329
Bennett, Michael (director-choreographer), 151
Bentley, Eric (critic), 197, 396
  on farce, 197
  on realism, 306
Berkeley Repertory Theatre (California), 81
Berliner Ensemble (East Berlin), 141, 206, 208, 223,
    243
Bernhardt, Sarah (actor), 112
*Better Class of Person: An Autobiography 1929–1956,
    A* (Osborne), 275
Between Theater & Anthropology (Schechner), 65
Birthday Party, The (Pinter), 276
Black box, 6, 349
Blackfriars (theatre), 42
Blakely, Colin (actor), 306
Blank verse, 215
Blocking rehearsals. *See* Rehearsals.
Boleslavski, Richard (actor), 118
  on acting, 118
Bond, Edward (playwright), 222, 277, 306
Booth-stage, 38
Boruzescu, Miruna (designer), 301
Boruzescu, Radu (designer), 301
Box set, 45, 46, 304, 342
Brand (Ibsen), 219
Brando, Marlon (actor), 10, 11, 15, 101, 113, 121,
    301, 326, 335
Bread & Puppet Theatre (Vermont), 59, 64, 71,
    72–74, 75
Brecht, Bertolt (playwright), 51, 52, 78, 79, 82, 98,
    99, 102, 141, 145, 154, 186, 199, 204–208,
    222–223, 224, 231, 232, 234, 243, 263–264,
    312, 313, 341, 344
  on alienation effect, 207
  on art, 186

Acknowledgments

Frontispiece: Courtesy Arena Stage; Opposite Brief
Contents page: Courtesy Richard Feldman/American
Repertory Theatre; Opposite Contents page: Peter
Cunningham/Courtesy Fred Nathan Co.; Opposite
Preface: Courtesy Arena Stage; p.2 Martha Swope; p.5
Courtesy Royal National Theatre; p.6 (both) Courtesy
Royal National Theatre; p.7 (top) Courtesy Guthrie
Theater; p.7 (bottom) Courtesy Oregon
Shakespearean Theatre; p.8 Courtesy Arena Stage;
p.11 The Museum of Modern Art/Film Stills Archive;
p.12 Vandamm Collection/The New York Public
Library at Lincoln Center; p.13 Courtesy *The Chapel
Hill Newspaper*; p.17 Donald Cooper/Photostage; p.19
Stan Wayman/Rapho-Guillumette; p.23 Courtesy
Shakespeare Centre Library, Stratford-Upon-Avon;
p.26 Chris Bennion; p.28 Courtesy Staatliches
Museum für Völkerkunde; p.31 Courtesy Greek
National Tourist Organization; p.32 The New York
Public Library at Lincoln Center; p.33 Courtesy Greek
National Tourist Organization; p.34 Courtesy Greek
National Tourist Organization; p.35 Bibliothèque
Nationale, Paris; p.36 Courtesy Columbia University
Press; p.37 From Glynne Wickham, *Early English
Stages*, Vol. 1 (1959), reprinted by permission of
Routledge & Kegan Paul and Columbia University
Press; p.38 Charles Genella/The Historic New
Orleans Collection; p.39 Courtesy Folger Shakespeare
Library; pp.40–41 Reprinted by permission of Oxford
University Press; p.42 Courtesy Shakespeare Centre
Library, Stratford-Upon-Avon; p.43 Courtesy Oregon
Shakespearean Theatre; p.46 (top) The New York
Public Library at Lincoln Center; p.46 (bottom)
Courtesy John F. Kennedy Center for the Performing
Arts; p.47 Robert C. Ragsdale/Courtesy Stratford
Festival Theatre, Ontario, Canada; p.48 Courtesy
Japan National Tourist Organization; p.49 (both)
Courtesy Japan National Tourist Organization; p.50
Courtesy Japan National Tourist Organization; p.52
From *Naniwa miyage* (Souvenir from Naniwa, 1738).
Courtesy of Torigoe Bunzō and C. D. Gerstle, *Circles
of Fantasy* (Harvard University Press); p.53 (top)
Martine Franck/Magnum; p.53 (bottom) Martha
Swope; p.56 Martha Swope; p.60 Zbigniew
Raplewski/KaiDib Films International, Glendale,
Calif.; pp.61–63 Photographs and drawings courtesy
H. M. Berg, Odin Teatret, Denmark; p.65 (top)
Richard Schechner Archives, Princeton University
Library; p.65 (bottom) Frederick Eberstadt/Courtesy
of Richard Schechner; p.66 AP/Wide World Photos;
p.67 (top) Gianfranco Mantegna/Courtesy Mark Hall
Amitin and Living Theatre; p.67 (bottom) Max
Waldman/Copyright Max Waldman Archives; p.68
(top) Martine Franck/Magnum; p.68 (bottom) Gilles
Abegg; p.70 Martine Franck/Magnum; p.71 (both)
Martine Franck/Magnum; p.72 (top) Martine Franck/
Magnum; p.72 (bottom) Dan Charlson/*Durham
Herald-Sun*; p.76 Chris Bennion; p.79 Courtesy Buena
Vista Distribution Co.; p.80 Allen Nomura; p.81 (top)
Allen Nomura; p.81 (middle) Gerry Goodstein; p.81
(bottom) Courtesy Ken Friedman; p.84 William B.
Carter; p.86 Robert Nemiroff; p.87 (top) National
Archives; p.87 (bottom) Fred W. McDarrah; p.88 (top)
Paul Harter/Courtesy Methuen, Inc.; p.88 (bottom)
Courtesy Stokley Towles, *The Patriot Ledger*; p.92
Gerhard Kassner; p.94 The New York Public Library
at Lincoln Center; p.95 The New York Public Library
at Lincoln Center; p.96 Culver Pictures; p.97 Courtesy
The Acting Company; p.98 Courtesy George Karger/
PIX; p.99 Martha Swope; p.101 Leo Friedman/The
New York Public Library at Lincoln Center; p.102
Courtesy Centre International de Recherche Theatrale;
p.103 Courtesy Music Theatre Group; p.103 J.P.
Zachariasen; p.104 Martha Swope Associates/Carol
Rosegg; p.105 Johan Elbers; p.106 Martha Swope;
p.108 Chris Bennion; p.110 Vandamm Collection/The
New York Public Library at Lincoln Center; p.113 The
New York Public Library at Lincoln Center; p.114
George E. Joseph; p.115 Stan Wayman/Rapho-
Guillumette; p.116 Bill Carter; p.117 Courtesy Theatre

Museum/Victoria and Albert Museum; p.120 The New York Public Library at Lincoln Center; p.121 The Lee Strasberg Theatre Institute; p.122 George E. Joseph; p.126 Eileen Darby; p.134 Richard Feldman/American Repertory Theatre; p.136 (top) The New York Public Library at Lincoln Center; p.136 (bottom) Arnold Rood/Courtesy Theatre Museum, London; p.137 Victoria and Albert Museum, London; p.138 Courtesy Mark Taper Forum Press; p.139 The New York Public Library at Lincoln Center; p.140 Eileen Darby; p.141 (top) The New York Public Library at Lincoln Center; p.141 (bottom) Courtesy KaiDib Films International, Glendale, Calif.; p.142 Courtesy KaiDib Films International, Glendale, Calif.; p.143 George de Vincent/Courtesy Arena Stage; p.145 (top) From Harold Burris-Meyer and Edward C. Cole, *Scenery for the Theatre*, copyright 1938, renewed © 1966, 1971 by Harold Burris-Meyer and Edward C. Cole. Reprinted by permission of Little, Brown and Company; p.147 The New York Public Library at Lincoln Center; p.149 Martha Swope; p.150 (top) Courtesy Patricia Zipprodt; p.150 (bottom) Bruce Goldstein/Courtesy Guthrie Theater; p.151 (top) Courtesy William Morris Agency; p.151 (bottom) Martha Swope; p.154 (top) Illustration of Pantalone from Jacques Callot's etchings, c.1622, of *commedia* actors in costume; p.154 (bottom) Courtesy Guthrie Theater; p.155 Martine Franck/Magnum; p.157 Photos courtesy Colortran; p.158 (top) Photo courtesy Kliegl Bros.; p.158 (bottom) Courtesy Colortran; p.159 Photos courtesy Colortran and Kliegl Bros.; p.160 T. Charles Erickson/Courtesy Yale University Office of Public Information; p.161 George E. Joseph; p.168 Gerry Goodstein; p.175 NYT Pictures; p.182 Annalisa Kraft/Courtesy Arena Stage; p.183 Courtesy Arena Stage; p.186 Chris Bennion; p.188 Donald Cooper/Photostage; p.190 Martha Swope; p.191 Courtesy French Press and Information Office; p.193 Martha Holmes; p.194 (top) Jerry Bauer/Courtesy Grove-Weidenfeld; p.194 (bottom) Courtesy French Press and Information Office; p.198 Martha Swope; p.199 Martha Swope; pp.201–203 All photos courtesy Peter Cunningham/Fred Nathan Co., except top photo p.203: Michelle V. Agins/NYT Pictures; p.205 Courtesy German Information Center; p.206 Courtesy Berliner Ensemble; p.207 Richard Feldman/Courtesy American Repertory Theatre; p.208 Courtesy Berliner Ensemble; p.209 Courtesy French Press and Information Office; p.210 Courtesy French Press and Information Office; p.211 Richart Feldman/Courtesy American Repertory Theatre; p.214 Joan Marcus/Courtesy Arena Stage; p.219 Culver Pictures; p.221 Robert C. Ragsdale/Courtesy Stratford Festival Theatre, Ontario, Canada; p.223 Courtesy Berliner Ensemble; p.225 Courtesy French Press and Information Office; p.227 Donald Cooper/Photostage; p.229 Donald Cooper/Photostage; p.230 George E. Joseph; p.231 Anthony Crickmay; p.232 Joan Marcus/Arena Stage; p.233 Peter Moore; p.234 Paula Court; p.240 Irene Haupt; p.242 Ralf Brinkoff/Courtesy Byrd Hoffman Foundation; p.243 Amnon BenNomis/Courtesy Mabou Mines; p.244 Courtesy American Repertory Theatre; p.245 Gerhard Kassner; p.246 Johan Elbers; p.248 Johan Elbers; p.252 Bruce Goldstein/Courtesy Guthrie Theater; p.256 Martha Swope; p.257 The Bettmann Archive; p.259 Anthony Crickmay; p.261 Robert C. Ragsdale/Courtesy Stratford Festival Theatre, Ontario, Canada; p.262 George E. Joseph; p.264 Courtesy Guthrie Theater; p.265 George E. Joseph; p.266 (top) Richard Feldman; p.266 (bottom) Martha Swope; p.267 (top) Ruth Walz; p.267 (bottom) Joe Giannetti/Courtesy Guthrie Theater; p.269 Courtesy Royal Shakespeare Theatre; p.271 Robert Ansell/Courtesy Performing Arts Services; p.273 Courtesy International Creative Management, New York; p.275 Courtesy UPI/Bettmann Newsphotos; p.277 Zoë Dominic; p.280 Gerry Goodstein; p.282 Gerry Goodstein; p.285 Joe Giannetti/Courtesy Guthrie Theater; p.289 Martha Swope; p.290 Eileen Darby; p.291 Gerry Goodstein;

p. 293 Donald Cooper/Photostage; p. 294 George E. Joseph; p. 297 Bob Marshak/Courtesy Williamstown Theatre Festival; p. 300 Joan Marcus/Courtesy Arena Stage; p. 301 (top) Joe Giannetti/Courtesy Guthrie Theater; p. 301 (bottom) The New York Public Library at Lincoln Center; p. 307 Douglas H. Jeffery; p. 309 (top) The New York Public Library at Lincoln Center; p. 309 (bottom) George E. Joseph; p. 310 (top) Zoë Dominic; p. 310 (bottom) © Max Waldman/Max Waldman Archives, Westport, Conn.; p. 311 (top) Martha Swope; p. 311 (bottom) Bruce Goldstein/Courtesy Guthrie Theater; p. 313 Richard Feldman/Courtesy American Repertory Theatre; p. 314 Kenn Duncan; p. 318 Courtesy Arena Stage; p. 320 Courtesy Greek National Tourist Organization; p. 324 Courtesy Jasper Johns and Leo Castelli Gallery; p. 325 UPI/Bettmann Newsphotos; p. 326 Eileen Darby; p. 327 (top) Peter Cunningham/Courtesy Fred Nathan Co.; p. 327 (bottom) © Wide World Photos; p. 328 Vandamm Collection/The New York Public Library at Lincoln Center; p. 329 Richard Feldman/Courtesy American Repertory Theatre; p. 331 NYT Pictures; p. 340 Martha Swope

Color Photo Essays
"Magic Time": all photos George E. Joseph
The "Creative" Director: p. 1 (top) Paul Slaughter; p. 1 (bottom) Martine Franck/Magnum; p. 2 (left) Martha Swope; p. 2 (top right) © Max Waldman/The Max Waldman Archives, Westport, Conn.; p. 2 (bottom right) Gilles Abegg; p. 3 (top) Richard Feldman; p. 3 (bottom) Arena Stage; p. 4 (top) Richard Feldman; p. 4 (bottom) Gerhard Kassner
The Musical: p. 1 Martha Swope; p. 2 (both) Martha Swope; p. 3 (top left and right) Peter Cunningham; p. 3 (bottom) Martha Swope; p. 4 Martha Swope
Makeup and Wigs for Cats: all photos Martha Swope.